THE CRISIS OF CAPITALIST DEMOCRACY

THE CRISIS OF CAPITALIST DEMOCRACY

Richard A. Posner

HARVARD UNIVERSITY PRESS
Cambridge, Massachusetts, and London, England   2010

Library of Congress Cataloging-in-Publication Data

Posner, Richard A.
The crisis of capitalist democracy / Richard A. Posner.
   p.   cm.
Includes bibliographical references and index.
ISBN 978-0-674-05574-2 (cloth : alk. paper)
1. Capitalism.   2. Democracy.   3. Financial crises.   I. Title.
HB501.P646 2010
330.12'2—dc22   2009050929

CONTENTS

INTRODUCTION

At this writing, it is more than two years since the beginning of a recession that turned into a depression in the fall of 2008, following the financial crisis in mid-September of that year. The financial circuits had become overloaded; the banking industry collapsed like the light bulb, shattered by an electrical overload, on the cover of this book. The first really frightening and dangerous economic crisis since the Great Depression of the 1930s, this depression already has had profound economic, political, institutional, and intellectual consequences, and the consequences may continue to be felt for many years to come. I am emphatic in regarding the economic downturn as a "depression." The issue is more than semantic, but to explain why would take up too much space here; I defer it to chapter 6.

I first analyzed the crisis in my book *A Failure of Capitalism: The Crisis of '08 and the Descent into Depression* (2009), which took the story up to February 2, 2009. The title alarmed some readers, who thought I meant that capitalism has failed us and we need something different. That was not my intention. I believe in capitalism. But capitalism is not a synonym for free markets. It is the name given to a complex economic system with many moving parts. The buying and selling and investing and borrowing and other activities carried on in private markets are only some of those moving parts. Others include a system of laws for protecting property and facilitating transactions, institutions for enforcing those laws, and regulations designed to align private incentives with the goal of achieving widespread prosperity. If the regulatory framework is defective, it must be changed, because competition will not permit businessmen to subordinate profit maximization to concern for the welfare of society as a whole, and ethics can't take the place of regulation.

One of the key regulatory institutions is a central bank, which in the United States is the Federal Reserve. The component of capitalism that consists of a private banking system is unstable and can fail, and if it fails can bring down much of the rest of the economy with it. That is one reason a capitalist system cannot consist just of free markets. A central bank has a key role to play in keeping a nation's banking system working, as do the government agencies involved in the regulation of banking, which include the Federal Reserve; indeed it is the most powerful of the bank regulatory agencies. A combination of unsound monetary policy and regulatory inattention brought on the banking collapse of September 2008.

The Federal Reserve was not created until 1913, and before then central banking in the United States was intermittent. An economic literature advocates returning to "free banking" (that is, no government creation or regulation of the money supply). And a return to the gold standard, for which there are more advocates, would curtail the power of the Federal Reserve. But realistically there is no alternative to a modern central banking system as typified by the Federal Reserve System.

The inherent instability of a capitalist economy is a fact, not a criticism. The average growth of the U.S. economy has long been about 3 percent a year, which is good and has made us the world's wealthiest large nation, as well as the world's most powerful nation. But the actual growth from year to year oscillates around that trend line—often dipping into negative territory—in an irregular, unpredictable fashion. This oscillation is the "business cycle," though the word "cycle" is misleading because it suggests a smooth wavelike motion, like a pendulum; the real motion is anything but.

One reason for the oscillation, perhaps the main reason, is feedback effects. There is an analogy to climate, another inherently unstable system. Carbon dioxide in the atmosphere raises surface temperatures by trapping heat radiated from the earth; the higher temperatures, among their other effects, melt the Alaskan and Siberian permafrost, releasing methane, another "greenhouse gas," which leads to a further increase in surface temperatures. Similarly, an asset-price bubble can form and then burst and in bursting trigger a recession that can feed on itself until it grows into a depression: demand falls, so output falls, so unemployment rises, so incomes fall, so there is a further reduction in demand as a result of which output declines further and unemployment rises further. Eventually, as inventories shrink and durables wear out and cash hoarding by businesses afraid to invest and consumers afraid to spend produces a savings glut, spending will increase, and the downward spiral will stop and then reverse. In either direction, feedback effects will amplify what initially may have been only a small change in economic behavior. Those effects can get out of hand. They did in the 1930s and again in the fall of 2008 and the winter and spring of 2009. To prevent them from getting out of hand requires active and intelligent government. Government has been active since the crash of 2008; how intelligent is another question.

February 2, 2009, did not end my interest in the crisis; nor did the economy and government obligingly stand still. Since then I have written on the crisis in my blog (sponsored by the *Atlantic Monthly*) called "A Failure of Capitalism" (http://correspondents.theatlantic.com/richard_posner/), in my separate blog with the economist Gary Becker ("The Becker-Posner Blog," recently moved to http://uchicagolaw.typepad.com/beckerposner/, formerly at www.becker-posner-blog.com/), and in the following published writings:

"Shorting Reason" (review of George A. Akerlof and Robert J. Shiller, *Animal Spirits: How Human Psychology Drives the Economy, and Why It Matters for Global Capitalism* [2009]), New Republic, Apr. 15, 2009, p. 30;

"Capitalism in Crisis," *Wall Street Journal,* May 7, 2009, p. A17;

"Reply to Akerlof and Shiller," *New Republic,* May 8, 2009, www.tnr.com/article/politics/disputations-case-misrepresentation;

"Our Crisis of Regulation," *New York Times,* June 23, 2009, p. A23;

"The President's Blueprint for Reforming Financial Regulation: A Critique—Part I," *FinReg21,* July 20, 2009, www.finreg21.com/lombard-street/the-president%E2%80%99s-blueprint-reforming-financial-regulation-a-critique-part-i;

"Treating Financial Consumers as Consenting Adults," *Wall Street Journal,* July 23, 2009, p. A15;

"The President's Blueprint for Reforming Financial Regulation: A Critique—Part II," *FinReg21,* Aug. 3, 2009, www.finreg21.com/lombard-street/the-president%E2%80%99s-blueprint-reforming-financial-regulation-a-critique-part-ii;

"Uncertainty Aversion and Economic Depressions," *Challenge,* Sept.-Oct. 2009, p. 25;

"How I Became a Keynesian," *New Republic,* Sept. 23, 2009, p. 34; and

"Financial Regulatory Reform: The Politics of Denial," *The Economists' Voice,"* Nov. 2009, www.bepress.com/ev.

I draw on these writings in this book, though on much else besides.

The book is not a sequel, picking up where the first one left off, though it does bring the story of the crisis up to date. Rather, it is an effort to deal in greater depth, and from a longer perspective, with a crisis that has continued to evolve, to elicit new response measures and new proposals for regulatory reform, to engender new concerns about the future and spawn new controversies about the past. More is known now about the background, causes, and course of the crisis; a richer narrative and fuller analysis are therefore possible. Current and former government officials who played an unwitting causal role in the economic collapse, such as Alan Greenspan and Ben Bernanke, have weighed in with their excuses. Academic economists, emerging from the shell shock that I described in my first book, have begun grappling with the profound economic issues presented by the crisis and the efforts to resolve it. I have joined the fray, and in the process amplified and sharpened the economic approach sketched in the first book.

That book was completed twelve days after Barack Obama's inauguration ushered in new efforts to contain the crisis. This book zeroes in on those efforts, and on the measures that have been proposed and in some instances adopted to prevent a repetition of the crisis. It is now possible to assess the success of the Obama Administration in responding to the crisis, and to evaluate proposals for financial regulatory reform, coming both from within and outside the government, that have acquired texture, that are not merely vague concepts. The politics of depression and recovery, and the practicalities of regulatory reform, have thus come into sharper focus. As recovery begins, moreover, careful scrutiny is required of the prospects for the recovery's continuing without interruption despite soaring deficits, which may be setting the stage for a painful depression aftershock, and perhaps even for a long-term deterioration of the American economy. Critics of the Administration are beginning to argue that the cure for the depression may turn out to be worse than the disease—and they may have a point.

Between the end of 2001, when the Federal Reserve pushed the federal funds rate (a benchmark short-term interest rate) way down, and the middle of September 2008, when the Fed and the

Treasury allowed Lehman Brothers to collapse, the government's management of the economy was miserable. Beginning in October and continuing through the enactment of the $787 billion stimulus package in February 2009 (and thus straddling the outgoing and incoming Administrations), the government's economic management was as good as could realistically have been expected. Since then, however, the government has stumbled again, as we shall see throughout the book, and in ways and for reasons that raise the question whether the American political system can preserve the nation's prosperity in the challenging conditions in which the economy now finds itself. Whether America is governable—whether its political institutions are still adapted to the challenges that the economic crisis has both highlighted and magnified—has been brought into question. The American polity is a fusion of a capitalist economic system with a democratic political system in which modern techniques of political manipulation overlie an eighteenth-century constitution. The economic downturn that began in 2007 and turned critical in September 2008 has acted as a stressor that has brought the resilience of our capitalist democracy into question. Hence the title of this book.

A depression raises complicated issues typically discussed, whether by economists or by journalists, in an esoteric business and economics jargon garnished with charts and statistics. One aim of my first book was to explain to the educated but nonexpert public, clearly and simply—stripping out all irrelevant detail—the economics of the business cycle and of finance, the causes and course of the crisis, the initial responses, and the dangers ahead. This book takes a further step. Different from its predecessor, it is more detailed, more wide-ranging, and requires greater involvement and attention from the reader. I want still to be understood by the nonexpert reader (formerly called the "general reader") who seeks understanding of a complex phenomenon that affects everyone. But I want to reach experts as well, especially a certain class of experts. The economic crisis caught unawares many persons who are professionally engaged with issues involving the crisis yet who are unfamiliar with the relevant macroeconomics, finance theory, and financial instruments and practices. This book seeks to equip them with the background knowledge they need in order to engage—whether as lawyers, accountants, congressional staffers, civil servants in the economic branches of government, or businessmen who buy rather than sell financial products or services—with the issues thrown up by the crisis. Even finance professionals, specialists all, may learn a little from seeing their field placed in a broader intellectual context.

As the crisis has evolved, as analyses have proliferated, as proposals for reform have become detailed and concrete, the challenge of lucid explanation has grown. And so, because intelligibility remains my overarching goal, I have had to decide whether to present essential background material (definitions, the operation of the Federal Reserve, the rival economic theories, and so forth) in a lump at the beginning of the book or to weave it into a narrative of the crisis. The first approach, though simpler to execute, would have bored the experts yet have been difficult for the nonexpert reader to digest. So rather than laying out all at once the essentials of business-cycle theory, the theory of money and banking, the structure of financial regulation, and the financial instruments that have figured largely in the crisis, I introduce these concepts, institutions, practices, and instruments as they become relevant to a chronological narrative that covers the run-up to the crisis, the crisis itself, how government and the market have responded, what reforms aimed at preventing a repetition of the crisis have been adopted or proposed, and what may lie ahead for the economy. I criticize several aspects of the government's response to the crisis, including the Obama Administration's program of financial regulatory reform, which seems to me premature, overly ambitious, too political, too interventionist.

That is the project of Part I of the book. Part II discusses lessons that we should bring away from the crisis and the responses. There is some repetition, but I think it will be helpful for readers to encounter key concepts first in a narrative context and second in a theoretical one. The central theoretical chapters are chapters 7 through 9; the concepts emphasized there, such as hoarding and uncertainty, will by then be familiar to the reader from the earlier chapters.

I argue that we need to understand the inherent fragility of a banking system and the danger therefore of slack regulation, including a loose monetary policy. And we need fresh economic thinking about the business cycle, but thinking that builds on the original ideas of John Maynard Keynes, as distinct from their revision by practitioners of the "New Keynesian Economics." Those ideas centrally include the importance of uncertainty as distinct from calculable risk in shaping economic behavior, the separation of savings from productive investment, and the role of confidence and optimism in shaping the business cycle. I extend the criticisms I made of present-day economists in the first book, emphasizing now not just their failure to anticipate the crisis, which was my emphasis in that book, but also failures of understanding that can be summarized as forgetfulness of Keynes.

Part III considers life after the depression. I canvass regulatory reforms that should be receiving serious considerations; generally these are not the reforms proposed by the Administration and under active consideration in Congress. I also discuss how the role of the United States in the world economy is being altered, probably for the worse and perhaps for a very long time, by the depression and its aftermath. It is not that the economic challenges that we face are insurmountable but that we may lack the governmental structures and political culture requisite for meeting them. I do not attempt to offer a theory of political failure, but I offer plenty of evidence of it.

The world will not stand still while I write a book and my publisher publishes it. I had thought when I began that by the beginning of the new year the economic and political outlook would be much clearer. It is not. It seems reasonably clear that the core of the proposals for financial regulatory reform that the Treasury Department made in June will be enacted by Congress in the first quarter of 2010, but the details of the legislation will be critical and they cannot be predicted. Economic recovery has begun, but how fast it will proceed cannot be predicted either; nor can its aftermath be foreseen. I can hope only to provide a lens through which to view with sharpened perception an economy in troubled transition.

Three simplifications in my presentation should be kept in mind. I use "Federal Reserve" to denote interchangeably the two principal organs of the Federal Reserve System, the Board of Governors and the Federal Open Market Committee. They can be regarded interchangeably because both are dominated by their chairman, who is the same person. Second, unless otherwise indicated explicitly or by context, I use "bank," "banking industry," "banking system," and other cognates of "bank" to refer to any financial intermediary—that is, any entity that lends borrowed capital, whether or not it is a commercial bank regulated by banking regulators. Third, I use "subprime" to refer to any home mortgage that would be considered unsafe under traditional banking principles because the mortgagor (the borrower) had little or no equity in the house, lacked an income adequate to assure his ability to make the monthly mortgage payments, was allowed to defer the making of monthly payments for several years, had a poor credit record, or had been given a mortgage without having to document his financial situation.

I thank Kevin Bensley, Ralph Dado, Gary DeTurck, Benjamin Foster, Anthony Henke, Martin Kohan, Sonia Lahr-Pastor, Alexandra Levy, Linda Shi, James Shliferstein, and Lara Vivas for very helpful research assistance. And I thank Michael Aronson, Douglas Baird, Francis Bator, Gary Becker, Larry Bernstein, Steven Eisman, Eugene Fama, Benjamin Friedman, Edward Glaeser, Hal Goltz, Ashley Keller, John Hagarty, James Heckman, Larry Hillibrand, William Landes, Jack Levin, Jonathan Lewinsohn, Yair Listokin, Robert Lucas, Gerard Minack, Roland Paul, Richard Porter, Kenneth Posner, Raghuram Rajan, Samuel Sax, and Stephen Schwarcz for very helpful conversations or correspondence about issues discussed in the book.

January 4, 2010

AN ANALYTIC NARRATIVE OF

THE CRISIS

I

THE CALM BEFORE THE STORM:

2001–2006

1

Low interest rates in the early 2000s set the stage for the economic collapse from which we are now gradually recovering. It was low interest rates that caused housing, stock market, and credit bubbles. The bursting of the bubbles brought on the depression. Low interest rates alone would not have had such consequences, though they would have produced inflation in one form or another. Had banking been safe, the bursting of the housing and stock bubbles would not have brought down the banks, and we would have been spared a depression.

Banking used to be safe. Made safe in reaction to the Great Depression of the 1930s, which had featured a banking collapse, banking became unsafe as a result of a financial deregulation movement that began in 1980, that culminated in 1999 with the repeal of a major 1930s banking reform (the Glass-Steagall Act), and that was succeeded by a brief, disastrous era of lax regulation, regulatory complacency, regulatory inattention, and regulatory ineptitude. The combination of low interest rates and inadequate banking regulation proved lethal. The contribution of low interest rates, and the responsibility for those rates, are the subject of this chapter. The failures of banking regulation are for later.

Low interest rates encourage people to borrow—and banks to

borrow, so that they can relend. As interest rates fell sharply in 2001 and remained very low until some months after a gradual rise began in 2004—for part of this period short-term interest rates were actually negative after adjustment for inflation—the amount of debt in the economy soared. Much of it went into the purchase of houses, a product bought mainly with debt (traditionally consisting of a mortgage equal to 80 percent of the purchase price). With the cost of debt such a big part of the price of a house, low interest rates increased the demand for housing. That led to an increase in housing starts. But because the housing stock is so durable, a steep increase in the demand for housing cannot be satisfied just by the construction of additional houses. Instead, with more people wanting to buy houses, the price of existing houses was bid up. As prices rose, many homeowners borrowed against their home equity—whether by increasing their first mortgage or taking out a second mortgage or a home-equity loan—to finance the purchase of other goods. This increased the amount of debt that people had, but they did not feel over-indebted because their principal asset—their house—was rising in value. Instead they felt wealthier, and so saved less. And so as a further consequence of low interest rates, rising housing and stock prices were accompanied by a decline in the personal savings rate.

Rising prices made houses seem a good investment. This attracted more buyers, and lenders too, because when house prices are rising, defaults are rare—a homeowner who has trouble making his monthly mortgage payments can sell his house for a profit rather than having to default and face foreclosure. And with the perfection, as it seemed, of debt securitization (discussed in the next chapter) as a method of optimally distributing risk, even mortgages that seemed extremely risky could be marketed. So credit standards for mortgage lending declined, which further increased the demand for housing; neither lack of money for a down payment nor a poor credit rating based on past difficulty in handling credit was any longer an insurmountable obstacle to buying a house.

Thus housing prices were rising because housing prices were rising—a spiral engendered by low interest rates. Prices continued rising until March 2006—and immediately began to fall. Mortgage interest rates had risen, owing to belated moves by the Federal Reserve, which feared inflation, though not in houses or other assets, to raise interest rates. The rise in interest rates made the purchase of a house a more costly undertaking, so the demand for houses fell, and therefore housing starts and housing prices fell. As housing starts fell, builders' incomes declined and unemployment in construction rose, while as prices of existing homes fell, homeowners—whose house was usually their principal asset—felt poorer and so reduced their spending if they could. Some homeowners abandoned their house because the unpaid principal amount of their mortgage exceeded the diminished market value of the house, making it seem a bad investment. These abandonments depressed housing prices further. People who had thought they could afford to buy a house because they would be able to refinance the mortgage at a lower interest rate after a rise in the value of the house gave them a substantial equity were shocked to discover not only that the value of their house had fallen rather than risen, but that lenders had raised credit standards because of the rising defaults. Many homeowners who had financed their house with an adjustable-rate mortgage could not afford the reset rate because of their financial distress. And although housing prices were falling, demand for houses remained weak, because houses no longer seemed a good investment.

The ingredients of a recession (a mild depression) were present; why it should have brought down the banking system is considered in the next chapter. For now I want to consider why interest rates fell and then rose in the early 2000s and whether the rise and fall in housing prices really was—as I intimated when I said that "housing prices were rising because housing prices were rising"—a bubble phenomenon.

There are two theories about the pattern of interest rates in the early years of the decade. One is the "global savings glut." This is a misleading term, because it implies that the world as a whole can have a surplus of saving over spending. The surplus money that some countries accumulate by exporting more than they import, so that they receive money in addition to goods in exchange for their exports, is offset by the deficits of their trading partners, which pay for the goods they import with a combination of their own exports and the money they pay to make up the difference between what they buy and what they sell.[1] China, along with some other developing countries, plus Germany, Japan, and the oil-exporting nations of the Middle East, were the savers, and the United States and some other wealthy countries—but the United States most of all—the borrowers of the savers' excess money.

Why some countries should want to export more than they import and so increase their money reserves rather than the goods enjoyed by their citizens is something of a puzzle, unless, as in the case of countries such as the Middle East oil-producing countries, which produce far more than their populations can consume, their domestic markets are too small to absorb imports commensurate with the countries' output. In some of the export-first countries, the population is exceptionally thrifty; it wants to hold large money balances rather than spend on consumption goods. (The standard example is Japan, although Japan's personal savings rate has been declining steadily since the early 1990s and is now about the same as the U.S. rate.) In other countries, such as Germany, the country's comparative advantage is

---

1. This is oversimplified, because it ignores earnings from foreign investment. For example, foreign earnings of U.S. companies reduce the net outflow of U.S. dollars caused by our negative trade balance.

the production of goods in strong demand in foreign countries. Many developing countries want to have large dollar balances as a buffer against financial crises such as those that swept East Asia in 1997, when weaknesses in the countries' economies caused huge withdrawals of money invested in them, causing economic distress.[2] If money starts flowing out of a country, interest rates will rise to ration a diminishing amount of money available to domestic businesses and individual borrowers; and as I'll be emphasizing, a rise in interest rates (at least if the rise is "real," rather than simply compensation for current or expected inflation) reduces economic activity.

China has the greatest imbalance of any major nation between exports and imports, in part because it has fixed an artificial rate of exchange between its currency and the American dollar that makes its currency cheap and the dollar expensive; the result is that China's exports to the United States are cheap and its imports from the United States dear.[3] As a result of its trade imbalance with this country, China owns more of our foreign debt than any other country—some $800 billion (though Japan is close behind).

What reasons could China have for such an old-fashioned policy ("mercantilism"—the maximization of a nation's cash or cash-equivalent reserves—famously attacked by Adam Smith more than two hundred years ago)? The immense exports that China's skewed exchange policy has fostered provide employment for a large number of Chinese. Their wages are low, but at least they have jobs. Of course, they might have jobs if the dollar were cheaper relative to Chinese currency. China would import more and export less. It would manufacture less, not only be-

2. Markus K. Brunnermeier, "Deciphering the Liquidity and Credit Crunch 2007–2008," *Journal of Economic Perspectives* 77 (Winter 2009).

3. Wayne M. Morrison and Mark LaBonte, "China's Currency: A Summary of the Economic Issues," Congressional Research Service Report, June 17, 2009, www.fas.org/sgp/crs/row/RS21625.pdf (visited Oct. 22, 2009).

cause of greater competition from imported manufacturers and reduced foreign demand for its manufactures, but also because many workers would be required for the expanded system of domestic distribution that would be necessary if domestic consumption soared. It would also manufacture a different mixture of goods, because of competition from imports. But above all it would need a much more elaborate system of wholesale and retail distribution, and perhaps a different commercial culture. The transition to a consumer society with its credit cards and product warranties and malls and the rest would be difficult; in the interim, unless the transition were very gradual, there would be widespread unemployment—shifting employees from manufacturing to distribution, or from one type of manufacturing to another, doesn't happen overnight. And China doesn't have the kind of social safety net that we do, to catch the unemployed before they reach the bottom. Because of the limitations of domestic consumption, Chinese are great savers, and this relieves the pressure the government would otherwise feel to provide social services. That provision might strain the government's administrative abilities. Moreover, China has a long history of political instability, of which its current government is acutely conscious; and there is tension between China's dictatorial communist government and its largely free-enterprise economy. Finally, the domestic Chinese economy is dominated by state-owned companies, and the government doesn't want to expose them to foreign competition. For all these reasons, the Chinese government is reluctant to take chances on changing the economy from one of producing manufactured goods for export to one of manufacture and distribution primarily for domestic consumption.

The dollar-surplus countries, like China, bought with their dollars bonds from the U.S. Treasury and other U.S. owners of debt, and as a result the U.S. money supply expanded. With more money available for lending, interest rates fell. In addition, because much of the foreign demand for U.S. securities was demand by foreign governments for Treasury securities, the yield

on those securities fell, and this drove other investors to riskier
securities,[4] such as the mortgage-backed securities that played a
starring role in the financial collapse.

When capital inflows from abroad increase the ratio of money
in circulation in the United States to goods and services bought in
the United States, the result is inflation unless the Federal Reserve
withdraws money from the economy. It does this (and the converse, which is to pump money into the economy to prevent
deflation—negative inflation) by what are called "open market
operations." An understanding of those operations is fundamental.

Suppose the Fed wants to increase the amount of money in
circulation. It used to do this by buying very short-term securities
(the equivalent of bonds) that are issued by the Treasury Department to help finance the federal government's operations. The
money that the Fed pays the bank or other seller of these securities, when deposited in the seller's bank account, expands the
amount of money that the bank can lend. The more money lent,
the lower the interest rate. The Federal Reserve creates the
money with which to buy securities by a bookkeeping entry that
increases the amount of cash reserves shown on the books of
Federal Reserve banks, which in this respect can be thought of as
branch offices of the Fed. It thus creates money out of nothing.

If the Fed wants to reduce the money supply, then instead
of buying Treasury securities it sells them, thus withdrawing
money from circulation. There is now less money in bank accounts, so the supply of lendable funds is diminished and as a result interest rates are higher. With interest rates higher, fewer
loans are demanded and supplied, and so there is less money in
circulation.

Nowadays the Fed doesn't actually buy and sell securities in

4. Ricardo J. Caballero and Arvind Krishnamurthy, "Global Imbalances
and Financial Fragility," 99 *American Economic Review Papers and Proceedings* 584 (May 2009).

its normal open market operations, but instead borrows and lends them by means of "repos" (repossession agreements). In a repo the borrower, instead of posting the security as collateral for the loan, sells the security to the lender but agrees to repurchase it at a specified future time (usually a very short time—from a day to three months) at a specified higher price. The difference between the price at which the borrower sells the security and the price at which he buys it back from the lender is the lender's compensation for having given the borrower the use of the lender's cash in the interim. The "seller" of the security is thus actually a borrower, which is what I have been calling him, and the "buyer" a lender, and the security that is sold and then repurchased is really the collateral for a loan, since the "buyer" will retain it only until he gets his cash back.

The repo form of lending is a detail so far as open market operations are concerned—there is little difference between the Fed's buying a security for cash and lending the cash with the security as collateral. But it is an important detail, because, as we'll see in the next chapter, repos are an important instrument in modern finance and played a role in the financial collapse.

I have said that the Fed engages in open market operations to influence the interest rate. But there are many different interest rates. Interest rates are determined by liquidity preference (the desire to have cash or its equivalent), credit risk (the risk that the borrower will default), and the risk of a change in the real value (purchasing power) of money due to inflation or deflation. In general, the longer the term of a loan, the higher the interest rate, because the lender is giving up liquidity (the cash he lent is tied up until the loan is repaid) and because default risk and inflation risk are greater the longer the loan is outstanding.

But in normal times (these are not normal times), the Federal Reserve gears its open market operations to regulating only one interest rate, and that is the "federal funds" or "overnight" rate. This is the rate at which banks make very short-term loans to each other secured by Treasury bills. The Fed focuses on this single, benchmark rate in order to make it easier for the private sector to assess the direction of monetary policy and hence interest rates in general.

Interbank lending is common because banks need "reserves" (cash) in order both to make loans and to satisfy regulatory requirements. Requiring banks to keep some of their capital in the form of cash reduces the risk of a bank's going broke should its loan portfolio or other assets lose value unexpectedly. Because cash does not earn interest, banks want to hold as little as possible except when they have a loan to make. So it makes sense that rather than accumulating cash they borrow the needed cash from another bank when the customer for a loan appears.

Similarly, a bank is usually happy to lend cash to another bank rather than let it sit idle, earning no interest. The bank might have received an influx of deposits at a time when the demand for loans by that bank was weak. Indeed, it is because receiving capital in the form of deposits and lending the capital are not coordinated that interbank lending is important to the efficient allocation of bank capital. When in September 2008 it became obvious that the banking industry had serious liquidity and solvency problems, banks became fearful about lending to each other because they were uncertain whether the borrower would repay, and the sharp drop in interbank lending that resulted disrupted the efficient allocation of bank capital. By aggressively increasing bank balances by means of open market operations and the purchase of other debt ("credit easing"), the Federal Reserve staved off a complete collapse of bank lending. But because lending remained constrained as a consequence of the gathering depression and the banks' solvency concerns, most of the cash that the Fed pumped into the banking system remained on the banks' books as excess reserves,[5] that is, as cash in excess of the amount

5. See Todd Keister and James McAndrews, "Why Are Banks Holding So Many Excess Reserves?" (Federal Reserve Bank of New York, Staff Rep. No. 380, July 2009).

required by the regulatory authorities to provide a margin of safety.

Interbank lending may seem too remote from mortgage lending for an interbank interest rate such as the federal funds rate to affect the mortgage interest rate, especially since the scale of open market operations required to raise or lower the federal funds rate is small in relation to the overall quantity of credit transactions. Moreover, it is a "notional" rate—a target rate announced by the Fed. Banks aren't required to lend to each other at that rate, a point that turned out to be important in the financial crisis.

But there are a number of ways in which changes in that rate affect other interest rates, including mortgage interest rates:

1. When the Fed buys short-term Treasury securities (or acquires them in repos), this increases the demand for and hence price of bonds generally, and so interest rates fall. A bond's price is inverse to its interest rate. The reason is that interest on a bond is specified as a percentage of its face value; that is why another name for bonds is "fixed-income securities." If the face value of a bond is $100 and the interest rate specified in the bond is 5 percent a year, the owner of the bond will receive interest of $5 a year. Suppose that the Fed (or anyone else) decides to buy bonds. This will increase the demand for bonds and so push up the price. Suppose the price of the $100 bond is bid up to $125. If the bondholder sells at that price, the buyer will receive interest of only 4 percent a year ($5/$125). So by increasing the demand for bonds by buying Treasury securities, the Fed reduces interest rates.

2. More important—because of the small scale of open market operations (again, in normal times)—the Fed signals its expectations concerning inflation by the federal funds rate that it picks. When the rate is low, the Fed is saying it doesn't fear inflation. That signal can be expected to reduce long-term interest rates, because such rates are strongly influenced by expectations

concerning inflation.[6] Of course, if the Fed is mistaken in thinking that there is no danger of inflation, its policy of keeping interest rates low may backfire, as indeed happened in the run-up to the banking crash.

3. A series of short-term loans is a close substitute for a long-term loan. Loans that are intended to be long-term often take the form of very short-term loans that are rolled over as they expire, as a way of reducing risk to the lender. Adjustable mortgage interest rates are another example of how short-term interest rates can turn into long-term rates: they turn a thirty-year mortgage loan into a series of shorter-term loans.

4. Many interest rates are floating rates based on a standard rate, such as the federal funds rate, the London Interbank Offer Rate (LIBOR),[7] or the Treasury bill rate, and the federal funds rate influences some of the other standard rates because of substitutability.

5. The lower the interest rate at which a bank can borrow reserves from another bank, the cheaper it is for the bank to lend, because the overnight rate is a cost of making a loan if the borrowing bank needs additional reserves in order to be able to make it. The lower the cost of borrowing, the lower the cost of lending the borrowed money. And so when banks can borrow reserves cheaply, competition among banks will tend to compress interest rates, including long-term interest rates.

A famous example of how the Federal Reserve can influence long-term interest rates through open market operations is its breaking of the inflation of the late 1970s. Inflation was running at an annual rate of 12 percent when Paul Volcker was appointed

6. See Hakan Berument and Richard Froyen, "Monetary Policy and U.S. Long-Term Interest Rates: How Close Are the Linkages?" 61 *Journal of Economics and Business* 34, 35 (2009).

7. Another interbank interest rate, but higher than the federal funds rate because LIBOR is a rate on unsecured three-month loans rather than on overnight secured loans.

chairman of the Fed in August 1979, and the federal funds rate was 11 percent. The Fed pushed it up to 20 percent in 1981. The prime-loan bank rate, 12 percent in August 1979, followed the federal funds rate up, reaching 21.5 percent in 1981. By 1983, inflation had fallen to 3 percent.

Some economists think Volcker's actions had nothing to do with any interest rate other than the federal funds rate, but that position is unconvincing. What is true is that Volcker *pretended* not to be raising interest rates, because no one likes high interest rates, especially at the astronomical levels that they attained during this period. Instead he said in effect that the Fed was providing the banks with the amount of reserves they needed to implement the Fed's target rate of growth of the money supply—no more and no less—and the high interest rates were the market's response, which the Fed does not control. He instructed the Federal Reserve Bank of New York to reduce bank reserves.[8] The federal funds rate is the price of reserves, so a reduction in the amount of reserves pushes up the rate, just as pushing up the rate by selling Treasury bills reduces the amount of reserves.[9] Volcker's action in maintaining high interest rates in the face of strong political pressures convinced the financial community that he was serious about breaking inflation. So expectations of inflation fell, and with them interest rates—and inflation.

What we experienced in the early 2000s was the Fed working

8. A recent book by a long-serving senior civil servant at the Federal Reserve explains Volcker's strategy: Stephen H. Axilrod, *Inside the Fed: Monetary Policy and Its Management, Martin through Greenspan to Bernanke* (2009). For empirical evidence that monetary shocks such as that engineered by Volcker's Fed indeed have the predicted effect of raising interest rates and causing output and employment to fall, see Christina D. Romer and David H. Romer, "Does Monetary Policy Matter? A New Test in the Spirit of Friedman and Schwartz," 4 *NBER Macroeconomics Annual* 121 (1989).

9. In practice, altering the amount of reserves and altering the federal funds rate are not quite equivalent. See Lawrence S. Ritter, William L. Silber, and Gregory F. Udell, *Principles of Money, Banking & Financial Markets* 406–409 (12th ed. 2009). But the differences are not important to my analysis.

the opposite side of the street: pushing interest rates down, to prevent deflation, rather than up, to break an inflation. At the beginning of 2000, the federal funds rate was 5.5 percent, and the average interest rate for a conventional thirty-year mortgage was 8.2 percent. Alan Greenspan, the Fed's chairman, feared deflation (erroneously, as it now seems) as a result of a recession caused by the collapse of the dot-com stock market bubble. So the Fed began pushing down the federal funds rate. By December 2003 it had fallen to 1 percent and the thirty-year mortgage interest rate had slipped to 5.9 percent—and housing prices had risen (since the beginning of 2000) by 42 percent. Beginning in July 2004, the Fed raised the federal funds rate in tiny steps, reaching 5.3 percent in July 2007. By then the mortgage interest rate had risen to 6.7 percent. After that, both interest rates began to decline. Housing prices had continued to increase until March 2006 and by then were more than 80 percent above their 2000 level, even though the mortgage interest rate had risen from its 2003 low of 5.2 percent to 6.4 percent.

If low interest rates drive up housing prices, high interest rates should (and eventually do) drive them down. Yet we have just seen that housing prices continued rising after interest rates started to rise. A leading housing economist, Edward Glaeser, has pointed out to me in correspondence that judging from studies of the responsiveness of housing prices to interest rates in other periods, it is unlikely that the fall in mortgage interest rates during the early 2000s accounted for more than 20 percent of the increase in housing prices.

What we are seeing in the numbers is a classic bubble phenomenon, a phenomenon that has been observed in a variety of markets in a variety of countries for centuries.[10] The low interest rates of the early 2000s pushed up housing prices both directly and indirectly: directly by reducing the cost of housing debt— and housing, as I mentioned, is bought mainly with debt—and

10. See John K. Galbraith, *A Short History of Financial Euphoria* (1993).

indirectly by pushing up the value of common stocks, which made people feel wealthier because their savings were increasingly concentrated in common stock, whether held in brokerage accounts, retirement accounts, college savings plans, health savings plans, or other forms. Feeling wealthier, people felt abler to afford to buy a house, or to use their existing house as collateral for borrowing money to buy other things, especially if its market value was rising. Banks, able to borrow capital at low rates for lending and thinking they could spread the risks of high-risk loans efficiently, were eager to encourage borrowing by relaxing their credit standards. So people who previously could not have qualified for a mortgage at any interest rate were able to obtain a mortgage at an affordable rate.

And despite my earlier point that short-term interest rates influence long-term rates, the bubble-making effect of short-term rates does not depend on that influence. Low short-term rates will incite risky lending even if long-term rates are high. Suppose there's a class of borrowers who are poor credit risks and would be willing to pay up to 10 percent for a loan but can't afford to pay more, and anyway no lender would lend at a higher rate because the higher rate would greatly increase the likelihood of a default. Suppose further that because the risk of default even at a 10 percent interest rate is high, a bank will not lend to these would-be borrowers if its cost of capital is more than 3 percent; it needs a 7 percent spread to compensate it for the risk of default. If the short-term interest rate falls to 3 percent, the bank will make the loan, which will increase the riskiness of the bank's loan portfolio. Greenspan's monetary policy thus contributed to the willingness of banks to lend against subprime mortgages. This not only increased the risk to the banks; it increased the demand for houses, and thus contributed to the housing bubble, by bringing into the market buyers who could not have obtained a mortgage at an affordable rate had it not been for the low short-term interest rates that induced the banks to reduce their credit standards.

The economist John Taylor has devised a rule for determining what the federal funds rate—the benchmark short-term interest rate—should be. The rule is based on how far below or above the desired inflation rate the actual rate is (as we'll see in chapter 3, the optimum rate of inflation is not zero) and on how far below its productive capacity the economy is operating. If the economy is in the doldrums and inflation is low, the federal funds rate should be set low, but if the economy is booming and inflation is nonnegligible, it should be higher.[11] Interest rates in the early 2000s were far below where they should have been according to Taylor's rule. That should have resulted in a high rate of inflation, which would have signaled to the Fed that it should raise the federal funds rate. But because of rapid productivity gains in American industry and because of cheap foreign imports, mainly from China, the prices of most goods and services, and hence the consumer price index, the most common measure of the price level, did not rise much. The Fed and most economists thought the Fed had succeeded in squaring the circle, maintaining low interest rates, which stimulate economic activity, without the inflation that rates so far below the level indicated by Taylor's rule would have led one to expect.

In fact there *was* inflation, but it was asset-price inflation—specifically, inflation in the price of houses (also commercial real estate) and of common stock. The inflation in housing prices caused a bubble, that is, an unsustainable rise in asset prices as a result of a misestimation of asset values. Once house prices

11. See John B. Taylor, *Getting Off Track: How Government Actions and Interventions Caused, Prolonged, and Worsened the Financial Crisis* 2, 62 (2009). The Taylor rule has been expressed variously, but in its simplest form (see id. at 67) states that the federal funds rate should equal $1.5i + 0.5y + 1\%$, where i is the inflation rate and y the difference between the rate of growth of GDP and its trend-line (that is, normal) rate of growth. Suppose GDP is 4 percent below its trend line (so that y is -4 percent) and inflation is 2 percent; then the federal funds rate should be 2 percent. If GDP were 2 percent above the trend line and inflation were 4 percent, the federal funds rate should be 8 percent.

started rising, mainly because of dangerously low interest rates, the increase acquired momentum. That is the classic bubble phenomenon and the explanation for the continued increase in housing prices after mortgage interest rates rose.

Buying in a bubble is not necessarily irrational behavior, as some economists believe, though it is risky. An increase in the price of an asset, after that increase has continued for a significant time, creates a belief that the asset is a good value. One sees other people bidding up the price of houses and assumes they know something that perhaps one does not; uninformed traders figure that the informed ones are driving the market.[12] Whether buying in a rising market produces a good or a bad investment depends on when one buys relative to the peak. People who buy in the early stages of a bubble may do fine, for even after the bubble bursts, the value of what they bought may be substantially higher than when they bought it.

And when officials and economists, and not just brokers and bankers, say that housing prices are rising because of "fundamental" changes in demand and supply that are likely to continue, the belief that a house is a good value, even though it costs a good deal more than it would have cost just a year or two ago, is fortified. As late as October 2005, as the housing bubble was beginning to leak air, Ben Bernanke, the chairman of the President's Council of Economic Advisers—and about to be appointed the chairman of the Federal Reserve—stated publicly that the rapidly rising housing prices were *not* the product of a bubble.[13] Reassured, the finance industry continued making

---

12. Gadi Barlevy and Pietro Veronesi, "Rational Panics and Stock Market Crashes," 110 *Journal of Economic Theory* 234 (2003). Irrational or not, momentum trading is well documented. See the discussion and references in Dimitri Vayanos and Paul Woolley, "An Institutional Theory of Momentum and Reversal" (Paul Woolley Centre Working Paper Series No. 1, EMG Discussion paper 621, Nov. 28, 2008).

13. Neil Henderson. "Bernanke: There's No Housing Bubble to Go Bust," *Washington Post,* Oct. 27, 2005, p. D1.

risky mortgage loans and selling risky securities backed by those loans to similarly reassured investors.

But because all that was sustaining housing prices was the expectation of continued price increases, when those increases ended because the Fed had finally stepped on the interest rate brakes, the demand for houses fell and so prices fell. The fall was precipitous, because many people could afford the high prices only on the premise that prices would continue to rise and by doing so increase the value of their houses and thus their wealth, rather than draining their money into meeting heavy monthly mortgage payments.

There were plenty of public warnings of a housing bubble, going back to 2002 and found even (indeed especially) in local newspapers.[14] But most economists missed the bubble, and so it was easy to dismiss the few who warned as alarmists, prophets of doom, naysayers, sourpusses, attention-seekers. The Federal Reserve shouldn't be criticized *too* harshly for accepting the conventional wisdom—although its failure to put two and two together and conclude that extremely low interest rates were causing asset-price inflation is pretty amazing. But its failure either to take the warnings seriously enough to evaluate them in depth (the Fed has some 250 Ph.D. economists), or to prepare contingency plans in the event that the ascent of housing prices proved indeed to be a bubble and the bubble collapsed and brought the banking industry (so heavily invested in housing) down with it, was inexcusable. As a result of the Fed's unpreparedness, when the banks began falling like ninepins in September 2008 the government was caught by surprise, improvised spasmodically, failed critically to prevent the bankruptcy of Lehman Brothers, and by its pratfalls deepened the downturn—as we shall see in the next chapter.

Some economists, such as Eugene Fama, disbelieve in bub-

14. See Richard A. Posner, *A Failure of Capitalism: The Crisis of '08 and the Descent into Depression* 118–119 (2009).

bles.[15] They think that markets are efficient mechanisms for aggregating and processing information and therefore that prices, including (or so Fama, at least, believes)[16] housing prices, reflect a realistic assessment of value. They argue that when housing prices rose rapidly between 2001 and 2006, it was because of a realistic belief that housing was in short supply relative to demand (maybe because land available for housing was shrinking, or the number of people who wanted and could afford to buy a house was growing, or interest rates would remain low for a long time), and that when housing prices collapsed, it was because of a realistic belief that a shock from the outside would hit the economy and make housing prices plummet.

The argument is not persuasive. There were no fundamental factors driving housing prices to the levels they attained. Nor was there any external shock to the economy that made houses suddenly worth less in March 2006. Housing prices rose first on low interest rates, then on momentum, and the inevitable though unforeseen collapse of those prices inaugurated a chain of events that triggered a widespread economic collapse which had an adverse feedback effect on housing prices. Some of the biggest increases in housing prices occurred in areas in which there was no shortage of land for housing, such as the desert surrounding Las Vegas.

Many conservative economists, such as Fama, strongly committed to an austerely rational model of human behavior, have exaggerated the degree to which businessmen and consumers make decisions based on sufficiently complete information, accurately processed, to avoid making huge mistakes. This exaggeration has prevented them from understanding the causes and

15. "The word 'bubble' drives me nuts." "Interview with Eugene Fama," Nov. 2, 2007, *The Region* (Federal Reserve Bank of Minneapolis), www .minneapolisfed.org/publications_papers/pub_display.cfm?id=1134 (visited Dec. 2, 2009).

16. See Eugene F. Fama, "Efficient Capital Markets: II," 46 *Journal of Finance* 1575 (1991). See also "Interview with Eugene Fama," note 15 above.

course of the depression. Some behavioral economists (economists who use the teachings of cognitive psychology to explain economic behavior) have gone to the opposite extreme of assuming that a great deal of human behavior, even in high-level financial maneuvers, is irrational from the standpoint of maximizing expected utility. The intermediate position, to which I subscribe, is that most human behavior, or at least the behavior of businessmen and consumers, is rational, provided that we are prepared to accept a more realistic concept of human rationality than many present-day economists are willing to accept. The more realistic concept acknowledges the role of irreducible uncertainty in decision making and the resulting influence of personality traits such as optimism or pessimism, and the prevalence of mistake. It accepts the results of "behavioral finance"[17]—a hybrid of finance theory and behavioral economics—but interprets them in a way that is consistent with the realistic concept of rationality.

In the case of investment bubbles, the three positions are personified by economists Fama, Robert Shiller, and Andrei Shleifer.[18] I will give an example of their differences that is unrelated to the bubble and then a bubble example. Money managers often sell underperforming stocks at the end of a quarter, though this timing does nothing to increase the value of their portfolios. To Fama this is anomalous, to Shiller an example of irrationality, but to Shleifer an example of rational behavior in the face of uncertainty. The money manager doesn't know how to beat the market (almost nobody does) and so must settle for average performance. He doesn't want his clients to notice underperforming stocks in his portfolio and ask embarrassing questions about why he made such poor picks. These client reviews are most

17. See Nicholas Barberis and Richard Thaler, "A Survey of Behavioral Finance," in *Handbook of the Economics of Finance,* ch. 18 (G. M. Constantinides, M. Harris, and R. Stulz eds. 2003).

18. See the lively discussion of their positions in Justin Fox, *The Myth of the Rational Market: A History of Risk, Reward, and Delusion on Wall Street,* ch. 14 (2009).

likely to occur at the end of a quarter, and so the money manager can minimize criticism by getting rid of the underperforming stocks then. This is rational behavior, though it distorts market valuations by clustering the sale of certain stocks at particular times and therefore pushing down their price for reasons unrelated to predictions of corporate earnings or other economically meaningful measures of shareholder values.[19]

A bubble-related example of stock market behavior goes by the name of "herding" or "going with the flow," which again to Fama is anomalous and to Schiller irrational but to Shleifer rational. If stock prices are rising, a money manager may suspect that the price increase is driven by ignorant "day traders" or by mistaken valuations by his fellow investment professionals. But he cannot be certain, for if certainty were possible, stock prices would never rise without a solid basis in economic value. So he may be mistaken if he sells, and if so he will stand out as a failure. If he goes with the flow and (as he suspects but isn't certain) he is buying into a bubble and stock prices later fall, he does not stand out from the crowd; they gain no competitive advantage from his failure, because they failed too. This is a rational strategy that helps explain bubbles.

A competitive mechanism that contributes more directly to the formation and expansion of a bubble is that short-run profits in a bubble tend to be very high because prices are rising rapidly. A bank that forgoes those profits out of fear that they are an artifact of a bubble that sooner or later must burst may lose key employees, whose compensation is geared to the profits they generate, and investors, especially those who, holding a well-diversified portfolio, would not be hurt by the collapse of one of the stocks in the portfolio. Because the price of a stock cannot

19. This example is from John Roberts, "Designing Incentives in Organizations" (Comment on Richard A. Posner, "From the New Institutional Economics to Organization Economics: With Applications to Corporate Governance, Government Agencies, and Legal Institutions") (forthcoming in *Journal of Institutional Economics*).

fall below zero but has no upper limit, the investor may want the company to take great risk, because risk and return are positively correlated in financial transacting.

Greenspan presided over the Federal Reserve when the housing bubble formed, and so has received criticism, to which he has responded in a series of papers. In the first, a narrative of the Federal Reserve's monetary policy between 1979 and 2004, he explains that the Fed during that period, under Paul Volcker's chairmanship and then his own, raised and lowered the federal funds rate in order to achieve, so far as possible, full employment with minimal inflation.[20] He notes the dot-com stock market bubble of the late 1990s and explains that the Fed did not try to puncture it by raising interest rates, fearing that to do so would cause "a substantial economic contraction and possible financial destabilization." He does not explain why he thought those consequences would have ensued.

He notes that after the bubble burst and a recession ensued in 2001, the Fed reduced the federal funds rate; by June 2003 it was at 1 percent, "the lowest level in 45 years." He thought (this was at the beginning of 2004) that such a reduction would not cause inflation because "both inflation and inflation expectations were low and stable." In fact, low interest rates had caused asset-price inflation—the housing and stock market bubbles, both well under way when he wrote. He didn't mention the possibility of a housing bubble, and anyway he had earlier said that rather than "trying to contain a putative bubble by drastic actions with largely unpredictable consequences," the Fed should "focus on policies to mitigate the fallout when it occurs and, hopefully, ease the transition to the next expansion.'"[21] We have learned that

20. Alan Greenspan, "Risk and Uncertainty in Monetary Policy," 94 *American Economic Review* 33 (2004).

21. This was also Bernanke's position. See "Asset 'Bubbles' and Monetary Policy: Remarks of Governor Ben S. Bernanke before the New York Chapter of the National Association of Business Economics," Oct. 15,

such policies, which were instituted beginning with the banking collapse of September 2008, can be immensely costly.

Greenspan's second paper, published in April 2008, after Bear Stearns, a major "shadow bank" (see next chapter), had collapsed in the wake of the bursting of the housing bubble, remarked that similar housing bubbles had emerged in more than two dozen countries besides the United States between 2001 and 2006.[22] He attributed these housing bubbles not to U.S. monetary policy but rather to a "dramatic fall in real long term interest rates." He did not acknowledge that the Federal Reserve should have started pushing up interest rates before 2004, adding that "regulators confronting real time uncertainty have rarely, if ever, been able to achieve the level of future clarity required to act preemptively." Tighter regulation of banking would have made no difference, because in his view the financial "misjudgments of the investment community" bore primary or even sole responsibility for the problems in housing finance. He added that the situation was stabilizing, and he repeated the view expressed in his 2004 article that the Federal Reserve should not try to prick bubbles.

Greenspan's third paper, published in March 2009, is, as one would expect, more defensive in tone, for by then, as he acknowledges, disaster had struck. The article argues that the housing bubble and the ensuing near-collapse of the international banking system were not at all due to the Federal Reserve's having pushed the federal funds rate way down and kept it there for years, but instead was the result of China's accumulation and

2002, www.federalreserve.gov/boarddocs/speeches/2002/20021015/default .htm (visited Dec. 3, 2009).

22. Alan Greenspan, "A Response to My Critics," *Economics Forum* hosted by the *Financial Times,* Apr. 6, 2008, http://blogs.ft.com/economists forum/2008/04/alan-greenspan-a-response-to-my-critics/ (visited Dec. 4, 2009).

investment of vast dollar reserves.[23] This had to be the cause, he argued, because the housing bubble was caused by low *long-term* interest rates—such as interest rates on thirty-year residential mortgages—while the federal funds rate is a short-term rate; and while short-term rates and long-term rates used to move in tandem, this relation was, he argued, shattered, beginning in 2002, by the flood of foreign capital into the United States.

The argument is doubly unpersuasive, for reasons I explained earlier: low short-term interest rates can feed a bubble even if long-term interest rates are high; and low short-term rates are likely to keep long-term interest rates low. It is important to bear in mind that the federal funds rate is a signal of the Fed's belief about inflation. If the rate is low, this implies that the Fed is not worried about inflation. Greenspan was a highly respected Fed chairman; his views about inflation prospects carried weight. His belief that inflation was not in the offing was calculated to push down long-term interest rates, because such rates are highly sensitive to expectations of inflation. Even economists such as Fama who are skeptical about the effect of Fed monetary policy on interest rates acknowledge that it affects the inflation component of those rates. Furthermore, given the popularity of adjustable-rate mortgages—which Greenspan beat the drums for[24]—short-term interest rates had a direct effect on the cost of mortgages during this period.

Greenspan's argument that the Fed had lost control of long-term interest rates because of inflows of foreign capital and therefore could not have lanced the housing bubble even if it had wanted to cannot be squared with the fact that the bubble burst when mortgage interest rates rose, though with a lag because of

23. Alan Greenspan, "The Fed Didn't Cause the Housing Bubble," *Wall Street Journal,* Mar. 11, 2009, p. A15.

24. See, for example, Sue Kirchhoff and Barbara Hagenbaugh, "Greenspan Says ARMs Might Be Better Deal," *USA Today,* Feb. 23, 2004, p. B1.

the self-sustaining character of a bubble. And it is plain from his earlier statements that Greenspan neither had been aware that there was a housing bubble nor would have lanced it had he been aware. He thought bubbles should be allowed to expand and burst and then the Federal Reserve would wake up, step in, and by reducing interest rates limit the effect of the bubble's bursting on asset prices ("mitigate the fallout when it occurs")[25]—which we have discovered it cannot do, at least by itself and without great cost to society. It was like saying the government should do nothing to prevent an epidemic, just swing into action after the epidemic hits. On the contrary, the government, through procurement of vaccines, medical research, and early-warning networks, engages in precautionary activity before an epidemic strikes; and the same should have been true, *mutatis mutandis,* regarding the financial "epidemic" that brought on the current depression.

Greenspan was in the grip of the monetarist fallacy that an economic collapse can always be averted by the Fed's reducing the federal funds rate to stimulate economic activity by increasing the amount of lendable funds that banks have. That doesn't work if the capital of the banking system is impaired, as it was when the housing market, in which the banks were so heavily invested, collapsed. For while by means of open market operations the Fed can flood the banks with money, they may decide not to lend it but instead to hoard it as a hedge against insolvency—which they have done. (You can lead a bank to money but you can't make it lend.) At this writing, the banks are sitting on $1 trillion in excess reserves—that is, lendable cash. The Fed under Bernanke, attempting to redeem its earlier mistakes, responded to the banks' reluctance to lend once disaster struck by going into the commercial banking business itself: buying mortgage-backed securities, credit card debt, commercial paper, and long-

25. Bernanke was of this view as well. Ethan S. Harris, *Ben Benanke's Fed: The Federal Reserve after Greenspan* 149–151 (2008).

term Treasury securities—just the sort of thing that commercial banks do.

When in 2004 the Fed began raising interest rates, Greenspan promised that the increase would be gradual, and it was. The policy, and its announcement, helped keep housing prices rising, by reassuring the market that interest rates would continue to be low for some time. Greenspan made another promise as well —and it was even more harmful. As Reinhart and Rogoff explain, "investors . . . relied on the central banks to bail them out in the event of any trouble. The famous 'Greenspan put' . . . was based on the (empirically well-founded) belief that the U.S. central bank would resist raising interest rates in response to a sharp upward spike in asset prices (and therefore not undo them) but would react vigorously to any sharp fall in asset prices by cutting interest rates to prop them up. Thus, markets believed, the Federal Reserve provided investors with a one-way bet."[26] A put is an option to sell a security to the issuer of the put at a specified price. It thus protects the buyer of the put from a fall in the price of the security below that price (the exercise, or "strike," price). The "Greenspan put" was an implied promise that if asset prices took a sudden dive, the Fed, by lowering interest rates, would place a floor under the drop ("mitigate the fallout"). By promising to limit the damage from any bursting asset-price bubble, while coupling the promise with denials that there was a bubble, the Fed helped the bubble expand. The Fed under Bernanke kept Greenspan's promise, lowering the federal funds rate as housing values plummeted, but by doing so failed to stave off the banking collapse.

Granted, raising interest rates—which the Fed should have done years earlier—is a costly way of stopping a bubble before it reaches a point at which it bursts with catastrophic effect, be-

26. Carmen M. Reinhart and Kenneth S. Rogoff, *This Time Is Different: Eight Centuries of Financial Folly* 291 (2009). See also Axilrod, note 8 above, at 147, 153.

cause higher interest rates curtail economic activity in general, not just overinvestment in housing.[27] A more targeted alternative would be a margin requirement for house purchases (see chapter 5), like the margin requirement for stock purchases. But that would be politically unthinkable. The only realistic method of stopping the housing bubble before it got too large, other than raising interest rates, would have been vigorous enforcement by the Fed and the Securities and Exchange Commission of their ample regulatory authority over financial intermediaries (the SEC regulates most shadow banks). That wasn't tried. Neither agency knew there was a housing bubble or what could happen if it was allowed to expand indefinitely. The Fed did raise interest rates eventually, but—thanks in part to the "Greenspan put"— too late and too slowly to prevent the bubble from becoming self-sustaining.[28]

Nor would the targeted alternatives to higher interest rates have gotten at the underlying problem—the violation of the Taylor rule. The bubble was the product of loose monetary policy, that is, of inflation. Inflation is inflation even if it is channeled into assets rather than consumables, and the only way to prevent inflation from getting out of hand is to raise interest rates. Had a bubble in housing been prevented by regulation, inflation would have taken another form, albeit one that might not have had as serious macroeconomic effects. A housing bubble is potentially disastrous because of the entwinement of the banking industry with the financing of housing—as the Federal Reserve should have realized.

One cannot be certain that there would have been no housing bubble had the Federal Reserve adhered to the Taylor rule. Interest rates, including mortgage interest rates, would have been

27. Bernanke, note 21 above, stresses this point.
28. There is growing, albeit belated, recognition within the Fed itself that its passivity regarding bubbles was a mistake. See Jon Hilsenrath, "Fed Debates New Role: Bubble Fighter," *Wall Street Journal,* Dec. 2, 2009, p. A1.

higher, but maybe not enough higher to avert the bubble. Even so, had it not been for the inadequacy of federal regulation of the banking (including shadow banking) industry, discussed further in the next chapter, the bursting of a housing bubble would not have brought down the industry and by doing so triggered a depression. We needed either sound monetary policy or effective regulation of banking. We got neither.

Housing debt in the United States is huge—something like $12 trillion, which is roughly the size of the national debt and almost as large as the gross domestic product (the market value of all goods and services sold in the U.S. economy during a year). When the housing bubble burst and housing prices fell sharply, the banking industry, being heavily invested in the financing of housing, including its financing by means of abnormally risky mortgages (subprime mortgages), collapsed. The collapse, as we'll see in the next chapter, brought on a depression. The collapse itself is traced in this chapter.[1]

1. There is a growing analytical literature of high quality on the financial crisis that crested in September 2008. Notable examples are Carmen M. Reinhart and Kenneth S. Rogoff, *This Time Is Different: Eight Centuries of Financial Folly*, pt. v (2009); Markus K. Brunnermeier, "Deciphering the Liquidity and Credit Crunch 2007–2008," *Journal of Economic Perspectives* 77 (Winter 2009); Harold James, *The Creation and Destruction of Value: The Globalization Cycle*, ch. 3 (2009); *The Road Ahead for the Fed* (John D. Ciorciari and John B. Taylor eds. 2009); *Restoring Financial Stability: How to Repair a Failed System* (Viral V. Acharya and Matthew Richardson eds. 2009); "Special Issue: Causes of the Financial Crisis," 21 *Critical Review* 125 (2009); Ben Steil, "Lessons of the Financial Crisis" (Council on Foreign Relations, Center for Geoeconomic Studies, Council Special Report No. 45, March 2009); Philip Swagel, "The Financial Crisis: An Inside View" (Brookings Institution, March 2009); Symposium: "The Mortgage Meltdown, the Economy, and Public Policy," 9, 3 *B.E. Journal of Economic*

Housing prices had started falling in 2006, and by July 2007 mortgage financing was understood to be in deep trouble. Countrywide, the nation's largest mortgage bank, almost collapsed the following month. Some hedge funds that had bought mortgages collapsed as well. Bear Stearns, a major shadow bank (a financial intermediary that provides banking or banklike services but is not a commercial bank), failed in March 2008 but was saved from bankruptcy by the Federal Reserve, which subsidized Bear's acquisition by JPMorgan Chase. Already in 2007 the Fed had created a "Term Auction Facility" to make it easier for banks to exchange their loans and other assets for cash, but there were few takers, because firms are reluctant to recognize a loss on their books and were afraid that using the facility would be seen as a sign of weakness. Early in 2008 Congress appropriated $168 billion for income-tax rebates to stimulate the economy, hoping that the recipients would spend rather than hoard the rebates; in retrospect, the rebates were a first installment in what in February 2009 became a much larger stimulus program. In the summer of 2008 the two giant federally sponsored though privately owned mortgage companies, Fannie Mae and Freddie Mac, tottered, and early in September they were placed in the equivalent of a receivership administered by the government.

The big financial collapse, however, did not occur until mid-September—after the government thought the situation had stabilized. In a period of weeks the government saved the major banks (plus American Insurance Group) from bankruptcy—all but one, Lehman Brothers. The abandonment of Lehman to its fate was, as we'll see, a colossal blunder.[2] A global financial col-

---

Analysis & Policy (2009), www.bepress.com/bejeap/vol9/iss3 (visited Oct. 18, 2009).

2. Very few doubt it was a blunder; whether "colossal" in consequences is more debatable. I argue that it was. See also William Sterling, "Looking Back at Lehman: An Empirical Analysis of the Financial Shock and the Effectiveness of Countermeasures" (forthcoming in *Journal of Musahi University*).

lapse ensued. The availability of credit plummeted despite the efforts of the Fed and of other countries' central banks to encourage lending by flooding banks with money. For a period in September the yield on Treasury securities was negative, meaning that people were not merely forgoing all interest but in effect paying interest for the privilege of holding wealth in an utterly safe form. Housing prices were falling so fast that prime mortgages, normally protected by the mortgagor's equity in his house, were endangered as well as subprime ones. By April 2009 housing prices would be 26 percent below their peak in 2006.

In seeking the causes of the collapse of the banking industry, one discovers a number of regulatory failures besides the failure of monetary policy discussed in the last chapter.

The industry had been transformed—in part as a result of a financial deregulation movement that had begun in 1980, had culminated in the repeal of the Glass-Steagall Act in 1999, and had been succeeded by a period of notably lax financial regulation during the Bush Administration—by the emergence and growth, to virtual parity with commercial banking, of the essentially unregulated shadow banking subindustry of financial institutions that provided a variety of banklike services. Commercial banks (including savings banks and savings and loan associations, now called "thrifts") had traditionally accounted for the lion's share of lending both to businesses and to consumers. Their capital had consisted to a large extent of demand deposits, which since the 1930s had been federally insured up to a modest ceiling, and on which the banks were forbidden to pay interest. But with the rise of the shadow banking industry—the assets of broker-dealers alone increased from less than 2 percent of the financial assets of the private sector in 1980 to 22 percent in 2007—and of new financing methods, the relative amount of lending done by commercial banks declined. In 2007 they accounted for only 17 percent of all lending in the American economy, though with the financial crisis that figure increased as lending by broker-dealers and other shadow banks declined.

(Broker-dealers—of which the best known before the crash were Goldman Sachs, Morgan Stanley, Merrill Lynch, Lehman Brothers, and Bear Stearns—broker, but also deal in, that is, buy and sell, securities, including commercial paper, bonds, and other debt securities, as well as common stock.)

Some forms of nonbank lending are old, such as the issuance of bonds and of preferred stock (which, despite the name, is a form of debt, but debt subordinated to the claims of the borrower's other creditors), as well as the financing of projects out of retained earnings, which amounts to borrowing from shareholders. Increasingly, however, highly creditworthy businesses financed their day-to-day operations by issuing commercial paper, which consists of unsecured short-term promissory notes and is bought by (that is, the lenders are) money-market funds, broker-dealers, and other shadow banks. The move to commercial paper deprived the banks of some of their best customers and by doing so nudged them into riskier lending to maintain the spread between the cost of capital and the return on capital.

In another important development, big corporations, instead of making bank deposits in excess of the limits on federal deposit insurance, began depositing their cash in financial institutions, such as broker-dealers, that would put up collateral in the form of securities of one kind or another to give the depositor protection against default. Commercial paper is short-term, and so are repos (see chapter 1), which enabled large deposits to be made in shadow banks' uninsured accounts with relative security. An incidental effect was to deprive the commercial banks of deposits that they would otherwise have had.

The rise of hedge funds (unregulated investment firms) induced broker-dealers to offer them what is called "prime brokerage," consisting of a variety of financial services. For example, a prime broker might hold a hedge fund's money while the hedge fund was between investments and needed somewhere to park its money. More commonly, the prime broker would lend the hedge fund money by means of repos secured by stocks or bonds posted by the hedge fund, to finance the hedge fund's lending and other investment activities.

And money-market mutual funds offered checkable accounts that were like conventional bank accounts except that—until the financial collapse, and again now—they were (are) not federally insured. The money-market funds paid interest on deposits, interest earned by lending the money in the depositors' accounts.

So commercial banks faced increasing competition for deposits, their safest form of capital, from a variety of shadow banks, and indeed from each other, because deregulation tore down the regulatory barriers that had limited interbank competition, such as state prohibitions on branch banking.

The growth of securitized debt, specifically mortgage-backed securities, was a major factor in the rise of the shadow banks, which specialized in originating and trading novel financial instruments. Not that securitized debt was new; a bond is a form of securitized debt. But traditionally a bank that made a mortgage loan (or bought a mortgage loan from the originating bank) held it to maturity. Alternatively, however, a number of mortgages could be packaged as a security—a kind of giant bond—the income on which was the sum of the interest paid by the mortgagors, though some of the income might go to the owner of the security itself, in the form of a return on equity. (The owner would also receive the principal of the mortgages as it was repaid by the mortgagors.) The advantage of securitized debt was that it enlarged the debt market: a person incapable of making or servicing a loan could still become a lender, by buying a debt security.

By the early 1980s Fannie Mae and Freddie Mac were originating (creating), buying, guaranteeing, and reselling mortgage-backed securities. The originator would be compensated for its work in creating the security by fees paid by purchasers, but often received additional compensation by acting as the "servicer" of the mortgages in the package—that is, attending to collection, modification, foreclosure, and other services incidental to the ownership of a mortgage.

The financial collapse has given securitized debt a bad name, as revealed in the title of an article about a planned new form of that debt: "New Exotic Instruments Emerging on Wall Street: Packaging Life Insurance Policies, Despite Fallout from Mortgage Meltdown."[3] When a person who has a life insurance policy surrenders it to the insurance company for its cash surrender value, he gets very little; yet he may have a desperate need for the money. If he sells the policy to someone who will hold it until the insured's death and then collect the full face value of the policy from the insurer, the price will greatly exceed the cash surrender value. Hence at any price between the cash surrender value and the face value of the policy (discounted to present value, since the buyer of the policy will not obtain the proceeds of the insurance policy until the insured's death), both the insured and the buyer of the policy are better off. By packaging these "life settlements" as securities, a bank or other originator can provide diversification (for the value of each settlement depends on the remaining life of the insured) as well as an investment opportunity to an investor who would not want to go into the business of negotiating life settlements.

There is nothing wrong with securitizing life insurance in this way, and there is nothing wrong in principle with the securitization of mortgages, even subprime mortgages. It is true that securitization not only enabled firms that would not have wanted to deal directly with a mortgagor to invest in the mortgage market (the investor might be in a different country—interests in American mortgage-backed securities were sold all over the world), but also facilitated a lowering of credit standards. But it was believed, not unreasonably, that the greater risk of default when credit standards are lowered would be offset by two features of the securities.

First, by combining mortgages from many different parts of the country, mortgage-backed securities achieved geographical

3. By Jenny Anderson, *New York Times,* Sept. 6, 2009, p. 1.

diversification of mortgage risk and thus made the package less risky than the individual mortgages in it. Second, each mortgage-backed security was sold in pieces (called "tranches"—French for "slices"), each of which had a different risk-return combination, which enabled investors to choose their preferred level of risk. (A tranche was thus a bond secured by an interest in a mortgage pool.) The senior tranche would be paid from the mortgage pool before any of the junior tranches, much as a debt holder's claim on a corporation's assets is senior to an equity holder's. So even if all the mortgages in the pool were substandard in terms of credit risk, the investment of the senior-tranche investors could be safe. How safe would depend on the size of the senior tranche relative to the junior ones. If the senior tranche was secured by 80 percent of the mortgage pool, the pool would have to lose more than 20 percent of its value before the owners of that tranche were hurt. The senior tranches were rated triple-A by the credit-rating agencies and were bought by commercial banks here and abroad. The junior tranches, because they were riskier, carried higher interest rates and lower credit ratings, and were bought by hedge funds and other investors willing to take greater risks in exchange for a higher expected return.

Although tranching had been used by Fannie Mae as early as 1983, the practice of packaging high-risk mortgages into mortgage-backed securities originated with what is now the JPMorgan Chase bank in 1987. It was widely imitated when the low interest rates of the early 2000s drove up the demand for houses and therefore for mortgages.

Another feature of securitization that allayed concerns about risk is that it appeared to address the fundamental cause of the inherent riskiness of banking, which is that banks borrow short (short in the sense of being either a loan that has a fixed short term or a loan of indefinite length that the borrower can terminate at any time, as in the case of a demand deposit in a bank) and lend long. One risk is that suppliers of short-term capital may suddenly withdraw it, pulling the rug out from under a bank that has committed the capital to long-term loans. Securitization gave banks a way of transforming a long-term loan (a mortgage) into a liquid, tradable asset; for as soon as the bank packaged its mortgages into a security and sold the security, the risk of default was shifted to the investors in the security and the bank recaptured its capital, which it could then use to make another loan. But securitization as a method of reducing the riskiness of banking was compromised by the banks' either retaining an interest in the securities that they sold or buying interests in securities originated by other banks. Any owner of such an interest was vulnerable to a fall in the value of the mortgages after they had been securitized.

Securitization contributed to the housing bubble in two ways. It attracted foreign capital to the mortgage market, which helped keep mortgage rates down (given the Fed's complacency about low interest rates). And by enabling credit standards to be lowered, because securitized mortgage debt was thought (not without reason) safer than conventional mortgage debt, it expanded the pool of people who could buy a house. With housing prices rising, people with bad credit histories thought they could swing a house purchase because its value would rise and enable them to refinance their mortgage at an affordable rate, since their equity in the house would grow with every increase in market value. Adjustable-rate and other subprime mortgages (remember that I am using "subprime" broadly to denote any mortgage in which the standard down-payment and credit-rating requirements are waived or substantially watered down) facilitated such purchases, but had been rare before tranched securitization because they seemed too risky. A high risk of default cannot be compensated for by charging a very high interest rate. Charging such a rate would increase the likelihood of default by straining the borrower's finances. And he might agree to the rate only because he didn't expect to repay the loan (he borrowed with his fingers crossed).

Because risky mortgages, when securitized, seemed a safe investment for buyers of senior tranches, mortgage-backed securities became the standard method of financing, as well as encouraging, subprime mortgages. Owners of the junior tranches were compensated by higher interest rates. These were not the interest rates on the mortgages themselves. Instead, the income generated by the mortgage pool was divided among the various investors in such a way as to compensate the owners of the junior tranches for the risk they were taking and to "compensate" the owners of the senior tranches for their lower return by giving them more protection against default. Tranching of securities backed by subprime mortgages thus offered safety to cautious investors and, to owners of the junior tranches, high yields in a period of low interest rates. By 2007, it is true, housing prices were falling yet securitizations continued. But even in a lousy housing market, mortgages continue to be issued, and so there remained opportunities for creating new mortgage-backed securities.

Two subtle risks of these securities seem not to have been widely recognized. First, because the most creditworthy borrowers prepay their mortgages at a higher rate than the least creditworthy ones, the riskiness of a mortgage-backed security increases over time. Second, although the mortgages backing each security were geographically diversified, they had the identical exposure to a nationwide collapse in housing values, in much the same way that a diversified portfolio of stocks is exposed to the risk of a general fall in stock values. The risk was not factored into the interest rate offered for the triple-A tranches, and the omission enabled the originators to offer higher interest rates to the purchasers of the junior tranches, thus stimulating the demand for those tranches.[4]

A partial corrective for this correlated risk was found in debt securities that pooled mortgage debt with other debt. In order to create additional risk-return combinations, which might be at-

4. Joshua Coval, Jakub Jurek, and Erik Stafford, "The Economics of Structured Finance," *Journal of Economic Perspectives* 3 (Winter 2009).

tractive to some investors, and in particular to create more debt securities that would be rated triple-A by the credit-rating agencies (which was important because many institutional investors are permitted to invest only in securities that carry that rating), banks created what were called "collateralized debt obligations." Generally these combined nonmortgage debt (credit card debt, for example) with junior tranches of mortgage-backed securities, though some CDOs had no mortgage debt. The CDO would be sliced into tranches, just like pure mortgage-backed securities, and this would permit a new low-risk tranche to be carved out and receive the coveted triple-A rating. The thinking was that by being included in the senior tranche of the collateralized debt obligation, an otherwise risky debt would not endanger the owner of the tranche, because he would be entitled to be paid ahead of the holders of the tranches junior to it out of whatever income the entire pool of debt generated. CDOs thus provided a way of satisfying any appetite for triple-A securities not already slaked by the triple-A tranches of mortgage-backed securities. In addition, the mixing in of nonmortgage debt with mortgage debt in a CDO provided further diversification for investors in the new security—product diversification.

The complexity of this form of securitization contributed to the eventual crisis by making the valuation of CDOs excessively difficult. The value of a collateralized debt obligation depended on, among other things, the value of the mortgage-backed securities the junior tranches of which had been securitized in the CDO. To make up a single CDO required pooling a large number of tranches from separate mortgage-backed securities, each tranche being backed by hundreds or even thousands of mortgages. The reason was that the triple-A tranche was normally by far the largest of the tranches in a mortgage-backed security, as in our earlier example, where the senior tranche was 80 percent of the security. Each of the junior tranches was therefore small, and it took a lot of them to make up a $500 million package, which would be a modest-sized CDO.

A further complication was that because the owner of a tranche was often difficult to identify, the originator of the CDO might, instead of buying the tranche, issue credit-default swaps to investors in the CDO; these are promises to pay the buyers of the swap a specified amount in the event of a default or other contingency affecting a debt (more on credit-default swaps below). The swap would take the place of the absent tranche, creating what was called a synthetic CDO. (The payment for a swap can be made equivalent to payment for the underlying bond that the swap insures.)[5] In addition, tranches of CDOs were combined to create additional CDOs.[6]

Because CDOs were built largely on high-risk tranches of mortgage-backed securities, the bursting of the housing bubble brought the CDOs down with the mortgage-backed securities. The CDOs' product diversification turned out to confer little protection, because the recession triggered by the fall in housing prices increased the default rate on other forms of consumer and business debt besides mortgage debt. Moreover, as the value of mortgage-backed securities plunged, banks started selling their good corporate loans to raise cash to increase their safe capital, creating a glut of loans for sale, which pushed down the price of bonds generally and thus the value of the CDOs, a type of bond.

Debt securitization is particularly attractive to banks when the demand for loans is high, because it enables them to make

5. Charles Davi, "Rethinking OTC Credit Derivatives," *FinReg21*, Sept. 28, 2009, www.finreg21.com/lombard-street/rethinking-otc-credit-derivatives (visited Oct. 24, 2009).

6. "Assume a hypothetical CDO2 [a collateralized debt obligation consisting of tranches of collateralized debt obligations, namely corporate bonds] held 100 CLOs [collateralized loan obligations—debt consisting of bank loans rather than corporate bonds], each holding 250 corporate loans—then we would need information on 25,000 underlying loans to determine the value of the security. But assume the CDO2 held 100 CDOs each holding 100 [mortgage-backed securities] comprising a mere 2,000 mortgages, the number now rises to 20 million!" Kenneth E. Scott and John B. Taylor, "Why Toxic Assets Are So Hard to Clean Up," *Wall Street Journal*, July 21, 2009, p. A13.

more loans than they could make were their money tied up in the mortgages. Not that securitization is strictly necessary to enable a bank to recycle its capital; it can sell individual mortgages, and should in principle be able to obtain in such a sale cash equal to the present value of the future stream of mortgage payments. But potential purchasers would be limited as a practical matter to people familiar with the local mortgage market. Securitization substitutes geographical diversification, and in the case of collateralized debt obligations product diversification as well, for local knowledge, as a protection against the risk of mortgage default, while enlarging the market for mortgages—for example, by attracting foreign investors, who would never consider dealing directly with American homeowners—and providing a variety of risk-return combinations for investors to choose among.

It is not surprising that on the eve of the financial collapse, two-thirds of all mortgage debt was securitized—and for the further reason that because the mortgage default rate was low, the triple-A tranches of mortgage-backed securities seemed to be safe assets for banks to hold. The Basel II Accords, an international standard for determining the safety of banks' capital structures, deemed those triple-A tranches so safe as to justify an increase in banks' leverage. "Leverage" is the ratio of debt to equity in a firm's (or an individual's) balance sheet. The higher the ratio, the riskier the firm, because debt, unlike equity, is a fixed obligation; it doesn't diminish just because the firm's revenues decline.

Because the credit boom induced consumers to take on more mortgage and other debt, in the ensuing bust they found themselves overindebted, which increased defaults and reduced demand for houses, adding to the downward pressure on housing prices. This is an illustration of the fact that leverage is "procyclical" (increasing in booms) for lenders but "countercyclical" (increasing in busts) for households. Demand for loans is higher in a boom, and with interest rates low it is cheaper for a bank to raise the capital it needs to meet the demand for loans by borrowing than by issuing stock. But a fall in the market value of a house reduces the owner's home equity and so increases the ratio of debt to equity in his balance sheet[7]—and a sharp increase in that ratio causes people to cut back on their spending. We can begin to see how the economy can experience negative feedbacks. In a bust, banks reduce their leverage to avoid bankruptcy and so have less to lend, while consumers find their leverage increasing dangerously and so try to reduce their debt. Both the supply of and the demand for credit plummet and with them economic activity.

When the housing bubble burst, mortgagors who could no longer afford their monthly mortgage payments—for example, because they had lost their job in the gathering recession—could not sell their house at a profit. Many of the subprime mortgages, moreover, were adjustable-rate mortgages that, because mortgage interest rates had risen, reset the interest rate at a level exceeding the mortgagor's ability to pay. As housing values tumbled, mortgage debt made houses seem poor investments for those mortgagors who because of the tumble had zero or even negative equity in their houses. A homeowner in that position may decide that he's made a poor investment and may abandon the house to the mortgagee rather than continue making monthly mortgage payments. He is unlikely to be sued for the unpaid balance of the mortgage, and in some states he can't be sued; mortgage loans in those states are by law "nonrecourse." Abandonments combined with foreclosure sales and falling demand further depressed prices, and so an increasing supply of houses for sale confronted a diminishing demand.

The bursting of the mortgage bubble devastated what had become a huge worldwide market in mortgage-backed securities. Housing prices fell more steeply than credit-rating agencies or the mortgage banking industry had thought remotely likely even

7. For a helpful discussion, see Tobias Adrian and Hyun Song Shin, "Money, Liquidity, and Monetary Policy," 99 *American Economic Review Papers and Proceedings* 600 (May 2009).

if prices eventually stopped rising and began to fall. Subprime mortgage lending was only part of the problem. Residential lending secured by subprime mortgages never exceeded 21 percent of all residential borrowing in a year, and the total amount of subprime mortgage lending did not exceed $1 trillion, which is less than 10 percent of total mortgage debt. Many prime mortgages had been packaged into mortgage-backed securities along with subprime mortgages, and the fall in housing prices was so steep that it undermined prime mortgages as well as subprime ones. And because the housing bubble, though bigger in some parts of the country than in others, turned out to be nationwide, the geographical diversification of mortgage-backed securities could not save the investors from loss even when they owned the triple-A tranches of the securities they had invested in.

The demand for new mortgage-backed securities composed of subprime mortgages dried up, because tranching could no longer be used to create triple-A-rated tranches of such securities. And with the default rate on subprime mortgages soaring, there was no market for high-risk tranches and therefore no cushion to protect the conservative investor. So neither the risk-preferring investors who had bought junior tranches nor the risk-averse investors who had bought senior ones were interested in buying into a new mortgage-backed security. Many investors, moreover, had lost their shirt as a result of the decline in the value of debt securities in which they had invested previously and could not afford to make a new investment. And with housing prices continuing to tumble, it was difficult to estimate the expected return on new mortgage-backed securities.

Not only was the banking industry heavily invested in mortgage-backed securities and collateralized debt obligations, but the suddenness of the crash caught many banks owning mortgages they had not yet securitized or mortgage-backed securities that they had created but not yet sold. Some banks had pledged their interests in mortgage-backed securities as collateral for loans, and when the collateral lost value, the lenders demanded either more collateral or repayment of their loans. But with collateral falling in value across the economy, coming up with additional collateral to satisfy lenders was in many instances impossible. And because tranches of mortgage-backed securities were tradable, there was pressure on the owners of the tranches to "mark [them] to market"—that is, carry them on their books at whatever the current market price was. So as prices fell, banks' balance sheets deteriorated. True, a bank that could make a case that it intended to retain its interest in a mortgage-backed security until the mortgages matured was permitted by accounting conventions to value it at the present value of the anticipated future income from the security. But that anticipated future income, and hence the accounting valuation of the security, was depressed by the collapse of the housing market.

A further complexity arose from the fact that instead of selling a mortgage-backed security in the conventional way, often the originating bank would sell it to a special-purpose corporation that it had created—a "structured investment vehicle." The main aim was to remove mortgage-backed assets from the bank's balance sheet in order to reassure the bank's regulators that the bank wasn't taking on too much risk. A related aim was to insulate the bank from liability for losses resulting from a decline in the value of the assets. It is another example of an effort to limit risk that miscarried.

The SIV would issue bonds or other securities backed by its mortgage-backed security. When the SIV's income from the security plummeted because of defaults in the mortgages underlying the security, it could not pay its investors the promised interest. Conceivably the originating bank could have abandoned the investors to their fate by allowing the SIV to default on the bonds, because a corporation generally is not liable for the debts of an affiliated corporation. But such abandonment would have been regarded as an extraordinary breach of faith. So instead banks would move the security onto their own balance sheet and thus assume the SIV's obligations to the investors. This contributed to the deterioration in the banks' balance sheets—and for the further reason that often the originating bank had backed up its SIVs with a standby line of credit that put the bank on the hook if the SIV defaulted. The sponsoring bank might also have issued a credit-default swap to the SIV, further insuring the bondholders against the SIV's defaulting.

The effect of the drastic loss of value of the mortgage-backed securities on the banks' balance sheets was amplified by the fact that the banks had increased their leverage. Because interest on debt is tax-deductible and the cost of equity capital is not, it is cheaper for a bank to increase its capital to meet an increased demand for loans by borrowing than by issuing stock. Also, issuing new stock would dilute the ownership rights of the existing shareholders. Expanding capital by taking on new debt was particularly attractive during the boom because interest rates were so low.

But the more leverage, the more risk. If a company has 25 times as much debt as equity, a 5 percent increase in the value of the company's assets will increase the company's equity by 130 percent $(25 + 1 = 26 \times .05 = 1.3/1 = 130 \text{ percent})$—and a 5 percent reduction in its capital will wipe it out.

By the middle of September 2008 it was widely believed that much of the banking industry—especially the shadow banking part of the industry—indeed was broke, or on the verge of going broke, as the combined result of high leverage and the plunge in the value of securitized debt. That was not a universal belief, however. An alternative theory, to which the Federal Reserve and the Treasury initially subscribed, was that mere *uncertainty* about banks' solvency was making lenders (including other banks) unwilling to lend to them and was making banks unwilling to lend to *anyone* lest their capital be further impaired. That would be a crisis of liquidity—a temporary unwillingness, until the situation was clarified, to part with cash, by lending or otherwise investing it—rather than a crisis of solvency.

The uncertainty has been blamed on the complexity of the debt securities. Often thousands of mortgages were packaged in a single security, and this is said to have made the valuation of the tranches owned by banks hopelessly difficult. Certainly the CDOs were hideously complex; and the banks' off-balance-sheet contingent liabilities made assessment of the banks' solvency difficult. It was difficult to value the mortgage-backed securities as well, but not because they were complex; rather because their value depended on future events that could not be predicted— namely the default rate of the underlying mortgages as housing values plummeted.

These uncertainties did create, for a time, a liquidity crisis, but it soon became apparent that a number of major banks were on —or even over—the brink of insolvency. Especially the shadow banks, of which the most important were the government-sponsored mortgage companies (Fannie Mae and Freddie Mac) and the principal broker-dealers—Goldman Sachs, Morgan Stanley, Merrill Lynch, and Lehman Brothers. (Bear Stearns had disappeared months earlier into JPMorgan Chase.) Most of the shadow banks were regulated by the Securities and Exchange Commission, which saw its role as protecting investors rather than assuring solvency. It was a helpless bystander as the industry collapsed, though the Federal Reserve was complicit, since Greenspan and Bernanke had faith in the self-regulating character of the entire banking industry. Critically, the shadow banks did not have federally insured deposits, so the suppliers of their short-term capital were likely to withdraw it at the first sign that a bank might be at risk of imminent insolvency.

Some very large commercial banks, such as Citigroup, and some major thrifts, such as Washington Mutual, also needed government money to avert possible insolvency, because their balance sheets contained significant amounts of securitized debt that had plunged in value. For a time, interbank lending froze even as the Federal Reserve began frantically reducing the federal funds rate. While lending at the federal funds rate was secure because the loans were backed by collateral consisting of Treasury bills, the rate had fallen to so low a level as to make lending at it unattractive, and anyway the banks were fearful of parting with capital, even short-term. For unsecured interbank lending, there is LIBOR—the three-month London Interbank Offer Rate—but because it is unsecured, it shot up when the banks began doubting each other's solvency.

The nation's biggest insurance company, American International Group—a huge issuer of credit-default swaps—went broke at the same time as the banks (September 2008) and had to be rescued at enormous cost (eventually $180 billion) to the federal government. For when the crash occurred and the risk of defaults spiked, purchasers of swaps from AIG exercised their contractual right to require that AIG post more collateral. AIG didn't have enough assets to meet these demands, in part because most of its counterparties (the buyers of its swaps) had not required it to post collateral at the outset of the swap purchase, or to hold reserves, in order to assure its ability to honor the commitments represented by the swaps; and with credit frozen, AIG couldn't borrow the money or securities it needed to meet the unexpected demands for collateral. The reason that saving AIG was so costly was that the government decided to honor all of AIG's swap obligations, lest defaulting on them plunge many of the company's counterparties (which included major banks such as Goldman Sachs) into insolvency.

The shadow banks' heavy dependence on short-term capital that was not federally insured was their Achilles' heel; it made them subject to devastating runs. I will illustrate with the collapse of Lehman Brothers, an event calamitous not just for Lehman but for the entire global financial industry, in part because of Lehman's dealings with other financial institutions, such as money-market mutual funds. The checkable accounts offered by those funds pay interest (which until 1986 commercial banks were not permitted to pay on demand deposits). The funds make their spread by buying interest-paying debt, such as commercial paper, with their depositors' money; as I noted earlier, commercial paper consists of short-term unsecured promissory notes issued by companies that have sterling credit records to finance their day-to-day operations. Sometimes these notes are issued directly to money-market funds, but more commonly they are issued to broker-dealers, who then issue their own commercial paper to the funds. The cash the broker-dealers receive in return (that is, the money they borrow from the funds, the commercial paper being their promise to repay) is what they use to buy commercial paper from—which is to say, lend to—the nonfinancial issuers of commercial paper. (This is not as complicated as it sounds. It's just a matter of nonfinancial companies borrowing from broker-dealers that borrow from money-market funds that borrow from their depositors.)

Lehman, besides being an intermediary between nonfinancial issuers of commercial paper and money-market funds, was a provider of prime-brokerage services to hedge funds. Hedge funds were both depositing their idle cash with Lehman and other prime brokers between deals and depositing securities with it to secure loans to them; that is, they were both lending to Lehman and borrowing from it. Federal deposit insurance was limited to $100,000 per depositor in September 2008 (it is now $250,000), so it did not protect a hedge fund that deposited millions of dollars in an account in a commercial bank. Instead the hedge fund might make a repo agreement to buy securities from a prime broker at a specified price for a short fixed period, after which the transaction would be reversed. These "deposits" were not federally insured, but the hedge fund would be protected by the collateral (the securities) that it had received from the prime broker and also by the very short term of a repo. The expectation was that the repo would be rolled over (that is, renewed), but this was not contractually required, and so the hedge fund could get its money back on short notice.

The short term of the repos was a bother for the hedge funds, so their prime-brokerage agreements allowed the prime broker to do the repos. Lehman Brothers would pool the hedge funds' money in its prime-brokerage accounts, use the pool of money to buy securities, and give the hedge funds a secured interest in the pool every time it did a repo.

Lehman's basic vulnerability, which it shared with the other broker-dealers, was that it borrowed short and lent or invested long. Its short borrowing mainly took the form of "tri-party repos." Instead of "selling" the lender collateral, it would "sell" the collateral to a bank. The bank would be like a clearinghouse; in fact the banks that provide this service, of which the leading one is JPMorgan Chase, are called "clearing" banks. The rationale of the tri-party repo is that if the collateral is held by a bank, the borrower is more comfortable than if it were held by the lender. But this means that, like a clearinghouse, the bank assumes the risk of a default if the borrower cannot repay the loan. It protects itself by insisting that the loan be very short term (typically overnight) and that it have a right to require the posting of additional collateral if the existing collateral loses value. Much of Lehman's borrowed capital—and most of its capital *was* borrowed, for as in the case of most other broker-dealers its balance sheet was highly leveraged—was in tri-party repos.

Lehman's $630 billion balance sheet included about $70 billion of mortgage-backed securities. Because it was so highly leveraged, even a small drop in the value of its assets could endanger its solvency. As the value of its mortgage-based assets fell, Lehman had to buy additional securities to post as collateral with the clearing banks, and that was a cash drain. As its short-term investors lost confidence in Lehman's long-term solvency and began withdrawing their money, Lehman needed more and more cash, to honor the withdrawals. But the more cash it needed, the harder it was to find someone who would lend to it. A run on Lehman had begun.

The run eventually killed Lehman. The run was largely independent of Lehman's prime-brokerage activities, which were only a small part of its business. But Lehman ran into problems in those activities too, as we'll see, and those problems were both important in their own right and illustrative of the vulnerabilities of the other, and larger, prime brokers.

The hedge funds were also, as I said, big borrowers from prime brokers by means of repos in which the hedge fund would deposit securities with the prime broker to secure the loan. When Lehman started to fail because it was so heavily invested in mortgage-backed securities that were rapidly losing value, the hedge funds realized that the securities they had posted as collateral might be frozen in a Lehman bankruptcy (as happened) and that they might be unable to replace their Lehman loans because they could not post the frozen collateral as security for new loans from other potential lenders. Moreover, Lehman had placed some of the securities that it had obtained when it lent money in hedge funds outside the United States. This meant that in the event of Lehman's declaring bankruptcy, a hedge fund trying to get its cash back or enforce a security interest would get entangled in a foreign bankruptcy proceeding. Lehman was doing business in twenty countries, all with their own bankruptcy laws, and investors could not be confident that those laws would give their cash or their collateral the same protection as U.S. bankruptcy law would.

The investors in hedge funds saw the same threat, and because their investments were not federally insured, they began withdrawing their money from the hedge funds, for fear they would collapse. They didn't withdraw money just from hedge funds that had borrowed from Lehman Brothers, either, for they were afraid that other prime brokers might go the way of Lehman Brothers. So a run on the prime brokers as well as on the hedge funds developed. Although the hedge funds' contracts with their investors usually limited the amount an investor could withdraw each quarter and also required advance notice of intent to withdraw, the hedge funds worried that if they stood on this right when their investors might be desperate for cash, they would be like banks that refused to honor the debts of their SIVs; they would be creating a lot of ill will among current and potential hedge-fund investors. Rather than do that, they tried to preserve their liquidity by pulling their money or securities out of the prime brokers.

The danger to the hedge funds was underscored by the fact that Lehman was permitted by its loan agreements (as were the other prime brokers) to "rehypothecate" (repledge) the securities that the hedge funds had deposited with it to secure its loans to them. Lehman thus had borrowed money from third parties, securing those loans with the securities that the hedge funds had deposited with it. So when Lehman defaulted, two sets of contracting parties tried to get at the same securities: the hedge funds wanted them back (they were their securities), and the borrowers from Lehman wanted to use the securities to satisfy their claims against Lehman.[8]

One might have thought that since the hedge funds were debtors of Lehman and the third parties were creditors, all that had to happen was for the hedge funds to pay what they owed Lehman to the third parties, who upon being repaid would release their claims against the hedge funds' securities. But that would not work if the securities were worth less than the third parties' unsatisfied claims. Suppose a hedge fund had borrowed $1 million from Lehman and posted collateral worth $1 million, and Lehman had rehypothecated the collateral to a firm from which it had borrowed $1.5 million (the collateral having increased in value), but that since then the collateral had fallen in value back to $1 million. If the hedge fund paid the firm the $1 million that it had owed Lehman, Lehman would still owe the firm $500,000, and the firm would try to satisfy that claim out of the same collateral. The law is not entirely clear, but it seems, be-

<hr>

8. See Steven L. Schwarcz, "Busting *Nemo Dat:* Intermediary Risk and the Consequences of Distorting Legal Concepts for Business Ends" (Duke University School of Law, Oct. 7, 2009); Schwarcz, "Intermediary Risk in a Global Economy," 50 *Duke Law Journal* 1541, 1594–1597 (2001).

cause of an amendment to Article 8 of the Uniform Commercial Code, that the lender's claim would be superior to that of the borrower (the hedge fund).[9] This was another reason for the hedge funds to try to pull out of Lehman as soon as Lehman seemed headed for collapse.

All the major prime brokers were in the same boat. Two of them, Bear Stearns and Merrill Lynch, were, with the government's financial backing, merged into solvent firms. The others were also saved—all but Lehman, which was forced to declare bankruptcy because the government would not lend it the money it needed to survive. After a last-minute effort to induce the large British bank Barclays to buy Lehman fell through, Lehman could have been saved only by a loan from the Fed of between $30 and $90 billion.[10] From what happened later, it is apparent that even a loan at the top of the range would have been a bargain for the U.S. economy, regardless of how much of the loan would ever have been repaid. When Lehman defaulted on the commercial paper that it had issued to money-market funds (that is, when it failed to repay the money it had borrowed from them), a run on those funds developed because they were not federally insured, until the government stepped in and agreed to insure their depositors temporarily. And since Lehman, broke, could no longer buy commercial paper, the nonfinancial issuers drew on the standby lines of credit that they had with banks—and as a result the banks had less money to lend to the many firms that were clamoring for bank credit in the crisis atmosphere of September 2008.

Lehman was not the only broker-dealer that issued commercial paper to money-market funds; in fact it was a minor player in that market. But its default awoke the funds to their vulnerability, and they realized or suspected that the other broker-dealers that borrowed from the funds were distressed as well,

9. See Schwarcz, "Busting *Nemo Dat*," note 8 above.
10. David Wessel, *In Fed We Trust: Ben Bernanke's War on the Great Panic* 20 (2009).

and as a result the commercial-paper market, in which the money-market funds were the ultimate lenders and the broker-dealers the intermediary lenders (remember that the broker-dealers bought the nonfinancial issuers' paper and the money-market funds bought the broker-dealers' paper), froze. The Federal Reserve then stepped in and began buying commercial paper in great quantity, and the market eventually revived.

Lehman was a big issuer of international letters of credit, which are essential in foreign trade, and for a time after it collapsed letters of credit were hard to obtain and foreign trade declined. It also was both an issuer and a buyer of credit-default swaps, and when it went broke the buyers of swaps from it did not know whether it would be able to honor the swaps and the sellers of swaps to it didn't know how much they would have to pay Lehman's creditors to honor the swaps. Greatly complicating Lehman's bankruptcy was the fact that Lehman had 433 subsidiaries in the 20 countries in which it operated,[11] and all those countries had their own bankruptcy laws, which were applicable to the subsidiaries' assets located there. The status of the Lehman assets remains uncertain to this day, as the bankruptcy proceedings drag on; there is no international convention providing for a unified bankruptcy proceeding for a firm that has assets in more than one country.

The consequences of the run that brought down Lehman and threatened to bring down the other major prime brokers were amplified by the fact that no one could figure out *why* Lehman had been allowed to fail, when Bear Stearns, a similar firm in similar straits, had six months earlier been saved, although its shareholders had taken a terrific loss. The hedge funds and their investors figured that if Lehman was insolvent, many of the other prime brokers—maybe all of them—were on the brink of insolvency; and since the government had refused to save Lehman, it

11. See Richard J. Herring, "Why and How Resolution Policy Must Be Improved," in *The Road Ahead for the Fed*, note 1 above, at 171.

might refuse to save other insolvent prime brokers. The financial community could not figure out what policy was guiding the Federal Reserve and the Treasury Department, which was acting in tandem with the Fed. (In fact there was no policy, just a series of ad hoc responses by a government caught by surprise.) The failure to save Lehman accelerated the rate at which hedge funds pulled their money out of other prime brokers, because they figured that since the government had refused to save Lehman, it might refuse to save the others as well.

Had the government not bailed out Bear Sterns, the other vulnerable banks would have scrambled to raise capital to avert its fate. Whether they would have succeeded is unknown. The worst of all possible courses of action that the government could have followed—and, alas, did follow—was to save Bear Stearns, thus creating the impression that the government was committed to saving the banking industry from a general collapse by bailing out any individual major bank that was in danger of collapse, yet let Lehman Brothers, a bigger bank than Bear Stearns, fail after the banks had been lulled by Bear Stearns' rescue into thinking they had a guaranty of survival from the government.

The Federal Reserve claimed—Bernanke continues to insist—that it lacked the legal authority to save Lehman from collapse by lending it the money it would have needed to stave off bankruptcy. The claim is unpersuasive. Section 13(3) of the Federal Reserve Act[12] authorizes the Fed to lend money to a nonbank in "unusual and exigent circumstances," provided that the loan is "secured to the satisfaction of the Federal reserve bank." Lehman did not have good security for the loan it needed, but in the emergency circumstances created by a collapsing global financial system the Fed could have declared itself "satisfied" with whatever security Lehman could have offered. The statutory term "secured to the satisfaction" of the Fed is defined nei-

12. 12 U.S.C. § 343.

ther in the statute itself nor in regulations issued by the Fed, and
although there is disagreement over its meaning, one commenta-
tor states that "the Fed was effectively granted [by section 13(3)
of the Federal Reserve Act] complete discretion to accept any
types of collateral for a [loan] made in 'unusual and exigent' circumstances.'"[13] In national emergencies, moreover, law bends to
necessity.[14] Bear Stearns had had lousy collateral[15] yet had been
saved anyway, months earlier, and this created suspicion that the
Fed's refusal to save Lehman Brothers must have some other, hidden basis. Wild rumors, emphasizing Secretary of the Treasury
Henry Paulson's past links to Goldman Sachs (he had been its
CEO), a competitor of Lehman Brothers, circulated.

The run on Lehman Brothers highlighted the difference between a liquidity crisis and a solvency crisis. The former, which is
associated with panics, refers to a situation in which markets
seize up, stop working. When Lehman collapsed, the government thought that the banking industry was undergoing a liquidity crisis. Banks were refusing to lend money to each other because they were uncertain about each other's solvency, though
(the government thought) they were solvent. A liquidity crisis is
the situation for which a central bank's role as "lender of last resort" is designed. The central bank has unlimited liquidity, because it creates the money it lends. But normally it should insist
that the loan be adequately collateralized. If it saved insolvent

13. Id. See Thomas O. Porter II, "The Federal Reserve's Catch 22: A Legal Analysis of the Federal Reserve's Emergency Powers," 13 *North Caro-
lina Banking Institute* 508 (2009); Stephen L. Schwarcz, "Systemic Risk,"
97 *Georgetown Law Journal* 193, 230 n. 232 (2008).

14. See Richard A. Posner, *Law, Pragmatism, and Democracy*, ch. 8
(2003). Cf. Sanford Levinson and Jack M. Balkin, "Constitutional Democracy: Its Dangers and Its Design" (forthcoming in *Minnesota Law Review*);
William E. Scheuerman, "The Economic State of Emergency," 21 *Cardozo
Law Review* 1869 (2000).

15. See Stephen H. Axilrod, *Inside the Fed: Monetary Policy and Its
Management, Martin through Greenspan to Bernanke* 154 (2009).

banks by making loans to them that, by definition of insolvency, in all likelihood they could not repay—and thus, realistically, gave them rather than lent them money—it would be creating "moral hazard," just as when an insurance company insures a building against fire for more than the building is worth.

This was the theory propounded in Walter Bagehot's classic, *Lombard Street: A Description of the Money Market* (1873), and was sound, given its assumptions. The crisis of September 2008 was in part one of liquidity because of uncertainty about the banks' solvency. But it was also a solvency crisis because many banks, especially shadow banks, were insolvent or about to become so. That was a critical problem because of the importance of the banking industry to economic activity in general. The problem could not be solved by the Fed's insistence that its loans to the banks be adequately collateralized, for with asset prices falling, banks found it difficult to obtain collateral with which to replace collateral now deemed inadequate.

Bailing out an insolvent firm creates not only moral hazard but also inflation. Bailing out a solvent firm does not. When the loan is repaid, the central bank, by retiring the cash that it receives, can restore the money supply to what it was before the loan was made; in contrast, bailing out an insolvent firm may well increase the money supply, because the loan is quite likely not to be repaid. Inflation and moral hazard resulting from bailing out insolvent banks are indeed costs of trying to avert a financial collapse, but they have to be traded off against the costs of the collapse.

Nor are liquidity and solvency readily separable. Withdrawal of short-term capital because of fear that the debtor is about to go broke deprives the debtor of liquidity, but that deprivation may be a signal of impending insolvency. The Federal Reserve's failure to save Lehman on the ground that Lehman couldn't post adequate collateral was interpreted to mean that the banking industry had a solvency problem because of the crumbling value of its housing-related securities, not just a temporary liquidity problem caused by a panicky rush to the exits by investors whose short-term capital was uninsured, like the rush of theater patrons panicked by a false cry of "Fire!" for the exits. But to some extent the credit freeze was due not to actual insolvency but to uncertainty whether a particular firm that was trying to borrow money was solvent, even if it was; and to that extent the freeze was a genuine liquidity crisis.

As far as the shadow banking industry was concerned, 2008 might have been 1929. There was virtually no regulation of the industry, because of the absence of federal insurance and the SEC's insouciance about the industry's solvency—in 2004 the SEC had allowed the broker-dealers to double their leverage—abetted by the Fed's complacency. Unlike most commercial banks, the shadow banks and their hedge-fund customers were heavily engaged in speculative lending and investing, including speculation in debt securities; and speculation by a highly leveraged firm is highly risky. While only economic ignoramuses consider "speculator" a pejorative term, the contribution to economic welfare of speculation on the scale that it reached during the boom years of the early 2000s is uncertain, and may not have been great. The gains from a successful trade are offset by the losses incurred by the other party to the trade; the only net social gain comes from the contribution that the speculation makes to bringing prices closer to underlying values, and that contribution is difficult to measure.

The absence of regulation of credit-default swaps was another factor in the runs that brought the banking industry low in September 2008. Credit insurance, issued by insurance companies, is old hat; so too the fact that contracts often contain an insurance component, because the promisor, by being liable for any damages caused by the breach of his contractual commitment, insures the promisee against any loss caused the latter by the breach. Credit-default swaps, however, which date only from

1997, are a novel form of credit insurance and in addition a novel vehicle for speculation.[16] As insurance, a credit-default swap is a promise to make good a bondholder's loss if the issuer of the bond defaults. The promisor need not be an insurance company, and it's an accident that the biggest issuer of credit-default swaps—American Insurance Group—was one. Its London office, which issued the swaps, was functionally a hedge fund. As a speculative instrument, a credit-default swap promises to pay the buyer of the swap the loss to a third party from a default on debt owned by that third party. The swaps could be and often were securitized.

Credit-default swaps resemble both forward and futures contracts. A forward contract is a promise to sell a commodity at some future time at the price specified in the contract. It might be a sale of wheat by a farmer to a grain elevator. By setting the price in advance of delivery, the forward contract hedges the farmer against an unexpected fall in the price of wheat between sale and delivery and the grain elevator against an unexpected rise in that price during that interval. A futures contract is similar, except that the parties do not intend to deliver and receive a commodity but merely to speculate on changes in price between when the futures contract is made and when it calls for notional "delivery." Instead of delivery, a futures contract is closed out by the purchase of an offsetting contract.[17]

The social function of the futures contract is to increase the

16. For a helpful discussion, see Squam Lake Working Group on Financial Regulation, "Credit Default Swaps, Clearinghouses, and Exchanges" (Council on Foreign Relations, Center for Geoeconomic Studies, July 2009).

17. To illustrate, suppose that A, a short seller, sells grain to B at a price of $1,000 for delivery in six months. A expects the price of grain to fall by then; B expects it to rise. Before the delivery date arrives, the price rises to $1,500, and A decides to cap his losses. The simplest way to do this is for him to buy from B the same quantity of grain that he had sold to B, paying $1,500. A now has offsetting contracts to sell and to buy the same quantity of grain; B now has offsetting contracts to buy and sell the same amount of grain; so neither has a delivery obligation.

amount of information about likely future prices by enabling persons who are not in the business of selling or buying commodities to profit from acquiring knowledge about those prices. The same is true when two parties to a credit-default swap speculate on the likelihood that a third party's debt to someone will lose value.

The macroeconomic problem that credit-default swaps created arose from the fact that swap contracts are traded over the counter, which is to say privately, rather than on an exchange, where trades are public. This made it difficult to assess the solvency of financial firms. If they had issued swaps, they had a potential liability that became actual when the financial ninepins started collapsing; if they had bought swaps, they had a potential asset. Neither the liability nor the asset could be assigned a dollar value without knowledge of the amount of swaps and the solvency of the counterparties, whether sellers or buyers of the swaps. So an additional reason for hedge funds to pull out of Lehman and other prime brokers, as it became clear that there were going to be many defaults, was that they didn't know what Lehman's exposure was as an issuer of credit-default swaps and to what extent that liability might be offset by credit-default swaps that Lehman had bought and whether the sellers of those swaps were solvent.

Only about a third of all credit-default swaps were collateralized, and in the meltdown of September 2008 the value of the collateral, consisting as it did of assets of endangered financial firms, was falling at a dangerous rate. In the end, however, the credit-default swaps performed on the whole quite well; most of the swaps were honored, without breaking the sellers. The reason seems to have been that there were fewer defaults than anticipated, because the bond market revived faster than was expected, enabling debtors on the brink of default to refinance their debt on better terms. But ignorance about the impact of credit-default swaps on the solvency of financial firms had done its work: it had contributed to pervasive doubts about their solvency, and such mistrust can create or accelerate a run on a firm that has short-term capital that is not federally insured.

Most forward and futures contracts are traded on exchanges, so that the total volume and price movements are public. Credit-default swaps are not, though like forward and futures contracts some are traded through clearinghouses. This minimizes the risk that the seller will not be able to pay the buyer at the settlement date. In trading through clearinghouses, seller and buyer do not deal directly with each other. Rather, each deals with a third party, the clearinghouse, which demands collateral—usually adjusted on a daily basis to track price movements in the traded contract—to make sure that it won't be left holding the bag on the settlement day. Clearinghouse trading was the reason why many credit-default swaps were adequately collateralized, enabling the buyers to collect the promised insurance proceeds despite the financial crisis.[18]

Another benefit of trading through clearinghouses is that it enables a trader's positive and negative exposures to cancel, further minimizing the risk of a default. If A has sold a swap to B, B to C, and C to A, the clearinghouse can credit A's account with the amount that C owes A, thus enabling A to make good on the swap it sold B, which in turn enables B to pay C, replenishing C's account after C's account was debited to liquidate C's obligation to A.

One reason not to demonize speculators is that speculation in credit-default swaps, by revealing changes in default risk, enables prompt adjustment of the amount of collateral to protect the buyer of the swap from a default by the seller. This is true even though credit-default swaps are, among other things, a device for short selling, than which there is no more unpopular (among the ignorant) form of speculation. Buying a credit-default swap is equivalent to selling short the debt that the swap

18. See Darrell Duffie, "Policy Issues Facing the Market for Credit Derivatives," in *The Road Ahead for the Fed*, note 1 above, at 123.

insures, because the swap will pay off if the debt is defaulted. But like other speculation, short selling adds information to the market: information that some investors believe that a security is overvalued. The temporary ban, at the height of the financial crisis, of short selling of financial stocks was defended on the ground that short sellers were driving down the price of such stocks by spreading false rumors that Morgan Stanley and other banks were going to go broke. Deliberately spreading false rumors to push down stock prices is a form of fraud, but the rumors may well have been true, or at least believed to be true by those who originated and who repeated them. The prime brokers might well have gone broke—Lehman being merely the first domino to fall—had it not been for federal intervention, and were it not for the short sellers, the banks' impending bankruptcy might not have been noticed until it was too late to avert another Lehman Brothers type of fiasco.

The other side of speculation, moreover, is hedging. Buying a credit-default swap on a bond that one does not own but thinks is inferior to one's own investments is a way of limiting one's possible loss should those investments fall in value; the bond will fall even farther (in all likelihood), and the credit-default swap will therefore have provided a significant offset to the fall.

This discussion may make it seem that requiring collateral for credit-default swaps, whether through clearinghouses or otherwise, is a magic bullet. But it is not, for two reasons. Insurance companies cannot be expected or required to have reserves, or reinsurance backed by reserves, or other collateral, against risks that cannot be estimated and that would cause a global depression or some equivalent catastrophe if they materialized.[19] If a nuclear attack killed 50 million Americans, the life insurance in-

19. There are now "catastrophe bonds" designed to insure against the consequences of catastrophes of unknown or very low probability of occurring, but if the cost of the catastrophe if it occurs is large enough, the issuer of the bond may not have the wherewithal to make good on his promise of insurance.

dustry would be bankrupt, because the industry is not required to maintain reserves against such an eventuality. Similarly, the issuer of a credit-default swap on a mortgage-backed security might be required to post 10 percent of the value of the security as collateral, the equivalent of an insurance reserve; if the value not only of that security but of a host of similar securities that the issuer had insured collapsed, the issuer might lack the resources to honor all its obligations.

The second problem, this one created by credit-default swaps that are not traded on an exchange, is part of the larger problem of off-balance-sheet contingent liabilities, and attends other derivatives as well. (A "derivative" is simply a security that is based upon another security; credit-default swaps are derivative from bonds, including tranches of securitized debt, and securitized debt is itself a derivative of the debt instruments that are securitized.) An example is interest-rate swaps: if one bondholder has a fixed interest rate and another, holding the same kind of bond, a floating interest rate, they might decide to swap their interest entitlements. Each bond would be listed on the balance sheet of the bond's owner, but the balance sheet would not reveal what the bondholder's entitlement to interest was—the interest rate in the fixed-interest bond might be higher or lower than the floating interest rate. Structured investment vehicles are another example of the information problem created by off-balance-sheet contingent liabilities.

Investors in and creditors of financial firms that were known to have issued many credit-default swaps or to have created large SIVs could not readily assess the solvency of such firms, because the contingent liabilities created by the swaps and the SIVs were opaque, as was the value of the swaps to the buyers. When realization dawned that the firms were in trouble—that the assets of the SIVs were depleted and the firms that had created them were likely to put them back on their balance sheets rather than allow them to default, and that honoring credit-default swaps might be very costly because so many defaults were occurring—the entities dealing with the firms became fearful that the firms would go broke, and they took defensive measures that increased the probability that the firms *would* go broke.

A final contributor to the runs on the banks was an accounting convention, the "mark-to-market" (or "fair accounting") rule.[20] The rule requires a firm to carry an asset on its books at its current market value if it's the kind of asset that trades, but not if it's the kind of receivable, such as a mortgage, that firms generally hold until maturity; the firm is permitted to record such an asset on its books at its full value, unless before maturity the firm should happen to sell or otherwise alter it (as by modifying a mortgage). The firm may also be able to convince its auditors that even though an asset is tradable, it intends to hold it until maturity, which in the case of a mortgage-backed security would be when the mortgages packaged in the security mature. But the owner of assets that could be traded but that the owner doesn't intend to trade is required to mark down their value to the present value of the anticipated income stream from them, a stream that in the case of mortgage-backed securities and other securitized debt was impaired. Had the firm posted a tranche of such a security as collateral, a markdown of its value might force the firm to come up with additional collateral, although markdowns based not on current market value but on value estimated from the anticipated earnings on the asset do not reduce the amount of capital that the firm is required by its regulators to have ("regulatory capital").

The mark-to-market rule was perverse to the extent that the financial crisis was one of liquidity rather than solvency. In a panic, when markets freeze because the participants do not know whom it is safe to do business with, the "market" value of an asset ceases to be a meaningful concept; the fact that no one will

---

20. For an excellent discussion, see Robert C. Pozen, "Is It Fair to Blame Fair Value Accounting for the Financial Crisis?" *Harvard Business Review,* Nov. 2009, p. 2.

buy the asset is due not to its being worthless but to uncertainty, in which event marking down its value to zero merely precipitates defaults, bankruptcies, and liquidations. So in the spring of 2009, the Fair Accounting Standards Board, the promulgator of accounting conventions, modified the mark-to-market rule by limiting it to "active" markets, as distinct from markets that had become inactive because of a liquidity crisis. The modification came too late, and in one respect impeded recovery from the financial collapse. Banks were reluctant to sell their "legacy" assets (the absurd euphemism for tranches of securitized debt issued before the collapse) because they would have to mark their value down to their sale price; by arguing that the market for such assets was still "inactive," they could continue to carry them on their books at cost. Who was fooled? Maybe no one; but reducing one's balance sheet can have serious consequences, as events that entitle a lender to declare a default are often defined with reference to the state of the debtor's balance sheet.

The financial collapse had begun in the summer of 2007. Yet as late as the summer of 2008, just months before the crisis hit with full force in September, the Fed was worrying about inflation. The worry was engendered by the spike in oil prices that summer. Besides reducing Americans' wealth and thus making them more vulnerable to an economic downturn, the spike fooled the Federal Reserve into keeping interest rates higher than necessary to prevent the recession that turned into a depression, doubtless because it remembered the inflationary effect of oil-price spikes in the 1970s.

The Fed had raised interest rates too late to prevent the housing bubble. Now it was lowering them too slowly and too late to prevent the bursting of the housing bubble from bringing down the banking industry. Granted, the Fed was in a box, albeit it had built the box. The reduction in interest rates that it engineered as housing prices sank, though too small to head off the collapse of the banking industry, contributed to a spike in gasoline prices that caused sales of motor vehicles to plummet, which created a recession in the automobile industry. Lower interest rates would have increased the industry's distress. But the Fed should have realized that because of the economic centrality of the nation's banking industry, which was dangerously invested in the housing industry, the critical need was for lower interest rates, which would have made it easier for mortgagors to refinance their mortgages and, by making houses cheaper to buy, would have encouraged housing starts. Housing prices would have continued to decline, but at a slower rate (because lower mortgage costs would have buoyed the demand for housing), and the disastrous fall in the value of bank assets might have been averted.

The entire government, including the Fed, was as surprised by the collapse of the international financial industry in September 2008 as the government had been surprised by the attack on Pearl Harbor or the 9/11 terrorist attacks—that is, completely surprised, despite abundant warning signs (more abundant in the case of the financial surprise). The government had no contingency plans to deal with a financial crisis, and appears not to have realized the macroeconomic significance of the shadow banks. I can think of no other explanation for the failure to save Lehman from bankruptcy. We shall explore the reasons for the government's lack of preparedness in subsequent chapters; for now it is enough to point out that its unpreparedness probably made the crisis much worse than it would have been had the Fed made timely efforts to head it off and, failing that, to contain it.

Although Bernanke was too slow to appreciate the significance of the bursting of the housing bubble and to respond appropriately,[21] and botched the initial response when the crisis struck in its full force by letting Lehman Brothers fail, he recovered quickly. He orchestrated the saving of the other principal broker-dealers, along with the endangered commercial banks; and by his policy of "credit easing" (see next chapter), he pre-

21. See Axilrod, note 15 above, at 155.

vented an even more calamitous drop in credit transactions. Another important measure the Fed took was to lend a great deal of money to foreign central banks to boost their dollar balances, a measure that if taken a few months earlier would have limited the global scope of the crisis.

Bernanke was part of a troika of government officials who ran U.S. economic policy until the end of the Bush Administration. The others were Timothy Geithner, the president of the Federal Reserve Bank of New York, and Henry Paulson, the Secretary of the Treasury.[22] They too had been blindsided by the financial crisis, but Geithner played a key role in advising Bernanke and implementing the rescue plans, and Paulson, though not as knowledgeable as the others about the technical details of banking and finance, had the advantage, in persuading Wall Street to go along with the rescue efforts, of being a prominent Wall Street insider. Our economic situation might be worse today had a different team been in charge—which is not to excuse the troika's failure to anticipate and take timely measures to prevent the financial collapse. It is odd that the nation's leading economic student of the Great Depression, Bernanke—who in addition had emphasized in his academic writings the critical role of bank failures in that depression—and the former CEO of Goldman Sachs, which was at the heart of the shadow banking system, and the president of the New York Fed, the Fed's link with Wall Street, should all have been surprised by a financial crisis that had been building for more than a year.

Bernanke's performance since the Lehman debacle has been

22. See the blow-by-blow account of the government's response to the financial crisis in Wessel's book, note 10 above. While praising the rescue efforts, Wessel is rightly critical of both Greenspan and Bernanke for allowing the financial crisis to develop in the first place. See id., chs. 3, 5–11, and summary at pp. 272–275. The number and gravity of Bernanke's errors are only now being realized. See Binyamin Appelbaum and David Cho, "Fed's Approach to Regulation Left Banks Exposed to Crisis," *Washington Post*, Dec. 21, 2009, p. A1.

marred by his embrace of a theory of the causes of the financial collapse that exonerates him from any responsibility for it by placing all blame on the private sector and on limitations of regulators' powers, such as the Federal Reserve's supposed lack of legal authority to save Lehman. The theory is being deployed in support of proposals for financial regulatory reform that are designed to solve a largely imaginary set of problems having to do with the mental and moral limitations of bankers (deemed greedy and reckless) and consumers (greedy and reckless) rather than the fundamental problem, which is inept regulation, prominently including inept regulation of the money supply by Bernanke and his predecessor and the failure of timely response (a failure in which Bernanke was joined by Geithner) to the gathering crisis in the months preceding Lehman's catastrophic collapse. When interest rates are low enough and regulators permissive enough, profit maximization on the banking side and utility maximization on the consumer side, in conjunction with human limits on the ability to acquire, absorb, and act on information, are a recipe for financial catastrophe.

Granted, other factors contributed to the government's failure to prevent the crisis, and, realistically, some were not preventable, for a variety of political and economic reasons. These include the tax deductibility of mortgage and home-equity interest, the favorable capital gains treatment of home resales, the favorable tax treatment of corporate debt versus equity, the limited liability of corporate shareholders, political pressures to lower mortgage credit standards, and profit—or, in the case of home buyers and other consumers, utility—maximization, which implies indifference to external costs.

External costs explain why it is a mistake to blame the bankers and the home buyers (or home-equity borrowers) for the banking collapse. Both groups took risks that, given the information that they had, seemed optimal. Bankers knew that they were heavily invested in residential real estate, that some people thought housing prices were a bubble phenomenon, and that if those people were right a bank heavily invested in residential real estate could go broke. Home buyers who had poor credit knew they might lose their house if a flattening in home prices made it impossible for them to refinance the mortgage at a lower rate. Of course there were fools in both camps, and crooks as well (mostly, it seems, among mortgage brokers), but they were not the main drivers of the collapse.

It is rational for a businessman to operate his business in such a way as to create a risk of bankruptcy—in fact, it's impossible to run a business any other way and survive, at least in a competitive market. Consumers likewise make rational decisions that nevertheless create a risk of bankruptcy. But neither group considers the possibility that if enough of them go broke at once, because their risks are positively correlated, the economy as a whole may experience enormous losses. Those losses are external to the firms and individuals creating them and thus are ignored by them.

This elementary point, and the corollary that an external cost is the responsibility of government to prevent because profit-maximizing firms will not do so on their own—to do so would reduce their profits—eluded Alan Greenspan. He had thought that markets in general and the financial market in particular were self-regulating, confessing in testimony before Congress on October 23, 2008, that "those of us who have looked to the self-interest of lending institutions to protect shareholder's equity (myself especially) are in a state of shocked disbelief."[23] Rational self-interest does not lead a firm to reduce its risk of bankruptcy to zero. If the consequences of a firm's bankruptcy for the economy are catastrophic, it is government's responsibility to force

23. Kara Scannell and Sudeep Reddy, "Greenspan Admits Errors to Panel," *Wall Street Journal,* Oct. 24, 2008, p. A15. See also Jon Hilsenrath, "Greenspan vs. the Greenspan Doctrine," *Real Time Economics* blog, hosted by *Wall Street Journal,* Feb. 17, 2009, http://blogs.wsj.com/economics/2009/02/17/greenspan-vs-the-greenspan-doctrine/ (visited Dec. 4, 2009).

the firm to take fewer risks than are in the firm's self-interest to take. It is no different from forcing a polluting enterprise to reduce its polluting at the cost of sacrificing some profits. It is odd that someone of Greenspan's experience should have overlooked this point.

At the root of the financial collapse, then, was a failure of regulation, compounded of unsound monetary policy and deregulation, nonregulation, and lax—excessively permissive—regulation of financial intermediation. Bernanke refuses to acknowledge that failure. In defense of that refusal he could point to the importance of public confidence in the nation's economic leadership. The morality of political officials is not that of private persons.[24] Officials must lie, dissemble, flatter, traduce, pander, to a degree that would be regarded as monstrous in private life. But there are costs to such dishonesty; in this instance, it is the Obama Administration's perverse proposals for preventing a recurrence of the financial crisis, which are the subject of chapter 5.

24. Max Weber, "Politics as a Vocation," in *From Max Weber: Essays in Sociology* 77 (H. H. Gerth and C. Wright Mills. trans. 1946); Richard A. Posner, *Affair of State: The Investigation, Impeachment, and Trial of President Clinton,* ch. 4 (1999).

The global credit freeze precipitated by Lehman Brothers' collapse galvanized the government. At the beginning of October 2008 Congress enacted the Troubled Asset Relief Program, authorizing the Treasury to spend up to $700 billion to buy "troubled" assets from financial institutions. The program quickly turned into one for recapitalizing the institutions rather than buying assets from them. Meanwhile the Federal Reserve was pushing down the federal funds rate—eventually nearly to zero —by flooding banks with cash in exchange for short-term Treasury securities. It also began buying private debt, such as commercial paper, credit card debt, and mortgage-backed securities, along with long-term Treasury debt, and thus began operating not just as the nation's central bank but as a substitute for a commercial bank.

So why, four months later, when Barack Obama became President, was the nation in a state of panic, with output and employment plunging and officials fearful of a deflationary spiral that might inaugurate a second Great Depression, and with the stock market 50 percent below its 2007 peak? Why, nine months after that, was the nation still deep in the economic doldrums, with output far below the GDP trend line and unemployment exceeding 10 percent, and, at best, a long, slow recovery in prospect? Why, in short, did a banking collapse quickly met with a huge infusion of federal money nevertheless precipitate a depression?

We must begin by noting that a modern economy lives on credit, and we should pause to consider why—one of those obvious questions with not-so-obvious answers. One answer is that it enables a smoothing of consumption. By borrowing when one is young and may have heavy expenses for child care or education and limited income, and by saving (which means lending, in order to obtain a return on the money saved) when one is older to have reserves for medical costs or other emergencies or for bequests, one can to a degree divorce consumption from income; for the desire to consume is independent of one's income. "Desire is boundless, and the act a slave to limit," as Shakespeare's Troilus put it.

Credit transactions (lending and borrowing) also match up people or businesses that want cash badly now with people who are happy to trade cash now for more later by lending at interest. The "payday loan" is the extreme example: a loan at an exorbitant interest rate, repayable at the borrower's next payday, to a person who cannot stretch his paycheck that far. In addition, businesses usually incur the cost of sale before receiving the revenue from it, and rather than keeping a large store of cash on hand to pay their expenses as they come due, they prefer to borrow the cash they need from someone who has a less urgent current need for it. The "someone" might be a bank, but the ultimate lenders would be the people who had entrusted to the bank capital that they didn't have a current need to spend.

Credit also serves an important role in bringing economic activity forward. Rather than saving up for years and buying a house with cash, a person can, by buying it with a mortgage, enjoy home ownership much sooner. The role of credit in accelerating consumption (and notice how the desire for such acceleration is implied by the life-cycle consumption/income hypothesis) is one reason why increasing the cost of credit causes economic activity to decrease. But a more important reason is that once an economic system is geared to a high level of credit transactions, anything that unexpectedly increases the cost of credit can disrupt the operation of the economy. For a time after the September 2008 collapse, the cost of credit was very high and for many borrowers infinite: no one would lend to them at any price. Banks and other lenders discovered that their capital was impaired, to a substantial though not precisely known degree, by the fall in value of their mortgage-backed securities, and they did not want to place their remaining capital at risk by lending it. They preferred the safe options of either holding cash or buying government securities. Lending is especially unsafe in a slump, because the risk of default increases as borrowers' incomes fall. Falling asset values further increase the riskiness of lending, by reducing the value of collateral.

Suppose the mortgage-backed securities in which the banks had invested so heavily had been backed by mortgages issued to foreign borrowers. The banks' capital would have been impaired, just as it was, and so the supply of credit to Americans would have shrunk; but the demand for credit by Americans would not have been affected. But because it was the prices of Americans' houses that had collapsed, it was their demand for credit, and their creditworthiness, that plummeted.

A house is the principal asset of most people, even when they have a large mortgage on it. The fall in housing and stock values left people overindebted, their assets having shrunk in relation to their debts. The shrinkage was especially great because many homeowners had cashed in on higher home values by borrowing against the equity in their homes and spending the borrowed money on consumption rather than on acquiring substitute assets.[1] This drove them deeper into debt. A natural reaction to be-

1. Atif R. Mian and Amir Sufi, "House Prices, Home Equity Based Borrowing, and the U.S. Household Leverage Crisis" (University of Chicago Booth School of Business, Chicago Booth Research Paper No. 09-20, July 5, 2009).

ing overindebted, unless one is totally impoverished and therefore needs all one's meager income for consumption, is to spend
less and save more, so as to reduce one's leverage; and to save in
safe, rather inert forms, so that one will have secure reserves
against emergencies, such as losing one's job.[2]

Banks did not stop lending. Some had preexisting obligations
to their customers as a result of having issued standby lines of
credit. Some had customers who they were confident would
weather the economic storm and not default. The government's
flooding of the banks with cash (both by making loans and other
direct investments in banks and by reducing interest rates in an
effort to increase the demand for loans and reduce the cost of
lending to the banks) enabled commercial banks to continue
lending at approximately their normal level throughout the economic crisis. But remember that bank loans are no longer the
principal source of credit in the American economy. The purchase of securitized debt alone, whether the debt consisted of residential mortgages, commercial mortgages, credit card receiv-
ables, or other debt, had by 2007 become a large fraction of the
credit market, ranging from 10 percent of automotive loans to
26 percent of mortgage loans. When, because of the rise in defaults, new securitizations plummeted, a major source of credit
dried up at the same time that the commercial-paper market was
seizing up because of the collapse of Lehman Brothers and the resulting distress of the money-market funds. Would-be borrowers
turned to the commercial banks; but they had also been weakened, and anyway, it's no fun lending into a depression. The
banks were happy to lend to nonfinancial issuers of commercial
paper, because they had excellent credit, but for other borrowers they raised interest rates and stiffened credit standards. This
dealt a severe blow to businesses (especially small businesses)

2. Overindebtedness as a causal factor in depressions is emphasized in
Richard C. Koo, *The Holy Grail of Macroeconomics: Lessons from Japan's
Great Recession* (2008), especially chs. 2–4.

and consumers, especially ones with less than sterling credit ratings.

The blow was all the more severe because of the "relationship" character of commercial bank lending. Banks, as we know, have to assume risk in lending. They can minimize the risk by getting to know their customers well, so that they can assess creditworthiness more accurately than by relying just on reports by credit-rating agencies. The goal is to identify borrowers who are less risky than other potential lenders consider them to be, so that lending to them at the going market rate will generate a return greater than necessary just to cover the risk of default.[3] The importance of relationship banking in reducing credit risk is one reason that commercial banks tend to be local (or, if they are big banks, to have local branches); it gets them nearer their customers, so that they can learn more about their creditworthiness.

If a bank customer loses his bank line of credit, as he is quite likely to do when his bank pulls in its horns, he may have difficulty reestablishing it in another bank, to which he is a stranger. The turmoil in the banking industry destroyed many relationships between banker and borrower that could not be reconstituted quickly. And unlike big businesses, small businesses and consumers cannot borrow at affordable rates outside the banking system; they cannot issue bonds or commercial paper.

The banking industry had been moving away from relationship lending before the crash. As debt securitization grew and big banks increasingly became originators and sellers of debt securities rather than conventional owners of debt until maturity, diversification and value-at-risk models replaced relationship-specific knowledge as means of controlling risk. Yet banks remained a major source of credit, and the credit system would have been devastated by their disappearance. Their assets would have been acquired by other lenders, but this would have taken time, and in

---

3. See Lawrence H. Summers, "Planning for the Next Financial Crisis," in *The Risk of Economic Crisis* 135 (Martin Feldstein ed. 1991).

the meantime the credit system would have been completely disrupted. A lender's knowledge of a borrower's creditworthiness is lost when the lender is dissolved and its staff scattered, and it is difficult, as I said, for a borrower to create forthwith a relationship with a new bank—let alone with a completely different type of lender—if his old bank fails.

A further disruption of the credit system occurred because the financial turmoil triggered standby credit commitments by the banks, leaving the banks with less money to lend to other borrowers. When the collapse of Lehman Brothers froze the commercial-paper market, the businesses that issue commercial paper began drawing on their bank lines of credit. Banks were happy to lend to big businesses in preference to the small businesses that depend critically on bank lending—before the era of commercial paper, big businesses had been the banks' best customers. The financial crisis hit small business especially hard.

The great danger to a capitalist economy is that a drop in economic activity will become self-sustaining. Businesses unsure of being able to obtain loans at reasonable rates anticipated a shortage of capital and therefore a reduction in their output, and so began laying off workers. (Why businesses tend to respond to a reduction in their output by laying off workers rather than paying them less is discussed below.) Anticipating that they would be operating on a smaller scale, these businesses had less need for loans—and the fact that they anticipated reduced sales also made them less creditworthy. Workers who are laid off suffer a loss of income, which makes them less creditworthy too. Banks with impaired capital become doubly reluctant to make risky loans as businesses contract and unemployment rises, because the risk of defaults is now greater and prospective borrowers have less collateral to offer. Lending to them is now riskier, and the increased risk cannot be offset by the bank's charging a higher rate without increasing the likelihood of the borrower's defaulting, because interest owed on a loan does not diminish just because the borrower's revenue falls; it is a fixed cost.

Laid-off workers may be desperate to borrow, but they cannot, because the risk of their defaulting is too great. And those who still have jobs but fear losing them are reluctant to take on greater debt. Instead they divert some of their normal consumption expenditures to saving. The result is reduced demand for goods and services, accelerating the tendency caused by a credit crunch for sellers to reduce output and therefore lay off employees. The unemployed, their incomes diminished, also spend less, further reducing demand for goods and services.

As the spiral accelerates, banks become increasingly gun-shy about lending. They don't mind that the Federal Reserve is replacing their short-term Treasury securities with cash accounts in Federal Reserve banks, because cash is a good thing to have in an uncertain business environment (and because the Fed is now paying interest on the banks' reserves). They have no desire to lose that good thing by lending the cash that the Fed has given them in order to encourage them to lend! We recall from chapter 1 that Alan Greenspan believed that bubbles should be allowed to burst without interference from the Federal Reserve, which he thought needed only to clean up the mess afterward by lowering interest rates. This solution doesn't work if the bubble engulfs the banks, even if the Fed pushes the federal funds rate all the way to zero. Indeed, at zero no bank has an incentive to lend to another bank. (That is what is called a "liquidity trap": if there is no reward for parting with liquidity—cash or instant access to cash—there is no incentive to lend, and the credit system freezes.) And a zero federal funds rate, rather than just signaling that the Fed does not expect inflation, signals major anxiety about the economy, an anxiety that induces banks to raise rather than lower the interest rates they charge for lending.

Thus the major effect of the Federal Reserve's reduction of the federal funds rate by its open market operations during the crisis was not to increase bank lending (although it helped prevent its decline) to take up the slack created by the collapse of other credit markets; it was to increase bank reserves. "Excess" reserves, which is to say cash beyond what the regulatory authorities require banks to retain in order to reduce risk, soared from just $2 billion in 2007 to $1 trillion in the fall of 2009. The banks were hoarding, as were many businesses and consumers. And much of what they were not hoarding they were using to pay generous dividends to shareholders, to buy other banks, and to buy low-risk bonds. The purchase of other banks reflected a judgment that such purchases were less risky or more profitable than lending into a depression (the motive for buying low-risk bonds rather than lending to small businesses and consumers was similar), while paying dividends is a hedge against bankruptcy. Shareholders (including bank managers, who invariably are shareholders as well as employees) would lose their equity in a bankruptcy but usually would not be required to return any dividends that they had received. But paying dividends reduces a firm's equity cushion and thus increases the riskiness of its debt—and did so at a time when many owners of debt were justifiably worried about its safety. In retrospect, the government should probably have forbidden the payment of dividends by the banks it bailed out, though the prohibition would have to have been temporary, lest it make it more difficult for banks to raise capital.

Banks could have tried to raise additional equity capital in order to reduce their leverage and therefore the probability that lending in risky circumstances would precipitate bankruptcy. But they didn't want to issue more stock (though the ones that had received government bailouts relented under government pressure); to do so would have harmed the existing shareholders, because the prices of bank stocks had fallen. Suppose that a corporation has 1,000 shares of stock outstanding, and the current (and very depressed) market value is $10 a share, although the book value of the company is $20,000, or $20 a share. Should the share price eventually double, making the company's market capitalization equal to its book value, each shareholder will have shares worth $20 apiece. Now suppose that at the bottom of the market the corporation sells another 1,000 shares, at $10 apiece, which increases the book value of the company to $30,000. On the assumption that in a normal market the company's market capitalization is equal to its book value (an arbitrary assumption, but adequate for illustrative purposes), and given that there are now 2,000 shares, the stock price will be only $15; the original shareholders will have been harmed by the dilution of their equity interest.

The government responded to the credit chill in a variety of ways, including "quantitative easing" or—a more descriptive term—"credit easing." The terms refer to the purchase by the Federal Reserve of debt other than just short-term Treasury securities. With banks reluctant to lend, the Fed decided to enter the credit market directly—for example, by purchasing commercial paper. It was not afraid to lend to businesses or consumers, as it cannot be made insolvent by defaulting borrowers. (That is one reason it needn't have balked at bailing out Lehman Brothers.)

One is thus to imagine the Fed buying an amount of commercial paper from, say, Procter & Gamble, with a check drawn on a Federal Reserve bank; adding the paper (that is, the amount of the loan to P&G) to the asset side of the Fed's balance sheet; crediting the Federal Reserve bank with the amount of the check; and adding that amount to the liability side of the Fed's balance sheet.

Credit easing increased the availability of credit but did nothing to strengthen the balance sheets of the banking industry. At first the Treasury wanted to buy the securitized debt from the industry, to increase the industry's cash. This was a bad idea, quickly abandoned, though hesitantly revived on a modest scale by the Obama Administration. If the Treasury paid the market price, it would do nothing for the banks' balance sheets, because it would just be replacing one asset with another. If it paid more, it would be making a gift to the banks, and why do that rather than lend them money? Some thought was given to buying the securitized debt not at its current, depressed market price but at the price it would command if held to maturity, the idea being that the current market price was depressed because the sudden global shortage of capital made it impossible to sell assets at higher than fire-sale prices, especially risky assets, as securitized debt had been revealed to be: in other words, there was a liquidity crisis. If a panic makes everyone all at once want to get out of risky assets, the price of those assets will be bid way down; and that was happening.

But the idea of paying the "fair" price for the securitized debt, as opposed to the fire-sale price, faded too, because it was not at all clear that the securitized debt was worth much more than its current market price. The price was depressed not just because a pell-mell exodus from risky assets had pushed down the price by suddenly and steeply increasing their supply, but also because the mortgages and other loans that backed the securitized debt had experienced a catastrophic fall in value—in other words, because banks had a solvency problem.

A bank that *wanted* to swap its nonperforming loans for cash could have sold them one by one, and similarly could have sold its mortgage-backed security tranches one by one. But the banks didn't want to acknowledge publicly, by a sale of a poor asset, how little capital they had, lest the government close them. Moreover, a sale, by establishing the market value of the asset, might have required the selling bank to mark to market the rest of its securitized debt—specifically, mark to the price at which it had sold the asset in question. Nor did the banks want the cash they would have received in exchange for the bad assets, because they didn't want to do more lending until the economic picture clarified. They wanted, in short, to be left alone.

Another idea that was popular for a time was to require the banks to place their "bad" assets in a separate "bad" bank, so that creditors would have an accurate idea of the "good" bank's assets. But since the bad assets were worth something, the good bank would have less capital and thus be weaker. So that idea was abandoned too, and the Troubled Asset Relief Program was reconceived as a program whereby the Treasury, instead of buying the bad assets, would lend money to banks that had a lot of securitized debt on their books, receiving in return preferred stock. The government would receive interest on its investment and the banks would receive safe capital, because unlike conventional loans, purchases of preferred stock do not have an expiration date—a date on which the buyer of the preferred stock can exchange the stock for the money he paid for it, plus any interest owed him.

Even after the banks were bailed out by the government's loans, there was concern that because the banks' securitized debt, which remained on their books, was difficult to value, until it was somehow taken off the books the banks would not be able to raise private capital to supplement what they were getting from the government and so complete the repair of their balance sheets. This didn't make a lot of sense. Most companies' balance sheets contain assets that are difficult to value, yet this does not prevent the companies from obtaining access to the capital markets.

Some thought was given to the government's buying common rather than preferred stock in the wounded banks, thereby becoming in all likelihood (because the market capitalization of the banks had diminished greatly) their controlling shareholder. That was a bad idea, and with a few exceptions was rejected. Controlled by government, the banking industry would become politicized, and probably incompetently managed to boot, unless the government was able and willing to sell the banks to private investors within a very short time. And that might have been impracticable, at least at any reasonable price, given the turmoil in the markets.

Not that the purchase of preferred stock was a completely satisfactory alternative. The issuance of preferred stock, because it's a form of borrowing, increases the bank's debt-equity ratio. The higher that ratio, the more profitable a successful transaction is, because the cost of debt is invariant to the profits generated by the borrowed money. By the same token, the higher the ratio, the more the firm loses if its transaction is unsuccessful. But if the firm is desperate, it will discount the downside risk, because given limited liability, losses to the owners of a corporation are truncated at zero. (The incentive of a firm at risk of insolvency to roll the dice is known as "gambling for resurrection.")

Besides the bailouts of financial enterprises, a notable rescue measure, undertaken at the very end of 2008, was a pair of government loans, to General Motors and Chrysler, to save them from the bankruptcy they would otherwise have been forced into by the end of the year. Because of the woeful prospects for the two companies and the scarcity of debtor-in-possession (DIP) financing (see next paragraph) at the time, which was due to the general shortage of capital, the two companies, if forced into bankruptcy at that time, might well have had to liquidate. That would have thrown hundreds of thousands of workers (the estimate at the time of three million was exaggerated, but the accurate number could well have been one million—both employees of the two companies and employees of their dealers and many of their suppliers) out of work. Some would eventually have been hired by Ford and by foreign auto manufacturers that have plants in the United States, but the transition would have been protracted.

When a company goes broke but wants to remain in business and so reorganizes in bankruptcy (and thus is a "debtor in possession"), it has to be able to borrow money to continue operating, just as it had to borrow money to operate before it went broke. The lenders who provide that money—the DIP financiers—have priority in repayment over the old creditors; otherwise they would not lend. But they are still taking a big risk, because most bankruptcy reorganizations fail and are converted to liquidations, in which all the creditors lose money. (The tendency of management to favor reorganization rather than liquidation, even if reorganization is unlikely to succeed, is another example of gambling for resurrection.)

There wasn't much optimism about the future of the two car companies, and that plus the continuing credit crunch made it unlikely that DIP financing could be obtained to enable the companies to reorganize. So the government stepped in. Had it not done so and the companies liquidated at the height of anxiety about the economy, the blow to business and consumer confidence could well have been catastrophic, and the danger of a 1930s-style deflationary spiral—prices fell by 25 percent between 1929 and 1933—real. I differ with conservative macroeconomists who discount the psychological aspects of the business cycle (as part of a general disdain for nonmathematical economics in general and the economics of John Maynard Keynes in particular) and so contend that the auto companies should have been allowed to go broke even if that would have resulted in their liquidation. A separate question concerns the further aid that the government extended to the two companies in the spring of 2009 to enable them to survive bankruptcy; but that is for a later chapter.

Furthermore, psychology to one side, the unavailability of private DIP financing may not have reflected a judgment that the auto companies had no going-concern value and should liquidate; it may have signified merely a liquidity problem—a temporary scarcity of capital caused by the turmoil in the banking industry. The government had no liquidity problem, so became the DIP financier of last resort.

The measures that the government took in the fall of 2008 slowed the downward spiral of the economy but did not arrest it. Indeed, the rate of economic decline, as measured either by gross domestic product or by unemployment (or by subtler measures of underutilization of the nation's economic resources, such as underemployment or the fall in the length of the average workweek), was greater in the first quarter of 2009 than it had been in the last quarter of 2008—the quarter that began two weeks after the collapse of Lehman Brothers. The reason for the accelerating decline was that a downward spiral of the economy tends to become self-sustaining rather than requiring further pushes after the push that got it started, provided the initial push is very strong, as it was in this instance.

With credit tight, economic activity slowed. Output fell, and with it employment. So incomes fell, and with that fall personal consumption expenditures fell—fell further, moreover, than they would have fallen had it not been for the very low personal savings rate, which when the crisis hit was only about 1 percent, compared to ten times that as recently as the 1980s. The personal savings rate had fallen because interest rates were low and the market value of assets had risen; people felt themselves well cushioned against adversity. But household wealth had risen because it was concentrated in housing and common stock. When the housing and stock bubbles collapsed, the market value of people's savings nosedived, and that made it difficult for them to maintain their level of consumption by drawing down their savings. Their reduced consumption, coupled with savings in forms not readily converted to productive investments, meant reduced production. So unemployment grew, incomes declined further, anxiety among the still-employed grew, and with these developments the propensity to save rather than spend kept growing—the personal savings rate would approach 6 percent for a time in 2009.

The global scope of the depression, moreover, reduced demand for U.S. exports. This in turn reduced production and therefore employment in industries that produce for export, and so imparted further momentum to the economy's downward spiral. Devaluation is a standard method by which a country digs itself out of a depression. By altering the exchange rate of its currency in favor of other currencies, it makes exports cheaper and imports more expensive. Domestic production rises and with it employment. But if all economies are depressed, none will benefit from devaluation, because all will want to devalue.

Similarly, when assets lose value, borrowers may be unable to repay loans as they come due without selling assets. When many borrowers are in this fix, their efforts to sell assets cause an over-supply and prices fall even faster.

When demand for goods falls unexpectedly, inventories swell, for they are the sum of the goods that have been produced but not yet sold. Goods in inventory yield no revenue. And storage and related costs, such as insurance against fire and theft, make holding goods in inventory costly apart from the revenue forgone (the "opportunity cost," as economists say). So sellers have strong incentives to sell goods that are piling up in inventory. But to do that in a weak market (the weakness being the reason for the swollen inventories), they have to reduce price. If the reduction creates an expectation of further reductions (reverse bubble thinking), people may hold off on buying, which will depress demand further. A reduction in prices increases the purchasing power of the dollar. In a deflation, cash, just like a loan that pays interest, grows in value—and you don't even have to pay income tax on the increment, as you would have to do if it took the form of interest or dividends. So you might as well sit on your cash rather than spend it immediately. Hoarding of cash by consumers incites further price reductions in order to move goods out of inventory in a weak market.

The other side of this coin is that a fall in prices increases the real supply of money (the same nominal amount of money buys more goods), which should reduce interest rates by increasing the supply of lendable funds and thus stimulate economic activity. But this has not happened in the current economic malaise, because banks are reluctant to lend even though they can borrow at very low interest rates.

An increase in the purchasing power of the dollar also precipitates defaults and bankruptcies. This is the "crushing debt" problem of deflation. Between 1930 and 1933, the dollar deflated at a rate of about 10 percent a year. This meant that, on average, a product that cost $1 in 1929 cost only 90 cents in 1930. The deflation rate in the current depression has been much lower; still, someone who took out a two-year loan at 8 percent in 2007, when the inflation rate was 5 percent, thought that he was paying real interest of only 3 percent. Yet by the beginning of 2009 the inflation rate was negative. This meant that the real rate of interest on the 8 percent loan was not 3 percent; it was more than 8 percent.

If deflation is bad, does this mean that inflation is good? In a depression, yes, though of course within limits. (In a boom, it is dangerous—think of the inflationary asset-price bubbles whose bursting brought the world economy to its knees. Everything is upside-down in a bust.) Inflation increases the price of the average house but not the unpaid balances of existing mortgages. So it increases the homeowner's equity and thus reduces the number of abandonments and foreclosures, which are burdens on the housing industry and on personal finances. The point is not limited to mortgage debt. Overindebtedness—a function of the amount of debt one carries relative to one's income—increases the propensity to save rather than spend. So by reducing the amount of debt in real terms that people carry, inflation encourages consumption, which results in increased production and so increased employment. When Roosevelt took the United States off the gold standard, shortly after his inauguration, deflation gave way to inflation. The gold standard ties a nation's money supply to the amount of its gold reserves, and though U.S. gold reserves had been growing, the Federal Reserve had "sterilized" gold imports—that is, had refused to allow them to be used to increase the money supply. Roosevelt ended sterilization, and the money supply grew rapidly. The resulting inflation contributed to the rapid economic recovery that began then, mainly by lightening debt, though the inflation was mild and a larger factor in the recovery was the effect of the expansion of the money supply in driving down interest rates[4] and therefore stimulating economic activity.

4. Christina D. Romer, "What Ended the Great Depression?" 52 *Journal of Economic History* 757 (1992).

Because it reduces the purchasing power of money, inflation is in effect a tax on cash balances (including banks' excess reserves) and thus penalizes hoarding. During an inflation people try to spend cash as fast as possible, because it's losing value by the minute. A related point is that inflation is a protection against the economy's falling into a liquidity trap. If the nominal interest rate is zero and there is inflation, then the real interest rate is negative, and borrowing becomes attractive—one is being paid to borrow. (For example, if the rate of inflation is 2 percent, a nominal interest rate of zero translates into a real interest rate of -2 percent.) Banks should be willing to lend, because inflation will erode the value of any cash that they sit on.

And inflation reduces the real wages of workers by raising prices, while if prices are falling, real wages will be rising even if workers receive no raises. A reduction in real wages reduces labor costs, which encourages companies to do more hiring and thus reduces unemployment. With more workers working, aggregate real wages may rise even though the real wages of some workers fall. And nonlabor income, at least, is not reduced.

Workers in a depression will tend to accept a reduction in their real wages because they fear being replaced by what Karl Marx called "the reserve army of the unemployed." They will be far more resistant to a reduction in their nominal wages; this paradox is explained below.

Creating inflation to fight depression is risky because of the difficulty of creating just the right amount at the right time. The ratio of money to goods depends on the amount of money in circulation, and if people are afraid to spend, just pumping money into the economy may merely increase the amount of money that is hoarded. The excess bank reserves that I have mentioned do not create inflation, because they are not spent (though a qualification is suggested below). The more money that piles up waiting to be spent, however, the greater the risk of unwanted inflation when confidence returns and the hoarded cash begins to be spent and the economy reaches its maximum output. When that point is reached, further spending will merely cause prices to rise, because more dollars will be chasing the same quantity of goods. Moreover, just the anticipation of inflation will tend to increase long-run interest rates, including mortgage rates, thus retarding the recovery of the housing industry. And as we'll see in later chapters, antidepression measures not aimed at creating even moderate inflation still may sow seeds of a dangerous future inflation.

The effect of the credit crunch on the downward spiral of the economy was amplified by a lack of confidence in the government's ability to arrest the spiral. That lack of confidence had several causes. One was that the measures taken in the wake of the September 2008 financial collapse, though drastic by historical standards, seemed only to have slowed the rate of economic decline, and all that a slowing of a downward spiral may mean is that a terrible bottom takes a little longer to reach. Another factor sapping confidence in the government was that the Federal Reserve and the Treasury, along with most academic and business economists, had so plainly been surprised by the events of September, and had responded to them initially in a spasmodic, disorganized manner exemplified not only by allowing Lehman Brothers to collapse after having saved Bear Sterns but also by the aborted effort to rescue the banking industry by buying its overvalued securitized debt. The reaction of the stock market to early signs that Obama's Secretary of the Treasury (Timothy Geithner) might be a weak custodian of the economy illustrates the economic importance of the business community's confidence in government's economic management.

When that confidence wanes, people take their own protective measures, which generally involve hoarding. The desire for cash (liquidity preference), even without the increase in the value of cash that deflation imparts, rises in economic emergencies, because people realize that they may need cash on short notice. So they curtail their spending on goods and services, and anything that does that keeps the downward spiral going.

Yet even if government is ineffectual, a depression will end eventually. And it will end sooner in the 2000s than it did in the 1930s, for a variety of reasons. One is that manufacturing and construction employ a much smaller percentage of the American workforce today than in the 1930s. They are the two major industries likely to be hardest hit in a depression. The purchase of durable goods can usually be deferred (they're durable, after all); most construction projects can be deferred as well. So these industries experience very sharp drops in demand during a depression. Their output plunges and many workers are laid off. That has happened in the current depression.

Another factor breaking the economy's fall is the "automatic stabilizers," which barely existed in the thirties. Because of the progressive income tax, a fall in pretax income reduces after-tax income by less than the reduction in pretax income. And unemployment benefits cushion the loss of income by persons who lose their jobs. Other government programs, such as Medicare, Medicaid, and Social Security, also help to offset the decline in the standard of living (and so in consumption expenditures) when incomes fall during a depression. Just the fact that such a large fraction of the American population today is retired or in prison (for the kind of people one finds in prison would have a high incidence of unemployment if they were free) cushions the economic effect of widespread unemployment. So does the fact that most married women now work; this reduces the drop in family income if a married man loses his job. But there is another side to this coin: housewives (and househusbands, a growing fraction of household producers) don't have to worry about losing their jobs. The larger the fraction of the population that is employed, the higher the potential unemployment rate.

The fact that most people nowadays have much more discretionary income than people did in the thirties provides a degree of offset to the effect of the automatic stabilizers. Affluent people can cut spending a great deal without experiencing hardship—and this has been happening and is reflected in sharply reduced sales by high-end retailers, resulting in turn in sharp reductions in employment in the retail sector. The effect is partially offset by gains to low-end retailers as many consumers downsize from Neiman Marcus to Walmart. The offset is only partial because the downsizers pay less in total—that's why they are downsizing—and because there are lags in repositioning the labor force. The salespeople laid off by Neiman Marcus don't get jobs the next day at Walmart.

For completeness I note that the automatic stabilizers trim booms as well as busts. They are financed by taxes, and taxes limit economic activity by raising prices, reducing disposable income, and impairing incentives to work and invest. This dampening effect may be a good thing. Anything that reduces the amplitude of the business cycle reduces the hardship caused by busts, though economists who embrace Schumpeter's Darwinian economics of "creative destruction" prefer a deep business cycle to a shallow one; it kills off more of the weak businesses and by doing so provides scope and impetus for entrepreneurs.

Even without the buffering changes since the 1930s—even with complete government passivity—depressions will bottom out. As durable goods begin to wear out, demand for them rises, and this acts as a spur to production and hence to rehiring laid-off workers. And as inventories become exhausted by inventory-clearing price reductions, production restarts and again laid-off workers are rehired, though gradually: unsure about the strength or durability of the recovery from a depression, employers try at first to increase production by working their existing, shrunken workforce harder, even if this means paying overtime. That is happening today.

As people's incomes fall, they save less, and eventually a point is reached at which they have to start spending from their cash hoard to avert real hardship. And the more that people save, the lower the interest rates on savings will be; as that rate falls, the propensity to consume rises, because saving becomes less attractive.

So depressions are self-limiting—eventually. Nevertheless the key point is the inherent instability of a capitalist economy—an economy in which economic decision making is decentralized and privatized. A boom tends to cause inflation, and inflation is bad in a boom, but it is good in a bust—yet in a bust, deflation is more likely than inflation. In a boom, banks increase their leverage because borrowing is cheap and demand for loans is great—and in a bust, banks "deleverage" by reducing loans and instead hoarding cash or investing in safe securities such as Treasury bills. Consumers are the opposite: their leverage falls in a boom because the value of their assets rises and so they spend more, and it rises in a bust because the value of those same assets (houses and common stock, notably) falls and so they save more. It would be better if banks and consumers saved in a boom and spent in a bust, just as it would be better to have deflation in a boom and inflation in a bust, rather than the reverse. Saving in a boom would make it easier to weather the bust when it comes, and spending (lending, in the case of the banks) in the bust would stimulate recovery. But there is no private mechanism for inducing this socially optimal behavior. The behavior of businesses and consumers in a bust is individually rational but collectively irrational. That is the case for government intervention, which is least controversial when it takes the form of automatic stabilizers rather than ad hoc interventions.

A critical accelerant of the downward spiral of a depression economy is unemployment, but the relation between depression and unemployment is complex. When as a result of an economy-wide shock, such as a sudden fall in household wealth because of the collapse of a housing bubble, people decide to spend less and save more owing to anxiety about the future, the average firm will experience a reduction in the demand for its output at the existing price. It might be expected to adjust by moving down its supply curve; an upward-slanting supply curve, which is the normal shape, implies that average costs increase with output (because as a firm increases its output it must pay higher prices for its inputs to bid them away from their existing users) and so fall as output falls. The result will be a lower output at a lower price. But this assumes that the firm's supply curve is unchanged—that the firm is just moving along it as demand shifts. Yet with the fall in the economy's demand for goods and services, demand for labor will also have fallen, and with it the equilibrium wage—the wage that clears the market for labor, leaving no workers who want to work unable to find jobs. By reducing its employees' wages to the new equilibrium level, the firm will have lower costs. This will lead it to charge still lower prices, and the result will be an increase in the demand for its output, and so its output will grow.

The end result should be full employment at lower wages, as shown in the graph below. With price on the vertical axis and quantity on the horizontal axis, and with D signifying demand as a function of quantity demanded and S signifying supply as a

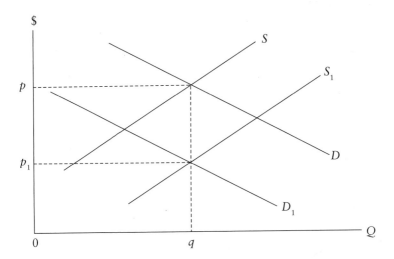

function of quantity supplied, the quantity supplied, q, is given by the intersection of D and S. If demand falls (to D_1) with S unchanged, so that the demand curve shifts downward but the supply curve remains where it was, the quantity supplied will fall. But if the supply curve also shifts downward (to S_1) because the employer has cut wages, and shifts by the same amount as the D curve, the quantity supplied will be q, as before.

But that is not what happens in the real world. When wages fall, so do incomes, and this causes a fall in the demand for goods and services and therefore in the demand for labor, which is derived from the demand for goods and services. This effect of a decline in wages on real income is unlikely to be fully offset by a fall in prices. A decline in a firm's costs is rarely passed on to customers in its entirety, and anyway labor costs are only one component of a firm's total costs. If labor costs are 50 percent of the firm's total costs and the firm reduces those costs by cutting wages and benefits in half, its total costs will fall by 25 percent. If half of that reduction is passed on to consumers in the form of a lower price, the price of the firm's product will fall by only 12.5 percent. In this example, wages have fallen further than prices, and so the price effects of a wage cut will not restore the demand for labor to its previous level.

Furthermore, when demand for a firm's products falls, the firm can adjust by reducing output, but it cannot do anything to reduce its fixed costs, such as debt. The result may be bankruptcy, which, even if the firm's depressed price exceeds its marginal cost, may result in liquidation rather than in a successful reorganization, because of the costs, delays, and uncertainty of a reorganization in bankruptcy. Liquidation will result in termination of all the firm's employees, though some will find jobs with competing firms or in other industries. Moreover, a fall in demand may, by preventing a firm from achieving economies of scale, cause its marginal cost (the effect on its total costs of a small change in output) to rise above the maximum price that the market will pay for the firm's products, and then reorganization will not be an option unless there is optimism about a quick economic recovery.

We recall that in a deflation, a failure to reduce a nominal wage (a fixed number of dollars per wage period) amounts to an increase in the real wage. But an employer could not persuade his employees to accept a reduction in their nominal wage on the ground that unless he reduces it, he will be giving them a (real) wage increase, which is an anomaly in a depression. Employees will not believe him. Nor in a depression will anyone feel better off just because his unchanged wage buys more goods because prices are falling. Anxiety about the economic environment, and (in our current depression, which has involved a huge loss in personal wealth as a result of the declines in housing and stock values) a desire to rebuild personal savings, will leave him feeling worse off even if he can buy goods and services at lower prices. In the Great Depression, the wages of many workers rose in real terms because their wages were not cut even though by 1933 the price level had fallen by 25 percent.

A further and more interesting explanation for workers' resistance to having their nominal wages cut in depressions, though they may accept a reduction in real wages caused by an increase in the costs of the goods and services that they buy, is that workers pay a great deal of attention to the relation of their wage to that of other workers in approximately the same line of work, especially if they have the same employer. They hate the idea of being paid less than a peer. They take it as criticism, and, human nature being what it is, are apt to think it unmerited criticism; or they suspect favoritism, or nepotism, or discrimination on invidious grounds; or they simply feel resentful, hurt, humiliated, or disrespected. (Employers may fear suits for employment discrimination if they treat workers in the same job classification differently.) Some economists describe workers' hostility to change in their relative pay as a preference for "fairness," but the hostility is more self-interested, and rational, than the word "fairness" implies. Moreover, "fairness" is a hopelessly vague word, which should be retired from social science.[5]

So while it might be attractive in principle to an employer to reduce wages selectively (not uniformly—for then he may lose his best workers to competing employers), he is likely to prefer to lay off his less productive workers instead. Notice the implication that workers of different productivity are nevertheless paid the same. This, though contrary to classical labor economics, which teaches that in a competitive market each worker is paid his marginal product (his contribution to the firm's profits), is implied by the analysis in the preceding paragraph: workers' resentment at wage differentials will not be allayed by telling them that some of them are better workers than others. Moreover, workers whose nominal wages are cut during a depression, and whose real wages therefore fall, will have trouble making ends meet. This will make them anxious and therefore distracted at work.

For these reasons and others, personnel officers generally advise their firm that if it needs to reduce its costs, it should lay off workers rather than cut wages, either selectively or across the board. The other reasons for this advice are:

(1) The entire workforce will be miserable with a wage cut (unless the cut is selective, but then it will create the problems noted above), whereas with layoffs, only those laid off will be miserable—and they will be off the premises and so their misery will not infect the remaining workforce.

5. See the penetrating deconstruction of "fairness" in Vernon L. Smith, *Economics: Constructivist and Ecological Forms* 161–167 (2008). The form of fairness that Smith identifies that relates to my analysis is "equality of outcomes," the rule that is "preferred by people in situations where they have no knowledge or means of identifying differences in individual merit or in their contributions to the total to be apportioned to individuals." Id. at 162.

(2) The employees who are retained will work harder, lest they be the next to get the ax.

(3) Layoffs enable the elimination of dead wood that had been hired when, because the labor market was tight, the employer had had to make do with whatever the labor market was offering.

(4) Layoffs eliminate fixed costs, such as costs of supervision, and wage cuts do not. And

(5) the reduction in the wage that would be necessary to achieve the desired economies might be so great that it would depress the wage below the workers' reservation wage, in which event it would be equivalent to a layoff.

Every firm, moreover, has indispensable workers, whose wages the employer would not want to cut, for fear of losing them. The brunt of any reduction in labor costs would thus be felt by workers whose wages would have to be cut drastically in order to achieve essential economies, creating wage disparities that would damage the morale of the workforce as a whole.

And from the employer's standpoint, it is easier to estimate the number of workers needed to satisfy the reduced demand for his products than to calculate the optimal wage cut, as he cannot be sure what the workers' response to the wage cut will be.

The last reason for laying off workers in a depression is that the employer may simply need fewer. Price cuts may not restore demand to its previous level, in which event output will fall and therefore the demand for labor will fall.[6] If it took 10 workers to produce x output, it may take only 5 to produce $x/2$ output. An alternative to laying off half the workers would be to pay each of them half his normal wage—maybe there wouldn't be enough work for all of them, and each would work half-time. This kind of sharing apparently was common in England during the 1920s

6. See Robert J. Barro and Herschell I. Grossman, "A General Disequilibrium Model of Income and Employment," 61 *American Economic Review* 82, 87 (1971).

and 1930s, but it is inefficient: the employer loses the opportunity to lay off his least efficient workers, and a drastic wage cut is likely to make a worker think himself better off quitting and looking for another job, meanwhile collecting unemployment benefits.

Notice that all these factors that incline employers to lay off workers in a depression operate independently of unionization, which in the United States today covers only a small part of the labor force outside of public employment—and public employment is largely insulated from the business cycle. In one respect, unionization of private firms slants the employer's choice in favor of layoffs, because union contracts rarely limit layoffs (for that could destroy a firm, and so it would never agree to such a term) but do limit wage and benefits reductions during the term (usually three years) of the union's collective bargaining contract with the employer, so that cutting wages and benefits requires renegotiating the contract. But in another respect unionization reduces the incentive to lay off workers: union contracts usually require that layoffs be strictly in reverse order of seniority, and so they cannot be used to prune dead wood.

In deciding whether to lay off workers, employers have also to consider how essential a particular worker is to their business (you need four musicians for a quartet), and how costly it will be to find and train a replacement when demand picks up. The simpler the work, the more likely the employer is to cut costs by laying off employees. That is one reason for the high rate of layoffs in construction, an industry in which many workers have only the most casual connection to a particular employer. When the cost of finding and training a replacement is high, employers may prefer furloughs (which differ from layoffs because the furloughed worker is promised his job back when conditions improve) or shortened work weeks to layoffs, which sever the employment relationship.

The fact that wages do not adjust much during a depression or recession strikes economists as anomalous because a fall in demand implies a fall in price. The expression used to describe the phenomenon—"sticky wages"—is not suggestive of efficiency. But we have just seen that the tendency of the quantity rather than the price of labor to decline in response to an economy-wide fall in demand for goods and services makes economic sense.

The analysis may help explain a puzzle that emerged at the end of the third quarter of 2009. Productivity (the ratio of output to input), which one thinks of as a major driver of economic growth, rose by an astonishing 8.1 percent that quarter. Yet unemployment rose (in September) to 9.8 percent, even though increases in productivity normally are associated with increased wages and employment. But we need to distinguish between different causes of productivity growth. If it is the result of technological innovation ("technology" in this context could include innovations in management, marketing, and other business methods unrelated to advances in the engineering sense), the effect of greater productivity on economic growth will indeed be positive. But the recent productivity spurt has been due not to innovation but to old-fashioned cost cutting, impelled not by technological advances but by economic distress. Facing declining demand and a frightened workforce, a firm can reduce its costs in a variety of ways unrelated to technological advances, including laying off workers, pushing its remaining workers to work harder, reducing wages and benefits, buying cheaper inputs, slowing delivery, paying its bills more slowly, and responding more slowly to customer complaints. Some cost reductions will not increase productivity, as they will be proportional to reductions in output. But others will, such as laying off the least productive workers or reducing quality in ways that do not show up in statistics on productivity (as they should—a reduction in quality is a reduction in the value of output).

Productivity gains based merely on adaptations to temporarily depressed economic conditions will be lost when conditions improve. As labor markets tighten, a firm will perforce hire workers who are less productive than the workers it retained in a slimmed-down workforce during the depression, and so productivity will decline.

The recent productivity gains could actually signal pessimism about the pace of the recovery from the depression. There are costs to reorganizing one's business in order to adapt to a reduction in demand. The shorter the expected reduction, therefore, the less reorganizing a firm will do. Indeed, often during a recession or depression there is "labor hoarding": if a restoration of normal demand is expected in the near future, a firm may be better off with a workforce larger than it needs in order to meet current demand for its output than it would be if it laid off workers and had to incur the expense of rehiring them, or hiring new workers, when demand for its output increases. There has been less labor hoarding in the current downturn than in previous ones, and this may be because employers don't anticipate an early revival of demand for their output. Such pessimism would be consistent with predictions made during the third quarter that unemployment would continue to rise for some months and thereafter decline only slowly, for with a very high rate of unemployment and underemployment—10.2 percent and 17.5 percent, as of the end of October, respectively (though these figures fell slightly, to 10.0 and 17.2 percent, in November)—demand for goods and services was likely to remain at a low level.

The election of a new Democratic President in the depths of what was shaping up as the first acknowledged depression since the 1930s made comparison with Franklin Roosevelt's election as the American economy was hurtling to the bottom it reached in March 1933, when he was inaugurated, inevitable. Beginning with his memorable inaugural address ("we have nothing to fear but fear itself") and continuing with a flurry of programs announced, enacted, and implemented with astonishing speed, Roosevelt presided over an immediate very sharp rebound of the economy, though because of a second depression in 1937 and 1938 (a period in which the unemployment rate, which had bottomed out at 25 percent in 1933, rose from 14 to 19 percent) before the first one had been overcome, the economy did not recover fully from what came to be called the Great Depression until 1941.

Something comparable was expected of Obama, quite unrealistically. The economy was not down nearly as far as it had been in March 1933. The population was far less desperate. The cult of the strong man (Hitler had taken power in January 1933, and Stalin and Mussolini were ruling their respective countries with an iron hand and Stalin was widely admired in the democratic countries, as even Mussolini was, to a certain extent) had faded. And American politics had become notably undisciplined. Obama has far less control over the Democratic majorities in both houses of Congress than Roosevelt had. Moreover, the executive branch of the federal government has become elephantine, smothered in red tape, racked by interest groups, and harassed by the media. On top of everything, Obama had no executive experience, whereas Roosevelt had been governor of the nation's most important state.

Eloquent though he is, Obama could not match Roosevelt's inaugural performance. And his critical economic appointment, that of Timothy Geithner as Secretary of the Treasury, was at first coolly received by the public, the Congress, and the media. (The fuss over Geithner's unpaid taxes exemplified the trivialization of American public discourse.) Worse, many people were startled—I certainly was—that Obama did not assume office with a comprehensive plan of economic recovery in hand. He had had a large, expert staff working on the transition from candidate to likely President from the summer of 2008, and by the middle of September it was obvious to everyone that economic recovery would be the major task of the new President, at least at first. Between then and January 20 the transition team had four months to devise a comprehensive plan; from election day, almost two and a half months.

But no plan was unveiled on inauguration day, and with the exception of the stimulus package, of which more shortly, the proposals that dribbled out in the following weeks, incomplete and unimpressive, indicated that no comprehensive plan existed. Two alternative inferences could be drawn, both damaging to the confidence of business and consumers in the new Administration: that it was no more (or not enough more) competent than its predecessor in economic matters; or that no one had a clue about what could be done to arrest the economic decline. The decline seemed in fact to be accelerating in the weeks after Obama's inauguration. The Dow Jones Industrial Average fell to 6,500 early in March, which was more than halfway below its peak of 14,000 in October 2007.

Further contributing to the economic deterioration was growing public anger about corporate compensation and other "lavish" expenditures (for example, on private aircraft and on meetings at fancy resorts), an anger quickly echoed and amplified by members of Congress. The uproar was connected with the tendency, abetted by the Administration, to blame "stupid, reckless, and greedy" bankers for the depression, rather than Greenspan, Bernanke, Geithner, and other officials on whose watch the financial collapse had occurred. Calling bankers greedy for taking advantage of profit opportunities created by unsound government policies is like calling rich people greedy for allowing Medicare to reimburse their medical bills.

As we know from the last chapter, a turn to thrift is the last thing one wants in a depression. Demagoguery about executive salaries and perks increased the uncertainty of the business environment, deflected senior executives from their core responsibilities to worrying about their personal finances and about retaining their best compensation-capped employees, and whacked the hotel and travel industries by deterring businesses, including nonfinancial businesses (including even some law firms), from holding meetings in pricey venues. Regulating the compensation of executives of financial corporations became an element of the Administration's program of financial regulatory reform. And even before that program was enacted, limitations were imposed on the pay of executives of firms that had received bailouts. Those limitations culminated in October 2009, when Kenneth Feinberg, the "pay czar" appointed by the Administration to regulate the compensation of executives at seven bailout recipients that had not yet repaid the government, placed limits on the compensation of top executives at those firms. Limiting the compensation of a handful of employees at a handful of firms can't have any effect except to benefit the firms' competitors by making them more attractive places to work; and this is not a merely theoretical concern.[1] Nor is the issue merely retention. Pay caps may make it impossible for a firm to attract desperately needed talent.

The caps are a form of scapegoating designed to appease public anger over the high incomes of financiers who precipitated an economic collapse that has caused widespread suffering, much of it among people who—unlike financiers, bumbling or inattentive government regulators, macroeconomists, members of Congress, and improvident home buyers and home-equity borrowers—played no role in the collapse.

None of the Administration's proposals for financial regulatory reform was aimed at helping the economy recover from the depression; their goal was, by limiting risky lending, to prevent a repetition of the financial crisis that had triggered the depression. They actually were impediments to recovery, because they further distracted financial executives from repairing their firms and getting on with lending and made businessmen fear that the government was antibusiness—and of course the Democratic Party does contain elements hostile to business, even though they don't parade under the banner of socialism. The limitations on compensation imposed thus far have been immensely complicated[2] and will only become more so if extended to the entire financial industry.

The Administration's major early effort to grapple with the

1. See, for example, Mary Williams Walsh, "AIG Chief's Mission: Save Executive Pay," New York Times, Nov. 11, 2009, p. B2; Louise Story, "Who Gets Paid What," Oct. 21, 2009, New York Times, p. B1; Mary Williams Walsh, "Ex-Chief of A.I.G. Is Busy Building a New Venture: Luring Familiar Talent: Concern That His Effort May Hamper Moves to Repay U.S.," New York Times, Oct. 27, 2009, p. A1; Tomoeh Murakami Tse and Brady Dennis, "Top Employees Leave Financial Firms Ahead of Pay Cuts: Grass Is Greener Where Bonuses Are Sky-High," Washington Post, Oct. 23, 2009, p. A20.

2. Robert C. Pozen, Too Big to Save? How to Fix the U.S. Financial System, ch. 11 (2009).

depression was a fiscal stimulus program—the American Recovery and Reinvestment Act of 2009—enacted a month after Obama's inauguration. The act authorized spending $787 billion in federal money over a roughly three-year period to fight the depression. There are three components: grants to states to enable them to avoid having to make drastic cuts in their public spending or to increase taxes; federal tax relief and other federal benefits to individuals (mainly tax relief, however); and public works, such as road building. The tax-relief component isn't literally an expenditure program. It does not consist of tax rebates, as the Bush Administration's anticipatory stimulus measure of early 2008 did, but rather of tax reductions. Like rebates, however, they put cash in people's pockets (though not necessarily immediately) by reducing the amount withheld from their paychecks for federal income tax, by reducing their estimated tax payments, and by increasing the size of the tax rebates they receive when they file their annual tax returns.

The theory of a fiscal stimulus as a measure for fighting a depression is straightforward, though controversial. Output, as measured for example by gross domestic product, is the sum of private consumption, private investment, and government expenditures. When private demand and hence personal consumption expenditures fall, government can step in and, by increasing its own consumption—its own purchases of goods and services —or, better, by investing in labor-intensive projects such as road building, restore total output to its former level. As output rises, so will employment, and the downward economic spiral will give way to an upward one.

A stimulus is financed either by the government's borrowing money or by the government's creating money. If instead the stimulus were financed by raising taxes, the government would be putting money into one pocket and taking the identical amount out of the other pocket.

Generally the most effective response to an economic downturn is monetary rather than fiscal—action by the Federal Reserve rather than by the Treasury.[3] By expanding the money supply, the Fed drives down interest rates, and the lower rates jumpstart economic activity. That is what the Federal Reserve did under Paul Volcker's chairmanship after engineering a severe recession by pushing up interest rates to break the inflation of the 1970s. The Fed could spur economic activity by expanding the money supply because the banking system was intact. But in a financial crisis, or in its aftermath, when the banks are still sick and credit is constrained, monetary policy may be ineffective—it was this time. When monetary policy loses its normal stimulative effect because no one wants to lend or borrow, fiscal stimulus comes into its own as an effective antidepression measure.[4]

The theory was imperfectly implemented in the stimulus bill that Congress passed. The two-thirds of the stimulus money that was earmarked for transfer payments to the states and for tax relief mainly for individuals was not a form of government investment, as building a road is. These were gifts. If gifts are used by their recipients to buy goods or services, then private consumption rises, which is fine, though, as we'll see, less fine than increased investment. But windfalls are to a great extent saved rather than spent. That happened with the Bush rebates in the spring of 2008, a forerunner of the larger stimulus program of 2009. Windfalls are what economists call "transitory" income, as distinct from "permanent" income. If taxes are cut in circumstances that lead people to believe the cut will be permanent, they infer that their permanent income has risen and that they can

3. Christina D. Romer and David H. Romer, "What Ends Recessions?" 9 *NBER Macroeconomics Annual* 13, 55 (1994).

4. Emanuele Baldacci, Sanjeev Gupta, and Carlos Mulas-Granados, "How Effective Is Fiscal Policy Response in Systemic Banking Crisis?" (International Monetary Fund, WP/09/160, July 2009); Miguel Almunia et al., "The Effectiveness of Fiscal and Monetary Stimulus in Depressions," *Vox*, Nov. 18, 2009, www.voxeu.org/index.php?q=node/4227 (visited Dec. 18, 2009). For a striking empirical study of the efficacy of fiscal stimulus in a depression, see Lester G. Telser, "The Veterans' Bonus of 1936," 26 *Journal of Post Keynesian Economics* 227 (2003).

adjust their standard of living upward—which means spending more. But if the increase in income is transitory, they will probably save more of it, because if they use it to increase their standard of living the increase will be temporary and they will have to retrench when the money runs out—a painful adjustment.

Poorer households, being liquidity-constrained, are more likely to spend than to save transitory income; and so the more severe an economic downturn is and the more overindebted people are, the higher the percentage spent of any transfer received will be. This provides some basis for thinking that a higher percentage of the transfer payment component of the 2009 stimulus would be spent than of the 2001 tax rebates (two-thirds spent within three months)[5] or of the 2008 tax rebates (half).[6]

And given the sluggishness of modern American government and the terror of government contract officers at the thought of being accused of allowing waste or fraud, the implementation of the public works component of the stimulus program was likely to be—and the evidence is that this one is and will continue to be—painfully protracted. And if much of the public works spending occurs toward the end of the planned duration of the stimulus program, coinciding with rising private spending, it will exacerbate what may by then be a problem not of economic decline but of too-rapid economic growth, with worrisome consequences discussed later in this book.

As the stimulus bill wended its way through Congress, the amount of money allotted to transportation infrastructure (mainly road and bridge construction, and repair and building projects such as the painting of schools) shrank, possibly because of political pressure: few women are employed in such projects.

5. David S. Johnson, Jonathan A. Parker, and Nicholas S. Soleles, "Household Expenditure and the Income Tax Rebates of 2001," 96 *American Economic Review* 1589 (2006).

6. Matthew D. Shapiro and Joel Slemrod, "Did the 2008 Tax Rebates Stimulate Spending?" 99 *American Economic Review* 374 (2009). Notice how much higher the savings rate of transitory income is than the normal personal savings rate.

Yet that is the class of expenditures that comes closest to satisfy-ing the conditions for an effective stimulus. It targets an industry, construction, in which the unemployment rate is very high; most of the projects financed by it can be started quickly if a deter-mined effort is made to cut red tape at the risk of inviting more than the usual amount of corruption and waste in public con-tracting; and there is an economic need, unrelated to the depres-sion, for improvements in the nation's dilapidated transportation infrastructure, so that the projects are likely to have value inde-pendent of their contribution to digging the nation out of its eco-nomic hole. At the opposite extreme are projects, such as the al-lotment of $17 billion to facilitating the digitization of medical records, that will be staffed by highly paid technical workers, most of whom have no difficulty holding or finding good jobs (especially in the medical industry, which has been least affected by the current depression), and that will not be completed until long after the depression ends. Moreover, no effort was made to concentrate public works spending in areas of the country in which unemployment is high.

A number of conservative economists oppose the stimulus on fundamental grounds (rather than because it was poorly de-signed and executed), and one must attend to their argument. In its simplest form, and with reference first to the public works component, it begins with the observation that the national in-come is the sum of consumption and investment, that savings is income minus consumption, and thus that savings equals in-vestment.[7] If so, then when the government borrows money to finance public investment, the amount of money available for private investment must fall by the identical amount. Only if the public investment is more valuable than a private investment of the same size is the public investment a worthwhile measure for fighting a depression.

---

7. Y [income] $- C = S$; $Y = C + I$; so by substitution $C + I - C = S$, so $I = S$.

What the argument misses is that not all savings are forms of *productive* investment. One form of savings, which is attractive in a depression, especially if there is deflation, consists of putting cash in a safe or a safe-deposit box, or even under one's mattress. Such money is not invested, and the motive for saving rather than spending it may have nothing to do with wanting to invest it in the future. The saver may be refraining from spending it not because of any definite intention of spending it in the future but because of a desire to have cash on hand to meet a possible urgent need for it—a common concern during a depression, and one that helps explain the surge in the personal savings rate since 2007. Not only are the cash reserves of nonfinancial institutions, as well as of the banks (as we know), much higher than in 2007,[8] but the amount of currency in the economy has increased substantially since then—by 2.8 percent in the year ending in September 2008 and by 10.3 percent in the year ending this past September. Even the sale of safes has increased.[9]

Critics reply that if the saver decides to *lend* his savings rather than hold them in cash, they will be borrowed by either a private investor or the government, and there is no reason to think the government will use the borrowed money more efficiently. Suppose I have $100 in a demand deposit account, meaning that I have lent the bank this amount. (Depositors do not own the money in their deposit accounts, as distinct from money in a safe-deposit box; they're just creditors of the bank.) The bank can lend it either to a business, another private enterprise, or a private individual or to the government, which to finance a public works project must borrow the project's cost.

But this picture is overdrawn. If the government doesn't borrow the money in the depositor's account from the bank, it

8. Tom McGinty and Cari Tuna, "Jittery Companies Stash Cash: After Crisis, Big Businesses Hoard Most Bucks in 40 Years," *Wall Street Journal*, Nov. 2, 2009, p. A1.

9. Ashley M. Heyer, "Stores See Boost in Sales of Safes," *Los Angeles Times*, Oct. 16, 2008, p. C7.

doesn't follow that the bank will lend it; the bank may instead decide to add the money to its excess reserves. In that event the depositor is not investing, because the bank isn't lending; the depositor is just building up the bank's capital so that *eventually* the bank will start lending. As the economist Eugene Fama has put it in correspondence with me, "The question is whether in current conditions the investment financed by a time-deposit in a bank is as productive as hiring unemployed construction workers to fill in potholes in the streets of Hyde Park. The time deposit will end up as investment, but perhaps not productive investment." Or the government may borrow not from an American bank but instead from foreigners, who finance so much of our public debt; and if the government follows that route, it won't be withdrawing any cash from the American economy. In either case, the government's borrowing will not reduce private investment. Some economists argue, as we'll see in chapter 9, that, knowing that future taxes must rise to repay the expense of the stimulus, people will reduce their consumption in order to save up for paying that uncertain future tax. The assumption is unrealistic and the prediction unconfirmed. No one knows when taxes will rise or what form they will take (higher marginal income tax rates? a VAT? inflation?) and what the effect will be on any given individual's income or wealth.

What is true is that any increase in the demand for capital will raise interest rates, which in turn will reduce the incentive for private investment. If the government finances a stimulus program by selling Treasury securities, the supply of debt will rise, the price will therefore fall, and so the yield will rise. Higher interest rates will, it is true, in turn tempt the cash hoarders and other ultrasafe savers to shift some of those savings into higher-yield investments that are more likely to fund productive activities. Nevertheless, the danger that public investment will crowd out private investment, causing no net increase in overall investment, is real; among other reasons is that competition between government and the private sector for scarce labor will push up wages and by doing reduce the marginal product of private capital investment.

But when private investment is severely depressed, as implied by, among other things, the extraordinary buildup of banks' excess reserves, and as a result interest and wage rates are low, the danger of crowding out is slight. There is also an important timing difference between private and public investment during a depression. A well-designed stimulus program spends as much money as possible as soon as possible in industries and areas of the country hardest hit by unemployment. Private investment of the same amount of money might proceed at a more leisurely pace, because it might be oriented not toward filling potholes (say) but instead toward building factories that might take years to be completed and employ few unemployed workers. Certainly the aim of private investment would not be to alleviate unemployment and to do so as quickly as possible.

And the *psychological* effect of a stimulus program must not be underestimated. The perilous and uncertain economic conditions in a depression engender fears that cause both business and consumers to freeze and hoard rather than invest and consume, and freezing and hoarding cause output to fall and unemployment therefore to rise. Confidence (hope, optimism) could not be restored by monetary policy and bank bailouts alone during the present economic downturn, because those measures were having only a limited effect in pulling the economy out of its hole; they slowed the downward spiral but did not arrest it. The government had to show the public and business its resolve to beat the depression, and the enactment of an ambitious program of deficit spending was the key to showing that.

The confidence-building effect of the program was probably its biggest effect in the early months after it was enacted, for in those months little of the stimulus money was actually spent, and what was spent consisted entirely of transfer payments (tax relief and payments to state governments), which have only a limited effect in stimulating spending. Moreover, the transfer payments were no more targeted on areas of the country that had the highest unemployment than the public works projects.

The valid criticism of even a well-designed stimulus program is that it creates a risk of future inflation because it adds to the national debt; and an addition of $787 billion to that debt, on top of all the other expenditures that in conjunction with the fall of tax revenues in a depression are causing the national debt to soar alarmingly, is no small potatoes. The fear of future economic harm from deficit spending to stimulate economic activity is an element of the "aftershock" problem that I discuss in chapter 6.

The stimulus was only one of the programs that the Obama Administration launched in an effort to arrest the economic decline and speed recovery. The banks, though saved by the hundreds of billions of dollars that the Fed and the Treasury had poured into them, remained a problem; despite all the money they had received, they were lending less than they had lent in the fall of 2008, at the height of the financial crisis. Rather than giving them more money, the Treasury announced a complicated plan (the Geithner Plan, later renamed the Public-Private Investment Program) for increasing banks' capital without a further infusion of federal money.

The plan involved subsidies to hedge funds and other private investors, including banks, in the form of guaranties (an example of the government's resort to off-balance-sheet liabilities) to induce them to buy securitized debt, mainly mortgage-backed securities, owned by banks. These assets, as we know, were carried on banks' balance sheets at what were widely believed to be inflated values, in order to fend off demands that the banks increase their capital; the banks were taking advantage of the relaxation of the mark-to-market accounting rule. The government's concern was that as long as the assets remained on the banks' balance sheets, uncertainty about their value would deter private investment in banks and thus leave them in a weakened state.

Corporate balance sheets usually list assets that are difficult for outsiders to value; that doesn't prevent corporations from raising money. The mortgage-backed securities created before the crash continue to trade. Hundreds of commercial banks have failed since 2008, owning interests in such securities that have to be valued when the banks' assets and liabilities are transferred to solvent banks with the financial assistance of the Federal Deposit Insurance Corporation. Still, these valuations are uncertain, because they depend on estimates of future default rates of the mortgages packaged in the security that have not yet matured. Nevertheless, it is unclear what would have been gained by inducing hedge funds and other investors (including strong banks) to buy the mortgage-backed securities still on bank balance sheets, for while the investors would be putting up some of their own money, and not just operating as a conduit for a government subsidy, the investors would be left with less of their own money to invest. There would be no net addition to lendable funds, except for the part of the cost borne by the government. Further problems with attempting to help banks in this way were that it would substitute a complex three-way transaction (government, private investor, and bank) for a simpler two-way transaction (government and bank), and that private investors would be loath to go into partnership with the government, lest under pressure from an angry public and Congress the government try to claw back any "exorbitant" profits that the investors made. And if the banks didn't want to lend, giving them more cash would just add to their reserves.

The plan went nowhere, as one might have expected; and impatience with it caused some economists to advocate the government's "nationalizing" weak banks and selling their questionable assets. That would have been a mistake—not only because of the inability of government to manage banks competently and avoid the politicization of credit, but also because the problem of valuing the overvalued assets would not be eliminated. The banks that were the targets for nationalization were not broke, so if the government had confiscated them, it would have had to pay the owners for the net value of their assets, including any overvalued assets that retained some value.

Maybe what the government should have done was to take (though again it would have had to compensate the stockholders) all the good assets of a bank, leaving the overvalued ones with the stockholders; then the bank's balance sheet would be "clean." But then what would the government do with the bank? Run it? Sell it? The practical complications would be immense. The amount of money that Congress would be required to appropriate in order to compensate bank shareholders would be immense too, though much of it would be recovered when the government, having cleansed the banks' balance sheets, sold the banks back to the private sector.

In lieu of nationalization, the Treasury decided to conduct a series of well-publicized "stress tests" on the banks that had received bailout money, and on the basis of the results of the tests order the banks to raise relatively modest amounts of additional equity capital. Most of the banks were able to raise the required sums with little difficulty, and by doing so and thus satisfying the Treasury that they were adequately capitalized, they could borrow money (remember that most bank capital is borrowed) in the private sector at lower rates than when their solvency was in question.

There was nothing novel about conducting stress tests on banks. They are conducted routinely by bank regulators. They involve examining a bank's balance sheet to see whether the bank needs additional capital in order to survive a hypothetical (but always possible) deterioration in economic conditions, which by increasing the default rate would reduce the value of the bank's loan portfolio, a major part of its capital. When the current stress tests were conducted, the government was correctly anticipating a further decline in the economy, and in particular an increase in unemployment, which would increase the default rate, and it wanted to make sure that the banks had enough capital to withstand a further deterioration in their loan portfolios.

What was notable about the tests was the publicity that the government gave to conducting them and to the results. It was trying to reassure the public about the essential soundness of the banking industry and hence (perhaps) of the economy as a whole. It was another confidence-building measure, like the stimulus.

Geithner was borrowing a leaf from Franklin Roosevelt, who immediately upon taking office declared a bank holiday, closing down the banks so that bank examiners could determine which were solvent. This was before deposit insurance; doubts about bank solvency were causing massive runs on the banks. After eight days most banks were allowed to reopen, having been declared sound. In fact, given the number of banks, the fewness of examiners, and the brevity of the bank holiday, it appears that, at best, only cursory examinations of the banks' books were made.[10] The bank holiday restored confidence in the banking system to a point at which a loose monetary policy, designed to reduce interest rates and replace deflation with inflation (see chapter 3), could become effective: the banks would stop hemorrhaging deposits, and with their capital thus stabilized would do enough lending to increase the amount of money in circulation. Geithner's stress tests were more serious than Roosevelt's, but not rigorous, which supports the inference that they were primarily designed for building confidence in the banking system.

Remember that the purpose of the tests was to determine the ability of the banks to survive, without further additions to their capital, if the economy continued to decline. Critical were the assumptions about how far and fast it might decline. The assumptions made were favorable to the banks. Unemployment was assumed to decline only to 8.2 percent by the end of 2010; within

10. William L. Silber, "Why Did FDR's Bank Holiday Succeed?" *Federal Reserve Bank of New York Economic Policy Review*, July 2009, p. 19.

weeks of the completion of the tests and announcement of their results, unemployment exceeded 9 percent, and by October it exceeded 10 percent. The discrepancy between predicted and actual unemployment rates was ominous, because there is a strong positive correlation between unemployment and loan defaults.

In addition, as the Harvard lawyer-economist Lucian Bebchuk has emphasized,[11] the stress tests considered likely defaults only through the end of 2010, ignoring loans that mature later. As the date of their maturity approaches, the prospects for their defaulting will weigh heavily on the banks' solvency and therefore on their ability and willingness to lend their excess reserves. This is more than a theoretical concern, because many banks remain heavily invested in commercial mortgages that will come due after 2010 and seem likely to default then.

A priority of the new Administration was residential mortgage relief. Mortgage defaults and foreclosures had reduced household wealth and thus increased the propensity to save, which one doesn't want in a depression, and had impaired the capital of the banks and of other investors in mortgage-backed securities. The goals of mortgage relief thus were twofold. First, anything that reduced homeowners' liabilities or increased their home equity would encourage them to spend money; they would be less indebted, and their savings, which included the net value of their home, would be worth more. Second, anything that increased the value of mortgages would increase bank capital, which remained heavily invested in mortgages and mortgage-backed securities. Of course there was potential tension between these goals, since mortgage relief could benefit the mortgagors at the expense of the mortgagees.

One of the early proposals was to amend the Bankruptcy Code to authorize bankruptcy judges to "cram down" first mort-

11. See, for example, Lucian Bebchuk, "Toxic Tests," *The Economists' Voice*, July 2009, www.bepress.com/ev/vol6/iss7/art3/ (visited Dec. 9, 2009).

gages on primary residences—that is, to reduce a mortgage to the current market value of the house so that the house wouldn't be worth less than the mortgage. The difference between the debt and the crammed-down mortgage would be an unsecured debt of little value, and so the effective debt burden of the homeowner—and his incentive to abandon the house—would be reduced. The proposal died because of strong opposition from mortgage bankers. But it never promised much relief. It would have required the borrower (the mortgagor) to declare bankruptcy in order to take advantage of it. A mortgagor whose house is worth less than his mortgage can, if he considers the house to have become a worthless investment, simply abandon it. Unless he is rich, he won't be sued for the unpaid portion of the debt, and remember that in many states he can't be sued. And while cram-down would have benefited some homeowners, it would have hurt lenders.

The Administration succeeded, however, in putting into effect other forms of mortgage relief under the umbrella of the Helping Families Save Their Homes Act, enacted in May 2009: a subsidy for first-time home buyers, in the form of an $8,000 tax credit, to stimulate the purchase of houses whose current owners could not afford them and thus to prevent defaults as well as to prop up house prices by increasing the demand for houses; subsidies to help some mortgagors with the interest component of their mortgage payments; the purchase by the Federal Reserve of mortgage-backed securities to reduce mortgage interest rates (remember that the greater the demand for some class of debt, the lower the yield—the interest rate); and the facilitation of mortgage modifications, to reduce foreclosures, by immunizing mortgage servicers from legal liability should a modification infringe the contractual rights of investors in some of the tranches of a mortgage-backed security.

The congressional appropriation for mortgage relief—$75 billion—was modest in relation to the total amount of mortgage debt ($12 trillion), much of it troubled, and the money dribbled out slowly because of stringent and complicated conditions on qualifying for subsidy money. Indirect subsidies in the form of increased lending by the Federal Housing Administration and the purchase of mortgage-backed securities by the Federal Reserve added to the federal largesse for homeowners. But these subsidies also increased concern about the federal deficit and hence fear of future inflation, and this fear for a time increased mortgage interest rates (since they are long-term rates), retarding the refinancing of mortgages and the purchase of new homes, though at this writing mortgage interest rates have come down again.

The most popular part of the program—the tax credit for first-time home buyers, which was due to expire on November 30, 2009, but was extended to April 30, 2010—may have been rather ineffectual, because most of the people receiving the credit might within a few months have bought a house anyway. In this it resembles the "cash for clunkers" program, discussed later. There is, moreover, a serious downside. In combination with the FHA's very generous mortgage terms, which require only a 3.5 percent down payment on the purchase of a house, the tax credit enables the buyer to purchase a house without any cash outlay at all. This invites speculative home buying that is likely to result in a high rate of default, further increasing the FHA's mounting losses.[12] Already 11 percent of all homes bought in 2009 are "under water,"[13] meaning that the unpaid principal of the mortgage exceeds the market value of the house, making abandonment an attractive prospect.

The grant of legal immunity to mortgage servicers, provided only that they acted in good faith, raised eyebrows; it seemed to authorize the servicer to revise the terms of the mortgages backing a mortgage-backed security and thus alter the priorities of the

12. Robert C. Pozen, "Homebuyer Tax Credits Threaten the FHA," *Wall Street Journal,* Nov. 24, 2009, p. A21.
13. Ruth Simon and James R. Hagerty, "1 in 4 Borrowers under Water," *Wall Street Journal,* Nov. 24, 2009, pp. A1, A4.

investors in the security.[14] Anyway the measure proved a flop, because few lenders (or their representatives, the servicers) are interested in modifying mortgages. A modification that reduces monthly payments without reducing the unpaid balance of the principal leaves the mortgagor with a debt that, given the fall in housing prices, may exceed his equity, and that is an incitement to abandon the house to the mortgagee as a bad investment. But mortgagees are adamant against reducing principal. Not only do they fear being inundated by requests for such modifications, but mortgages are carried on a bank's balance sheet at full value until there is a default—or a modification—and banks, as we know, don't like to write down the value of their assets before they have to. It is true that firms are not required to mark to market loans they intend to hold to maturity, or even (since the relaxation of the mark-to-market rule for assets in inactive markets) tranches of mortgage-backed securities. But once there is a transaction, such as the modification of a mortgage, the firm must alter its valuation of the mortgage, and of similar mortgages on its balance sheet as well. Even the prospect of modifications that just lower monthly payments without reducing the unpaid balance can generate a flood of requests—and worse: threats by mortgagors to default, made in the hope of inducing a modification. Modifications also involve significant transaction costs.

The Administration assumed that modification is superior, from a mortgagee's as well as a mortgagor's perspective, to foreclosure as a method for dealing with a mortgage default, but that securitization of mortgages, by severing the relationship between the originator of the mortgage loan and the borrower, impedes modification and so contributed to the drop in housing prices and the increase in foreclosures. Both assumptions are plausible but appear to be incorrect. In a very large sample of res-

14. See Steven L. Schwarcz, "Fiduciaries with Conflicting Obligations" (forthcoming in *Minnesota Law Review*).

idential mortgages, only 3 percent of seriously delinquent borrowers obtained a modification that reduced their monthly mortgage payments in the year after they got into trouble.[15] It seems that most delinquent borrowers either resume their mortgage payments without a modification ("self-cure") or default irrevocably within a short time. In either event, little is to be gained by a modification—and much is to be lost. Modification not only reduces the monthly payments received by the mortgagee but also entails negotiation costs. And by postponing foreclosure, it lowers the price that the mortgagee will receive, either because house prices are continuing to fall or because financially stressed homeowners do not maintain a house adequately. So the mortgage loses value between modification and eventual foreclosure.

Surprisingly, the study found no significant difference in the modification rate depending on whether the mortgage had been securitized. One reason may be that the incentives to modify are very weak even if the originator of the mortgage still owns it. And while there are reports that servicers of mortgage-backed securities lack the staff needed to handle all the modification requests they are receiving—which is plausible, because these securities often pool thousands of mortgages—the banks that service the mortgages in fact have very large staffs and may be discouraging applications for modification simply because they don't think the costs of processing them are worthwhile, given how few modifications are in a mortgagee's best interests.

It is nice to have the Federal Reserve study that makes these points, and no doubt it took months to complete. But this does not excuse the government's failure to have realized that modi-

15. Manuel Adelino, Kristopher Gerardi, and Paul S. Willen, "Why Don't Lenders Renegotiate More Home Mortgages? Redefaults, Self-Cures and Securitization" (Federal Reserve Board Public Policy Discussion Paper No. 09–4, July 2009). Another skeptical analysis of modification is Christopher Foote et al., "Reducing Foreclosures: No Easy Answer" (NBER Working Paper No. 15063, June 2009).

fication might not be the magic bullet that its mortgage relief plan assumed it would be, and that securitization of mortgages might not have been the culprit in the housing crisis that it was thought to be. All that would have been necessary to get to the same conclusion that the Fed economists reached would have been to talk to a few mortgage bankers. Once again we encounter the government's surprising ignorance of the economy that it is trying to regulate. It's not as if the federal government is new to the mortgage market. The banking industry is deeply invested in that market and pervasively regulated by the federal banking agencies, and the Federal Housing Administration is a major insurer of home mortgages.

At best, efforts at mortgage relief (which basically mean efforts to increase the demand for houses) are unlikely to do much for economic recovery. Those first-time home buyers are people who before buying a house were renters (unless they lived with their parents), so when they buy houses the vacancy rate rises, and with it rise defaults on commercial real estate, in which the banking industry is also heavily and riskily invested. And because there are so many unsold houses, a program that makes it easier to buy or finance a house is unlikely to do much to stimulate housing starts and thus aid the construction industry, with its very high rate of unemployment; most sales of houses will simply reduce existing inventories, which will decline very slowly.

A major initiative of the Obama Administration was the reorganization of General Motors and Chrysler in bankruptcy. In the last chapter I defended the loans to the two companies that were made in December 2008 to avert their being forced to declare bankruptcy. With the economy in a tailspin that was beginning to remind observers of the Great Depression of the 1930s, the bankruptcy of the two firms would have been experienced as a dangerous shock to the economy. They would have needed tens of billions of dollars of debtor-in-possession loans to keep operating, and they could not have obtained that amount of private money. The bailout thus purchased an insurance policy against macroeconomic calamity, at the relatively modest cost of $17 billion.

The auto companies' inability to obtain DIP financing may, moreover, have been due to the liquidity constraints of the embattled banking industry rather than to the nonviability of the companies in a bankruptcy reorganization. To explain, the *average* cost of producing a car is the total cost incurred by the manufacturer, including interest on its debts, divided by the number of cars it produces. That cost exceeded the price at which GM (and Chrysler, but I'll use GM to illustrate) could sell an appreciable number of its vehicles, which is why it was broke. GM's *marginal* cost, however, is the addition to its total costs of producing one more vehicle. That cost does not include interest on existing debt, because the interest is a fixed amount rather than varying with how many cars GM builds and sells. It was the fixedness of its debt that made the company insolvent when the demand for its vehicles plummeted in the fall of 2008; it could not reduce the debt by reducing its output.

As long as GM's cost of making a car, apart from any costs arising from its debts, is less than the price at which it can sell its cars, efficient resource allocation requires that it remain in business, because bankruptcy would wipe out its debts, and the wipeout would be a transfer payment (from GM's creditors to GM) rather than a net social cost. But the credit crisis prevented GM from obtaining the cash it needed to remain in business. In February 2009, bankruptcy experts cautioned that "the tightness of the credit markets" was a factor keeping potential private lenders from providing DIP financing to GM and Chrysler.[16] And it has been estimated that DIP loan rates may have climbed as

16. Jeffrey McCracken and John D. Stoll, "Bankruptcy Funding Solicited for Car Makers," *Wall Street Journal,* Feb. 23, 2009, p. B1.

high as 10 percent above LIBOR (which in January 2009 was about 2 percent) in 2009.[17] So it made economic sense, apart from the impact of a liquidation on employment and on business and consumer confidence, for the government to step in and take the place of the temporarily constrained banks and become GM's banker.

But that was then. Five months later, with the auto bailout money spent, credit was less constrained. GM's continued inability to obtain debtor-in-possession financing may have reflected not a liquidity problem but a judgment by the private sector that GM had no long-run future and therefore could not repay a debtor-in-possession loan large enough to keep the company going. Moreover, those five months saw a partial, and because it was gradual, an orderly partial, liquidation of both GM and Chrysler. The companies closed many of their plants, laying off (for good, probably) many hourly and salaried employees and terminating many dealerships. As a result of these measures, which, being spread out over months, had a more limited psychological impact than if the companies had liquidated completely in December, the shock effect of the companies' declaration of bankruptcy diminished greatly, and for the further reason that the government's promise to guarantee any bankrupt automaker's warranties began to sink in and reassure consumers. When Chrysler finally declared bankruptcy in May 2009 and GM followed suit a few weeks later, the perturbation to the economy was negligible. Bankruptcies that would have been real shockers five months earlier could now be taken by the economy in stride.

But this may have been only because the government agreed to pour tens of billions of dollars more into the companies, mainly General Motors. The scale of the government's invest-

17. "DIP Financing: A Rough Road to Recovery," July 28, 2009, http:// uscorporate.practicallaw.com/2-386-7115 (visited Nov. 1 2009).

ment was so great in relation to the market value of the companies' assets—the investment was anticipated to reach $50 billion in the case of GM ($30 billion in new money, on top of the $20 billion in prebankruptcy bailout money), though much less in the case of Chrysler, which has in effect merged with Fiat—that it made the government a minority owner of Chrysler and the majority owner of GM.

Had it not been for the government's intervention, the bankruptcies might well have resulted in the liquidation of the auto companies' remaining assets. There may not have been enough optimism about the companies' long-run viability to interest DIP lenders. The economy was still declining, albeit at a slower rate than in the first quarter of 2009, and a liquidation of the remaining assets of the two auto companies would have been a blow to a very weak economy, though not so heavy a one as it would have been in December of 2008. So there was a case for what the government did. The specifics of the deals, however, were problematic in several respects, though not in one respect that drew sharp criticism. It was argued that the reorganized companies would be controlled by the United Auto Workers and therefore managed inefficiently, as worker-managed firms typically are. But it is not true that the UAW would be managing the companies. Not the union, but the union-management retirement plan, a separate entity, is a shareholder in the reorganized companies, and it has a fiduciary duty to maximize shareholder value rather than to increase the earnings and benefits of the current workers; as far as I am able to determine, such fiduciary duties generally are discharged honestly.

In any event, whether the companies are managed efficiently or inefficiently has little macroeconomic significance. Chrysler is an unimportant company in a highly competitive global industry. If it is inefficiently managed, it will disappear and its place will be taken by better-managed rivals in the United States and abroad. General Motors is much bigger, but its gradual disappearance as a result of displacement by more efficient producers would have no greater consequence for the economy as a whole.

More troublesome is the fact that the workers and their retirement plans were better treated in the reorganizations than more senior creditors, including secured creditors (neither the workers nor the retirement plans were secured creditors). This is worrisome because it unsettles creditors' expectations and by doing so may lead them to raise interest rates, which is the last thing one wants during a depression. But to evaluate this concern requires careful attention to the details of the bankruptcy procedure. Although I have said that the companies were "reorganized," that is not technically correct. The valuable assets of the two companies were sold to newly created corporations, successors to the old GM and the old Chrysler, under section 363 of the Bankruptcy Code. Section 363 authorizes the bankruptcy judge to auction off the assets of the bankrupt firm if that is the best deal for the creditors; the proceeds of the auction are distributed to the creditors according to the usual priority rules. Section 363 sales have become a common alternative to corporate reorganizations in bankruptcy.[18]

The kicker is that the first bidder, which in the case of these two bankruptcies was the federal government, proposes to the bankruptcy judge the structure of the bids. The government proposed that every bidder be required to offer as much as the government was willing to offer to the union retirement plans. The bankruptcy judge agreed. The consequence was that the auction was unlikely to, and did not, attract any bids that would honor the priority of the senior creditors. To illustrate, suppose senior creditors have claims of $4 billion and the bid structure proposed by the government and accepted by the judge requires that any bidder promise $3 billion to the union retirement plans. Suppose

18. See Douglas G. Baird and Robert K. Rasmussen, "The End of Bankruptcy," 55 *Stanford Law Review* 751 (2002).

further that the government's bid is $5 billion, so that the senior creditors would get only $2 billion. Conceivably some other prospective bidder (it might even be one of the senior creditors, or a consortium of them) might have been willing to pay senior creditors' claims in full but unwilling to both do that *and* pony up another $3 billion for the retirement plans, for suppose it valued the company's assets at only $4 billion. That bidder's bid, which would make the senior creditors whole, would be ineligible.

It can be argued that refusing to allow the bid violates the principle of "absolute priority"—that in bankruptcy the claims of senior creditors must be satisfied in full (if possible) before any junior claimants get anything. (Note the analogy to the rights of the owner of a triple-A tranche of a mortgage-backed security, or of a first mortgagee relative to a subsequent mortgagee or the owner of the mortgaged property.) But suppose that the senior creditors, unconvinced that the company has any future as a going concern, offer $4 billion for the assets with the intention of selling them piecemeal, thus liquidating the company. The government, in my example, being unwilling to pay more than $5 billion yet thinking that paying the retirement plans $3 billion would be necessary to give the company a reasonable chance of surviving as a going concern, would not outbid the senior creditors' bid if they were entitled to terms of sale that would pay them ahead of all junior creditors, such as the retirement plans.

That would be an unattractive result, because it would yield a lower price for the assets—$4 billion rather than $5 billion. A company thought by one bidder to be worth more as a going concern than in liquidation would be sold for a lower bid and liquidated. A major goal of bankruptcy law is to maximize the value of the debtor's estate,[19] and, as in my example (and proba-

19. Toibb v. Radloff, 501 U.S. 157, 163 (1991); In re Chrysler LLC, 576 F.3d 108, 119 (2d Cir. 2009); 12a *Collier on Bankruptcy* § 28.31[2] (Alan N. Resnick & Henry J. Sommer eds., 15th ed. 2009). The *Chrysler* decision was later vacated as moot; that does not eliminate its significance as a precedent that might be relied on in a future case.

bly in the GM and Chrysler bankruptcy cases as well), sometimes that goal can be achieved only at the expense of the senior creditors. I incline to the view that section 363 authorizes the sale at the higher price, as the court of appeals held in the Chrysler bankruptcy.[20] Earlier cases had refused to apply the absolute-priority rule to section 363 sales unless the sale was a *"sub rosa reorganization"*—an effort to defeat the rights that senior creditors would have in a Chapter 11 reorganization.[21] And there was judicial authority that a sound "business justification" for a sale of the debtor's assets, as distinct from an unrelated reason for favoring junior creditors, was enough to defeat classifying the sale as a *sub rosa* reorganization.[22] (There was also contrary judicial authority, however.)[23] Maximizing the value of the debtor's estate should be a sound business justification for a sale of the debtor's assets.[24]

An inference of unwarranted favoritism would arise if the government's plan were *too* favorable to labor, but there are two reasons to doubt that it was in the Chrysler and GM cases. The first, which is related to, though in some ways the converse of, the question discussed in the last chapter of whether an em-

20. In re Chrysler LLC, note 19 above.

21. See, for example, In re Continental Air Lines, Inc., 780 F.2d 1223, 1227–1228 (5th Cir. 1986); In re White Motor Credit Corp., 14 B.R. 584, 588 (Bkrtcy. D. Ohio 1981); but see In re Gulf Coast Oil Corp., 404 B.R. 407 (Bkrtcy. S.D.Tex. 2009).

22. See, for example, Motorola, Inc. v. Official Committee of Unsecured Creditors (In re Iridium Operating LLC), 478 F.3d 452, 466 (2d Cir. 2007); In re Lionel Corp., 722 F.2d 1063 (2d Cir. 1983); see also In re UAL Corp., 433 F.3d 565 (7th Cir. 2006). The Chrysler and GM bankruptcies have already generated a significant literature. See, for example, Ralph Brubaker, "The Chrysler and GM Sales: §363 Plans of Reorganization?" *Bankruptcy Law Letter*, Sept. 2009; Mark J. Roe and David Skeel, "Assessing the Chrysler Bankruptcy" (Harvard Law School and University of Pennsylvania Law School, 2009).

23. Notably In re Braniff Airways, Inc., 700 F.2d 935 (5th Cir. 1983).

24. In re Chrysler LLC, note 19 above, at 118–119; 12a *Collier on Bankruptcy*, note 19 above, § 28.31[2]; cf. In re Chateaugay Corp., 973 F.2d 141, 145 (2d Cir. 1992).

ployer is better off laying off workers in an economic downturn or cutting their wages, is that firms that take over a bankrupt firm which they intend to operate as a going concern prefer that the bankruptcy court treat the workers (or their retirement and welfare-benefits plans) better than other creditors. The workers will remain with the firm and may be the key to its success; the disgruntled creditors will be gone.

There is also a macroeconomic reason to squeeze the creditors of a firm saved by the government. A principal concern about bailouts is that a firm that for whatever reason will not be allowed by the government to fail can borrow money at a lower interest rate than its competitors, because its creditors are not at risk of having to try to collect their money from a bankrupt debtor. The message of the auto companies' bankruptcies is that the government can keep firms from failing (liquidating) in bankruptcy proceedings on terms that are hard on the firms' creditors, including their secured creditors.

But since these were difficult cases, testing the outer boundaries of section 363, the speed with which the bankruptcies were rushed through the bankruptcy court, and, even more tellingly, the speed with which the higher courts rebuffed challenges to the bankruptcy court's decisions—from start to finish, Chrysler's bankruptcy took forty-two days and General Motors' thirty-nine days—suggest the reluctance of judges, ever since the Supreme Court got into trouble by invalidating major New Deal programs, to buck the President in a national economic emergency, which was the sense of the nation's economic condition in the spring of 2009.[25] This should reassure creditors who fear that the resolution of the two bankruptcy proceedings establishes a precedent likely to be followed in normal times. But if this is wrong and the two cases come to be seen as precedents, the question will arise of the impact of the rulings on the cost of secured debt. If the risk is known and calculable, then probably it will lead to

25. Cf. the discussion and references to law in emergencies in chapter 2.

higher interest rates; if incalculable, it may lead instead to higher credit standards, since there is no premium that is actuarially equivalent to an unquantifiable risk.

I am worried, however, by the President's criticism of purchasers of secured, and for that matter unsecured, debt from the original lenders to the auto companies. He called them "speculators," and the context suggests that it was a pejorative term. In fact speculation has an economic function: it makes traders in markets better informed. And the form of speculation that he criticized makes debt more liquid by providing a market for it rather than requiring the original creditor to hold the debt until maturity. There are downsides to speculation, as we'll see, but it must not be condemned out of hand.

The government's investment in General Motors should not have taken the form of cash for common stock, which, given the amount of cash, made the government GM's owner. As owner, it is vulnerable to the political pressures that the United Auto Workers and other entities that have a financial stake in General Motors can be expected to exert on members of Congress and on the President—and they are doing so.[26] The problem is bigger than GM. "Executives [of bailed-out firms] say congressional demands gobble up time and make a rocky business environment even more unpredictable. Bank chief executives say incessant calls from Capitol Hill, combined with threats of legislation, were among the main incentives for them to pay back money injected by the government and escape Washington's clutches."[27] The bankruptcy bailout of GM should have taken the form of a purchase of preferred stock, though paying cumulative rather than current dividends so as not to affect GM's current cash flow.

The government has promised not to interfere in management decisions even though it owns General Motors. The promise is

26. Neil King, Jr., "Politicians Butt In at Bailed-Out GM," *Wall Street Journal,* Oct. 29, 2009, p. A1.
27. Id., p. A18.

fraudulent, unless by "management" the government just means day-to-day operating decisions. The Administration wants to use GM as a "chosen instrument" of U.S. policy, much as Pan American World Airways was once the United States' "chosen instrument" for international air travel. But at least Pan Am was a private company, albeit heavily regulated. If the government insists that GM subordinate profit maximization to the achievement of national goals, the prospects of the government's recouping its $50 billion investment, which are not good, will diminish further.

The goals for the automotive chosen instrument are two. One is to reduce carbon emissions by requiring General Motors to build more fuel-efficient cars. The goal is worthy, but the chosen-instrument approach is unsound. A coherent environmental policy cannot treat competing firms differently. If GM's competitors are subject to the same environmental requirements as GM, that is fine but does not require the government to own GM or interfere in its management. If instead the government uses its control to make the company promote environmental goals more vigorously than its competitors because it gives less heed to profit, it will place it at a competitive disadvantage and accelerate its demise and the loss of the government's investment—which will do nothing for the environment.

The second goal of public ownership of General Motors is to enforce a national commitment to the United States' remaining a major manufacturer of motor vehicles. That is a ridiculous goal, and one hopes just a rhetorical flourish. Nowhere is it written that the United States shall produce motor vehicles, any more than that it shall produce television sets, which it no longer does. If other countries, such as Japan, produce better motor vehicles (from the standpoint of price and quality—and of the health of the environment and of reducing our dangerous dependence on oil produced by unstable or hostile foreign countries) than the United States, we should import their motor vehicles and reallocate the resources that go into the domestic manufacture of motor vehicles to other productive activities. The reallocation would proceed automatically in accordance with the law of supply and demand, without need for any government intervention.

Even if GM (and Chrysler) liquidated, there would be a thriving U.S. automobile industry. There would be Ford's production, and there would be the foreign cars that are manufactured in the United States. Toyota and the other foreign producers that have factories in the United States are part of the American automobile industry; their ownership by foreigners has no significance.

The cost of the government-managed bankruptcies of General Motors and Chrysler has thus been higher than the $60 billion of government subsidy, for it includes an implicit commitment to further support, at least of General Motors, and an enhanced danger of government interference in private business.

The last new recovery program—actually a small part of the stimulus package, but worth separate discussion because of the enormous publicity it generated in the summer of 2009—was the $3 billion "cash for clunkers" program, which cleaned out many automobile dealers' inventories. The government offered to give anyone who turned in (to be destroyed) a car with low gas mileage between $3,500 and $4,500 to buy a new car that would get better gas mileage by a specified margin. Some 700,000 new cars were sold under the program. Like the bailout of the auto companies, the program had dual environmental and economic recovery goals, although the former was trivial; the aggregate improvement in gas mileage from the program was minuscule, and possibly negative because the new cars will be driven more since their operating costs are lower.

The contribution to economic recovery was probably very small as well, though not negative. The program was one of transfer payments, not government investment. It is true that people who participated in it couldn't just pocket the money they received from the government, as they could with the other transfer payments included in the stimulus; they had to buy a new car. But giving money to people to buy cars is less stimulative than paying a road contractor to build a new highway. The contractor has to go out and hire people to build it, from a pool that contains many unemployed workers, so employment rises. The purchase of a new car merely reduces a dealer's inventory, and whether the reduction leads to new production will depend on the size of existing inventories in relation to producers' estimates of future demand. Those estimates are likely to be inverse to the success of the "cash for clunkers" program. The program may to a large extent merely have caused people to accelerate a previously determined intention to trade in their old car, which would reduce future demand—and in fact sales of new cars plummeted in September, the month after the program ended.

Timing is important; had the "cash for clunkers" program been put into effect in the winter of 2009, the buying spurt that it induced might have had a bracing effect on consumer confidence. But by the summer the economy had sufficiently improved that the need for confidence-boosting measures that had no other effect on economic activity had waned.

The "cash for clunkers" program illustrates the sluggish execution that has characterized the rescue efforts since the flurry of Federal Reserve and Treasury actions focused on the banking industry that began in September 2008 and that, with the exception of the stress tests, were largely completed by the end of the Bush Administration. The plan for a "public-private partnership" to buy mortgage-backed securities from the banks never got off the ground, and the mortgage relief program progressed very slowly. The stimulus moneys were doled out slowly, the Administration having failed to appoint an expediter to try to cut the red tape that was bound to entangle any large new federal spending program. (The expediter's slogan, borrowed from Macbeth, would have been "If it were done when 'tis done, then 'twere well / It were done quickly.") Vice President Biden was designated to oversee the program, but he has no business, economic, or managerial experience, no executive authority, and little time to devote to the program. Even so simple and modest a component of it as "cash for clunkers" was started too late to have the intended effect.

A traditional and valid criticism of fiscal responses to recession or depression is that by the time they are implemented, the need for them may have passed. Between the enactment of such a program and spending by consumers of the funds appropriated for it many months may elapse, though the enactment itself may stimulate spending by convincing consumers that better times are coming. The stimulus program should have been enacted in the fall of 2008 and been heavily weighted toward public works concentrated in areas and industries of high unemployment, with provisions for cutting red tape even at the risk of a higher incidence of fraud and waste, which are unavoidable in government programs.

So how, in sum, should the recovery efforts by the Obama Administration be rated? Or, for that matter, by the Bush and Obama Administrations, since there has been such continuity in personnel as well in policy? Bernanke has been a constant, and it appears that he was the author of most of the recovery efforts taken during the Bush Administration. The role of Henry Paulson, the Secretary of the Treasury, appears to have been one largely of negotiation with the banking industry, with which he was intimate as a former CEO of Goldman Sachs. Geithner played a large role,[28] even though during the Bush Administration he was only the president of the Federal Reserve Bank of New York—but that is the second most important position in the Federal Reserve. The Bush Administration's troika of Bernanke, Geithner, and Paulson metamorphosed into the Obama Administration troika of Bernanke, Geithner, and Lawrence Summers. Monetary policy and policy toward the banking industry remained largely unchanged, and the Obama Administration's program of mortgage relief, while considerably more ambitious

---

28. David Wessel, *In Fed We Trust: Ben Bernanke's War on the Great Panic* 106–107, 113 (2009).

than the Bush Administration's very limited program, had only a modest impact.

The Obama Administration's distinctive contribution to the recovery effort was the $787 billion stimulus program, though a scaled-down version might have been enacted under a Republican Administration (at least if Congress had remained in the control of the Democrats), even though no Republican members of Congress voted for it when it was introduced in Congress after the change in Administrations. I don't think any Administration would have taken a chance on a further decline of the economy and invited the accusation of having done nothing when it could have done something that many economists were urging. In the spring of 2008, with the economic situation far less frightening, the Bush Administration had pushed a $168 billion tax rebate program through Congress—a form of stimulus. Had a new Administration announced in January 2009 that although monetary policy had failed to stop the rot and the bailouts of the banks and the automakers likewise, the government had run out of ideas and therefore the American people would just have to grin and bear the downward spiral of the economy, the effect on public morale might have been devastating—especially since, despite the lengthy transition period, the Obama Administration took office with no detailed plans for dealing with the crisis.

Anything that increases the uncertainty of an already uncertain economic environment is likely to reduce investment and consumption further. A sense that the government itself is uncertain about what to do in an economic crisis is particularly ominous, because only government can prevent an economy from spinning down to its "natural" bottom.

Besides being unprepared with a recovery plan, the Obama Administration failed to resist blind populist rage against "Wall Street" and by this failure further unsettled the business environment. The President's joining in the attack (though briefly) on the payment of bonuses to employees of American Insurance Group, and his leading the attack on the resistance of Chrysler's secured

creditors when the government was desperate to encourage lending, including by lenders who would not lend without collateral
(which normally would give them a favored position in a bankruptcy proceeding of a borrower), frightened business. I don't re-
tract what I said earlier about the appropriateness of forcing
Chrysler's secured creditors to the back of the bus, as it were;
what I criticize is the Administration's rhetoric of populist hostility to creditors. Particularly unfortunate was Obama's reference
to Chrysler's creditors as "speculators." All he could have meant
by this was that some of them had bought Chrysler bonds from
other bondholders, rather than having been original purchasers
of the bonds from Chrysler. It is absurd to criticize someone for
buying a bond! Or to denounce "speculators." They perform
a social function, that of moving prices closer to true values,
though we're about to see that successful speculators may be
overpaid from a broad social standpoint. (That is a subtle point;
speeches by government officials eschew subtlety.)

The bonuses for AIG's employees were authorized by the
company's dollar-a-year federally appointed chief executive officer for traders and middle management, not for senior management. De facto control of the board of directors by the senior
management of corporations does conduce to excessive compensation—of senior management. But senior managers have no incentive to overpay their subordinates. The finance industry is
thoroughly international, and the best financiers have opportunities to work for enterprises here and abroad whose compensation is not regulated by government. They will go where the pay
is best. The loss of key employees reduces a bank's efficiency and
thus the value of the government's large investment in banks.
And it reduces the willingness of banks and other financial intermediaries to accept or retain federal money even if their refusal
means less lending and thus impedes economic recovery. So senior management has to pay its traders and loan officers and
other key employees generously.

I have a different reaction, however, to public anger over the

report in October 2009 that Goldman Sachs was on course to
pay more than $20 billion in compensation (not just bonuses,
however, as erroneously reported by some journalists and repeated by some politicians) to its employees in 2009. The controversial bonuses that AIG had wanted to pay had been intended to
reward performance before the company collapsed, and most of
the intended recipients had not been responsible for the decisions
that precipitated the collapse. The Goldman compensation pool,
in contrast—in particular the amount allotted to bonuses—was
based on Goldman's profits in 2009. The profits were huge, and
reflected skill as well as luck. But the opportunity to reap huge
profits had been created by the government's bailout of Goldman
in September 2008, when it appeared that upon Lehman's declaration of bankruptcy, Morgan Stanley and Goldman Sachs might
soon have to follow suit[29] as the hedge funds and other investors
withdrew their capital from broker-dealers. Goldman's share
price, $169 on September 8, 2008, plunged to $86 on September
18. The plunge reinforced its creditors' anxiety, and further withdrawals would have caused the share price to fall faster and farther. Goldman was rescued by $10 billion in bailout money;

29. See Andrew Ross Sorkin, *Too Big to Fail: The Inside Story of How
Wall Street and Washington Fought to Save the Financial System—and
Themselves* 178, 432–442, 448 (2009); Joe Hagan, "Tenacious G: Inside
Goldman Sachs, America's Most Successful, Cynical, Envied, Despised and
(in Its View, Anyway) Misunderstood Engine of Capitalism," *New York
Magazine,* July 26, 2009, http://nymag.com/news/business/58094/ (visited
Dec. 7, 2009); Carrick Mollenkamp and Serena Ng, "Report Rebuts
Goldman Claim: TARP Audit Suggests AIG Collapse Could Have Resulted
in Big Losses," *Wall Street Journal,* Nov. 18, 2009, p. C1. "Goldman would
not exist without Washington's rescue of Wall Street. No matter how bril-
liantly hedged it might have been, it could not have survived a systemic collapse. Today, Goldman continues to benefit from government support: both
from the explicit state-backed financial safety net all the Wall Street firms
can rely on, and from access to state-underwritten funding." Chrystia
Freeland, "Global Insight: Goldman's Claims to Genius," *Financial Times,*
Nov. 24, 2009, www.ft.com/cms/s/0/04b02580-d928-11de-b2d5-00144
feabdc0.html (visited Nov. 29, 2009).

by the government's giving American Insurance Group enough money to enable it to honor its credit-default swaps in full, including those it had sold to Goldman Sachs; by being permitted to convert from a broker-dealer to a bank holding company; and by a general sense that after Lehman's demise the government simply would not allow another major financial institution to fail. Conversion to a bank holding company entitled Goldman to borrow from the Federal Reserve, unlike Lehman, denied a Fed loan on the spurious ground that it was not a bank. Just the loan from the government, plus the money that the government passed through AIG to Goldman, added $23 billion to Goldman's capital at a crucial time—and it was by speculating with its capital that Goldman obtained the profits out of which to pay large salaries and bonuses.

Moreover, the dramatic reduction in short-term interest rates engineered by the Federal Reserve as part of its efforts to arrest the economic collapse enabled Goldman to obtain capital for its profitable speculations very cheaply. This point bears on proposals for financial regulatory reform, so is worth dwelling on for a moment. It can be grasped with the aid of the concept of the "yield curve." In the figure on page 146, the interest rate of a loan (yield) is plotted against its maturity (loan length). The yield is higher the longer the maturity of the loan. This is the essence of banking, as we know from earlier discussions. If the maturity is *very* short, so that the interest rate and the maturity are both close to the origin, the bank will be able to borrow very cheaply, while if the yield curve is steep, the bank will be able to charge very high interest by making a long-term loan with its cheap borrowed capital. (Maturity should be understood as just a proxy for risk—obviously there are short-term loans that are as risky as or riskier than long-term loans.) The government's rescue enabled Goldman to attract short-term capital at very low rates and to relend or otherwise invest or speculate with that capital at the top of the yield curve, because the government had made it clear that Goldman would not be permitted to fail.

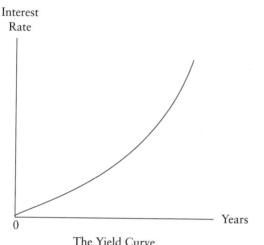

The Yield Curve

Without government aid, no $20 billion-plus in salaries and bonuses for Goldman Sachs's employees in 2009—maybe no bonuses; indeed, maybe no Goldman Sachs. Against that background, the amount set aside for compensation was indeed egregious, and suggests that the government drove a bad bargain when it bailed out Goldman—it should have demanded a big chunk of Goldman's future profits. Against this it can be argued that a generous bailout was justified by the need to strengthen the banks so that they would lend. And I agree. It is true that the banks haven't increased their lending by the amount of money they received from the government, but had they not received it, they would be lending even less than they are. Goldman's 2009 profits—the source of the compensation pool—were not from lending, however, but from proprietary trading. Goldman used its capital to buy stocks and bonds and sell stocks and bonds short and engage in other speculative maneuvers.

There is nothing wrong with speculation, as I keep saying, but remember that its social value is not equal to the profits of successful speculators. Speculative profits are not net additions to economic welfare, because they are offset by the losses of the speculators on the other side of the successful speculators' trades. Speculation creates social value by bringing about improved matching of prices to values, which encourages investment in productive activities. But the amount of profit that a speculator makes is not the measure of that social value.

Not by a long shot. In theory, it is true, stock prices discount expected corporate profits, and bond prices discount expectations regarding inflation, default risk, and other determinants of interest rates. But the swings, especially in stock prices, greatly exceed the swings in corporate profits and other objective measures of value, in part because much trading is based on expectations of what other traders will do. A great deal of the speculation in stocks does little or nothing to align stock prices more closely with the value of the assets of the companies whose stocks are traded. This is another reason to doubt that the profits of successful stock speculators are closely related to the information value of speculation, and to suspect that too much IQ is being sucked into finance. Goldman Sachs's traders probably are "overpaid" in the sense that their incomes send a bad signal to the labor market from an economic standpoint. Many of the Ph.D.'s in physics lured to Wall Street by the prospect of outsized incomes would contribute more to national welfare by using their scientific skills in business, government, or academia.

It might be argued that the high incomes paid to financial executives merely compensate them for career risk. Think of actors. A tiny handful have huge incomes, but most earn so little that they abandon acting as a career. The lucky handful are like lottery winners, and the only way you can motivate people to buy a lottery ticket is to offer a jackpot for winning. The only way you can motivate people to attempt a career in acting is to provide a jackpot for the tiny handful of aspirants who succeed.

Could finance be the same, since it too is a risky business? The answer depends in part on what happens to traders if they devise or approve a very risky deal and the deal is a flop. Are they exiled from the industry? Do they end up as waiters? If so, the huge incomes of successful financiers would be justified as compensation for the risk of failure. My impression is that the failed traders, deal makers, etc., do not end up as waiters or in other relatively impecunious jobs. (I say "relatively" because waiters in elite restaurants are well paid by ordinary standards.) Their training and experience equip them for a variety of good jobs in the financial industry. Since they can look forward to a soft landing, it is unlikely that the high incomes of the most successful financiers are compensation for the risk of failure.

It is true that anyone who is risk-averse will seek compensation for taking risks, but the people who gravitate to risky occupations are unlikely to be risk-averse. Put differently, as long as there is an ample supply of risk preferrers an employer will not have to pay a premium based on risk aversion. And as I have just suggested, the career risks in being a trader or deal maker for Goldman Sachs are probably very small.

The worst consequences of the Goldman "bonuses" (as politicians insist on referring to the entire compensation pool) belong to political economy rather than to economics narrowly understood. The degree of economic equality in a democratic society is bounded at both ends of the income distribution. If incomes are made too equal, say by heavily redistributive tax and spending policies, incentives for innovation, enterprise, and hard work will dwindle and the wealth of the society will decline, and these effects will put pressure on government to relax its egalitarian policies. But if incomes are allowed to become too unequal, because an absence of redistributive measures gives differences in skill and luck full rein to determine how poor or wealthy a person shall be, the resentments of the have-nots will create debilitating social tensions and political antagonisms and by doing so will exert pressure for redistributive measures. Neither extreme, therefore, is an equilibrium.

The Goldman "bonuses" could become a symbol of excessive inequality in American society and a spur to equalizing measures. Their revelation coincided with high and growing unemployment and widespread economic misery and anxiety. It looked as if the government had gratuitously enabled a handful of wealthy traders to become still wealthier at a time when much of the population had just become poorer. The news that Goldman planned to give $200 million—1 percent of the compensation pool—to charity recalls John D. Rockefeller's tossing nickels and quarters to passersby. When Goldman's CEO said he is "doing God's work," one knew that the banking industry was its own worst enemy.[30]

Goldman belatedly realized that it had committed public relations hara-kiri, apologized insincerely, and committed another $500 million to the charity kitty.[31] The show of contrition was inadequate, so later Goldman announced that its top executives' pay for 2009 would be in the form of Goldman stock that they could not sell for five years. The lesson, which will not be lost on the bankers, is that in a period of public hostility to banks and "speculators," bankers had better master public relations. Goldman might have pointed out that the reason half its revenues go to pay its employees is that its employees are its most important factor of production; its nonlabor inputs are trivial relative to those of a manufacturing company. Because its key factor of production is its professional employees, it cannot risk losing them to competitors by failing to pay competitive compensation, however outlandish the compensation may appear to people who earn less than a tenth of the *average* compensation (more than $700,000) that Goldman's employees will receive in 2009.

In the wake of the revelation of Goldman's financial success in 2009, a controversy arose over the government's decision, when it took over AIG, to pay AIG's credit-default swap creditors—in-

30. John Alridge, "I'm Doing 'God's Work.' Meet Mr Goldman Sachs," *Sunday Times,* Nov. 8, 2009, www.timesonline.co.uk/tol/news/world/us_and_americas/article6907681.ece (visited Nov. 12, 2009).
31. Graham Bowley, "$500 Million and Apology from a Bank," *New York Times,* Nov. 1, 2009, p. A1.

cluding Goldman—the full amount AIG owed them. The government could have driven a harder bargain, but that's like saying that the government could have allowed the entire banking industry, which includes Goldman Sachs, to have gone down the drain with Lehman Brothers. AIG's creditors included prominent U.S. and foreign banks that the United States and foreign governments didn't want to see fail. Making AIG's creditors whole was part of the overall bank bailout strategy.

The Goldman "bonus" issue provides a sidelight on the stimulus program. The American public has been patient with the failure of capitalism in the current downturn. The anger at "Wall Street," fanned by demagogues, has yet to incite serious efforts to bring about a radical change of our economic system. But the longer the economy remains in the doldrums, and in particular the longer unemployment and underemployment and wage cuts and benefits cuts persist, the greater the danger of political instability. There is latent instability in American politics (think of the period from the Democratic Convention of 1968 to Nixon's resignation in 1974), just as there is in the economy. If the stimulus has even a modest positive effect on employment and wages, it may contribute significantly to keeping our politics on an even keel.

The failure to drive a hard bargain in bailing out Goldman Sachs was a stumble of the Bush Administration. A stumble by the Obama Administration was the enactment by Congress, at the behest of the Administration, of a law banning certain practices by issuers of credit cards. This law, the Credit Card Accountability, Responsibility, and Disclosure Act of 2009,[32] is a part—the first, indeed, to be implemented—of the Administration's ambitious program of financial regulatory reform, which I discuss in the next chapter. But the credit card law, like the other

32. Pub. Law 111-24, 123 Stat. 1734; for the text, see www.gpo.gov/fdsys/pkg/PLAW-111publ24/html/PLAW-111publ24.htm (visited Dec. 7, 2009).

components of the reform program, is designed to head off a future crisis. It is not a recovery measure—it is an anti-recovery measure, because anything that limits the rights of creditors causes them to raise interest rates, thereby reducing economic activity. For example, one provision of the act forbids a credit card issuer to raise the interest rate to a borrower because it has learned that the borrower has defaulted on a debt owed someone else. That other default is a signal that the borrower is likely to default on his credit card debt as well, and the credit card company raises its interest rate to compensate for the increased risk. Forbidden to use such a signal, the credit card issuers will charge higher interest rates from the start.

The Administration has been trumpeting the message—which both misstates the causes of the economic crisis and will slow recovery from it—that "Wall Street" should be blamed (China also, or instead, in some versions, as Geithner once suggested) and must be punished. This hostility and air of menace make financial firms reluctant to get into or stay in bed with the government and thus impede the bailout efforts. Criticism of the Goldman "bonuses" would not be amiss. But the major culprits in our present economic distress— government officials, such as Alan Greenspan, and academic economists—are getting off lightly because they are obscure and there is more political mileage in denouncing "Wall Street." How many Americans actually know who Alan Greenspan is, or what a macroeconomist is? How many have even a vague idea of what the Federal Reserve is or does?

It doesn't help that on the ground that a crisis should not be wasted—in other words, that the depression should be treated as a pretext for the launch of expensive social programs that might be politically infeasible in calmer times, as if Franklin Roosevelt had announced the day after the Pearl Harbor attack that he would use the occasion of a world war to complete the enactment of his New Deal program—the administration is piling trillions of dollars of proposals for long-term social reform on top of the trillions of dollars of emergency spending committed to fighting the depression and the trillions of dollars of "normal" federal budget deficits augmented by the decline of federal tax revenues in a depression. The ambitious long-run proposals are ill-timed because by further unsettling the business environment, they are slowing down the economic recovery.[33]

Six months after Obama took office, the economy was still deep in the doldrums, indeed still declining, albeit at a slower rate. Then came the surprising news that after declining by 6.4 percent (on an annualized basis) in the first quarter of 2009, the economy had declined by only 1 percent (on the same basis) in the second quarter. The Administration naturally wanted to take credit, since the second quarter was the first full quarter in which Obama had been President. Yet most of the Administration's programs for fighting the depression were either continuations of the Bush Administration's programs or disappointments, such as mortgage relief and the attempt to subsidize the purchase of the banks' overvalued debt securities, and the latter would at best have been merely more of the same, for remember that the bank bailout began in an attempt, wisely abandoned, to buy those securities.

The only thing brand-new and not a flop was the stimulus. So on August 6, 2009, Christina Romer, the chairman of the President's Council of Economic Advisers, gave a talk entitled "So, Is It Working? An Assessment of the American Recovery and Reinvestment Act at the Five-Month Mark."[34] Her answer to the question in her title was "Absolutely" (p. 1). Despite the reference to "five months" in the subtitle, her analysis is limited to the second quarter of 2009, and her claim is that the stimulus had a

33. For evidence, see, for example, Gary Fields, "Political Uncertainty Puts Freeze on Small Businesses," *Wall Street Journal,* Oct. 27, 2009, p. A1.
34. http://blog.prospect.org/blog/weblog/DCEconClubprint.pdf (visited Dec. 7, 2009).

dramatic effect on output and employment during that quarter, which ended on June 30. I do not think that her analysis is responsible, and it is a matter for concern when academic economists, upon becoming either public officials or public intellectuals (like Paul Krugman), leave behind their academic scruples.[35]

Romer argues in her talk that by the end of the second quarter, "more than $100 billion" of stimulus money had been "spent" ("absolutely going out the door," as she also put it) (p. 5). Untrue. The government's stimulus website—recovery.gov—states that $60 billion was spent during the quarter, and so the $100 billion must include the tax relief granted in the quarter, which was approximately $40 billion and mysteriously is not reported on the stimulus website. Had that $40 billion consisted of rebate checks, it should indeed have been included in the total outlays of the stimulus program. But very little of it consisted of rebates. Most of it consisted of reductions in taxes owed by individuals and businesses. We do not know how much of the total reduction represented cash flow to the taxpayer. If a reduction was reflected in reduced withholding or a reduced payment of estimated tax by people who filed estimated returns on April 15, 2009, it should have been counted as stimulus spending in the second quarter, because it put money in people's pockets then. But to the extent that it merely reduced their future tax liability, it should not have been counted.

A deeper problem is the difference between what the government disburses to state treasurers, business firms, and individuals and what the recipients spend—especially, since my concern is the accuracy of Romer's talk, what they spend in the same quarter as the disbursements. She acknowledges that "the fact that consumption fell slightly in the second quarter after rising slightly in the first quarter could be a sign that households are

35. This is one of the themes of my book *Public Intellectuals: A Study of Decline* (2001), and Krugman was one of my examples of the phenomenon. See also chapter 10 of the present book.

initially using the tax cut mainly to increase their savings and pay off debt" (p. 15). If that's what they're doing, they aren't doing anything to stimulate economic activity. I agree with Keynes that consumption is the motor of the economy (see chapter 8) and that what government needs to do when personal consumption expenditures drop is to increase government expenditures. But they should be expenditures that finance public works, which employ people, rather than transfer payments, which may largely be saved rather than spent. Romer says that public works (she calls them "direct investments," but the meaning is the same) "have short-run effects roughly 60 percent larger than tax cuts" (p. 18). She doesn't indicate where she gets the number, but it is further evidence that she believes, as she should, that transfer payments are not as efficient in stimulating economic activity as public works are. And earlier she had said that "large proportions of temporary tax cuts are saved, blunting their stimulatory impact on output and employment."[36]

Transfer payments are at two removes from putting the unemployed to work. The amount of a transfer that is saved by the recipient in a savings account or other safe haven is (by definition) not spent, and so does not increase demand. The amount that *is* spent is spent at a store or other retail outlet, to purchase a good that has already been produced. It is buying from inventory. Only when the store's inventory runs down to the point at which the store has to order a new supply of goods from the manufacturer is there any stimulation of production, and thus of hiring. The dive that the economy took in the wake of the September 2008 financial collapse was unanticipated, and as a result sellers found themselves with excess inventories; until they were worked down, production would remain depressed.

Moreover, the stimulation provided by consumer spending

36. Christina Romer and Jared Bernstein, "The Job Impact of the American Recovery and Reinvestment Plan," Jan. 9, 2009, p. 5, http://otrans .3cdn.net/45593e8ecbd339d074_l3m6bt1te.pdf (visited Nov. 8, 2009).

need not be stimulation of production by an industry, or in an area, of high unemployment. It might, for example, be spending on imported goods. Its effect on employment could be nil.

A further complication is that unless a stimulus program is carefully targeted on industries in which the unemployment or underemployment rate is high, the initial effect may simply be to replace another funding source; and then one has to ask where the replaced funds ended up. Suppose a state receives a federal grant for a construction project that it had planned to pay for with state funds, and it uses the state money that it has saved to pay down the state debt. The effect of that expenditure on employment would be indirect, deferred, and probably trivial. A federal grant of stimulus money for mass transit *was* nullified by reductions in state expenditures on mass transit.[37] What happened to the money the state saved? Maybe it funded a tax reduction, in which event state taxpayers would have more money in their pockets. But to assess the effect on current spending, one would have to determine how long it took to get the money to the taxpayers and how much of it they spent rather than saved.

All the $100 billion disbursed or committed to stimulus in the second quarter consisted of transfers, not of investments, and no one seems to know how much was actually spent rather than squirreled away. I noted earlier the tendency of people to save rather than spend transitory income (the tendency Romer herself acknowledged with reference to tax relief), and all the transfer payments authorized by the stimulus program are transitory. Moreover, given the inevitable lag between disbursement and the expenditure of disbursed funds by the recipient of the disbursement, disbursements made toward the end of the second quarter could not possibly have affected output and employment in that quarter.

Romer might reply that just the prospect of receiving stimulus

37. Michael Cooper, "States Cut Back and Layoffs Hit Even Recipients of Stimulus," *New York Times,* Sept. 5, 2009, p. A1.

money can stimulate spending. And I agree! My criticism is only that her speech, presumably for political reasons, exaggerated the effect on the economy of the limited amount of actual stimulus spending as of June 30, 2009. The effect of a stimulus on the confidence of business and consumers is important and is to a considerable degree independent of the precise schedule of stimulus spending. If businesses and consumers know they're going to get tax reductions or other benefits, this may affect their current spending.

Economists both left and right systematically neglect the psychological dimensions of a depression. An exception, however, is Daniel Indiviglio, who is not an academic economist. He argues that "perhaps knowing that the government was throwing $787 billion at the economy in order [to] try to reduce the pain of the recession helped the sentiment of business as well. Maybe businesses decided that the economy can't possibly continue to suffer given such extraordinary government intervention, so built more plants, ordered more equipment and ramped up inventories in the hopes of imminent recovery built on that government action."[38] In the same vein, with regard to the transfer payments, he points out that the "money must be going somewhere, so where is it going? Maybe it's being used to pay down debt; maybe it's being used for investment; or maybe it's just being saved. I would argue that, though not consumption, those are still actions that ultimately help a stumbling economy get a little healthier. Having more money in your pocket certainly makes you feel better, and consumer sentiment matters a lot during a recession, even if that doesn't translate to immediate consumption. Maybe people would have saved even more and spent even less without the payments, for example."[39]

38. "The Stimulus Didn't Work—or Did It?" *Business,* Sept. 17, 2009, http://business.theatlantic.com/2009/09/the_stimulus_didnt_work_—_or_did_it .php# (visited Nov. 1, 2009).
39. Id.

The Administration's political problem is that the confidence-building effect of the stimulus cannot be quantified. The meaningless number $100 billion gives a false sense of precision to Romer's claim that the stimulus was responsible (she did not say how responsible, but implied that it was primarily responsible) for the drop in the rate of economic decline from the first to the second quarter. The effect of the stimulus in the second quarter cannot be estimated responsibly. It probably had some positive effect because of its confidence-enhancing character and because some fraction of $100 billion—though no one seems to know how large a fraction—undoubtedly was spent by recipients of stimulus money. If half of the $100 billion was actually received by the ultimate intended recipients, and half of that amount was actually spent by them in the second quarter rather than saved, the total amount of actual spending in that quarter attributable to the stimulus program was $25 billion, which is roughly two-thirds of 1 percent of that quarter's GDP. That is not a negligible amount, but whether it explains much or all or a little of the reduction in the rate of decline of GDP from the first to the second quarter is unproved—and unprovable.

It is unprovable because so much else was happening at the same time to stimulate an economic recovery, including things unrelated to government recovery measures. Some people doubtless had to dissave during the quarter—turn savings into expenditures—because their income had fallen (maybe because they had become unemployed and their unemployment benefits and other resources were dwindling) below the level necessary to cover their basic expenses. Some people had to replace durables that wore out. Foreign demand for U.S. products rose some, and exports net of imports stimulate domestic output. Dissaving, replacing durables, and increasing exports are standard *private* spurs to recovery from a depression and are among the reasons that depressions bottom out even if the government is passive. But the government has not been passive; it has been doing a lot to stimulate recovery besides the stimulus—has in fact expended or guaranteed trillions of dollars in an effort to increase the amount of lending, which is essential to economic activity.

But the same criticism—the difficulty, probably the impossibility, of separating one development that might have reduced the rate of decline of output in the second quarter of 2009 from other developments that might have had the same effect—can be turned against critics of the stimulus. John Cogan and his coauthors note in a piece in the *Wall Street Journal*[40] that the transfer payments (the major component of the stimulus that was actually implemented in the second quarter) appear not to have resulted in any measurable increase in personal consumption expenditures during that quarter; they constituted transitory income and therefore were largely saved. The authors attribute the reduction in the rate of decline of GDP in the second quarter to military spending unrelated to the stimulus and to a slowing of the rate at which business investment was declining that began in January, before the enactment of the stimulus law. But the fact that personal consumption expenditures didn't increase—in fact decreased—after the stimulus program was enacted is inconclusive, because had it not been for the transfers they might have decreased further. The fact that the increase in military spending was unrelated to the stimulus *law* doesn't mean it wasn't an effective form of stimulus. And the slowing of the rate of decline in business investment in January may have been in anticipation of the stimulus, as it was certain by then that there would be a stimulus program.

In academic work not mentioned in her speech, Romer had warned against fiscal measures that are not implemented until the recession or depression reaches its nadir.[41] For then the stimulus spending comes too late to do much good, and it risks overheating the economy. It is not the Obama Administration's fault

40. John F. Cogan, John B. Taylor, and Volker Wieland, "The Stimulus Didn't Work," *Wall Street Journal,* Sept. 17, 2009, p. A23.

41. Romer and Romer, note 3 above, at 55–56.

that the stimulus package was not enacted, as it should have been, in the fall of 2008. But the unavoidable fact is that it was not enacted until late February 2009 and that on August 6, with economic growth seeming about to restart, most of the stimulus money remained to be spent. If it was spent after the economy picked up steam, there would be a danger of inflation.

When Vice President Biden, the nominal stimulus "czar," gave a widely publicized speech on September 3 echoing Romer's praise of the stimulus, it was apparent that the Administration was reacting to the surprising fact that the program was unpopular. Any effect of Romer's and Biden's talking up the stimulus was soon undercut when the Administration, in another futile effort at quantification, offered statistics riddled with fraud, error, and implausible assumptions on the number of jobs saved by the stimulus.[42] The statistics treated as jobs saved any jobs financed by stimulus money, ignoring the possibility that the person hired had not been unemployed but had simply switched jobs. The jobs they had vacated might be filled by unemployed persons or might not be filled at all, or at least not for a long time.

Probably the most important reason for the growing unpopularity of the program was the controversy over the Administration's ambitious plans for revamping the health-care industry. The plan was to cost the government $1 trillion over ten years—and the promoters of expensive spending programs almost always underestimate the costs. And it soon became evident that despite vague talk of economizing on the provision of health care, the Administration had no workable, politically feasible plans for funding the $1 trillion in projected cost. The estimate of economies could not be taken seriously, and raising taxes to pay for the health-care program seemed likely to be blocked by congressional opposition.

42. See, for example, Michael Cooper, "Stimulus Watchdog Says White House Numbers May Not Be Accurate," *New York Times,* Nov. 20, 2009, p. A16.

It began to seem that the Administration was insouciant about the rapidly mounting federal deficits, and that the $787 billion stimulus program was a giant pork-barrel project by an Administration indifferent to fiscal prudence. The almost $1 trillion stimulus plan merged in the public mind with the $1 trillion healthcare program, although they were unrelated. The hundreds of billions of bailouts for "Wall Street"—on top of the stimulus— were also unpopular, and made more so by the denunciation of financiers by the Administration, and especially by Congress. People began to think that the Administration's slogan was too much, too soon, too costly—an unsettling thought, inimical to economic recovery. A loss of credibility set in. The more Administration officials talked about the need to reduce the deficit, and the more they talked about the need to keep the dollar strong, the more it seemed that their intentions were the opposite of their avowals.

The economy took an upturn in the third quarter of 2009; GDP rose at an annual rate of 2.2 percent. The Administration, and many neutral observers as well, attributed the increase in GDP in part to the stimulus, though, for reasons explained earlier, no one can know how big a part. Much of the increase may have been due to what are better described as "accelerants" than stimulus—the "cash for clunkers" and new-home buyers' tax credit programs, which may largely have just shifted consumption forward by a month or two, setting the stage for a future drop.

Then came the news that unemployment had surged in October to 10.2 percent and underemployment to 17.5 percent. Left-leaning economists urged a new stimulus program. They had a point. The figures indicate a great quantity of idled productive resources that could be put to work on projects initiated and financed by the government. But more and more people were beginning to think that "stimulus" was shorthand for the government's taking money out of their pockets and throwing it away on pork-barrel projects. They began worrying, possibly prematurely, about future inflation and tax increases. There are grounds for that concern; the question is timing and response, which I will address in chapter 6.

The then incoming Obama Administration had blundered in predicting back in January 2009 that the stimulus plan that it was in the process of formulating would reduce the unemployment rate from 8.2 percent to 7 percent by the fourth quarter of 2009.[43] By the beginning of that quarter, the unemployment rate stood at 9.8 percent, en route to 10.2 percent in October. Administration spokesmen explained that they had underestimated the gravity of the economic crisis. That was a common error, and not culpable. What was culpable was making a promise that might be impossible to keep, for when it was broken, many people lost confidence in the government's ability to manage the economy.

Opponents of the stimulus pounced on the error as proof that the stimulus was a flop.[44] It was not proof. By the beginning of November 2009, some $168 billion in stimulus money had been disbursed.[45] Although no estimate of the effect of this amount of stimulus spending on unemployment is worth much, it is likely to have had some effect on the unemployment rate, as the figure is equal to about 2 percent of the GDP for that period. Suppose— though this is pure conjecture—that the unemployment rate would have been 11 percent rather than 10.2 percent without that shot in the economic arm. That would be the highest rate of unemployment since the 1930s depression and might have had a seriously deleterious effect on business and consumer confidence and hence on economic recovery.

But with much of the public taking the rise in unemployment as evidence that the Administration's recovery program was a

43. Romer and Bernstein, note 36 above, at 4 (fig. 1).

44. See, for example, "Washington and the Jobs Market" (editorial), *Wall Street Journal*, Nov. 8, 2009, p. A16.

45. Christopher Favelle and Jeff Larson, "Stimulus: How Fast We're Spending Almost $800 Billion," *ProPublica*, http://projects.propublica.org/tables/stimulus-spending-progress (visited Dec. 7, 2009).

failure, the President hosted a "jobs summit" on December 3 to explore ways of reducing the unemployment rate. One possibility considered at the summit—it has been tried in Europe recently, apparently with some success—is to pay employers, through tax credits or otherwise, to hire workers. This is fiscal stimulus—Keynesian deficit financing—by another name. It is like the government's paying a construction company to build a highway, which requires the company to enlarge its workforce. All that might seem to distinguish the job subsidy is that the link between funding and jobs is more direct, which increases its political appeal.

A common objection is that a job subsidy will encourage fraud—employers will fire workers and then rehire them to obtain the subsidy. Some workers may even quit their jobs and join the ranks of the unemployed in the hope of getting a better job with a subsidized employer. More likely some employers will lay off workers and hire replacements in order to obtain the subsidy. A more serious problem is that if demand for goods and services is down, employers will not need more workers, and the fact that an additional worker will not add as much to the employer's wage bill as he would without the subsidy will not induce the employer to hire him.

A further objection to a job subsidy, which is also an objection to the design of the original stimulus program, is that if only for administrative reasons it probably would not be targeted on industries or areas of above-average unemployment. Even in an area of low unemployment, an employer will have an incentive to hire workers in order to obtain the subsidy. But he may do this by hiring workers who already have a job. In that event, the net effect of the subsidy on unemployment will depend on what the hired worker's former employer does—maybe just pay him to stay.

There are other ways of stimulating employment, at lower cost and probably with greater impact. One would be to reduce the federal minimum wage, which over a three-year period beginning in 2007 will have risen from $5.15 to $7.25 an hour—a 40 percent increase. As time passes, unemployment becomes less a matter of layoffs and more a matter of failing to provide jobs for new entrants to the workforce, and a reduction in minimum wage would make these new entrants—inexperienced workers with modest wage expectations—far more employable.

Another way to reduce unemployment would be to amend the stimulus law to redirect the remaining unspent funds to areas and industries of high unemployment. Still another would be to reduce payroll taxes, including the unemployment insurance tax and the employer's share of the Social Security tax, for payroll taxes are part of the cost of labor. The effect on the employer would be similar to that of a wage cut, and so would increase the demand for labor. Since Social Security and unemployment benefits (as opposed to taxes) would be unaffected, the tax reduction would not reduce the employees' full wages and so spark demands for higher wages. The employer's net labor cost would therefore fall and his demand for labor rise.

The problem is that the government's deficit would increase. That would also be true of a subsidy for hiring, though it would not be true of a reduction in the minimum wage. The Administration had put itself in a box. Its ambitious spending plans, on top of a large and rapidly growing federal deficit, created an impression of fiscal irresponsibility. In seeming to squander money, it had squandered a good deal of political support.

Perhaps because the jobs summit made little impression on the public, the President returned to banker bashing. He summoned the leaders of the industry to a meeting at the White House on December 14 at which he told them to increase lending. The day before, he had publicly referred to them as "fat cat bankers." He argued that in gratitude for the bailouts of the banks, the bankers should be lending more. Even as political rhetoric, banker bashing is questionable because it feeds criticisms of the Administration as being too soft on bankers. If they are such a despicable crew, why are they allowed to earn "obscene" profits?

A further question arises: if as the Administration keeps saying the economic crisis was the result of excessive risk taking by banks, then, since the obvious reason for the banks' constrained lending is the riskiness of lending in the present very troubled economic environment, isn't the Administration urging the banks to resume the risky practices of the boom years? And if they do so and come a cropper, won't that give them a moral claim to be bailed out once again?

But the "fat cat" rhetoric and the meeting may just be political theater. By allowing all the major bailout recipients to pay back their bailout money, the Administration has relaxed its control over them; and it surely does not want banks to take risks that might precipitate another banking collapse. It may just want to impress on the public its zeal in trying to speed up the slow-seeming recovery from the depression.

On June 17, 2009, the Treasury Department issued an 88-page report entitled *Financial Regulatory Reform: A New Foundation: Rebuilding Financial Supervision and Regulation.* A blueprint for reforms of financial regulation intended to prevent a repetition of the financial crisis of September 2008, it was followed up by detailed legislative proposals. With the economy seeming to improve, the Administration's attention was shifting to measures for preventing the next financial crisis. As 2009 drew to a close, the House of Representatives passed a series of bills based on the Administration's proposals, though with many alterations. The Senate has yet to act. What the final statute will say cannot be predicted, but that a statute will be passed seems certain, and that it will be broadly similar to the Administration's proposals is likely.

The Treasury report was a political document; an air of unreality hangs over it. Premature and overambitious, it manifests reorganization mania and FDR envy. It is natural for a new President, taking office in the midst of an economic crisis, to want to emulate the extraordinary accomplishments of Roosevelt's initial months in office. Within what seemed the blink of an eye the banking crisis was resolved, public works agencies were created and hired *millions* of unemployed workers, and economic output rose sharply. But that was seventy-seven years ago. The federal government has since grown fat and constipated. The program proposed by the Treasury could not be implemented in months, in years, perhaps in decades—as would be apparent had the report addressed costs, staffing requirements, and milestones for determining progress toward program goals and attempted an overall assessment of feasibility.

The report was premature in three respects. The first was that it advocated a course of treatment for a disease the cause or causes of which had not been discovered, or at least acknowledged. Not that it is always necessary to understand a cause in order to be able to eliminate an effect. Someone who has typical allergy symptoms may get complete relief by taking an antihistamine and not think it necessary to find out what he's allergic to. But generally, and in the case of the economic crisis of 2007–2010, unless the causes of a problem are well understood an effective solution is unlikely. Yet the Great Depression of the 1930s ended sixty-nine years ago and economists are still debating its causes. That may seem to make the search for the causes of the present crisis futile. But it would be more accurate to say that a search is unlikely to yield a definitive account. It would be sure to improve on the Treasury report, which embraces the implausible (and embarrassingly self-serving) explanation that the collapse of the banking industry in September 2008 was due to a combination of folly—a kind of collective madness—on the part of bankers, credit-rating agencies, and consumers (gulled into taking on debt, particularly mortgage debt, that they could not afford) and of defects in the regulatory structure. The report overlooks the errors of monetary policy by the Federal Reserve that pushed interest rates down too far in the early 2000s—errors unrelated to regulatory structure. It omits mention of the Bush Administration's huge annual budget deficits, even though they have made it difficult for the government to dig the economy out of its hole without setting the stage for rampant inflation, heavy taxes, devaluation of the dollar, or increased dependence on foreign lenders—the aftershock danger that I discuss in the next chapter.

Nor is there mention of the deregulation movement in banking, which enabled—in fact compelled—banks to make riskier loans than in the old days, when regulation had discouraged competition in banking; and, even more important, which allowed the growth of a huge unregulated shadow banking system. Deregulation often begins (in telecommunications, for example, as well as in finance) in simply not regulating firms that provide substitutes for regulated services. Competition from those firms impels the regulated providers to pressure the regulatory authority to relax regulation so that they can compete with the unregulated upstarts on an even playing field. Competition increases bankruptcy risks by compressing spreads; that is why I said that deregulation *compelled* the banks to take more risks.

The Treasury report also fails to mention lax enforcement of existing regulations, and the broader problem of regulatory inattention that resulted in a lack of information on which to base effective regulation. Regulatory errors are tepidly acknowledged and ascribed to defects in the regulatory structure, the sort of thing a government reorganization might repair—and the report goes on to propose an ambitious reorganization. It seems that the desired solution to the problem of financial collapse was chosen first and the diagnosis of the problem then fitted to the solution.

The regulators of money and banking—of monetary policy and financial intermediation—were asleep at the switch. That is the elephant in the room that the report ignores. Apart from all the other examples of regulatory inattention that might have been but were not mentioned, the Federal Reserve, though well aware that bank holding companies were creating subsidiaries to make subprime mortgages, and having been warned repeatedly of the risks of such lending, turned a blind eye.[1]

1. Binyamin Applebaum, "As Subprime Lending Crisis Unfolded, Watchdog Fed Didn't Bother Barking," *Washington Post,* Sept. 27, 2009, p. A1.

Testifying in Congress in October 2008, Alan Greenspan acknowledged that he had "made a mistake in presuming that the self-interest of organizations, specifically banks and others, were such [that] they were best capable of protecting their own shareholders and their equity in the firms."[2] That was a whopper of a mistake for an economist to make. It was as if the head of the Environmental Protection Agency, criticized for not enforcing federal antipollution laws, had said he thought the self-interest of the polluters implied that they are best capable of protecting their shareholders and their equity. They are indeed best capable of doing *that*. The reason for laws regulating pollution is that pollution is an external cost of production, which is to say a cost not borne by the polluting company or its shareholders, and in making business decisions profit maximizers don't consider costs they don't bear. Banks consider the potential costs of bankruptcy to themselves in deciding how much risk to take but do not consider the potential costs to society as a whole.

The Treasury report is scathing about the financial incontinence of bankers and consumers but complacent about regulatory failures, perhaps because officials responsible for the report (to which Bernanke subscribes, though it was issued by the Treasury Department) were implicated in that failure and because the failure was bipartisan; the deregulation of banking had begun in the Carter Administration with the Depository Institutions Deregulation and Monetary Control Act (1980). Since many of the report's authors are economists as well as officials, it is unsurprising that the report also omits mention of the complacency of the economics profession and its errors of understanding as causal factors in the crisis. Bernanke has been shameless in refusing to assign any share of responsibility for the crisis to mismanagement of monetary policy by the world's central bank-

2. Quoted in Jon Ward, "He Found the Flaw?" *POTUS Notes* blog, hosted by *Washington Times,* Oct. 24, 2008, http://washingtontimes.com/weblogs/potus-notes/2008/Oct/24/he-found-flaw/ (visited Oct. 20, 2009).

ers;[3] he was one of the mismanagers. The failure to cite budget deficits as a causal factor in the crisis may reflect the fact that the Obama Administration's programs, if enacted in anything like the form proposed, are likely to create immense deficits.

The emphasis the report places on the folly of private-sector actors ignores the possibility that most of them were behaving rationally given the environment of dangerously low interest rates, complacency about asset-price inflation (the bubbles that the regulators and, with the occasional honorable exception, the economics profession ignored), and light and lax regulation. The

---

3. See Ben S. Bernanke, "Reflections on a Year of Crisis," speech given at the Federal Reserve Bank of Kansas City's Annual Economic Symposium, Jackson Hole, Wyoming. Aug. 21, 2009, www.federalreserve.gov/ newsevents/speech/bernanke20090821a.htm (visited Oct. 13, 2009), and the appropriately sarcastic commentary on his speech by Lauren Silva Launghlin and Edward Hadas, "Bankers as Heroes," *New York Times,* Aug. 25, 2009, p. B2. See also Stephen Roach, "The Case against Bernanke," *Financial Times,* Aug. 25, 2009, p. 7; Jon Hilsenrath, Sudeep Reddy, and David Wessel, "After Slow Start, Fed Chief Found His Groove," *Wall Street Journal,* Aug. 26, 2009, p. A4. A key passage in Bernanke's talk is the following effort to justify the Fed's failure to save Lehman Brothers from bankruptcy in September 2008: "As the Federal Reserve cannot make an unsecured loan, and as the government as a whole lacked appropriate resolution authority or the ability to inject capital, the firm's failure was, unfortunately, unavoidable. The Federal Reserve and the Treasury were compelled to focus instead on mitigating the fallout from the failure, for example, by taking measures to stabilize the triparty repurchase (repo) market." This, as we know, is false. A further mea non culpa from Bernanke—Ben Bernanke, "The Right Reform for the Fed," *Washington Post,* Nov. 29, 2009, www .washingtonpost.com/wp-dyn/content/article/2009/11/27/AR20091127023 22.html (visited Nov. 30, 2009)—elicited this pert comment from another macroeconomist: "The arrogance of this column is almost beyond belief. This man is incredibly lucky to still have his job at time when millions of other workers have lost theirs as a direct result of his incompetence." Dean Baker, "Bernanke Forgets His Role in Causing the Great Recession," Nov. 29, 2009, http://tpmcafe.talkingpointsmemo.com/2009/11/29/bernanke _forgot_about_his_role_in_causing_the_grea/ (visited Nov. 30, 2009). See also the Appelbaum and Cho article cited at page 76, note 22 of this book.

government had created that environment, albeit under pressure from the finance industry. Moneyed interest groups, dispensing the quasi-bribes known as campaign donations, exert a powerful influence on American government.

But when I say the report puts misplaced emphasis on the behavior of the market participants as distinct from the regulators, I mean misplaced on the basis of what we know, or at least what I think I know. I may be wrong. The important point is that it is too soon to draw confident-enough conclusions about the causes of the crisis to base radical policy changes on those conclusions. The causal account in the report is thin, one-sided, unsubstantiated, and implausible. And yet the soundness of most of its proposals hinges on the accuracy of that account.

The report is premature in a second sense, one illustrated by the proposals (discussed further below) for limiting the provision of credit to high-risk borrowers. Tightening credit at the bottom of the business cycle is badly timed. And while the report creates the impression that high-risk borrowers are feckless consumers unable to curb their greed for material goods, many high-risk borrowers are small businesses dependent on credit card credit to finance their business. More important, throwing a raft of proposals at a banking industry struggling to regain its footing is sure to distract the banks' management, not to mention the Administration's economic team, from more important issues. There is a danger, in short, of information overload, both for business and for government. Some of the report's proposals are contradictory, which reinforces their effect in increasing the uncertainty of the business environment. For example, the banks are not to make unsafe loans, but the Community Reinvestment Act, which encourages the making of mortgage loans to persons in low- and moderate-income neighborhoods, is to be vigorously enforced, even though many of the individuals intended to be helped by the act are poor credit risks.

The third respect in which the report is premature is that enacting its proposals would impede the negotiation of an international treaty for regulating the global financial system, even though such a treaty is both necessary and a declared objective of the Administration's economic policy. By the time such a negotiation gets going in earnest, Congress will have passed legislation altering the U.S. financial regulatory structure, and the alterations will prevent the government from acceding to foreign proposals inconsistent with them and will thus erect a barrier to successful negotiations.

It borders on the ridiculous for the government to create an investigatory commission that will report on the causes of the financial crisis *after* the measures for preventing a recurrence of the crisis are adopted, and to conduct negotiations with foreign countries about the creation of a system of global financial regulation *after* the United States has unilaterally adopted regulatory reforms that may be inconsistent with a system acceptable to the international community.

The proposals in the Treasury report are presented as if their merit were self-evident. A more thoughtful document would have discussed the objections to each proposal and explained why the authors thought the objections could be overcome. Consider the proposals for a substantial reorganization of the regulatory structure. Government leaders typically respond to a government failure (in this case, the failure to prevent the economic crisis that has engulfed us) by proposing a governmental reorganization, because such reorganizations are relatively cheap, highly visible, and easily explained with the aid of organization charts. More precisely, *plans* for reorganizations are cheap, visible, etc.—and plans are the easy part; it is at the stage of implementation that our government falls down. A serious plan would confront the obstacles to successful implementation.

Even when a reorganization plan leads to an actual reorganization, the reorganization usually fails to improve government performance. It fails because of inertia, turf warfare, passive resistance, and lack of follow-through, leaving in its wake merely more bureaucracy.[4]

> Most reorganizations in the federal government are only partially completed. Agency heads, after first fighting the merger, will next aim to send their weakest performers to the new agency and keep their very best. Temporary inconveniences associated with the reorganization—moving people into new office buildings, for instance—will be argued as detracting from day-to-day pursuit of the urgent mission of homeland defense. Government unions, strong in some of the agencies included in the new [Department of Homeland Scrutiny], will scrutinize personnel policies. Congress will need to disband influential committees with established relationships and constituencies. All this is necessary but difficult. A reorganization done halfway could make things worse.[5]

The Treasury report urges the creation of a powerful new agency for the protection of consumer borrowers, and this agency, if it is created, will overlap and scrap with the Securities and Exchange Commission and the Commodity Futures Trading Commission. Another proposal, to create a National Bank Supervisor, will if adopted incite conflict with the Comptroller of the Currency, who regulates national banks. (The Comptroller is to give up his "prudential responsibilities" to the National Bank Supervisor.) There is also to be a council of regulators (the Financial Services Oversight Council) layered over the regulatory agencies themselves, and if the council is not merely a committee of kibitzers—as it probably will be, for it seems to be a renaming

4. See, for example, Richard A. Posner, *Preventing Surprise Attacks: Intelligence Reform in the Wake of 9/11* 127–131 (2005); Arthur S. Hulnick, "Intelligence Reform 2007: Fix or Fizzle?" 20 *International Journal of Intelligence and CounterIntelligence* 567 (2007); James R. Locher III, "Has It Worked? The Goldwater-Nichols Reorganization Act," *Naval War College Review* 94 (Autumn 2001); Craig W. Thomas, "Reorganizing Public Organizations: Alternatives, Objectives, and Evidence," 3 *Journal of Public Administration Research and Theory* 457 (1993).

5. Ashton B. Carter, "The Architecture of Government in the Face of Terrorism," *International Security* 5 (Winter 2001/2002).

of the President's Working Group on Financial Markets, which failed to anticipate the financial crisis—it will complicate and slow the regulatory process.

We have seen a similar process at work in the national intelligence field. After the security agencies failed to prevent the 9/11 attacks, the system was reorganized by the creation of the Department of Homeland Security, the Office of the Director of National Intelligence, the National Counterterrorism Center, the National Security Branch (in the FBI), and other entities. The main result, after several years, has been new layers of bureaucracy, turf wars, overstaffing, and confusion.[6]

The Treasury report is uncritical about the regulatory process. Politics, a ubiquitous impediment to effective regulation, is not mentioned. The report worries about actions by private persons that can precipitate an economic crisis but not about actions (or inaction) by regulators. Its concern with market failures is not matched by a concern with regulatory failures, regulatory distortions due to interest-group pressures, regulatory capture by interest groups, regulatory culture, the timidity of civil servants, the mutual dependence of regulators and regulated (which resembles that of prison guards and prisoners), and the power of the "office consensus" to marginalize independent thinkers for failing to be "team players."

And if brilliant bankers screw up, why not not-so-brilliant regulators? Don't the enormous disparities in income between successful bankers and financial civil servants have implications for the relative competence of the latter? Have we set sheep to watch over wolves? And isn't there a revolving-door problem?

The Securities and Exchange Commission is an example of an agency that, though responsible for regulation of an important sector of the modern banking industry—broker-dealers— fell down completely. And we have learned in the wake of the extraordinary fraud committed by Bernard Madoff that the SEC

6. See references in notes 4 and 5 above.

has in recent years lapsed into incompetence across a broad range of its responsibilities.[7]

Congressman Barney Frank made a perceptive comment in a television interview with Charlie Rose in the fall of 2008. He said that the basic problem with the regulation of banking is that financial regulation lags financial innovation. Regulatory agencies are forced by procedural requirements to move slowly in promulgating new rules, but the regulated industry can begin to game those rules as soon as they go into effect, and once it has succeeded in pulling their teeth, the agency must start over. Regulatory lag becomes embedded in regulatory culture. As explained by Kenneth Posner in correspondence, "Banks move at T+1, and regulators react at T+2. That's why so much of the function of regulators is to resolve failed institutions. They behave similarly to debt investors, who impose covenants (when they think of it) and stand ready to foreclose. Debt investors, rating agency analysts, regulators—this is the slow-moving crowd, which generally has lower and less risky compensation."

The problem of lags is further compounded by the regulators' dependence on information supplied to them by the regulated firms, which of course have superior knowledge of their own businesses, and by the reluctance of agency staff to antagonize firms for which they may hope someday to be working (or at least they want to leave that door open). If and when the proposals in the Treasury report are implemented, or even before, the banking industry will be probing for loopholes and openings for counterstrategies. And therefore the next financial crisis won't

7. See, for example, Steven M. H. Wallman, "Commentary on Redesigning the SEC: Does the Treasury Have a Better Idea? 95 *Virginia Law Review* 825 (2009); Jill E. Fisch, "Top Cop or Regulatory Flop? The SEC at 75," 95 *Virginia Law Review* 975 (2009); and two devastating reports, both issued on September 29, 2009, by the agency's inspector general, H. David Kotz, lambasting the commission's Office of Compliance Reports and Investigations and Division of Enforcement.

look like the current one and the regulators may again be unprepared and ineffectual.

And if one may judge from the current crisis, which is global, regulatory organization is uncorrelated with failures of financial regulation. National regulatory structures are diverse, yet none is pointed to as a model for the United States. The pathologies of regulation are not rooted in tables of organization or curable by adding new bureaucratic layers. So before adopting a new structure, why not try improving the performance of the existing one? I make some suggestions in chapter 11.

The Treasury report is deficient in detail. It has nothing about the cost of implementing its proposals, the staff required to man the new agencies and to shoulder the new regulatory responsibilities that are to be imposed on the existing agencies, the time it will take for implementation, or the methods of determining the capital requirements of financial institutions believed to create "systemic" risk (of which more presently).

So there is a sense in which the 88-page report is at once too short and too long: too long to be a statement of principles, which would provide a basis for productive discussion; too short to enable an assessment of the desirability and feasibility of the specific proposals that the report makes.

Among them, the most important is to give the Federal Reserve responsibility for regulating financial companies that it deems to create "systemic risk." Runs on commercial banks are rare, because depositors are federally insured; and while banks have uninsured creditors as well, the usual sequel to a bank failure is for the bank's liabilities as well as assets to be assumed by another bank with the financial assistance of the Federal Deposit Insurance Corporation. Commercial banks can protect themselves from insolvency caused by lack of liquidity (which might occur because the bank could not sell assets fast enough to meet withdrawal demands) by borrowing from the Federal Reserve. This is called "borrowing at the discount window," an archaic phrase that confuses people about how the Federal Reserve operates. There is no window, and "discount" just means loan. Morgan Stanley and Goldman Sachs reorganized as bank holding companies to be able to borrow from the Fed without having to satisfy the misunderstood criteria discussed in chapter 2 for a Fed loan to a nonbank.

The September 2008 banking crisis centered on the shadow banks, which are not regulated as commercial banks. Commercial banks were also heavily invested in securitized debt, but the combination of federal deposit insurance and the ability to borrow easily from the Fed, along with the Fed's ability to flood them with cash by purchasing or lending against Treasury bills, cushioned the effect of the financial crisis on them—though it was still considerable.

The Treasury wants the Federal Reserve to be authorized to classify any financial intermediary—that is, "bank" in the broadest sense—as a "Tier 1 Financial Holding Company" and, having done so, to place restrictions on the bank's capital structure, management, and operations (including its compensation practices) designed to prevent the bank from failing or, if it fails, from setting off a chain reaction.

The basis for the classification would be that the bank posed a "systemic risk," meaning that its failure, like that of Lehman Brothers, could endanger the financial system and through it the larger economy. Usually this would be because of the firm's web of relations with other participants in financial markets—in Lehman's case, money-market funds, nonfinancial issuers of commercial paper, banks that had provided standby lines of credit to those issuers, purchasers of letters of credit, hedge funds that lent to and borrowed from Lehman, and banks with which it had credit-default swaps. Sheer size would presumably be another criterion for classifying a bank as a Tier 1 FHC, because the larger a bank is, the more its failure could have a ripple effect.

The simplest solution to the systemic risks created by large broker-dealers (though at the moment all five of the former principal broker-dealers are either parts of bank holding companies or, in the case of Lehman Brothers, have disappeared) would be to forbid them to trade on their own account or engage in any other speculative or highly risky financial activities; and perhaps that is what the Federal Reserve would do to broker-dealers that it classified as Tier 1 FHCs. Nor would it stop with broker-dealers, since other financial intermediaries that are critical nodes in the global finance network might also carry much of the financial structure down with them if they collapsed. In 1998 the collapse of a single hedge fund, Long-Term Capital Management, caused a global financial crisis, while the current crisis was precipitated in part by speculation in credit-default swaps by American Insurance Group. But the Treasury report does not indicate the range of measures that the Fed would consider. It also rejects specifying criteria for classifying a firm as a Tier 1 FHC because it does not want to tie the Fed's hands or enable a firm to skirt classification by keeping just under whatever threshold—in terms of size and nature of assets, leverage, or interconnectedness with other financial intermediaries—Congress or the Fed might establish.

Other measures for limiting systemic risk created by Tier 1 FHCs could include requiring a bank to hold more of its capital in debt convertible to equity at the direction of the regulatory authority (such debt has been termed a "regulatory hybrid security") should the bank get into trouble during a period of general financial stress.[8] The conversion would reduce the bank's debt load at critical times, yet without requiring a government bailout. Moreover, a lender of the convertible debt, having no protection in bankruptcy (equity holders usually are completely wiped out in a bankruptcy), might insist in his loan covenant on

8. For a good discussion, see Squam Lake Working Group on Financial Regulation, "An Expedited Resolution Mechanism for Distressed Financial Firms: Regulatory Hybrid Securities" (Council on Foreign Relations, Center for Geoeconomic Studies, July 2009).

measures to reduce the risk of his borrower's bankruptcy—might in other words be a more zealous monitor of his borrower's solvency than a lender who did not face the risk of involuntary conversion of his loan to an equity investment. Monitoring by lenders is attractive from a macroeconomic standpoint because lenders are more sensitive to risk than management is; unlike management (and shareholders), they don't have upside risk, as they do not receive any share of the firm's profits.

Banks will fight hard against being required to issue this kind of convertible debt. At the time of conversion, the price of a bank's stock will be low (the bank, by definition, is in trouble); but if the price later recovers, the value of the original stockholders' equity will be diluted by the stock issued to the lenders upon conversion of their loans. A bank that got into trouble might prefer selling assets or reducing lending to issuing stock, yet those measures, if taken at a time of impending financial crisis, could have adverse macroeconomic consequences.

There are objections to regulatory hybrid securities as the answer to systemic risk, however. The securities would be unattractive to conservative investors because of the added risk but attractive to firms that saw an opportunity to buy a company on the cheap should the conversion trigger be pulled. Such firms would exert pressure on regulators to pull the trigger and might sell the company's stock short to make default more likely.

A more serious problem would be deciding whether to pull the trigger. The Federal Reserve (the agency designated by the Treasury report to be the systemic risk regulator) would be hesitant, since the act of pulling the trigger could set off a panic. The alternative would be an automatic trigger, but it would be extremely difficult to specify the triggering conditions (rate of withdrawal of short-term capital, percentage fall in the Dow Jones Industrial Average, etc.). Then too the government can never make a fully credible commitment to an automatic response to a crisis—can never promise credibly not to disarm the Doomsday bomb at the last minute.

Another possible weapon in the systemic risk regulator's arsenal might be requiring banks to increase the ratio of equity to debt in their capital structure (that is, reduce leverage—which is also what happens when debt is converted to equity) when the market value of banks' loans and other capital rises. The market value of a bank's capital rises in the boom phase of the business cycle and falls in the bust phase, so reducing its leverage in the boom would make it better able to weather the bust that followed. But limiting risk by limiting leverage is easier said than done. A lender can increase the riskiness of its transactions without increasing leverage, simply by making riskier loans, which will command higher interest rates and thus offset the effect on profits of a regulatory ceiling on leverage. Although the Fed limits bank leverage now, it does so to reduce bankruptcy risk rather than to reduce banks' profits in booms.

If there is to be a systemic risk regulator, there are pros and cons to making it the Fed.[9] The Fed can flood the economy with money in a financial emergency such as hit the banking industry in September 2008, and it has considerable political independence (though the basis of that independence is statutory rather than constitutional). But these are not compelling points. Flooding the economy with money is a response to a financial crisis rather than a preventive measure. And granting the Fed uncanalized discretion to subject firms to draconian restrictions would threaten the Fed's political independence. As long as the Federal Reserve just manages the money supply and regulates commercial banks, which are its instruments for managing the money supply in normal times (because in normal times it regulates interest rates, and thus the money supply, by altering banks' cash balances by means of open market operations), it is engaged in a limited, technical, even esoteric activity that does not involve

9. See Squam Lake Working Group on Financial Regulation, "A Systemic Regulator for Financial Markets" (Council on Foreign Relations, Center for Geoeconomic Studies, July 2009).

picking and choosing among individual firms outside the commercial banking industry. (How many Americans have the faintest idea of what open market operations are?) Once the Federal Reserve has a roaming jurisdiction to place the mark of Cain on whatever firm it deems, on whatever ground (since the criteria for classifying a firm as a Tier 1 FHC are to remain uncodified so that the banks cannot game them), as a potential source of systemic risk, it will be accused of playing favorites. That will incite political interference by the Administration and Congress. If the Fed acted with a light touch, permitting banks to go on as before, and there was another crash, it would be completely discredited. If instead it ruled with an iron hand, it would be constantly clipping bankers' wings, thereby inflicting large costs on politically powerful firms. The Fed's choice would be between impotence and infamy.

The Treasury report does not examine how the banks might try to game the Federal Reserve's systemic risk authority, but try they would. Some might actually try to become Tier 1 FHCs. They might think that since the Fed will not allow such a firm to fail, lest the potential systemic risk that by definition such a bank is believed to pose should become actual, the firm will be at no risk of bankruptcy and therefore will be able to borrow money at lower interest rates than its competitors that are not Tier 1 FHCs. That might not seem a winning strategy; recent experience teaches that when the government bails out a failing firm, it can and will impose conditions that wipe out not only shareholders and managers but also, as in the case of the bailout of the auto companies, major creditors, even secured ones. The report recommends giving the Federal Reserve the power to "resolve" a failing Tier 1 FHC. The term refers to the streamlined administrative bankruptcy procedure that bank regulatory authorities employ when a commercial bank or a thrift goes broke.[10] As

10. See Federal Deposit Insurance Corporation, *Resolutions Handbook*, www.fdic.gov/bank/historical/reshandbook/ (visited Dec.7, 2009).

in conventional bankruptcy, the usual consequence is that the shareholders are wiped out and the unsecured creditors recover only a small fraction of their claims. But even secured creditors of a "resolved" bank have less legal protection than the Bankruptcy Code gives them,[11] though the treatment of Chrysler and General Motors by the bankruptcy court has narrowed the gap. Recalling creditors' unhappy experience in those bankruptcies, a firm classified as a Tier 1 FHC may find itself unable to borrow at attractive rates because lenders may fear that if it gets into trouble and has to be "resolved" it will be dealt with mercilessly by the regulatory authorities as a macroeconomic culprit.

The resolution power, unlike conventional bankruptcy, doesn't depend on a bank's becoming insolvent. The resolution authority can step in at an earlier time, when it determines that a bank's balance sheet has become so risky that there is a clear and present danger of bankruptcy. Banks, especially the shadow banks that would become subject to the resolution power under the Treasury proposal, might wish to tiptoe closer to the brink of bankruptcy than the resolution authority would permit.

Not that it is certain that resolution would be the fate of a Tier 1 FHC that got into financial trouble. The Fed might conclude that the shock value of resolving a big bank would be too unsettling for the economy, or that the mechanics of taking over and running a giant financial institution would be too much for the Fed, or for any other regulatory agency. If so, the Fed might decide that the institution should be bailed out with minimum harm to creditors, as was done in the September emergency (except with respect to Lehman Brothers). Government has problems with precommitment; it cannot tie its hands as a private firm can, and it does not want to. Creditors can always hope that when the chips are down, the government will balk at allowing Tier 1 FHCs to fail, especially since the big banks are even bigger

11. Cf. Hope W. Olsson, "The RTC Intrusion into Bankruptcy: A Crisis Solution at the Expense of Equity?" 42 *Buffalo Law Review* 901 (1994).

now than they were at the time of the crash, because of acquisitions encouraged by the government. A Tier 1 FHC would be resolved only if it were on the verge of failure in circumstances suggesting that its failure might trigger a broader financial collapse, and in the face of such a collapse the government would be inclined to save the creditors in order to contain the damage to the financial system, of which banks' creditors are an important part. A notable example was using federal money to pay AIG's credit-default debt to Goldman Sachs.

In addition, Tier 1 FHCs are to be regulated with a view toward making them less risky—less leveraged, for example. That would reduce the risk of lending to them, and hence the likelihood that they would ever *have* to be resolved. So such firms might be able to borrow at lower interest rates after all, which might compensate them for the added regulatory burdens of their status.

Some firms that would be candidates to be classified as Tier 1 FHCs might cringe at the prospect and decide they'd do better to spin off enough of their operations to avoid the classification and therefore the restrictions that come with it. For example, a broker-dealer that was both a dealer in commercial paper and a trader on its own account might do better to spin off its trading operations, thereby giving its shareholders shares in two companies, than to continue in its dual role and be subjected to restrictions that might make its trading unprofitable by preventing it from making attractive deals that were highly risky. Those restrictions could, moreover, make Tier 1 FHCs noncompetitive with foreign banks regulated under looser standards. It is a terrible fate to be a regulated company forced to compete with an unregulated, or even a less severely regulated, company.

Even if all firms that were thought to create systemic risk decided—in order to avoid classification as a Tier 1 FHC—to shrink, or to reduce their interactions with other financial firms, systemic risk would not be eliminated. Such risk is a property of the financial system rather than of individual firms. Systemic risk is *correlated* risk. If the entire banking industry were heavily invested in home mortgages and a housing bubble caused a precipitous fall in the value of those mortgages, it wouldn't matter if the industry consisted of 10,000 banks of equal (and therefore equally small) size that had no dealings with other financial firms; the entire industry would be brought down. Not would it matter if the banks had no transactions with each other (were not "interconnected").

Making the Fed the systemic risk regulator would not only compromise its independence; it would distract it from its core function of managing the money supply. Since its mismanagement of the money supply was a major cause of the financial crisis, it hardly needs an additional distraction. If the financial collapse is rooted in regulatory mistakes, expanding the responsibilities of the regulatory agency that made the most serious mistakes seems a perverse response.

The restriction that the Federal Reserve could impose on Tier 1 FHCs that would most alarm a bank would be to limit the level or regulate the structure of executive compensation. But we need to separate issues of compensation of senior executives from issues of compensation of traders, loan officers, and other executives at the operating rather than management level. The Fed would be authorized to regulate compensation at both levels, but at the top level the aim would be to make management a more faithful agent of the shareholders, while at the operating level it would be to curb the risk-taking incentives of financial executives by requiring that much of their compensation be deferred. The deferred component might consist of stock that could not be sold for a period of years or cash bonuses that could be recovered by the company if the deals for which the bonuses were a reward later soured.

The two aims—better aligning executives' incentives with those of the shareholders and reducing the riskiness of executives' compensation—are inconsistent. Shareholders in a publicly held corporation are generally less risk-averse than executives because they have a smaller stake in the enterprise, as they can diversify away any risk that is peculiar to the enterprise by holding a diversified portfolio of securities. Top executives have much more to lose, in reputation and future earnings prospects, from the collapse of their company. And they are in control, and so are able—up to a point, at any rate—to manage the company in their own interest rather than that of the shareholders.[12] That is bad from a microeconomic standpoint but may be good from a macroeconomic one, as it implies that if top financial executives were allowed to remain *im*perfect agents of the shareholders they would establish procedures for preventing traders, loan officers, and other subordinate executives from taking excessive risks. It is not in management's interest for a trader to make a deal that will get him a bonus on which he could retire but that is likely to blow up shortly after the bonus is paid.

The analysis is not changed by shifting the focus from the shareholders to the board of directors. To the extent that the directors are honest agents of the shareholders, they will be no more risk-averse than the shareholders are. As far as their personal interests are concerned, they are likely to worry more about the company's going broke than the shareholders would, because it would be an embarrassment. But it would be an embarrassment shared with the other directors, and the loss of income and career prospects would be much less than that of the company's chief executive officer and the other senior managers. And if the directors are either insiders or pals of the CEO, they will not be independent, and if they are independent, they are unlikely to know much about the company, or learn much, since they will be part-timers and the information flow will be controlled by management.

12. See, for example, Lucian A. Bebchuk and Jesse M. Fried, "Executive Compensation as an Agency Problem," *Journal of Economic Perspectives* 71 (Summer 2003); Richard A. Posner, "Are American CEOs Overpaid, and, If So, What If Anything Should Be Done about It?" 58 *Duke Law Journal* 1013 (2009).

But while the directors have less to lose than management from risk taking, they also have less to gain. So they might, after all, try to curb some of the risky but profitable activities of the corporation. But they wouldn't try very hard, because there wouldn't be much in it for them, and they would be at a serious disadvantage with respect to both information and expertise in arguing with management over specific practices.

Although management has an incentive to prevent subordinate employees from taking excessive risks, "excessive" means something different to private businessmen from what it would mean to a systemic risk regulator. Risks that are cost-justified from a corporation's standpoint may be unacceptable from a broader social standpoint because of their potential for bringing down the entire financial system and in its wake the nonfinancial economy as well. Nevertheless, government regulation of compensation is unlikely to be effective, especially given the global nature of the market for financial executives.

Placing ceilings on compensation would be worse, but altering the compensation structure is bad enough. There is a reason why the compensation of traders and other financial executives is not backloaded to the degree the advocates of reform want. Many things can affect a stock's price besides a trader's deals, as critics of stock options as devices for compensating top executives point out, and the longer the period in which a seller cannot sell the stock he receives as a bonus for a successful-seeming deal (to make sure it's a durable success), the less his conduct will affect the price of the stock and thus the size of his bonus. Retractable cash bonuses make it difficult for recipients to manage their finances. Nor does the government have the staff resources or analytical tools to establish compensation structures for thousands of financial executives in thousands of financial firms (or for that matter in hundreds or just dozens of firms).

Lucian Bebchuk, the leading critic of existing corporate compensation practices, does not want the government to restrict the compensation of executives at the operating level but just at the managerial level, to motivate them to limit the risk-taking activity of their subordinates.[13] The Fed might require the CEO of a Tier 1 FHC to place two-thirds of his salary and bonus in an escrow account, from which he could withdraw the money only after five years. This would motivate him to establish and enforce procedures that would reduce the likelihood that deals made anywhere in the company would blow up and destroy the company and by doing so perhaps create the kind of chain reaction illustrated by the collapse of Lehman Brothers. But that chain-reaction effect would not be his concern; his concern would be the loss of his escrowed compensation.

Bebchuk's suggestion is superior to the recommendation of the Treasury's report to loose the modestly paid civil servants of the Federal Reserve on the entire compensation structure of Tier 1 FHCs. Motivated to limit risks that may cause losses to themselves, the top executives may, for example, decide (as under the other regulatory pressures exerted on Tier 1 FHCs, which I discussed earlier) to shrink the firm, because control of subordinates is more difficult the larger a firm is, or to spin off its riskiest parts. Combining different organizational cultures—one of safe lending, for example, and the other of risky trading—in the same firm is problematic. Because trading is more profitable, the safe lenders will have an incentive to take risks so they can generate profits large enough to avoid being dominated by the traders. A separation of the two parts into separate companies would solve this problem, leaving one part, at least, safe.

13. See, for example, Lucian A. Bebchuk, "Fixing Bankers' Pay," *Economists' Voice*, Nov. 2009, www.bepress.com/ev; Bebchuk and Holger Spamann, "Regulating Workers' Pay" (forthcoming in *Georgetown Law Journal*); Bebchuk, "Let the Good Times Roll Again?" *Project Syndicate*, July 2009, www.law.harvard.edu/faculty/bebchuk/opeds/07-09_Project Syndicate.pdf (visited Oct. 13, 2009); U.S. Congress, House Committee on Financial Services, "Hearing on Compensation Structure and Systemic Risk: Written Testimony Submitted by Professor Lucian A. Bebchuk," 111th Congress, 1st Sess. 11 (June 2009).

Bebchuk's proposal has serious drawbacks, however, besides the obvious one that regulators lack the expertise required to create, at *any* level of management, compensation systems that balance a firm's competitive needs against the macroeconomic risks that rewarding risky financial decisions can create. Errors by the regulators will create openings for non–Tier 1 FHCs, including foreign firms that may be identical to Tier 1 FHCs in all but regulatory constraints, to skim the cream of the Tier 1 FHCs' financial executives. The employment market for financial executives is global, the language of finance English, and American financiers will relocate abroad—and brilliant foreign financiers decline offers from American firms—if the Fed puts the screws on executive compensation.

And the specifics of financial compensation practices may not even have been a significant factor in the financial collapse. A careful study has found no connection between how much a bank lost in the collapse and how risk-rewarding the bank's method of compensating its CEO was.[14] The study also found that CEOs incurred large personal wealth losses, which implies that they didn't think they were taking "excessive" risks. The first finding implies, according to the logic of Bebchuk's argument, that the CEOs had an incentive to adopt methods of compensating their subordinates that would prevent the latter (traders, loan officers, etc.) from taking risks that might (with a probability sufficient to alarm top management) bring the company down. This implication is further supported by the experience of Merrill Lynch, which in 2006 had instituted compensa-

14. Rüdiger Fahlenbach and René M. Stulz, "Bank CEO Incentives and the Credit Crisis" (NBER Working Paper No. w15212, July 2009). See also Steven N. Kaplan, "Should Banker Pay Be Regulated?" *Economists' Voice*, Dec. 2009, www.bespress.com/ev; Mark Hulbert, "Did Bankers' Pay Add to This Mess?" *New York Times Sunday Business*, Sept. 27, 2009, p. 6. Kaplan's paper is an especially compelling criticism of proposals to restrict the compensation of financial executives.

tion reforms that Bebchuk approves of yet nevertheless sustained immense losses in the financial crisis.[15]

A still deeper objection is that financial penalties are unlikely to change the incentives of financial executives to avoid creating a macroeconomic crisis. Suppose the Nuclear Regulatory Commission ordained that the CEO of any electrical utility that owned a nuclear power plant must place half his salary in escrow for five years. If at the end of that time there has been no nuclear accident (such as at Three Mile Island or Chernobyl), the money is released to him; if there is a serious nuclear accident, it is not. His decisions would not be affected; the risk of a nuclear accident is so slight that he would regard the money in escrow as securely his. The probability of a financial crisis that precipitates a depression or severe recession is probably higher than that of a serious nuclear accident (judging from the relative frequency of the two types of accident), though no one knows, but it probably is too low for modest financial penalties, such as partial deferral of compensation, to influence financial management.

So suppose a firm buys the triple-A tranche of a mortgage-backed security and there is a 1 percent annual risk that the investment will turn out to be worthless and bring down the firm. A financial executive paid salary or bonus based on the expected profit from such a deal would have an incentive to make it despite the slight chance that it would blow up eventually. Suppose 50 percent of the bonus he received on the deal was placed in escrow for five years. Then he would face a 5 percent chance of losing half his bonus. That would be too small an expected penalty to dissuade him from making the deal. The penalty could not be made sufficiently heavy to dissuade him without depriving him of most of his current income.

In light of the foregoing analysis, what is one to make of the Fed's suggestion that it regulate the compensation practices of *all*

---

15. See Louise Story, "In Merrill's Failed Plan, Lessons for Pay Czar," *New York Times,* Oct. 8, 2009, p. B1.

federally regulated banks—not only the handful of Tier 1 FHCs —and that the regulation should encompass the compensation not just of senior executives but of all bank executives?[16] This seems madly ambitious. Where will the Fed find the staff for such regulatory oversight? And what is the need to regulate the compensation practices of small banks? And given Bebchuk's point that if senior executives are compelled to be compensated in ways that would penalize them if their company got into trouble and needed a bailout, they will be motivated to prevent their subordinates from taking risks that might trigger such consequences, why does the Fed think it has to reach down and review the methods by which banks compensate traders, loan officers, and other nonsenior executives? Why can't that be left to properly incentivized senior management? But probably the Fed is just talking tough, to soothe public anger at the financial industry, and lacks either the desire or the staff to regulate bankers' salaries.

It is taken for granted that the finance industry will fiercely resist any regulation of compensation. That is probably correct, but not quite so obviously correct as one might think. To see this, we need to understand the converse of monopoly, which is monopsony. A monopolist reduces output in order to push price above the competitive level. A monopsonist reduces his purchase of an input in order to drive the price of the input below that level. If a firm faces an upward-sloping supply curve—meaning that the more it buys, the higher the prices it must pay—then by buying less and thus moving down the supply curve it will pay lower prices for its inputs. (Recall the figure illustrating this dynamic in chapter 3.) Suppose the input is labor. If the relevant labor market is competitive, monopsony won't be feasible; workers offered a lower than market wage will quit and work elsewhere. But if all the firms in an industry conspire to reduce

16. Edmund L. Andrews and Louise Story, "Fed Considers Sweeping Rules on Bank Pay," *New York Times*, Sept. 18, 2009, p. A1.

their hiring, wages will fall, because the affected workers will not have good alternatives.

But such conspiracies are illegal. Without industry-wide—which means worldwide—caps on financial executives' compensation, imposed by government(s), a reduction in compensation is not an equilibrium. A given financial firm, especially the immensely successful Goldman Sachs, might be able to get away with limiting its employees' compensation in the short run. But in the long run it would lose superior employees to competitors. Such defections could be critical for Goldman, since its major asset is its human capital, and this is true of the rest of the banking industry as well.

If pay caps were imposed and were effective, the firms subject to them would be more profitable, provided the caps were imposed on a sufficiently broad range of companies, both foreign and domestic, to minimize poaching of superior employees by companies not subject to the cap. In effect, the government would be the enforcer of a finance industry monopsony, which the industry might be expected to welcome. But the monopsony would be a leaky sieve. And the pay-capped employees would still be under heavy pressure to engage in risky transactions—especially if management were subjected to more effective control by shareholders—because of the positive correlation of risk and return.

So it is not clear what would be accomplished by pay caps. The emphasis on them can be understood only in political terms. Many members of Congress, and of the public, and much of the media, seem able to understand the financial crisis only in the crudest populist terms, as the product of the machinations of greedy, reckless, overpaid, perhaps criminal denizens of "Wall Street." Systemic causes of the financial crisis, such as unsound monetary policy, deregulation, lax regulation, unsound economic theories, complacency, the tax code, deficits, Chinese trade policy, mindless governmental promotion of homeownership, and so forth, are beyond them.

The government is willing to play to the ignorant partly because government in a democracy must always treat popular views deferentially; partly because it doesn't think the public, Congress, or the media (except for the most sophisticated financial journalists) can understand economic analysis; and partly because the populist account conveniently deflects attention from the failures, in which the current economic leaders of the nation were complicit, that led to the crisis. Of course, if the officials who screwed up *said* they'd screwed up, the people and the Congress would be reluctant to entrust them with responsibility for redesigning the regulatory system. So they must find scapegoats, and where better than among the wealthy inhabitants of "Wall Street"?

In a speech on September 14, 2009, the President acknowledged that "Congress and the previous administration took necessary action in the days and months that followed. Nevertheless, when this administration walked through the door in January, the situation remained urgent." And so "this administration . . . moved quickly on all fronts, initializing a financial stability plan to rescue the system."[17] The implication is that, the previous Administration having failed to stop the rot, the new one had to move quickly to create and execute a recovery program. In fact all the new Administration did, apart from the stimulus and the stress tests and an ambitious but not very successful mortgage relief plan, was to continue the policies of the previous Administration. But the stimulus and the stress tests, at least, were important new initiatives.

The speech goes on to describe the recovery program, and, while acknowledging that "the work of recovery continues," adds that "we can be confident that the storms of the past two

17. "Remarks by the President on Financial Rescue and Reform," Sept. 14, 2009, www.whitehouse.gov/the_press_office/Remarks-by-the-President-on-Financial-Rescue-and-Reform-at-Federal-Hall/ (visited Nov. 27, 2009). I assume "initializing" is a misprint for "initiating."

years are beginning to break." The implication is that they are beginning to break because of the program. Actually they are beginning to break as the result of the natural recuperative strengths of the economy plus the combined efforts of successive Administrations.

The speech then turns to the causes of the economic crisis. The failures of government policy that precipitated the crisis go unmentioned. Acknowledgment of them would strike a discordant note, and not only because the President has appointed Bernanke to another term as chairman of the Federal Reserve and because Geithner was the President's choice for Secretary of the Treasury (not only held over, but promoted from his job as president of the Federal Reserve Bank of New York). The Administration wants to enlarge the powers of the Fed, yet the Fed under Alan Greenspan was a major cause of the economic crisis because of its bubble-blowing monetary policy, and the Fed under Bernanke, as we know, failed to take measures that might have headed off the crisis.[18] Acknowledgment of these errors would raise questions about the appropriateness of rewarding the Fed for its failures by giving it enhanced powers.

Blame has to fall somewhere, and in the President's speech it falls on the "reckless behavior and unchecked excess at the heart of this crisis, where too many were motivated only by the appetite for quick kill and bloated bonuses. Those on Wall Street cannot resume taking risks without regard for consequences, and expect that next time, American taxpayers will be there to break their fall." But American taxpayers *will* be there next time to break their fall, because according to Bernanke the bank bailouts were necessary to avert a second Great Depression, and they will be necessary to do the same thing the next time we're in the same fix. And nobody in a position of authority on "Wall Street" takes risks without regard for consequences. The problem is that they

18. See also John Cassidy, *How Markets Fail: The Logic of Economic Calamities* 304–327 (2009).

do not have regard for consequences for the economy as a whole, because that is not the business of business. That is the business of government.

One thing that was new in the President's speech was a discussion of "resolution" authority, the streamlined bankruptcy process that the Federal Deposit Insurance Corporation uses on insolvent commercial banks and thrifts. The speech suggests that if only there had been authority to "resolve" the insolvency of the nonbank banks, the taxpayer would have been spared having to bail them out. That doesn't make sense. Broke is broke, whatever the mechanics of liquidation or reorganization; and if you don't want to have an insolvent banking system, you have to bail out the broken banks. No one thinks bankruptcy a bad way to "resolve" a bankrupt auto manufacturer; the bankruptcies of GM and Chrysler were orderly and prompt—yet the government still poured in tens of billions of dollars to save them from liquidation.

Moreover, whatever changes we make in our procedures for winding up a bankrupt financial institution will not deprive foreign countries of control over the assets of such an institution that are located in foreign countries, which has protracted the Lehman bankruptcy.

Another novelty in the speech (I think it's a novelty) is the suggestion that bonuses for senior executives should be subjected to a vote by the company's shareholders. What would that do? Probably the senior executives would substitute higher salary, more stock options, bigger severance packages, and other forms of compensation for bonuses. And *that* would prevent the next financial crisis? And remember: shareholders are less risk-averse than managers, not more.

The most questionable proposals in the Treasury report concern the protection of investors and consumers from false, misleading, or "unfair" practices by the banking industry (as always, broadly construed to include the shadow banks) and by the credit-rating agencies. Three of the proposals are particularly important (and misguided): that originators of mortgage-backed securities and other securitized debt be required to retain at a minimum a 5 percent equity interest in the securities that they sell; that oversight of credit-rating agencies be increased; and that a new agency be established—the Consumer Financial Protection Agency—to protect consumers from making mistaken or foolish decisions regarding taking on debt, such as credit card and mortgage debt.

The premise of all three proposals is that the financial and broader economic crisis in which the nation finds itself is due on the one hand to the irrationality and sharp practices of bankers and on the other to the irrationality and gullibility of their customers. The bankers are fools and knaves and the consumers are fools. This is to blame the errors of the regulators on the regulated.

Especially implausible is the idea that *sophisticated* investors were gulled, and therefore that requiring the originators of securitized debt to retain an interest in the securities when they sell them will make them less likely to sell securities that they know to be worth less than the selling price. It is true that the seller of a complex product usually knows more about its possible flaws than the buyer, that a security that consists of a package of thousands of mortgages is as a practical matter impossible for the buyer to inspect, and that the seller's retention of first-loss exposure ("skin in the game," also called "eating your own cooking") is a conventional method of reducing the risk to the buyer that the product may be defective; in effect, the seller gives the buyer a hostage—the seller's retained interest, which will die if the product explodes.

But all this was well known by the banks, pension funds, sovereign wealth funds, and other buyers of tranches of mortgage-backed and similar securities. These interests were sold not to hapless consumers but to professional investors. Such investors, if they want a seller of a financial product to have first-loss exposure as a guaranty of the quality of the product, can negotiate for such a provision in the contract of sale—as some did and do. They don't need the government's protection.

This is further suggested by the fact that banks that originated securitized debt often bought interests in such debt from other originators.[19] They would not have done that had they been skeptical about the value of such securities—and they would have been skeptical had they been deceiving the buyers of the securities that they originated. At least this is true in general; for it is possible that banks might tacitly agree to buy each other's overpriced assets. Suppose Bank A has a security worth $1.5 million that it sells to B for $2 million, and later B sells a security worth $1.5 million to A for $2 million. If each bank records the value of the security that it has bought at its purchase price of $2 million, each bank's balance sheet will have increased by $500,000.

The proposal to tighten oversight of credit-rating agencies also invites a skeptical reaction. It is true that the agencies gave triple-A ratings to the senior tranches of mortgage-backed securities and other debt securities that later plunged in value. But the limitations of the credit-rating agencies were well known to professional investors (and securitized debt is sold only to such investors, not to hapless individuals): the agencies are paid by the issuers of the securities that they rate; they advise on the design of such securities; they are under pressure to rate securities triple-A because many institutional investors are forbidden to invest in lesser-rated securities; they do not pay high salaries by Wall Street standards and as a result do not hire the cream of the financial analyst crop; and they are reluctant to downgrade a debt issue because of changed circumstances after they have

19. Viral V. Acharya and Matthew Richardson, "Causes of the Financial Crisis," 21 *Critical Review* 195, 200 (2009).

rated it, as that places a cloud over the creditworthiness of the issuer—their customer.[20] Professional investors who knew all this
and failed to treat their ratings of complex securities with a degree of skepticism had only themselves to blame.

And yet it is unclear whether, in spite of the agencies' institutional limitations, their ratings were inaccurate. That depends on
how likely it seemed that the securities they rated triple-A would
tank. To most observers, including regulators, financial journalists, economists, and the professional investment community, the
probability seemed remote. We must be wary of hindsight bias, a
potent source of unjust blame.

Still, it is reckless to make a large investment on the strength
of a credit rating alone, and if that recklessness was indeed widespread before the crash, it will not be from now on; the investors
will have learned their lesson. (Much of the Treasury report consists of recommending closing the barn door after the horses
have escaped.) I do think that some reforms of credit rating are
warranted, however; I discuss these in chapter 11.

The case for the government's trying to protect consumers
of financial products, as distinct from sophisticated investors, is
stronger. But efforts should probably be limited to protecting
consumers from fraud. If so, the creation of a Consumer Financial Protection Agency (which is to be given the consumer financial protection powers and staff of the Federal Reserve, the
Comptroller of the Currency, the Federal Deposit Insurance Corporation, and the Federal Trade Commission) is a step in the
wrong direction. There are plenty of remedies against financial
fraud, including criminal laws as well as special laws protecting
borrowers, such as the Truth in Lending Act and the Fair Debt

20. On the history, regulation, and practices of the credit-rating agencies, see the excellent discussion in Lawrence J. White, "The Credit Rating Agencies and the Subprime Debacle: Understanding Their Centrality
and What to Do about It," *FineReg21*, Oct. 19, 2009, www.finreg21.com/
lombard-street/the-credit-rating-agencies-and-subprime-debacle-understand
ing-their-centrality-and-wh (visited Oct. 25, 2009).

Collection Practices Act, and plenty of enforcers, including not only the Justice Department, the Securities and Exchange Commission, the Federal Trade Commission, and their state counterparts but also lawyers who file consumer class-action suits. The proposed new agency, however, is to have the additional assignment of protecting consumers of financial products from themselves. The Treasury report argues that oversight of financial markets should be based on "actual data about how people make financial decisions," and it is apparent that the authors believe that consumers do not make rational financial decisions because they cannot understand financial products.

The report has the new agency designing "plain vanilla" financial products, such as a thirty-year fixed-payment mortgage, and requiring that they be offered to prospective borrowers along with the lender's own product. The agency-created products, according to Harvard law professor Elizabeth Warren, who first proposed such an agency, would be "designed to be read in less than three minutes."[21] Sellers of these products would have a safe harbor from being sued, while sellers bold enough to offer an alternative would be courting litigation. If this didn't move the market toward the plain-vanilla products, the agency could draw another arrow from its quiver and restrict the terms that lenders offer in their own products if it believed that the benefits of the restriction would outweigh the costs. Since no responsible cost-benefit analysis would actually be conducted, the agency would have carte blanche to impose its view of optimal mortgage terms on the housing market.

The proposal was fleshed out, shortly after the Treasury report was published, in a 152-page draft statute prepared by the Administration and entitled the Consumer Financial Protection Agency Act of 2009.[22] The aim of the statute is that "consumers

21. Elizabeth Warren, "Consumers Need a Credit Watchdog," *Business Week,* July 15, 2009, p. 76.

22. www.financialstability.gov/docs/CFPA-Act.pdf (visited Oct. 13, 2009).

[of financial products] have, understand, and *can use* the information they need to make responsible decisions" (p. 19). The phrase I have italicized is the tip-off that the agency would not be limited to requiring the provision of information to prospective mortgagors. Regarding the plain-vanilla products, the agency could forbid the seller to offer his own product if the offer would "cause substantial injury to consumers" that "is not reasonably avoidable by consumers and . . . is not outweighed by countervailing benefits to consumers or to competition" (id.).

The statute would authorize the new agency to require reports from providers of consumer financial products and to conduct surveys, for example of the consumers themselves, aimed at determining the risks to consumers and consumers' understanding of those risks. Given the number of sellers of financial services to consumers, not to mention the number of consumers, the potential costs, both to those providers and to the agency, of reporting and monitoring could be astronomical.

The statute would authorize the agency to prevent, both by rule making and by enforcement actions, "unfair, deceptive, or abusive acts or practices" (p. 29). To declare a practice "unfair," the agency would have to determine that it "causes or is likely to cause substantial injury to consumers which is not reasonably avoidable by consumers and such substantial injury is not outweighed by countervailing benefits to consumers or to competition" (id.). So vague a standard would confer enormous discretion on the agency, especially as there is no attempt to define "abusive" ("deceptive" is reasonably clear).

In an earlier era, all this verbiage might have been dismissed as hot air. Ever since the late 1930s the Federal Trade Commission has had the authority to prevent "unfair or deceptive acts or practices," but in practice this has usually meant preventing false labeling and advertising. What is new in the proposal for the Consumer Financial Protection Agency, though not mentioned anywhere, is "behavioral economics," the application of cognitive psychology to economic phenomena. The literature of behavioral economics, which appears to be influential with the Obama Administration, emphasizes cognitive deficiencies that make it difficult even for people of normal intelligence and good education to act in their best interests even when fully informed. The teachings of behavioral economics could be employed by the new agency to go far beyond typical consumer protection measures.

The act's defenders maintain that many consumers were unable to respond sensibly to the mortgage offers they received during the housing boom of the early 2000s. The mortgage bankers and other sellers of residential mortgages often did not require prospective buyers to demonstrate that they had the wherewithal to repay the mortgage; mortgages that required no down payment were sold to people of quite limited financial means; prepayment penalties were specified, which make it costly to refinance a mortgage to take advantage of lower interest rates; and many mortgages were ARMs—adjustable-rate mortgages that specified low "teaser" rates for the first few years followed by higher rates when the rates were redetermined at the end of the teaser period. Some loan agreements required no monthly payments for years. The monthly payments then due would be higher than in a standard thirty-year mortgage because the loan would be repaid in a shorter time: the payment schedule for a thirty-year mortgage with no monthly payments due for the first five years is equivalent to the payment schedule for a twenty-five-year mortgage.

Oren Bar-Gill, a law professor and economist, argues that many consumers made themselves worse off by taking out mortgages during the boom because they could not respond rationally to the offers they received.[23] Many could not compare the terms

23. Oren Bar-Gill, "The Law, Economics and Psychology of Subprime Mortgage Contracts," 94 *Cornell Law Review* 1073 (2009). See also Michael S. Barr, Sendhil Mullainathan, and Eldar Shafir, "The Case for Behaviorally Informed Regulation," in *New Perspectives on Regulation* 25 (David Moss and John Cistermino eds. 2009).

of alternative mortgages (say, a conventional thirty-year mortgage and an ARM) because the terms were not stated in an intelligible fashion. In addition, Bar-Gill argues, here borrowing from behavioral economics, during the bubble many consumers were afflicted by "myopia" and "optimism." "Myopia" in this context means inability to give proper weight to future costs—for example, higher interest rates when the mortgage resets. Many prospective buyers do not look behind the teaser rates even though the reset rates are disclosed. By "optimism" Bar-Gill means exaggerating one's future economic prospects—unrealistically believing that either one's income will increase or housing prices will continue rising and by doing so enable one to refinance the mortgage on attractive terms because one's equity will have increased, the principal amount of the mortgage being fixed.

Bar-Gill's concern with inadequate disclosure of the interest rate on alternatives to the conventional thirty-year fixed-payment mortgage does not present a novel regulatory issue. The Truth in Lending Act requires disclosure of the annual percentage interest rate (APR) of a mortgage or other consumer loan, and if the requirement is defective (Bar-Gill believes that the APR is not required to be disclosed early enough in the negotiations over the mortgage to influence a consumer's decision), the act can be amended, and likewise if violations are not punished severely enough to deter. Bar-Gill just recommends requiring earlier and clearer disclosure of the APR, though he describes this as merely a first step in purging the mortgage market of irrationality.[24]

He does not make clear what he means by "rationality." It cannot mean full information, or the ability to process information flawlessly, because these conditions are rarely met in any area of human activity. It presumably does not mean a high order of intelligence, for that would label much of the American popu-

24. See Bar-Gill, note 23 above, at 1140–1151.

lation as irrational. The word does, however, imply consistency and the avoidance of fallacies that cause serious harm, financial or otherwise, to people who harbor them. But it is unclear that either myopia or optimism in the sense in which Bar-Gill uses these terms is irrational. It might seem that if the discounted present cost of an adjustable-rate mortgage is greater than that of a fixed-rate mortgage, anyone who prefers the former is irrational: he is paying more than he has to. But that conclusion depends critically on assumptions about discount rates, which differ from person to person.[25] Some people have very low discount rates; they save a lot of money, or they incur substantial costs to get an education that will yield a compensating increase in earnings only after many years. Other people have high discount rates; they live for the present. These people are not irrational, though they may turn out to be mistaken concerning their preferences when the future that their decisions are shaping arrives—but that is just to say that the future is uncertain. The difference between them and people with low discount rates, like differences in risk aversion, is a matter of personality rather than of rationality.

If you have a high discount rate, the low teaser rate in an adjustable-rate mortgage may be much more attractive than the high reset rates. You are "irrational" only from the perspective of a person who has a low discount rate, such as Professor Bar-Gill, who has two doctorates, two master's degrees, and a total of thirteen years of education after high school.

Nor is the only function of an adjustable-rate mortgage to entice people with low discount rates. It is a method by which mortgagees sort mortgagors, and it is sometimes superior to imposing heavy creditworthiness requirements at the outset. It thus

25. A discount rate is a rate that equates the utility of a future receipt to a present one. A person who would prefer $5 today to $10 a year from now would have a discount rate of 50 percent. A person who preferred $5 today to $5.50 a year from now would have a discount rate of 10 percent.

can work to the advantage of both parties to the mortgage. The resetting of the interest rate after (usually) two years is a credit test: some mortgagors pass (they pay the reset rate), some fail, and some are given another two years at the teaser rate and thus in effect scheduled for a further credit check then.

Optimism, like a personal discount rate, is a personality trait, and, as it happens, one essential to progress because of the uncertainty of the economic environment. Someone who invests in building a factory that will not produce anything for years is taking a big risk of failure. And because it is a risk that cannot be reliably quantified, he is making a leap of faith, which he probably wouldn't do unless he happened to have an optimistic outlook. It is not that rationality implies such an outlook (or its opposite), but that rationality is not inconsistent with it. Optimists are often disappointed but sometimes richly rewarded for the risks they take; and as long as the prospect of such rewards makes them happier than more cautious, pessimistic decisions would do, they are not behaving irrationally. "Nothing ventured, nothing gained" is the credo of the optimist. The pessimist's is "Nothing ventured, nothing lost." Neither reaction is irrational. The optimist and the pessimist just have different personalities. Bar-Gill has made a value judgment rather than an economic or cognitive one.

Economists traditionally worried that there is *too much* risk aversion in economic life. Risk aversion can result in less investment in risky undertakings, such as invention, than is socially optimal.[26] A project may have net expected benefits, yet risk aversion may deter an entrepreneur from undertaking it. The financial collapse of 2008 has given risk a bad name. That is unfortunate because the willingness to take financial risks is essential to economic progress.

26. Kenneth J. Arrow, "Economic Welfare and the Allocation of Resources for Invention," in *The Rate and Direction of Inventive Activity: Economic and Social Factors* 609, 610–614 (1962).

Here is another example of the ambiguity of "rationality." Most rules of contract law are "default" rules; they govern the interpretation of a contract unless the contract says otherwise; that is, they can be "contracted around." Yet studies have found that these rules often are not contracted around even if they are inefficient.[27] This seems irrational—and indeed the authors attribute it to "status quo bias," which they regard as a cognitive quirk—and is the sort of finding that is used to justify the government's intervention in the contractual process, as the Consumer Financial Regulatory Agency would do. Actually there are reasons for thinking such behavior rational. Very few contract disputes result in litigation, and therefore the transaction costs of adding a term to negate a default rule will often exceed the benefits, even if one party or the other doesn't like the rule. And it's not just a matter of deleting a term in the contract; it's a matter of finding appropriate language by which to negate an otherwise applicable rule of contract law without injecting new interpretive uncertainty. Moreover, one party's raising an issue about a default rule may make the other party search for default rules that *he* might wish to object to. And to raise in a negotiation issues about the background rules of contract law, as distinct from the idiosyncratic terms of the contract governing price, quantity, delivery dates, and so forth, may worry the other party that the raising of those issues is an attempt to create an escape hatch from the obligations created by the contract (and contract law). The seeds of suspicion thus sown may doom the negotiation.

The kind of wet-blanket regulation that Bar-Gill might favor if he thought it feasible—the kind of regulation the sponsors of the Consumer Financial Regulatory Agency Act favor—might be

27. Omri Ben-Shahar and John A. E. Pottow, "On the Stickiness of Default Rules," 33 *Florida State University Law Journal* 651, 654 (2006); Russell Korobkin, "The Status Quo Bias and Contract Default Rules," 83 *Cornell Law Review* 608 (1998). See also Lisa Bernstein, "Social Norms and Default Rules Analysis," 3 *Southern California Interdisciplinary Law Journal* 59, 71–72 (1993).

defended on macroeconomic grounds, as conducing to economic stability. Had there not been in the early 2000s a strong market for risky mortgages, there would have been fewer defaults when the housing bubble burst and therefore less damage to the solvency of the banking industry. But whether the proposed act would do anything to limit risky mortgage lending is unclear, unless it actually outlawed such mortgages. If people have high discount rates and/or are highly optimistic, the provision of safe alternatives (the plain-vanilla products that the agency would design) is unlikely to affect their choice.

Notice that if those products resulted in lower interest rates, Americans would borrow more, setting the stage for a future financial crisis, while if the products resulted in higher interest rates, the recovery from the present crisis would be delayed. Higher interest rates are the likelier consequence. The proposed statute would pile more rights on consumers, which would raise the costs of the finance companies and might reduce the amount of consumer indebtedness. Reducing it would be a good effect—in a boom, though, not in a bust[28]—since overindebtedness was one of the contributors to the economic crisis.

The new agency would complicate the regulation of banking. Its creation would divide regulation between the new agency and the banking agencies. This would not be a problem were the new agency concerned just with protecting consumers against deception (although if that were all it were concerned with, there would be no need to create it, given the existing agencies). But its immense discretionary authority over the marketing of consumer financial products ranging from mortgages to credit cards could, if exercised aggressively, have significant effects on the economics of the finance industry—effects that could increase systemic risk and thus bring the new agency into conflict with the Federal Reserve and the other banking regulators.

28. One is reminded of Saint Augustine's prayer (before he became a saint, of course): "Make me chaste, O Lord, but not yet."

And were the people who during the housing boom bought homes with adjustable-rate mortgages, or mortgages with pre-payment penalties, or mortgages that required a low or even no down payment, really such fools, when the *government* was denying that the rapid increase in housing prices, which made such mortgages seem a good investment to people who could not otherwise afford a home, was a bubble? It's not as if the products that were offered conferred no advantages on the buyer. Adjustable-rate mortgages are cheaper than fixed-rate ones, be-cause they shift the risk of interest-rate fluctuations from lender to borrower. And mortgages that provide prepayment penalties, though they make refinancing a mortgage more costly, carry a lower interest rate. No doubt some mortgagors don't grasp the significance of a prepayment penalty, but the choice among these alternatives is not beyond the cognitive competence of the aver-age home buyer. Must the entire financial products market be turned upside down because an unknown number of *really* unso-phisticated consumers can't understand the terms of any mort-gage except a nonadjustable mortgage with no prepayment pen-alty? Robert Shiller, the prominent behavioral economist (see chapter 1), has expressed doubt that a consumer financial protec-tion agency would have headed off the housing bubble and re-sulting financial crisis.[29]

Another prominent behavioral economist, however, Richard Thaler, who is said to have influence in the Obama Administra-tion,[30] supports the Consumer Financial Protection Agency Act and may have helped to inspire it. He calls himself a "libertarian paternalist."[31] That is an oxymoron. He is a paternalist with a velvet glove. Through a combination of carrot and stick, an

29. Robert Shiller, "Financial Invention vs. Consumer Protection," *New York Times,* July 18, 2009, p. B2.

30. Franklin Foer and Noam Scheiber, "Nudge-ocracy," *New Republic,* Apr. 29, 2009, p. 22.

31. Cass Sunstein and Richard Thaler, "Libertarian Paternalism Is Not an Oxymoron," 70 *University of Chicago Law Review* 1159 (2003).

agency inspired by behavioral economics will steer consumers to those financial products it thinks best for them, whatever they naïvely think.

Thaler's backing of the proposed agency is ironic. For many years he has been questioning the size of the "equity premium"— the amount by which the return on common stock (equity) exceeds the return on bonds (debt). He has argued that people exaggerate the riskiness of equities and has urged them to invest more of their savings, including their retirement savings, in common stock, since college and university "faculty who had allocated all of their [retirement] funds to stocks would have done better in virtually every time period, usually by a large margin," and "those [who invest] in all-stock portfolios often do better by very large amounts" than investors in portfolios that contain debt as well as equities. Thaler finds "the case for equities compelling," but believes that "myopic loss aversion"—investors' failure to aggregate returns over time (where they would see their losses offset by gains)—prevents people from investing as much in equities as they should.[32]

Invest all your money in stocks? Many people who followed that advice—advice based on the kind of myopia (much criticized in postmortems on our current economic crisis) that bases predictions about the future on naïve extrapolation from the past—find themselves in trouble today. People who, being loss-averse, adopted more cautious investment strategies did better. One of our most prominent behavioral economists succumbed to the second type of myopia, that of naïve extrapolation. Should behavioral economists who labor under the same cognitive limitations as consumers be designing systems of consumer protection?

In response to these criticisms, Thaler has analogized con-

---

32. Shlomo Benartzi and Richard H. Thaler, "Myopic Loss Aversion and the Equity Premium Puzzle," 110 *Quarterly Journal of Economics* 73 (1995).

sumer financial protection to the regulation of baby cribs.[33] Noting the death of a friend's infant as the result of a defectively assembled crib, Thaler argues that instructions on its proper assembly would have been unlikely to prevent the accident, because people notoriously fail to read instructions. Therefore "cribs should be designed to be fail-safe in the sense that they should not be dangerous even if the user has not read the instructions." And Thaler asks rhetorically whether mortgages and credit cards are "all that different" from cribs.

Well, they are. Death is a more costly consequence of misunderstanding than taking on a mortgage that proves to be onerous, and so a risk of death warrants stronger preventive measures. And while the menace of a misassembled crib, as of other defects in physical products, is hidden, a financial product is identical to its description. If you tell a person the terms of a mortgage, you have told him everything he needs to know in order to decide whether to accept them, except whether he can afford the mortgage, and he should know that better than anyone.

There is a problem with instructions, even in the crib case, that Thaler doesn't mention. One of the reasons people don't read instructions is that a combination of government safety regulations and producers' fear of lawsuits has resulted in a proliferation of warnings. The proliferation increases the time required to read warnings, which—since time is a cost—impels many people to skip them, especially since an increasing number of product safety warnings are ridiculously obvious, such as "flame may cause fire" (warning on a cigarette lighter), "never drive with the cover on your windshield," "peel cellophane from fruit before eating," and "remove used tampon before inserting new one." Might consumers treat a plain-vanilla financial product as the equivalent of a government-mandated warning, and ignore it?

At a time when the credit system is fragile, to propose a novel

33. See www.pbs.org/newshour/businessdesk/2009/07/thaler-responds-to-posner-on-c.html (visited Dec. 7, 2009).

approach to consumer financial regulation (coming hard on the heels of the Credit Card Accountability, Responsibility, and Disclosure Act of 2009, which, as I noted in the last chapter, will increase the costs of credit card borrowing) is likely to retard the economy's recovery by further unsettling the economic environment of the finance industry. The proposal caused the credit industry to mobilize its resources to oppose enactment, when the industry should have been devoting all its time and energy to self-repair.

The mobilization was effective, at least to the extent of killing the proposed provision that the agency require sellers of consumer financial products to provide plain-vanilla versions of those products. That was fortunate, because the proposal had become a captive of consumer advocates and behavioral economists concerned with marketing rather than with economic stability. The macroeconomic problem was not, or at least not primarily, that consumers had been bamboozled into taking on more risk than was wise for them. It was that risk taking by millions of home buyers, like the risk taking of the banks that financed it, created an external cost in the form of a global financial collapse.

There is a more straightforward solution to the problem of risky mortgage lending than creating a Consumer Financial Protection Agency, though it is not feasible politically. One of the causes of the financial collapse in the Great Depression was what were called "brokers' loans": banks made loans to stockbrokers on margin (collateral) of only 10 percent, which encouraged speculation. If the stock doubled in price, the broker's customer obtained a profit equal to ten times his investment minus the interest on the loan. (For example, if he put up $10 to buy a $100 stock which then doubled in value, he would have $200 worth of stock minus the $90 loan, for a $100 gain, minus the interest on the loan, on his $10 investment.) But if the customer lacked the resources to repay the loan in the event that the stock became worthless, he would have lost only $10. The down payment on a mortgage loan is a form of margin, and traditionally it was 20 percent of the purchase price of the house. If only a 10 percent down payment is required, the margin is the same as in the brokers' loans of the 1920s, and the purchase of a house begins to seem a speculative transaction, especially if the mortgage loan is legally or effectively nonrecourse (that is, if the collateral is worth less than the mortgage debt, the mortgagee cannot sue the mortgagor for the difference). If the purchaser has a poor credit rating, the speculative element of the transaction is amplified; and if he is not planning to live in the house but instead to "flip" (sell) it when the price rises, it is a purely speculative transaction. When millions of people engage in speculation financed by banks, there is a threat to the entire economy.

In the wake of the Great Depression, the Federal Reserve was empowered to set margin requirements on loans for the purchase or sale of securities. If the speculative borrowing in the housing market is deemed a significant factor in the financial collapse of September 2008, the Fed can be empowered to set margin requirements for mortgage lending.

It might seem that even requiring 20 percent margin (that is, a 20 percent down payment) would not have averted the housing crash, because housing prices fell by more than 20 percent. But apart from the fact that a homeowner's equity grows as principal is paid back, requiring a 20 percent down payment would reduce the demand for homeownership, so housing prices would not have risen as far as they did and therefore would not have fallen as far.

DEPRESSION AND AFTERSHOCK:

2007–?

6

Economists' joke: A recession is when your neighbor loses his job; a depression is when you lose your job.

The point of the joke is that neither "recession" nor "depression" is well defined, and so the line between them is indistinct to the point of vanishing. (Economists can joke about depressions and recessions because they are untouched by them if they have tenure.) Until the 1930s depression, the busts that punctuated the business cycle were referred to as "panics" or "crises." The Hoover Administration called the economic collapse that began in 1929 a "depression," in an unsuccessful effort to alleviate anxiety. The earlier busts were then renamed "depressions," and since the 1930s depression was the gravest in modern times, it came to be called the "Great Depression." Oddly, when that happened, the word "depression" was retired; all future downturns, unless as severe as the Great Depression (which was unlikely, if only because of the growth of the service sector relative to manufacturing and construction, other economic changes, the automatic stabilizers, and greater resolution to fight a severe economic downturn at any cost), would be called "recessions." It's as if after World War II no armed struggle of any lesser magnitude would ever again be called a "war"; we would speak instead of the "Korean fight" or the "fight in Vietnam," while continuing to refer to the "Franco-Prussian War" and the "Boer War."

So: economic downturns before 1929 are still called "depressions"; the depression of the 1930s is "the depression" or the "Great Depression"; all subsequent depressions are "recessions"; but to mark the fact that the current "recession" is far more serious than any of the previous recessions (which is to say, any of the depressions since the Great Depression), it is now being called by some the "Great Recession."[1] What lexicographic chaos! We should call all our economic busts "depressions," distinguishing between the mild and the severe and reserving the term "Great Depression" for the 1930s depression, because it appears to have been the most severe and consequential in U.S. history, although we cannot be certain of this because of

1. In a talk I gave on April 29, 2009, at a meeting of members of the federal Senior Executive Service, I presented the following eleven reasons for regarding the current depression as qualitatively more serious than its predecessors since the Great Depression: "(1) the global scope [of the depression], creating a drastic fall in international trade and a surge of protectionism, (2) the failure thus far of monetary policy, because of the distress of the banking industry, (3) the enormous fall in household wealth, (4) the hoarding of cash by consumers and banks, creating a risk of deflation (Bernanke's policies suggest that he fears deflation), (5) the extraordinary expenditures by the Treasury on bailing out giant banks and the auto industry, (6) the unprecedented (and inflation-risking) purchase by the Fed of long-term, risky private debt, (7) the public and media hysteria (for example over the AIG bonuses), (8) the unprecedented fiscal stimulus program, surprisingly endorsed, in principle at least, by conservative economists like [Martin] Feldstein, though he disagrees with the details, (9) the bafflement of the macroeconomists, (10) the likelihood of radical, and probably very dumb, regulatory changes, and (11), related to (10), the possibility of a fundamental change in the relation of government to the economy." As Carmen M. Reinhart and Kenneth S. Rogoff put it in their book, *This Time Is Different: Eight Centuries of Financial Folly* 208 (2009), "The global financial crisis of the late 2000s, whether measured by the depth, breadth, and (potential) duration of the accompanying recession [which the authors call the "Second Great Contraction," the first "Great Contraction" being the 1930s depression] or by its profound effect on asset markets, stands as the most serious global financial crisis since the Great Depression. The crisis has been a transformative moment in global economic history whose ultimate resolution will likely reshape politics and economics for at least a generation."

the incompleteness of economic statistics before the twentieth century.

All that I may seem to have shown is that Americans are serial abusers of language, with a near-fatal proclivity for euphemisms and clichés. And you knew that. But there is more. The word "recession" is belittling. It doesn't sound like anything to get excited about. And so it tends to occlude the suffering caused by massive involuntary unemployment and threat of unemployment. The economist Daron Acemoglu displays this tendency toward belittlement when he writes that "despite the ferocious severity of the global crisis—and barring a complete global meltdown—the possible loss of GDP for most countries is in the range of just a couple of percentage points—and most of this might have been unavoidable anyway, given the overexpansion of the economy in prior years. In contrast, within a decade or two, we may see modest but cumulative economic growth that more than outweighs the current economic contraction."[2]

It is not true that the only cost of a depression is a temporary, and relatively minor, decline in the gross domestic product. This ignores negative effects on economic growth[3] resulting from reductions in research and development, worker training, and product design.[4] It ignores the profound psychological effects of a depression,[5] including the anxieties of those who lose their jobs

2. "Daron Acemoglu, "The Crisis of 2008: Lessons for and from Economics," 21 *Critical Review* 185, 190 (2009).

3. See Gadi Barlevy, "The Cost of Business Cycles under Endogenous Growth," 94 *American Economic Review* 994 (2004).

4. See Michael Mandel, "The GDP Mirage: By Overlooking Cuts in Research and Development, Product Design, and Worker Training, GDP Is Greatly Overstating the Economy's Strength," *Business Week,* Nov. 9, 2009, p. 34.

5. See the classic study by Truman E. Bewley, *Why Wages Don't Fall during a Recession* (1999). Cf. Satyajit Chatterjee and Dean Corbae, "On the Aggregate Welfare Cost of Great Depression Unemployment," 54 *Journal of Monetary Economics* 1529 (2007). For evidence regarding the current depression from an opinion poll conducted by Rutgers University, see Bill Marsh, "Jobless, Sleepless, Hopeless," *New York Times Week in Review,*

or their homes or their retirement incomes, or fear losing them. It ignores the long-term economic consequences of the immense costs that governments incur to halt a severe economic decline and speed recovery, and the political effects that bring economic consequences in their train—consequences such as a permanent increase in the size and intrusiveness of government.

My criticism of how economists talk about the costs of depressions is related to criticisms of GDP as an imperfect measure of welfare. By ignoring depreciation, natural calamities, crime, and other sources of losses of value (also by ignoring both improvements and deterioration in products and services), it exaggerates the correlation between increases (or for that matter decreases) in GDP and changes in economic welfare. When GDP falls because of a financial crisis, economic welfare falls with it; but the percentage drop in GDP may be smaller or larger than the welfare loss.

The fact that "most of [the loss of GDP] might have been unavoidable anyway, given the overexpansion of the economy in prior years" does not mitigate the severity of the downturn. The idea seems to be that people were living high on the hog because of excessive borrowing and the day of reckoning has now arrived. But most of the people hurt were not living high on the hog during the boom years; of the millions of people involuntarily unemployed as a result of the depression, how many acquired enough wealth during the boom years of the early 2000s to compensate them for the loss of their jobs?

A related point is that the return of GDP to its predepression

Sept. 6, 2009, p. 4. For other evidence, see Michael Luo, "Recession Exacts an Emotional Toll on Children," *New York Times,* Nov. 12, 2009, p. A1. And Irasema Alonso and Jose Mauricio Prado, in their paper "Ambiguity Aversion, Asset Prices, and the Welfare Costs of Aggregate Fluctuations" 2 (Yale Department of Economics and IMT Lucca Institute for Advanced Studies, June 26, 2008), show that because of people's aversion to uncertainty, the welfare loss caused by the business cycle is much greater than other economists have believed. I discuss uncertainty aversion in chapter 9.

level will not wipe out the cost of the depression, because many and perhaps most of the beneficiaries of the higher GDP will not be the same people who lost out in the bust. We must not ignore the phenomenon of "job destruction." Many jobs lost in a depression never come back; their occupants are not rehired by their former employer or an employer in the same line of business and so must either leave the workforce or find other types of job, which usually pay less.[6] The chance of an unemployed worker's obtaining as good a job as the one he lost may be dim if prospective employers infer that he lost his job because the economic downturn caused his employer to cull its least productive workers. And he will find himself competing for a job with young workers who have been laid off, plus more young workers entering the workforce for the first time as they graduate from school; and employers may prefer young workers for reasons that include their lower expectations of pay and lesser interest in joining a union.[7] So for many older workers who become unemployed, unemployment means involuntary early retirement from the workforce and consequently a decline in permanent income. (This is another reason why the rate of personal savings tends to rise in a depression: transitory income becomes a larger fraction of total income because permanent income is down, and there is a greater propensity to save transitory than permanent income.)

Furthermore, unemployment figures can, and the unemployment figures for the current depression do, understate the severity of unemployment because of the "combined data" fallacy. At the lowest point of the 1979–1982 depression, the

6. See Steven J. David, John C. Haltiwanger, and Scott Schuh, *Job Creation and Destruction* 31 and chs. 5–6 (1996); Robert E. Hall, "Lost Jobs," *Brookings Papers on Economic Activity* 221, 253–256 (1995). Hall notes a "downstream" unemployment effect: a worker who loses his job in a recession or depression is at high risk of losing any future job that he manages to get.

7. Unions offer greater benefits to older, settled workers, because collective bargaining agreements usually key job security to seniority.

unemployment rate reached 10.8 percent, compared with "only" 10.2 percent in October 2009. Yet the unemployment rate was actually higher, among both college-educated and non-college-educated workers, in 2009 than in 1982. The reason the combined rate was lower was that the unemployment rate is lower among college-educated than other workers and the percentage of college-educated workers has risen since 1982, and the latter increase dominated the increase in the percentage of unemployed college-educated workers.[8] To illustrate the principle, suppose that at time t, 20 percent of workers are in service industries and their unemployment rate is 4 percent, while the unemployment rate of workers in manufacturing is 10 percent. So the combined unemployment rate is 8.8 percent (.20 × .04 + .80 × .01). Suppose that at time $t + 1$ the unemployment rate of service workers has risen to 5 percent and of manufacturing workers to 12 percent, but the percentage of service workers has risen to 60 percent. Although the unemployment rate has risen for both groups, the overall rate has dropped from 8.8 percent to 7.8 percent (.60 × .05 + .40 × .12).

Some economists have argued that a depression has a "cleansing" effect on the labor force; the least efficient firms are forced to liquidate, freeing up their resources, including their workers, for more productive employments. But this effect is outweighed by the tendency—very marked in the current depression because of the depletion of retirement assets—of workers not laid off in a depression to cling to their jobs, which retards the matching of workers with their most productive job opportunities.[9] Even so,

8. Cari Tuna, "When Combined Data Reveal the Flaw of Averages," *Wall Street Journal*, Dec. 2, 2009, p. A21.

9. See Gadi Barlevy, "The Sullying Effect of Recessions," 69 *Review of Economic Studies* 65 (2002), and references cited there. In another paper Barlevy points out that if more-efficient firms tend to borrow more, efficient resource allocation will suffer if credit is constrained in a depression, as it has been in this one. Barlevy, "Credit Market Frictions and the Allocation of Resources over the Life Cycle," 50 *Journal of Monetary Economics* 1795 (2003).

the net effect of a depression may be to increase productivity. But if this is done mainly by pushing those workers who are not laid off to work harder, the effect may, as I said in chapter 3, be dissipated when the depression ends and firms hire more workers.

Statistics of output and employment also overstate the costs of a depression by excluding nonmarket output, such as household production. If a woman who has been a full-time housewife (a "household producer," an economist would call her) takes a job in the market, her full salary in the job will be counted in the gross domestic product, but the loss of her household production will not be subtracted even though it is a real loss in economic value. Volunteer work—any work done "for free"—is also not included in GDP even though it has economic value.

Some people who lost their jobs in this depression did substitute household production.[10] And although the sum of their monetary and nonmonetary income fell—otherwise they would have quit their market jobs earlier rather than waiting to be laid off—it did not fall to zero, yet was valued at zero for purposes of calculating GDP.

There is even a sense in which there is no such thing as "involuntary" unemployment; the unemployed are people who are either working for something other than a wage—such as leisure, if they're treating unemployment as vacation time, or the nonmonetary returns from taking care of their children, preparing meals, making home repairs, or producing other nonmarket goods and services—or looking for a job that will pay enough to compensate them for giving up their leisure and household production and for incurring the cost of moving (if they cannot find an acceptable job in their community) or changing occupations.[11] But there is also what economists call an "income effect":

10. See, for example, Mary Pilon, "Per Capita Savings: Home Barbering Grows in Recession, with Hairy Results," *Wall Street Journal*, Aug. 31, 2009, p. A1.

11. As emphasized in Robert E. Lucas, Jr., and Leonard A. Rapping,

the less money one has, the more utility one derives from having a little more money, and so a reduction in money income by reason of having lost one's job will increase one's desire to find another job. More important, the nonpecuniary compensations of unemployment are minor offsets to the reduction in money income. They are outweighed not only by the loss of money income but also by the nonmonetary costs of unemployment in anxiety, fear for the future, embarrassment, and humiliation. Some of these costs are also borne by people who have not lost their jobs but fear they will.

Nevertheless, because of the protraction of the Great Depression and the incredible fall in output and employment in its initial phase (1929–1933), anything that falls far short of Great Depression statistics (duration, output, employment, deflation) is apt to seem rather minor. Yet the effects of the Great Depression that are least susceptible of statistical measurement were the most momentous. These were the political effects, which included the New Deal, British socialism, the spread of communist ideology, and, perhaps, World War II, Hitler having been swept to power by the Great Depression, which was particularly severe in Germany. The political consequences of what I insist is our present depression are likely to be great too, though not so great as those of the Great Depression. The line that separates the sphere of business from that of government is shifting in the direction of government, and America's global hegemony is declining as we rack up enormous deficits in fighting the depression—deficits that may weaken us in much the same way that the enormous costs that Britain incurred in two world wars weakened it: weakened it politically as well as economically. Generally, eco-

---

"Real Wages, Employment, and Inflation," 77 *Journal of Political Economy* 721, 748 (1969); Robert E. Lucas, Jr., *Models of Business Cycles* 54–69 (1987). Lucas and Rapping are careful to add, however, that they do not mean to "imply that high measured-unemployment rates are socially costless." Lucas and Rapping, above, at 748.

nomic power is political power and economic weakness is political weakness.

There is no longer an accepted definition of a depression except "comparable to the Great Depression," the word having lost all but historical referents. Some economists say that if gross domestic product were to decline at a 10 percent or greater annualized rate for some unspecified period of time, that would be a depression. But that is just round-number thinking. It would be better, as I have suggested, to call all nontrivial economic downturns depressions, distinguishing mild from severe ones, with severity measured by total social costs. These would include not only the costs I have discussed thus far but also—an obvious point surprisingly overlooked—the cost of fighting the depression. Suppose a depression that would have caused damage comparable to that of the Great Depression is headed off at a cost of $5 trillion, which is enormous and might do serious long-term damage to the economy. If an economic bust that inflicted a total loss of $5 trillion would be classified as a depression, a depression reduced to a mere "recession" at a cost of $5 trillion should likewise be called a depression—in fact a worse depression, because its costs would not be limited to the $5 trillion spent on limiting its severity.

With the word "depression" relegated to economic history, attention has shifted to criteria for a recession. The media define it as two consecutive quarters in which GDP falls, which is crude but serviceable, except that it doesn't enable the beginning of the recession to be pinpointed to a month. The National Bureau of Economic Research uses a similar measure but looks at other economic indicators besides GDP, such as unemployment, but cannot "call" a recession when it starts because protraction is one of the criteria. It took NBER a year to decide that the current "recession" had begun in December 2007.

The more important question is when a recession ends. The media and many business economists regard it as ending when GDP stops falling, some business economists when it starts rising, and NBER when several key indicators start rising. These definitions are misleading, as the statistics of the current situation show. Normalize GDP in 2007 to 100. In 2008 it was less than four-tenths of 1 percent greater, hence 100.4. In the first quarter of 2009 it fell at an annual rate of 6.4 percent: that is, it declined by 1.6 percent of 100.4, to 98.8. In the second quarter it declined at an annual rate of .7 percent, which means that it fell by .175 percent of 98.8 that quarter. Hence, by the end of June, GDP was 98.6, compared to 100 in 2007. It rose at an annual rate of 2.2 percent in the third quarter (so .55 percent for that quarter), and assume it rises at the same rate in the fourth quarter. Then GDP for 2009 as a whole will be 99.7.

That looks like only a slight decrease since 2007. But this ignores the GDP trend line. GDP grows at an inflation-adjusted rate of about 3 percent a year on average. Hence GDP in 2008 "should" have been 103, and in 2009 106; at 99.7, it would be more than 6 percent below trend. And at this writing GDP is not expected to grow by more than 3 percent in 2010. If so, then as 2011 begins, GDP will still be more than 6 percent below trend. Nonetheless, most journalists, economists, and government officials are saying that the recession ended in the third quarter of 2009.

If that's right, then the Great Depression ended in 1933, when GDP began to rise, though GDP was a third below its 1929 level and unemployment was at 25 percent. In fact the Great Depression persisted until rearmament began in earnest as we prepared to join in World War II. (This is acknowledged, which means that our understanding of when recessions or depressions end is incoherent.) Or suppose that, as in Japan in the 1990s, year after year after year our GDP grows much more slowly than it did on average before; that would be a real depression—a "growth depression."[12] (Another oxymoron, like "jobless recovery.")

12. Paul Krugman, *The Return of Depression Economics and the Crisis of 2008* 67 (2008, with 2009 epilogue).

Another objection to declaring that the current depression ended in the third quarter of 2009 is that the 2.2 percent increase in GDP in that quarter may have been due largely to the government's stimulus expenditures, and if so, then what we were seeing was an economy on life support. GDP in the third quarter was about $3.6 trillion, and 2.8 percent of that is $79 billion. Stimulus expenditures in that quarter were about $100 billion, and there were other emergency antidepression expenditures, such as mortgage relief (including heavy purchases by the Fed of mortgage-backed securities) and the tax credit for first-time home buyers. A recession or depression ends when the economy is taken off life support—not before.

And remember that the cost of a depression includes the cost of fighting it. Perhaps that cost should be subtracted in calculating depression GDP. According to the thoroughly respectable Committee for a Responsible Federal Budget,[13] as of December 2009 the government had spent, guaranteed, or been authorized by Congress to spend the astonishing total of $10.7 trillion to fight the depression (this includes TARP, the stimulus, mortgage relief, the expansion of the Federal Reserve's balance sheet, the auto bailouts, the cost to the government of resolving failed commercial banks and thrifts, a variety of guaranties, and more), though the actual amount spent was "only" $3.8 trillion. Almost half of that represents purchases of debt by the Federal Reserve rather than net transfers. And some of the $3.8 trillion was spent in the last quarter of 2009. A conservative estimate (though really just a guess) is that the government had pumped a net of $1 trillion into the economy in the year ending September 30, 2009 (that is, the 2009 fiscal year). Much of the money has gone to banks, and has stayed there, as excess reserves. Still, had it not been for these expenditures (assuming no crowding-out of private investment), GDP in fiscal 2009 would have been even lower than it was. Suppose it was 2 percent lower (another con-

13. http://stimulus.org/ (visited Dec. 19, 2009).

servative estimate, since 2 percent of GDP is less than $300 billion). Subtracting that would reduce the GDP index from 6 to 8 percent below the GDP trend line. And this assumes no multiplier effect (see chapter 8) of the government's antidepression expenditures.

It would give a more realistic picture of the business cycle to say that a recession (or depression) ends when GDP returns to its trend line, for until that happens, the economy is in trouble and measures to speed recovery should continue to be considered. Otherwise, when GDP begins to grow, however modestly—or even when it just stops falling—people will say that the recession is over, so let's forget about the economy for a while—even if unemployment is still growing, foreclosures are increasing, defaults and bankruptcies are increasing, and, in short, the economy is performing in a dangerously unsatisfactory manner and could at any time resume declining.

Maybe nothing can be done when GDP begins to climb from its depression depths but to let economic "nature" take its course. But complacency should be avoided, as should the insensitivity to the plight of the involuntarily unemployed that is implicit in such common terminology of economists and journalists as "jobless recovery"[14] and unemployment as being a "lagging indicator." It is true that unemployment often continues increasing after an economic recovery begins. The standard explanation is that firms prefer not to incur the cost of hiring or rehiring workers until they are sure that demand for goods and services is increasing. An alternative explanation is tacit collusion: firms may hesitate to expand output as demand rises, hoping that their competitors will follow suit, since the more slowly supply rises in

14. A comment posted on my Atlantic blog on August 3, 2009, states: "There isn't a single person on 'Main Street' who defines 'recovery' as jobless, or ties it to GDP. Most people outside of Washington and Wall Street define 'recovery' as becoming gainfully employed in a job that will show real increases in income over time, not in a job that provides stagnant wages over decades."

response to rising demand, the more prices and profits will increase.

But it is only after a depression is over that one can recognize
an increase in unemployment as a lagging indicator. It would
have been ridiculous to observe the steep decline in employment
in 1930 and be reassured that since unemployment is a lagging
indicator, the depression was over. It had just begun. As long as
unemployment is rising and incomes therefore falling, the downward slide in production and consumption may resume.

Yet by midsummer 2009 the depression *was* weakening. And
with its weakening, people began looking beyond the recovery,
to the long-run effects of the depression. One of those effects
goes by the name of "moral hazard" and is best illustrated by the
tendency to be less careful if one is well insured against the consequences of one's carelessness than if one is not. If the government is expected to make vigorous efforts to dampen the consequences of a bust, investors and consumers will be less cautious
in a boom. (That is the problem of the "Greenspan put," discussed in chapter 1.) In particular, if secured creditors of large
financial institutions feel insulated against the consequences of
their debtors' defaulting, they will not only lend more to such institutions but also make fewer efforts (which are costly) to po-
lice their debtors' conduct. The shellacking that Chrysler's secured creditors took in its bankruptcy is thus the silver lining of
the cloud that the outcome of the bankruptcy proceeding placed
over secured credit.

There is speculation that Americans will not return to their
"free-spending," debt-financed ways as the economy improves.
The personal savings rate bounces around a lot. It was 10 percent in 1980, declined pretty steadily after that, reaching negative territory in 2005, but after the financial collapse of September 2008 rose from 1 percent to almost 6 percent before falling
to 4 percent, its current level. The question is whether it will remain there or instead return to the 1980 level. I am skeptical that
we are entering an era of thrift. Memories are short, and our usu-

ally low savings rate is due in part to the impressive ability of the modern marketing profession to separate people from their money—and that ability is growing.

But the *composition* of people's personal consumption expenditures may change. This depression has been marked not only by a shift from consumption to savings but also by a change in consumption. A wealthy friend of mine who owns three cars that he used to turn over every two years has decided, in reaction to the modest losses in his investment portfolio that he experienced at the depth of the economic downturn, to wait another year before buying a new car. Because modern cars are highly durable and annual design changes generally modest, he may discover that changing cars every two years isn't worth the expense and bother. People who have reacted to their losses by moving a notch down the luxury-goods hierarchy from Neiman Marcus may discover to their surprise that they are content with the switch.

An economist might think such reactions implausible—that if, for example, a person would have been better off had there been no depression in replacing his car every four years rather than every three he would have done so. Manufacturers would have bragged about the superior durability of their cars. But this is uncertain. Unless only one manufacturer can plausibly represent that his cars are good for four years and the cars of his competitors for only three, his advertising that his cars can be kept for four years without loss of utility will simply provoke matching advertising by his competitors, and all will end up with fewer sales. Moreover, people are skeptical about advertising claims and loath to abandon a habit without a good reason. If economic distress jars them out of their habitual behavior, they may learn that that behavior was second best, though had there not been that stressor, inertia would have kept them in their accustomed groove—much as inertia kept General Motors and Chrysler from changing their business strategies until it was too late. Both companies had long been in decline owing to poor management. It took a depression, which bankrupted them, to change their management and direction.

The reason is related to the theme of uncertainty, which is fundamental to my analysis of the depression (see chapters 8 and 9). Changing a business strategy is extremely risky because the full consequences can only be guessed at. That is why innovations generally come from outsiders to an industry. As long as a firm is doing all right, even if it is slowly declining, a risk-averse management may prefer to ride the decline rather than embrace uncertainty by embarking on a daring course change. GM and Chrysler (especially GM) were relatively profitable companies until the depression struck, even though they had been losing market share for many years to foreign-owned companies that made better cars at lower cost.

So suppose that demand for the output of a major industry, such as automaking, does not return to its previous level. (That would be in contrast to a depression in which sales of every category of consumer product fall by the same percentage, so that when demand returns to its pre-recession level sellers rehire laid-off workers and increase their purchases of supplies and materials until sales are back to that level.) Then some of the laid-off workers in that industry will have to find jobs in other industries—jobs for which they are not trained—and those jobs may be in other parts of the country. Suppliers to the industry may have to retool. The need for such adjustments in labor and materials supply will delay recovery. This is one reason why the recovery from the current depression may be slow and job destruction extensive.

There are other reasons as well. The fall in the stock market and in housing prices since 2007 has reduced household wealth dramatically, resulting in increased savings and repayment of debt and what would be a decline in personal consumption expenditures were it not for the stimulus program and other government transfers. Unemployment has also taken a toll on spending, as have the wage cuts that are a distinctive feature of employers' response to this depression. It may be years before consumption returns to trend. The access of small business and consumers to credit has declined and will remain limited as long as the banks feel undercapitalized, and that too may be years, because of uncertainty about future default rates on long-term bank loans secured by residential and commercial mortgages.

Consumer default rates are correlated with unemployment, which may still be increasing and in any event is expected to remain abnormally high for years. A number of banks have failed, and others, including the largest, Citigroup, are troubled though solvent. State and local government budgets are in terrible shape. And the Administration's campaign to reform financial regulation and health insurance may delay recovery by increasing the uncertainty of the economic environment for business.

The slower the recovery, the stronger the case for continuing the recovery programs rather than cutting them back to reduce the risk of inflation, which is the primary aftershock threat. The government administered very strong medicine to a very sick patient. The patient lived, but faced a protracted convalescence during which a serious relapse was possible. Such a relapse occurred in 1937; a recurrence of the depression pushed output and employment sharply down long before they had returned to their 1929 levels. A confluence of factors appears to have been responsible: a reduction in federal spending, a tax increase, and a tightening of monetary policy (higher interest rates). Well, we won't make those mistakes again, will we? We may; and they may not even be mistakes.

The government has created a great deal of money, and borrowed a great deal of money, to finance the bailouts and the stimulus package and increase the amount of money in circulation in order to encourage lending. If, when demand for credit rises, the banks, freshly recapitalized, lend their $1 trillion of excess reserves, the ratio of money in circulation to the output of goods and services will rise steeply—and this will mean inflation. The ratio will rise further, and the danger of rampant inflation will grow, if the government decides to finance some of the immense additional debt that it is incurring as a result of its recovery expenditures by increasing the money supply. A low rate of inflation is manageable and does little economic harm and can even, as we know, assist recovery. But a high rate of inflation is very harmful and usually can be brought down only at the cost of a sharp economic downturn when the Fed raises interest rates in order to reduce the amount of lending and hence the amount of money in circulation. That happened in 1979–1982, when the Federal Reserve broke the inflation of the 1970s with very high interest rates and caused a severe downturn. History may repeat itself a few years from now.

The danger would be less acute were it not for the Bush deficits, which doubled the national debt, and the Obama Administration's ambitious, and costly, programs in the fields of health care and climate change. Fiscal stimulus as a treatment for depression is most effective when there is plenty of "fiscal space," which is to say low public and private debt, so that the increase in public debt caused by borrowing to finance the stimulus does not cause a significant increase in interest rates, which would impede recovery.[15] Since Treasury bonds are close substitutes for private bonds, anything that raises the interest rate that the Treasury must pay to finance a stimulus program will cause interest rates on private bonds to rise also, reducing private investment. Lack of fiscal space thus undermines monetary policy, which uses low interest rates to try to stimulate economic activity. It also creates uncertainty about when and what kind of tax increases or other measures will be imposed in the future to deal with the deficit created by the spending program. Every increase in economic uncertainty retards recovery.

It is paradoxical that conservative economists should be argu-

15. See Emanuele Baldacci, Sanjeev Gupta, and Carlos Mulas-Granados, "How Effective Is Fiscal Policy Response in Systemic Banking Crisis?" (International Monetary Fund, WP/09/160, July 2009).

ing, as some do, that rather than enacting the stimulus package Congress should have enacted a permanent tax cut. It is true that a smaller percentage of a permanent tax cut than of a temporary one would be saved (in accordance with the permanent-income hypothesis), and so the permanent cut would be more effective than the third or so of the stimulus package enacted by Congress that consists of temporary tax cuts. But in the fiscal bind in which the nation finds itself, the very idea of a "permanent" tax cut is incoherent. It would increase the annual budget deficits; and sooner or later, by hook or by crook, those deficits will have to be paid off, whether by inflation, devaluation, or other painful measures—including higher taxes. Indeed, economists who believe in "Barro-Ricardian equivalence" (see chapter 8) should doubt that a permanent tax cut would have *any* stimulative effect; people would simply spend less, in anticipation of their lower after-tax incomes in the future, when painful measures would have to be taken to close the fiscal gap created by the tax cut. Some conservatives would reply that a permanent tax cut is bound to increase tax revenues by reducing the benefit of tax avoidance. But that is true only within limits—otherwise tax revenue would be maximized when the tax rate was zero!

A tax cut laser-beamed to encourage production, such as an increase in the investment tax credit, might be an effective component of a stimulus program. Or might not. If firms are uncertain about the future demand for their products, they will be reluctant to invest even if it would reduce their tax bill.

The Administration's proposed health-care program has riveted public attention on the national debt, at present almost $13 trillion. Of that, $7.5 trillion is public debt—debt owed to lenders other than federal agencies. The rest consists of guaranties and obligations of various sorts that are not firm legal commitments to pay definite amounts. These include the guaranties that the government has issued as part of its economic recovery efforts, but the main components are the Social Security and Medicare trust funds. Like corporate reserves (for depreciation, for bad debts, etc.), they are estimates of what the government will have to pay current and future recipients of Social Security and Medicare to meet its statutory obligations to them; only the actual expenditures are included in the annual federal budget.

Concern with the national debt focuses on the public debt component because failure to honor the obligations that the government has assumed to the owners of that debt would be a default, whereas Congress can always decide to curtail Social Security and Medicare obligations by amending the statutes that create those obligations. Were Congress to do that, it would not perturb our international relations or increase the interest rates that the Treasury would have to pay in order to borrow.

The nation's public debt has reached its highest point, relative to the size of the economy, since World War II—and is growing rapidly. Federal tax revenues are way down because of the depression, while federal spending is rising because of the stimulus and other recovery programs and because the continued aging of the population and continued rapid increases in the cost of new medical technology are increasing the cost of the Medicare program; the aging of the population is increasing the cost of the Social Security program as well. The federal budget deficit in fiscal 2009 (which ended on September 30) was $1.4 trillion—an enormous addition to the public debt. The slowness of the recovery may keep tax revenues depressed for years. Estimates of future deficits are notoriously unreliable, but, for what they are worth, the public debt is predicted to rise to $12.6 trillion by 2014.

About 45 percent of the public debt is owned by foreign governments and other foreign investors. Much of it is relatively short-term, which means that the government is constantly doing new borrowing even when the public debt is not growing. In the first three quarters of the 2009 fiscal year, the government borrowed a total of $1.37 trillion, $533 billion of it from foreigners. These are staggering figures, unprecedented in modern American history except for World War II. And while that debt was rapidly unwound after the war ended, the conditions that made this possible do not exist today. Owing to the catastrophic effects of the war on the economies of many nations, the United States ran a strong current-account surplus (that is, a trade surplus), which meant that foreigners owed us money rather than vice versa. And because of rationing during the war, which had curtailed consumption expenditures, Americans had saved a great deal of their incomes, which enabled most of the public debt to be financed internally (and anyway foreigners had little money to lend). Inflation during the war (only masked by wage and price controls) wiped out much private debt, which facilitated internal financing; people were much less burdened by debt than they had been in the 1930s. And the high income-tax rates imposed during the war were retained. Had these conditions not obtained, inflation might have been the only way of reducing the deficit to a tolerable level.

If the current economic downturn has reached bottom, and if, moreover, the climb from there will be swift, there is an argument for shifting from stimulation of the economy—whether through deficit spending or the purchase of debt by the Federal Reserve in order to keep interest rates low—to deficit reduction. If, contrariwise, the economy is likely to stay at or near the bottom of the business cycle for a long time, the danger of inflation is remote and more stimulus may be indicated, and certainly no cutting back. In November 2009, more than a year after the financial collapse, the economy was still in a seriously depressed state, with the unemployment rate at 10 percent (the "underemployment" rate, which includes workers who have stopped looking for jobs and workers who are involuntarily working only part-time, was 17.2 percent), with personal consumption expenditures and housing prices both still very low, private investment negative, the banking industry still shaky, and a new wave of defaults in both commercial and residential lending expected. With the consumer price index having fallen since 2008, anyone who had borrowed money in 2007 or early 2008, when interest rates included an inflation component, found himself having to repay the loan (if it came due now) with dollars worth more than he had anticipated. Unexpected debt burdens precipitate defaults and bankruptcies.

Many economists believed that with the economy still so depressed and likely to remain so for years, inflation would not be a serious risk for a long time. Others, pointing to the immense and growing deficits, disagreed and warned that the more the deficits were permitted to grow, the worse the aftershock would be, and the deficits would grow faster the slower the recovery. It is not possible to choose between these predictions on the basis of data, but only on the basis of temperament (optimism versus pessimism) and politics (belief in weak government versus belief in strong government). And temperament may be influenced by politics. The liberal may be pessimistic about the economic prospects because he wants the fragility of the economy and the salvational role of government to be demonstrated; the conservative may be optimistic about those prospects because he is embarrassed that the economy should fall so far that government has to step in and replace private with public demand.

If business-cycle economics were a scientific field, economists' conclusions would be "observer independent" rather than inflected with each economist's political outlook. It is when science and other methods of exact reasoning (such as logic and mathematics) give out that a person's political preconceptions are apt to influence his professional opinions. Different macroeconomists look at the same evidence, the same phenomena, and see different things. Conservative macroeconomists see a self-regulating economy, which achieves and maintains equilibrium (or an approximation to it) with minimal government regulation but is vulnerable to disruption by heavy-handed government regulation. Liberal macroeconomists see a naturally unstable economy that requires aggressive government intervention to keep it from running off the rails.

When it's impossible to make an objective choice between two courses of action—here, between stepping on the economic brakes and stepping on the economic accelerator—on the basis of which is more likely to yield the greater benefits, it may still be possible to make a rational choice by considering the consequences of error. If mistakenly stepping on the brakes would produce worse consequences than mistakenly stepping on the accelerator, we should step on the accelerator. But which would be the graver error can't be determined either. If we step on the brakes, this could reignite the depression, as happened in 1937. Even a modest increase in short-term interest rates could destabilize banking by increasing the banks' cost of capital while doing nothing to increase their revenues, which would be determined to a large extent by the interest rates on their existing long-term loans.[16] But if we step on the accelerator, the resulting increase in the budget deficit might set the stage for an inflation that could, like the inflation of the 1970s, precipitate a depression when, the inflation threatening to get out of hand, the Federal Reserve pushed up interest rates steeply.

About $2.5 trillion of federal government debt will mature in 2010 and thus will have to be rolled over. Anything the Fed does to raise interest rates will increase the interest rate that the government has to pay on new debt. An alternative is to take measures to reduce the deficit without exacerbating the economic downturn. The concern with inflation and related methods, also harmful to economic activity, to which the government might resort to deal with a swelling public debt is a concern about future government revenues and expenditures; deficit spending and mild inflation are pluses during the downturn. Tabling programs, such as health-care reform, that do not contribute to recovery from the depression (the health-care reform plan under consideration by Congress would not take effect until 2013) would alleviate the concern about a future inflation and by doing so reduce long-term interest rates (which contain an inflation premium),

16. Stephen H. Axilrod, *Inside the Fed: Monetary Policy and Its Management, Martin through Greenspan to Bernanke* 56 (2009).

and that would speed recovery. I am not impressed by suggestions that radical health-care reform would cut the public debt by reducing the rate of increase of health-care costs. The only kind of reform that would do that would be reform that reduced the amount of health care that Americans receive, and the political obstacles to such reform seem insurmountable.

As the summer of 2009 approached and the economy seemed to be improving, the interest rate on ten-year Treasury bonds rose to almost 4 percent and the interest rate on thirty-year mortgages to almost 6 percent. These rate increases contributed to a continued decline in housing prices and rise in foreclosures, which reduced the value of mortgage-backed securities and so contributed to the distress of the banks as well as reducing household wealth.

The increase in long-term interest rates suggested that an expectation of future inflation was forming. Such an expectation does not increase prices immediately and does not affect short-term interest rates, but it does increase long-term interest rates. One might think that an increase in interest rates that was due to an anticipation of inflation would have *no* effect on economic activity, including housing prices, because borrowers would expect to be paying the higher interest rates in cheaper dollars. But this ignores liquidity constraints. If you want to refinance your mortgage, or to finance the purchase of a house with a fixed-payment mortgage, and the mortgage interest rate has risen in anticipation of a future inflation, you will have to shell out more cash each month starting now, and you may be unable to afford to do that because your wages will not have increased in anticipation of inflation.[17]

The surge in long-term interest rates didn't last. By the end of

17. Unless you are represented by a union. Since collective bargaining agreements, which fix wages, are usually for three years, the inflation rate anticipated for that period will be a subject of negotiation between the union and the employer.

November the yield on ten-year Treasury bonds had fallen nearly to 3 percent and the thirty-year mortgage rate was under 5 percent. These declines reflected pessimism about the pace of the economic recovery. But a long-run inflation threat remained. Between May 2008 and May 2009 the Federal Reserve's balance sheet had ballooned from $1.3 trillion to $2.2 trillion; as late as mid-December it was still $2.2 trillion. The concept of the Federal Reserve's balance sheet is obscure, however, and let me pause to explain it. Like a firm, the Fed has a balance sheet in which assets equal liabilities. The Fed's major assets in normal times are the Treasury bills that it borrows and lends in order to jigger the federal funds rate. The Fed's major liabilities are money, both currency and the cash accounts in Federal Reserve banks. It is odd to think of cash as a liability. But it is, in the sense that currency, plus money in Federal Reserve banks, are what the Fed "owes"—what it must give out—to obtain assets, such as Treasury bills. The increase on the liability side of the Fed's balance sheet since the crash of 2008 consists largely of accounts in Federal Reserve banks on which banks can draw to make loans or other investments. They are thus the excess reserves of which I have spoken. They are sitting in the commercial banks' bank accounts in Federal Reserve banks, and the banks can draw on them at any time. Because they are not doing so, however, the amount of money *in circulation* is not rising yet. As long as newly created money is not in circulation, that is, is not being used to buy goods and services, it does not create inflation.

But suppose the economy turns up and the hoarded money is put into circulation and spent, and in fact is spent faster than the increase in the output of the recovering economy. Then prices will rise. The Fed can check this tendency by selling Treasury securities and retiring the cash it obtains in the sales, thus reducing the amount of cash in the economy. But by doing so it will push up interest rates. Maybe it will be afraid to do that because high interest rates slow economic activity. In that event there will be inflation, which can get out of hand.

After the financial collapse of September 2008, the Fed began paying interest on banks' excess reserves in order to prevent the federal funds rate from dropping all the way to zero. Since interest paid by the Fed is risk-free, no bank would lend money at a lower interest rate, so the Fed's rate put a floor under all bank interest rates, including interbank rates. There is an element of paradox in trying to encourage interbank lending by placing a floor under the federal funds rate, but remember that that rate is a notional rate, which has an important signaling function. If it falls to zero, this tells the banks, Don't lend; put your cash in Treasury securities. By paying interest on excess reserves, then, the Fed was encouraging the banks to expand their reserves rather than use their cash to buy Treasury securities, for those reserves formed at least a potential source of credit.

Paying interest on excess reserves has a further significance, however; it enables the Fed, by adjusting the interest rate, to check the speed at which those reserves are lent and by being lent increase the amount of money in circulation. The higher the interest rate, the smaller the danger of a sudden emptying of bank accounts thick with excess reserves into the "real" economy of spending on goods and services. The interest rate that will curb that danger doesn't have to be as high as private interest rates are because there is no default risk to worry the borrower.

In assessing the risk of inflation, we must also bear in mind that the $1 trillion in excess reserves are a liability, offset by an equivalent amount of assets that include the private debt that the Fed acquired as part of its program of "credit easing." As that debt is paid back, or if it is sold by the Fed to private lenders, the banks' excess reserves will drop correspondingly. Suppose, for example, that the Fed sold some of the credit card debt that it has acquired to a bank. The bank would pay the Fed cash equal to the value of the debt, and both sides of the Fed's balance sheet would decline and with it the amount of excess bank reserves, which, remember, are deposits in Federal Reserve banks.

The obstacles to using the interest rate on reserves, or other measures, to prevent excess reserves from being converted into loans at too rapid a rate, therefore causing inflation, are ones of timing and politics. They are serious obstacles (to which I'll return) to the Fed's ability to engineer an inflation-free elimination of excess money from the economy without raising interest rates steeply. If it does raise them steeply, there may be a double whammy, because the Treasury may be doing the same thing by selling Treasury securities in great quantity to finance the ballooning federal budget deficits. The more it sells, the higher the interest rate that it will have to pay, and that will force up all interest rates as well as increasing the national debt.

When the bill is presented for the costs incurred in fighting the depression, it may be too large to pay either by raising taxes or by continued borrowing. At that point the only alternatives may be drastic reductions in government spending, which are likely to be politically infeasible, or inflation, which can wipe out a debt completely and can be engineered smoothly by what is called "monetizing" the national debt. That means that instead of selling Treasury bonds to investors, the government would sell them to the Federal Reserve. (In fact the Fed has bought $300 billion of such bonds in order to reduce the interest rate that the Treasury would have to pay if it tried to borrow all the money required to finance government spending.) The Fed would pay for the bonds by creating money, thus expanding the money supply relative to the output of goods and services. Inflation would soar, given annual deficits expected to exceed a trillion dollars for the indefinite future.

Remarks by Paul Krugman can help to bring the inflation aftershock problem into focus.[18] Krugman had been trying for some time to correct a misunderstanding by the prominent historian (and author of an excellent book on the history of bank-

18. At a panel discussion of the economic situation. Paul Krugman et al., "The Crisis and How to Deal with It," *New York Review of Books,* June 11, 2009, p. 10.

ing) Niall Ferguson. Ferguson had argued that the monetary and fiscal responses to a recession or depression—reducing interest rates by expanding the supply of money and increasing the demand for goods and services by deficit financing of public works —operate at cross purposes. The cost of public works has to be financed by borrowing, and any increase in borrowing raises interest rates and therefore reduces the effectiveness of the monetary response. But as Krugman points out, the fall in private demand for goods and services, which provides the rationale for deficit spending as a spur to economic recovery, has been matched (not dollar for dollar, however) by the rise in personal savings. Deficit spending on public works is a way of using the pool of savings to increase investment and therefore employment. "Keynesian policy . . . takes excess desired savings and translates them into some kind of spending. If the private sector won't do it, the government will."[19]

The relation between savings and productive investment can be seen most clearly by imagining that the government decided to finance the public works program by selling "Victory [over Depression]" bonds to the general public. Because the bonds would be safe (the risk of the United States' defaulting on its obligations is close to zero), most of the hoarders would be quick to buy them in lieu of holding cash that carries no interest at all; and so the government would not have to pay a high rate of interest. The government isn't financing the public works program in this way, but the economic effect may be the same. If a money-market mutual fund in which a person has placed some of his savings buys government securities in order to be able to pay interest on its money-market accounts, the account holder is indirectly financing the government.

Ferguson might not disagree, because his real concern may be not with the impact of the stimulus program on interest rates but with the cumulative effect of *all* current and planned federal ex-

19. These and subsequent quotations are from the panel discussion.

penditures on the long-term solvency of the U.S. government, including expenditures financed by the creation of money by the Federal Reserve. That is a legitimate concern, although it does not prove that the stimulus program is unwise. The longer and deeper the depression, the bigger will be the federal deficit; so if the stimulus program makes the depression shorter and shallower, it may not increase the total public debt.

Krugman is an advocate of universal health care and other costly social programs, and he argues that the depression has underscored "the importance of a strong social safety net," such as Europeans have. Their generous safety net has reduced the human costs of the depression to them "because Europeans don't lose their health care when they lose their jobs. They don't find themselves with essentially no support once their trivial unemployment check has fallen off. We have nothing underneath. When Americans lose their jobs, they fall into the abyss." But safety nets are costly, and, Krugman continues, "there are people who say we should not be worrying about things like universal health care in the crisis, we need to solve the crisis. But this is exactly the time when the importance of having a decent social safety net is driven home to everybody, which makes it a very good time to actually move ahead on these other things."

He is saying that the time is ripe in a *political* sense for a basic change in the management of the American economy. He may be right. One effect of a European-style safety-net economy is to reduce the amplitude of the swings that we call the business cycle, and at the moment that amplitude, the human costs of which are increased by the absence of a strong safety net, is hurting many Americans. Because the European-style safety net raises labor costs, in part by making it difficult to lay off workers, unemployment is higher in Europe than in the United States in boom periods; employers are reluctant to hire if it will be difficult for them to lay off workers when the boom ends. In the current bust our unemployment rate has been about the same as the average

European rate (after correction for differences attributable to different definitions of unemployment),[20] rather than higher, as Krugman's analysis would seem to imply. But he is right that unemployment inflicts greater hardship in the United States than in most European countries.

Even if the European approach were thought preferable to ours and compatible with our political and social culture, the costs of moving toward it in the present economic setting would have to be estimated and given their due weight, which Krugman is unwilling to do. The costs are of two kinds: A costly and ambitious program of social reform increases the uncertainty of the economic environment,[21] which is a downer from the standpoint of economic recovery. And the costs of ambitious social reform, when added to the costs of the depression recovery programs and to the "normal" budget deficit augmented by the decline of tax revenues in a depression, may result in a catastrophic increase in the national debt.

Krugman has derided what he calls "the big inflation scare."[22] He acknowledges that the Federal Reserve "has been buying lots of debt both from the government and from the private sector, and paying for these purchases by crediting banks with extra reserves." But that creates no danger of inflation because "banks aren't lending out their extra reserves." Instead they're "just sitting on them—in effect, they're sending the money right back to the Fed. So the Fed isn't really printing money after all." The

20. See Matthew Saltmarsh, "Jobless Rate in Europe Rises Further," *New York Times*, June 2, 2009, p. B5.

21. Kathleen Parker, in "Anxiety Attacks," *Washington Post*, Aug. 8, 2009, p. A15, quotes a friend as saying: "Angst about health care is real because people are just anxious in general. They don't have jobs, and those who do are worried about losing them. They're saying, 'Holy crap, I've got $10,000 on my credit card, and you're talking about change? Guess what, dude, I can't handle any more change right now.'"

22. Paul Krugman, "The Big Inflation Scare," *New York Times*, May 28, 2009, p. A25.

Bank of Japan "purchased debt on a huge scale between 1997 and 2003," yet there was no inflation. Nor are huge budget deficits, whether financed by borrowing or by increasing the supply of money, bound to create inflation. The United States "emerged from World War II with debt exceeding 120 percent of G.D.P." yet did not have to resort to inflation to reduce the burden of the national debt to a tolerable level.

I noted earlier that conditions are different today. But there is at least a faint echo of the earlier experience, because the personal savings rate is now rising, and a reduction in private debt makes it easier to repay public debt. Some of the increased savings has taken the form of increased purchases of Treasury securities—no surprise, considering people's economic fears. Buying Treasury securities (government bonds) means lending to the government, and at low rates because there is no default risk and because the demand for private borrowing is weak. That was Krugman's point with regard to the effect of the stimulus on interest rates; it would be small given the amount of private savings. But the point has a broader significance.

Krugman is right that the danger of inflation *in the short run* is small. To see why, imagine that the national income is $1,000 and is spent entirely on consumption goods, which consist solely of ten 1983 Chevrolet Caprices. Then the average price of a Caprice will be $100. The following year, all the Caprices bought the previous year have rusted away, so ten more 1983 Caprices are brought to market. Only this time the government has doubled the supply of money. Again the entire national income, now $2,000, is spent on the Caprices, so the average price is now $200. That is inflation—an increase in price due solely to an increase in the ratio of money in circulation to the goods available for purchase.

But "in circulation" is vital. For suppose that in this second year the people become fearful and decide to stuff half their income under their mattresses. As a result, only $1,000 is spent on

Caprices, and so the average price is unchanged, even though the supply of money has doubled. For it is only money that is put to use to buy things that influences prices. The depression, as we know, has caused both banks and individuals to hoard cash. But the curtailment of spending is, we hope, a temporary condition. As the economy improves, the banks will start to lend, and individuals will spend more. It is misleading to say as Krugman does that the Fed hasn't really created money by increasing the banks' reserves because the banks are sitting on them. When they start lending, they will be increasing the amount of money in circulation (before the onset of the current depression, total excess bank reserves were only a few billion dollars), and there will be a risk of inflation.

And the money the Federal Reserve has created in an effort to lower interest rates and stimulate economic activity is only a small part of the liabilities that the government has assumed in an effort to fight the depression. The grand total of current and planned commitments, both actual and contingent (guaranties), has been estimated at almost $11 trillion, though most of that amount will be recouped or avoided—eventually.

We have, besides the liabilities specially incurred to combat the depression, a "structural" budget deficit of some $500 billion a year; I call it structural because it seems to be deeply embedded in the "normal" economy. The deficit swells in a depression because tax revenues plummet and the cost of unemployment benefits soars. And it is growing annually because of the growth in Social Security and Medicare spending. Some of the Obama Administration's long-range program of social and economic improvement will be enacted—without being fully funded. And quite apart from the health-care and climate-change components of the program, the Administration hopes to make programs that account for $140 billion of the $787 billion in planned stimulus spending permanent. I do not know how much annual spending on such programs is contemplated, but if, say, it were $50 billion, this would raise the $500 billion structural deficit by 10 percent.[23]

So the nation indeed has a long-run budget problem. What it does not have is a politically feasible long-run solution. There is much wasteful government spending—but try cutting it! We have low taxes by international standards and by comparison with tax rates in the 1950s, when our economic growth was more rapid than it is now—but try raising them! Americans are not so heavily taxed that financing an increase in the national debt by higher taxes would be intolerable. But Congress and the public seem adamant against any nontrivial tax increases, even when they take the form of closing ridiculous loopholes, and against spending reductions as well, even in fossil programs such as farm subsidies.

Every sensible path to a long-run solution to the nation's long-run fiscal problems, which have been greatly exacerbated by the depression, seems blocked by special interests and political demagoguery. We are likely to be left with either inflation, the standard debtor's remedy, or an increased dependence on loans by foreign nations and foreign investors—and at increasing interest rates, because the more we borrow, the higher the interest rates we have to pay. If we borrow 2 percent more per year and the interest rate rises by 1 percent a year, after one year we are paying 3 percent more interest and after five years 16 percent more. Interest paid on loans from abroad drains American wealth when the loans are financing budget deficits distended by inefficient government programs.

We can't be comforted by Japan's example of promiscuous money creation that does not lead to inflation, because the Japanese people were great hoarders until recently; in economic jar-

---

23. Alex Brill and Amy Roden, "A Sickening Deficit," *Forbes,* Oct. 19, 2009, www.forbes.com/2009/10/18/health-care-stimulus-deficit-opinions-con tributors-alex-brill-amy-roden.html (visited Dec. 7, 2009).

gon, their "propensity to consume" was much lower than Americans'. We can't take comfort in our situation at the end of World War II either. Besides the points I noted earlier, the end of the war led to a conversion of military to civil production that resulted in a large increase in the sale and purchase of consumer goods, which sopped up the money that had accumulated in people's savings accounts because of the high wages that full employment in a wartime economy (with rationing, which pushed up the savings rate by reducing the goods and services available for consumption) had generated.

Yet in July of 2009 Bernanke told Congress that there was no danger of inflation (and he has repeated this since, right up to the end of the year), even though the Fed had decided to keep short-term interest rates very low and the banks were awash with excess reserves. Bernanke explained that if unwanted inflation was looming, the Fed could head it off in a variety of ways. I explained two of them earlier (paying high interest on bank reserves and selling the Fed's private debt to the banks); he mentioned others as well. But there are two clouds in this otherwise sunny sky. The first is that the device for reducing the amount of money in circulation with which Bernanke led in his testimony—paying interest on bank reserves on order to increase interest rates—has not been tried before. It sounds as if it would work, but until it is tried, no one can be sure.

Second is a statement made shortly after Bernanke's testimony by Richard Fisher, the president of the Federal Reserve Bank of Dallas and thus a member (albeit no longer a voting member) of the Federal Open Market Committee, the branch of the Fed that regulates the money supply. After summarizing Bernanke's "exit strategies" from the current "easy money" Fed policy, Fisher said that "we [that is, the Fed] know full well that monetary policy trickles in with a lag and that we will have to 'pull the trigger' of tightening policy *well before it is politically convenient.*"[24]

24. Richard W. Fisher, "Two Areas of Present Concern: The Economic

What I think he meant was the following. As the economy recovers, cash hoarding will decline and cash in circulation will
therefore increase. The ratio of cash to goods and services will
therefore rise, probably faster than output, and so inflation
will increase. But before it increases significantly, the increase in
lending will have stimulated economic activity, speeding recovery from the depression. Even if the Fed has the technical capa-
bility of stopping the rising inflation in its tracks (as Fisher, like
Bernanke, is confident it does), it may by doing so slow or even
stop the recovery—and at a time when the unemployment rate
will probably still be high. We know from experience in 1979–
1982 that high interest rates, engineered by the Fed to stop inflation, can coexist with both high inflation and high unemployment—a politically unpopular combination that helped
Reagan beat Carter in 1980. For high interest rates do not automatically stop inflation in its tracks. If people think that the increase in interest rates is temporary and that inflation will continue, they will keep on borrowing and spending because they
will not think the high interest rates "real"—they'll think they'll
be able to pay back their loans with cheap money. In that event
the ratio of money in circulation to goods and services will not
diminish.

Partly because of Paul Volcker's forceful personality and com-
manding presence (he is six foot eight), which helped convince
the nation that he was serious about stopping inflation no matter
at what cost, and partly because of Reagan's ideology, the Federal Reserve was allowed to crush inflation at the cost of a severe
recession in the early years of Reagan's presidency. Reagan got
some protective coloration from the fact that Volcker had been
appointed by Reagan's predecessor, Carter, a Democrat. Obama

Outlook and the Pathology of Too-Big-to-Fail: Remarks before the Senior
Delegates' Roundtable of the Fixed Income Forum," July 23, 2009, www
.dallasfed.org/news/speeches/fisher/2009/fs090723.cfm (emphasis added)
(visited Oct. 22, 2009).

will not have that protection, because he has decided to reappoint Bernanke, who will preside over a Volcker-type induced recession should there be one.

If history repeats itself and inflation looms, I have no doubt that Richard Fisher will want to pull the trigger, because he is a famous inflation hawk. But will Bernanke? And a majority of the Federal Open Market Committee? We are to imagine banks sitting on hundreds of billions of dollars in excess reserves while businesses and consumers are clamoring for credit. The Fed does not operate in a political vacuum. It has no constitutional independence from the political process. It is unpopular in Congress, and Democrats are not as hawkish about inflation as Republicans are, because the debtor class tends to support Democrats. Fisher may be overoptimistic about the Fed's willingness to "pull the trigger" regardless of "political inconvenience." At the other end of the political spectrum, liberal economists like Krugman are too optimistic about price stability. They argue that inflation is no danger, period. But I suspect that what they actually believe is different—that inflation, unless it gets out of hand (unless it exceeds 10 percent, say), is not such a big deal. Inflation is a tax on cash balances and on fixed-interest loans. It is not an efficient tax, but few taxes actually imposed in our political system are efficient. It would be interesting to see a serious economic study of the social costs, and possible social benefits, of allowing inflation to rise above normal levels in the recovery phase of the economy.

Yet even Krugman does not advocate paying down our public debt by inflating. Nor, I think, does he want to increase our dependence on foreign lenders, at what undoubtedly would be increasing interest rates as our public debt grows. I am sure he does not favor outright repudiation of the public debt, runaway inflation, or a formal devaluation of the dollar. But neither does he want to shrink government spending. That leaves higher taxes as the only way to bring our deficits under control. On the Sunday television talk shows on August 2, 2009, Lawrence Summers and Timothy Geithner, the President's top economic advisers, sensibly refused to rule out tax increases not limited to persons with incomes above $250,000. The next day the President's press secretary stated without equivocation that the President would not agree to any increase in taxes paid by persons with incomes below that level. The only solution to our fiscal woes had been taken off the table.

Or had it? The President is a lawyer. Lawyers are masters of equivocation. Perhaps what has been taken off the table is just increases in *income tax rates* until the economy *recovers* from the current depression. Perhaps the door has been left ajar for other forms of tax increase, such as cutting deductions (which do not affect the nominal tax *rate*) and increasing federal income tax rates in a year or two when (one hopes) the gross domestic product will have returned to its trend line; or even for imposing other taxes, such as a federal value-added tax, a tax on financial transactions, or a tax on online sales.

Let us hope that there is that much running room; the alternatives seem either less feasible politically (such as cutting spending) or more harmful to the nation—as Summers and Geithner well know.

WHAT LESSONS HAVE WE
LEARNED FROM THE CRISIS?

II

7

The economic crisis that began late in 2007 has been a calamity the effects of which may be felt for many years. The desire to avoid a repetition of it is intense. That desire is more likely to be fulfilled if we can pinpoint the causes of the crisis, but that is not easy to do because there is as yet no authoritative study of the causes. Congress has created a ten-member Financial Crisis Inquiry Commission, headed by a former state treasurer, to investigate the causes. The commission is bipartisan rather than nonpartisan; there are six Democrats and four Republicans, and most of them have strong partisan affiliations, as revealed by their campaign contributions. I am skeptical that the commission's inquiry will be impartial and professional, and for the further reason that none of its members is a professional economist, though several have experience in economic policymaking. Nor is its executive director an economist—he is an antitrust lawyer. The commission has also been sluggish in staffing up—six months after its creation, the executive director was its sole employee. Given the complexity of the economic issues and the commission's limited economic expertise, its inquiry is likely to devolve into an investigation of frauds and errors (and there were plenty of both, I am sure) of lenders and borrowers during the housing and credit bubbles. There may be some value in such an investigation, but it will not get at the root causes of the crisis or point the way toward sensible reforms. Anyway the report, not due till December 15, 2010, will postdate statutory and regulatory reform of financial regulation.

Without awaiting the results of an authoritative study, people are pointing fingers of blame in all directions. Many of these are people who are eager to deflect blame from themselves or who see some other career advantage in pointing the finger in the direction they do. The left is blaming the stupid, greedy, reckless, and overpaid bankers (as it deems all bankers to be), and is being joined by Congress and many in the media, who sense political and commercial advantage, respectively, in a simplistic populist explanation for economic failures. Some on the left are also blaming financial deregulation and lax enforcement (during the Bush Administration) of the remaining regulations and conservative macroeconomists and conservative finance theorists for arguing that depressions were a thing of the past and asset-price bubbles an illusion. The right is blaming the government for encouraging mortgage lending to people with poor credit. Investors are blaming credit-rating agencies for rating the top tranches of mortgage-backed securities triple-A. Behavioral economists are blaming everyone in sight, including bankers and borrowers, for exhibiting irrational exuberance during the boom that preceded the bust. The chairman and members of the Federal Reserve are blaming the fragmented structure of financial regulation, the limitations of the Fed's legal authority and economic power, the global "savings glut," and mistaken assessments by bankers of the risks created by novel financial instruments. There is little *disinterested* analysis of the causes of the depression; most of it seems motivated by political or career concerns.

A disinterested analysis begins with recognition that banking (by which, I remind the reader, I mean financial intermediation in general) is both inherently risky *and* critical to economic stability. If it were critical but safe, there would be no problem. If it were risky but not critical (like the airline industry), there would be no problem. It is because the banking industry is inherently risky that it can collapse without careful macroeconomic management by government, and it is because it is critical to a modern economy that if it does collapse, it can bring the rest of the economy down with it, as September 2008 proved.

Banks were safe for so long that it became difficult to comprehend their inherent riskiness. They can be made safe by regulation, but that is not their natural state, and so if regulation is removed they may career out of control. Remember that to cover administrative costs and generate a return for its shareholders, a bank has to borrow its capital at a lower cost than it lends it. It can do this by borrowing short-term and lending long-term, since short-term interest rates are lower. But they are lower because the lender has less risk, which means that banks can earn the spread between cost and revenue that they need in order to survive only by placing their capital at risk. And it is at risk not only because they are lending long but also because, having borrowed short, they are at risk of having to return their borrowed capital when their capital is tied up in long-term loans. The rug may be pulled out from under them at any time.

Because the lending of borrowed capital is the essence of banking, we expect a bank to have much higher leverage—a much higher ratio of debt to equity—than a nonfinancial firm. And that is what we observe. The ratio is not considered excessive for a commercial bank unless it exceeds 20 to 1. What holds down leverage in nonfinancial firms is that as it rises, the risk of bankruptcy increases, because debt is a fixed cost and so does not fall when revenue falls. Also the greater the risk of bankruptcy, the higher the interest rate that the firm must pay on the debt it takes on. Borrowing short holds down the interest rate by minimizing the lender's risk, but the short-term credit needs of nonfinancial firms are limited. Banks, in contrast, being in the business of providing a market for short-term lenders, such as demand depositors, cannot avoid taking on a great deal of short-term debt. And unless the interest-rate spread between short- and long-term debt is very large, the bank needs to maintain a high ratio of debt to equity, because otherwise the spread would not be large enough in relation to the amount of equity to compensate the shareholders adequately. Only if the bank makes *very* risky loans does a fat equity cushion make sense. That is the business model of hedge funds. Hedge funds use short-term capital to make highly risky investments because their investors seek abnormal returns (but protect themselves by their right to withdraw their money on relatively short notice should the fund get into trouble), and as a result they have less leverage than commercial banks.

The lower interest rates are, the greater is the demand for loans, which makes it attractive for banks to borrow cheaply and thus increase their leverage (if the regulatory authorities permit) and with it both risk and expected return. And by securitizing debt, banks discovered, they could turn over their capital faster and thus do more lending. Instead of waiting for a mortgage loan or other type of loan to be repaid, they could sell the loan in the form of a security and use the proceeds of the sale to make another securitized loan. As long as interest rates stayed low and prices of houses and other assets rose, the collateral for loans was increasing in value and the default rate was falling, and on both counts the loans backing the securities seemed safe, which made the securities seem safe, which further encouraged banks to increase their leverage.

Securities created from residential mortgages were vulnerable to a nationwide fall in housing prices. But how much weight should the banking industry have given to the risk of a decline steep enough to bring down the securities? That risk was what statisticians call "tail risk." The well-known "normal distribution" of probabilities, and variants of it such as the student's t-distribution, form a bell-shaped curve the ends, or "tails," of which denote very small probabilities. If the mean of a normal distribution is 500 and the standard deviation is 100, then 99.7 percent of the observations comprising the distribution will fall between 200 and 800, and hence fewer than one-third of 1 percent of them will be smaller than 200 or larger than 800.

The perceived probability in 2005 that housing prices reflected a nationwide housing bubble that would burst and drive the banking industry into a condition of near insolvency (indeed, without the bailouts, the banking industry, most of the assets of which were and are owned by a handful of big banks, would have been insolvent by the fall of 2008) was small—a tail risk. And unlike the example I just gave, the risk could not be quantified; it was an example of "uncertainty," as distinct from calculable risk—a distinction that will figure importantly in the next chapter.

There are always tail risks. But why should businessmen worry about them? They have plenty else to worry about. They are well aware of the riskiness of their business and take measures to control risk and uncertainty.[1] But a tail risk is likely to occur only in the long run, and in the long run we're dead. The point that commentators on the economic crisis keep overlooking is that a risk too small to worry a banker may create an expected cost to the economy as a whole that is great enough to warrant close regulation of bank risks. And regulation is the responsibility of government. Markets are not "self-regulating," as Alan Greenspan believed, with the serious consequences that we are living with. (To his credit, Greenspan has acknowledged being mistaken, unlike Bernanke, who made the same mistake. Greenspan has not, however, acknowledged the consequences of his mistake.)

On May 1, 2009, a macroeconomist at Northwestern University, Robert Gordon, predicted that the depression would bottom

1. See, for example, Alexandra Michel and Stanton Wortham, *Bullish on Uncertainty; How Organizational Cultures Transform Participants* (2009).

out (in the sense that GDP would stop declining) in that month or the next.[2] He based the prediction on "a surprisingly tight historical relationship in past US recessions between the cyclical peak in new claims for unemployment insurance . . . and the subsequent trough." His prediction was based entirely on past data. It was an exercise in induction. It assumed that the future would be just like the past. But there was a tail risk that the future would not repeat the past, and Gordon made no effort to estimate that risk. This is not a criticism; it could not be estimated. Similarly, the risk that housing prices would dive to a level at which the triple-A tranches of debt securities would lose most of their value, like the risk of a terrorist attack or of an attempt to assassinate the Pope, could not be quantified.

As Keynes famously wrote (see next chapter), the "urge to action" induces businessmen to take risks that cannot be calculated. It induced Professor Gordon to predict when our current economic downturn will reach its nadir. And it motivated, and motivates, risky lending.

What is undeniable is that many of the mortgages packaged in mortgage-backed securities were highly risky; and it is at this point that the political right swings into action, arguing that making mortgage loans to persons who were at high risk of defaulting was a consequence of government policy rather than of private business decisions. The government subsidizes home ownership, for example by allowing the deduction of mortgage and home-equity interest from income tax but not (in the case of individuals as distinct from businesses) other interest and by exempting home sales from capital-gains tax; and laws such as the Community Reinvestment Act of 1977, along with measures by the Clinton and Bush Administrations, encouraged risky mortgage lending.

2. Robert J. Gordon, "Green Shoot or Dead Twig: Can Unemployment Claims Predict the End of the American Recession?" *Vox*, May 1, 2009, www.voxeu.org/index.php?q=node/3524 (visited Dec. 7, 2009).

The particular *bêtes noires* of conservative analysts are the Federal National Mortgage Association (Fannie Mae) and the Federal Home Mortgage Association (Freddie Mac), the huge mortgage companies that financed much of the housing bubble and, facing bankruptcy, were taken over by the government. Their business was to buy residential mortgages, thus expanding the market for such mortgages. They were pioneers in mortgage securitization, packaging the mortgages they bought into mortgage-backed securities that brought additional capital into the mortgage market.

Fannie and Freddie were "government-sponsored enterprises," though until they were taken over by the government they were private corporations. Their pertinacious and well-informed critic, Peter Wallison of the American Enterprise Institute, contends that these GSEs, along with the laws that encouraged them to make risky mortgage loans, were primarily responsible for the housing bubble.[3]

I have no truck with the GSEs. Harbingers of the crony capitalism that one finds in countries like Russia and China, they illustrate the dangers of trying to hybridize business and government. Because of their official government sponsorship, lenders assumed correctly that they would not be permitted to default, and so the GSEs could borrow at very low interest rates (almost as low as the interest rates at which the U.S. government borrows) to finance their activities. This enabled them to earn huge profits; the quid pro quo was their cooperation with the govern-

3. See, for example, Peter J. Wallison, "The True Origins of This Financial Crisis" (American Enterprise Institute for Public Policy Research, Feb. 2009); Wallison, "Worse Than You Think: What Went Wrong at Fannie and Freddie—and What Still Might," *National Review,* Nov. 3, 2008, p. 36; Wallison and Charles W. Calmomiris, "Blame Fannie Mae and Congress for the Credit Mess," *Wall Street Journal,* Sept. 30, 2008, p. A29. Wallison is not alone. See Johan Norbert, *Financial Fiasco: How America's Infatuation with Homeownership and Easy Money Created the Economic Crisis,* ch. 2 (2009), for a more dispassionate treatment of the issue.

ment's policy—irresistible because bipartisan—of promoting a nation of homeowners.

I disapprove not only of GSEs but also of encouraging home-ownership—and I note that an economic advantage of a nation of renters is that relocation to a different city or state to pursue new job opportunities is easier when one rents rather than owns one's home, and job mobility is one of the great strengths of the American economy. And were it not for the policy of encouraging homeownership, and the implementation of that policy by government-sponsored institutions (and by the Federal Housing Administration, a government agency), there would be less homeownership and fewer mortgages, and so less risk of a financial crisis triggered by the collapse of a housing bubble financed by the banking industry. But I doubt that this was a big factor in the financial crisis. Wallison exaggerates the effect of the Community Reinvestment Act, the GSEs, and the Clinton and Bush Administrations' "ownership society" propaganda in fostering the risky mortgage lending that got the banking industry and through it the nonfinancial economy into such deep trouble.

Wallison contends that the GSEs and the government's encouragement of risky mortgage lending caused loose lending practices to spread to the prime loan market, vastly increasing the availability of credit for mortgages and thereby leading to speculation in houses and ultimately to the housing bubble. It is true that the GSEs provided a market for mortgage-backed securities backed by subprime mortgages and thus encouraged the creation of such securities. But when the default rate on the mortgages that they had bought skyrocketed, the loss fell on the GSEs rather than on the banking industry as a whole, and the government quickly took over the GSEs, assuming their debts. The economic impact of the irresponsible lending, fostered by its implicit federal guaranty, was contained.

The broker-dealers and other banks that created mortgage-backed securities by securitizing mortgages sold to them by mortgage specialists, and that then sold interests in the securities to other banks, hedge funds, and other investors, did not do this because of the GSEs. The GSEs' provision of a market for substandard mortgage loans and mortgage-backed securities was irrelevant to the decision of private investors to invest in such securities. Had the banks and other investors thought subprime mortgage loans excessively risky, they would have ceded this part of the market entirely to the GSEs. There was no governmental pressure on anyone to create or invest in mortgage-backed securities.

The Community Reinvestment Act doesn't even apply to financial intermediaries other than commercial banks and thrifts. And while the commercial banks and the thrifts were major originators of mortgages, including subprime mortgages, that were securitized, they did not do so because of the act. These were lucrative transactions.

And finally it's not even clear that the loans that the GSEs bought and packaged into mortgage-backed securities were of lower average quality than the ones that were issued privately. There was government pressure, but it was pressure exerted against an open door. There were profit opportunities in subprime loans, and the opportunities were eagerly grasped by profit-making institutions—including the GSEs.

Which brings me back to the basic point that banks engaged in highly risky lending—with their eyes more or less wide open—because such lending was vastly profitable: too profitable for the good of the economy as a whole, but too profitable only because interest rates were too low and banking regulation too lax. Everything else, I believe, was secondary.

At this point another coterie of suspected culprits swims into view—the credit-rating agencies that gave triple-A ratings to the senior tranches of mortgage-backed securities. This is said to have lured unwary investors into buying those tranches. I expressed my skepticism concerning this allegation in chapter 3.

The compensation practices of the banks have also been

blamed for the financial collapse. It is another claim about which I expressed skepticism in that chapter. Demand for loans was rising, and was being met to a great extent by the creation and sale of tranches of debt securities, which are highly complex financial instruments, as are the credit-default swaps and other derivatives that played an increasing role in financing. With these developments, the banks' demand for financially sophisticated staff soared. Competition to hire the best and brightest led to high salaries and generous bonuses, which did reward risk taking. More important, however, was the sheer increase in the size of banks and in the number of bankers required to service the increased demands for credit. Between June 2000 and June 2007 the number of persons employed in the financial services industry (minus insurance) grew from 5.2 million to 6.1 million, or by almost 20 percent. (By June 2009 it had fallen to 5.5 million.) When businesses expand rapidly, they suffer a loss of control. In the banking industry this took the dangerous form of a loss of control over trading, lending, and other investment decisions of lower-level executives—traders, loan officers, and other investment officers. Since risk and return are correlated and a small though nonnegligible risk is unlikely to materialize within a short time, performance-based compensation may tempt an investment officer to make an investment even if its expected value over the long run is negative. Many of their managers were technically sophisticated, but the longer they had been in management, the less likely it was that their technical skills were up to date. The rapidity with which investment methodologies progressed widened the knowledge gap between the latest hires and their supervisors and made it more difficult for the latter to rein in the former.

The math whizzes whom the banks hired to manage risk are being blamed for having failed to calculate it correctly. More likely, the growing size of banks elongated the management hierarchy by increasing the number of supervisory levels, causing the limitations of the mathematical models of risk—though communicated by the math whizzes to their immediate supervisors—to fade from corporate consciousness as they were relayed through multiple layers to the top of the hierarchy. Senior managers had difficulty in assessing and limiting highly risky deals put together by members of a younger generation equipped with the latest tools of what came to be called "financial engineering." Novel financial instruments were invented in an effort to maximize loan volume at acceptable levels of risk, but as with most innovations there were unintended consequences, which turned out to be negative.

I said in the last chapter that we mustn't let the financial collapse of 2008 give risk a bad name. But this advice is hard to follow because hindsight turns risk into certainty. Once a calamity occurs, it is seen as inevitable. This is not an illusion: it *was* caused, and once the causes were in place, the effect *had* to happen. "Hindsight bias" is not a misunderstanding about causality but a confusion of actual with perceived probability. The actual probability of the financial collapse was 100 percent, because it happened; but the perceived probability was very much lower—otherwise it would not have happened. A financial collapse such as occurred in 2008 was always a possibility, but it could not be quantified, and it seemed to most people, including most experts inside and outside the banking industry, to be slight.

Banks were doing what they are supposed to be doing in a capitalist society, which is satisfying demand for their products at the lowest possible cost and the highest possible price. Profit maximization impels firms to minimize cost and, by producing what consumers most want, maximize revenue. Firms that succeed in creating a large margin of revenue over cost attract new entry, which forces cost lower and promotes product improvement and innovation. The push for better products requires emphasis. Firms do not merely meet existing demand; they also create demand. The finance industry tried to create financial products that would attract consumers and investors. Some of these products, such as subprime mortgages, were risky; and no doubt many buyers didn't fully understand the risks. But with housing prices rising and expected to continue doing so, the risks, even when fully understood, would have seemed to many people worth taking. As we know from chapter 1, buying into a suspected bubble is not necessarily irrational. It might be the only way one could afford to become a homeowner, so if one prized homeownership the risk might be worth taking. Housing prices fell so far because they had soared so high, and they had soared so high in part because the availability of subprime mortgages had drawn to the demand side of the housing market many people who could not have qualified for a conventional mortgage.

The responsibility for preventing or remedying disasters that transcend the capabilities of the private market to avoid is a governmental responsibility, which our government failed to discharge. I continue to be perplexed by how government (except for its promotion of home ownership, a secondary cause of the crisis) has managed to escape most of the blame for our current economic state. The answer has partly to do with efforts by the responsible officials to shift suspicion to others but more with the fact that blaming bankers and home buyers (or homeowners who borrowed against their home equity to finance other consumption) for being stupid, greedy, and reckless makes for a much simpler story than blaming monetary policy or banking deregulation. This doesn't make it a true story. Most bankers are pretty smart, and some of them are brilliant. If they are "greedy," it is in the sense in which most Americans (most anyone, I imagine) could be called "greedy"; they like money a lot. Yet even they don't derive *all* their job satisfaction from their monetary compensation. There is the challenge and excitement of trying to excel in a high-risk, highly competitive profession. There is also the joy of outsmarting competitors—in which respect financiers resemble highly paid athletes: in both cases the money the stars are paid not only enhances consumption opportunities but also indicates relative performance. Money is a scorecard of success. Professors have a different scorecard: for money income are substituted citations, prestigious appointments, the satisfaction of self-expression and perhaps honorary degrees, a modicum of fame, prizes. That does not make them nobler human beings.

With "reckless" we get a little closer to the truth, which is that banking is, as I keep emphasizing, an inherently risky activity. Many of the critics of banking are risk-averse, or at least averse to the kinds of risk that a businessman takes. These critics have difficulty accepting the fact that the taking of business risks implies a positive risk of bankruptcy. Bankers couldn't survive in business without taking such risks; and though they took risks in the early 2000s that were excessive from the standpoint of overall economic stability, they were encouraged—indeed, as a practical matter caused—to do so by the government. The financial deregulation movement that began in 1980 primarily involved allowing nonbanks to provide close substitutes for bank services and then allowing the banks to respond by providing the same services as the nonbanks. Even before that, in the mid-seventies, the abolition of fixed commission rates for stockbrokers—the end of the brokers' cozy cartel—had encouraged broker-dealers to maintain their profitability by engaging in risky proprietary trading—more dealing, less brokering.

Money-market mutual funds were allowed to offer interest-paying checkable accounts, which are close substitutes for demand deposit accounts in commercial banks, and the latter, to meet the money-market funds' competition, were then allowed for the first time to pay interest on deposits.[4] The combination of these two measures increased the riskiness of the banks' capital, because no longer did banks have capital on which they paid no interest, so no longer could they obtain a spread by making very safe, low-interest loans. If one needs a 3 percent spread and borrows at 3 percent, one has to charge 6 percent interest on the loans one makes with that borrowed capital. If one borrows at

4. This change was made in the Depository Institutions and Monetary Control Act of 1980.

zero interest, one needs to charge only 3 percent interest to make one's target spread.

Other federal laws preempted state restrictions on branch banking and on maximum interest rates (usury laws); allowed savings and loan associations to compete more directly with commercial banks; and by removing restrictions on commercial banks' making real estate loans enabled those banks to compete more directly with thrifts. Allowing branch banking increased competition among banks, and abrogating usury laws enabled banks to make riskier loans.[5] In 1999 banks were permitted for the first time since the early 1930s to engage in investment banking,[6] and in 2004 the Securities and Exchange Commission raised the ceiling on leverage of broker-dealers, a major component of the shadow banking industry.[7] Along the way some measures to increase regulatory control over banking were adopted,[8] but the current flowed strongly against regulation.

In the pro-business atmosphere of the Bush Administration, against a background of substantial economic stability since the early 1980s and exaggerated respect for Alan Greenspan,[9] the ef-

---

5. These laws were the Gain-St. Germain Depository Institutions Act (1982), the Riegle-Neal Interstate Banking and Branching Efficiency Act (1994), and the National Securities Markets Improvement Act (1996).

6. Gramm-Leach-Bliley Act (1999).

7. Securities and Exchange Commission, "Alternative Net Capital Requirements for Broker-Dealers That Are Part of Consolidated Supervised Entities; Supervised Investment Bank Holding Companies; Final Rules," 17 C.F.R. pts. 200, 240, www.sec.gov/rules/final/34-49830.pdf (visited Oct. 19, 2009).

8. See, for example, the Financial Institutions Reform, Recovery, and Enforcement Act (1989), which increased regulatory control over savings and loan associations, and the Federal Deposit Insurance Improvement Act (1991), which expanded the FDIC's authority to close down failing banks. For general discussions of bank regulation, see Carl Felsenfeld, *Banking Regulation in the United States* (2d ed. 2006); Alan Gart, *Regulation, Deregulation, Reregulation: The Future of the Banking, Insurance, and Securities Industries* (1994).

9. See, for example, Edmund L. Andrews, "The Greenspan Effect: The Doctrine Was Not to Have One," *New York Times,* Aug. 26, 2005, p. C1.

fect of deregulation in promoting risk taking by banks was augmented by laxity in enforcing existing regulations. There was also a lack of attention not only to specific warning signs of possible economic disaster but also to industry changes that were increasing the likelihood of such a disaster. They included the diminution in federally insured deposits as a source of capital for lending, the concomitant rise in a huge unregulated shadow banking industry, and the proliferation of off-balance-sheet contingent liabilities, such as structured investment vehicles and credit-default swaps.

Along with its other pratfalls, the Federal Reserve made an unsound trade-off between prevention and remediation. The greater the confidence in being able to remedy a problem if it occurs, the less effort will be made to prevent the problem from occurring. The economics profession had come to believe that cleaning up the debris caused by the bursting of an asset-price bubble (the possibility of which was, however, denied by some prominent economists) would be preferable to pricking the bubble before it grew large enough for its bursting to cause significant damage. Pricking was resisted by the Fed because of the difficulty of determining when an increase in asset prices was a bubble rather than a response to changes in real relative values and because of the political backlash that is stirred up whenever the Fed raises interest rates (which is one way to burst a bubble in a product bought largely with debt, another being to require more collateral for borrowing, as by raising the margin requirements for buying stock on credit) and thus curtails economic activity.

It was thought that when the housing bubble (if that's what it was) burst, damage to the economy could be contained simply by a reduction in the federal funds rate, which would restart economic activity chilled by the bursting of the bubble and the

Greenspan's political conservatism endeared him to the right; his easy-money policy endeared him to the left.

resulting plunge in asset values. This thinking turned out to be erroneous. It was a major failure of economic analysis. For macroeconomics, the era that ended abruptly in September 2008 was not the "Great Moderation"—the mistaken belief of most economists that the Fed had finally learned how to maintain price stability without high unemployment. It was the Great Complacency.

Am I saying that deregulation *made* bankers and through them borrowers take risks that were excessive from an overall social standpoint? Yes, once we recognize that competition will force banks to take risks (in order to increase return) that the economic and regulatory environment permits them to take, provided the risks are legal and profit-maximizing, whatever their consequences for the economy as a whole. Competition compresses the spread between cost and revenue and by doing so reduces profits, reduces the equity cushion, and hence increases the risk of bankruptcy. Specifically and ominously, compressing a bank's spread exerts pressure on the bank to increase its leverage in order to enhance the effect of its spread on its profits.

Some commentators on the economic crisis believe that boards of directors should be encouraged to govern their corporations with an eye not only to maximizing shareholder value but also to protecting broader social interests, such as avoiding systemic risk. That would not only be commercial suicide in a highly competitive industry; it would mingle social duties confusingly. It would be like telling a doctor to consider not just how to treat a patient but also whether the patient is worth saving, all things considered, including the federal deficit. Society assigns discrete functions to the various professions and vocations, and creates government to integrate the functions.

Additional causes of the financial crisis can be assigned. The deductibility of mortgage and home-equity interest from federal income tax encourages these potentially risky forms of borrowing, and the nondeductibility of the cost of equity capital encourages leverage. The policy of countries like China, Japan, Germany, and the oil-exporting nations of the Middle East of exporting more than they import and investing the resulting accumulation of cash balances in the United States reduced interest rates for U.S. borrowers and so contributed to the rapid expansion and risky policies of our banks.

But when attributing blame, some background causes must be taken as constraints rather than treated as choice variables. One of the causes of a fire is the oxygen in the atmosphere, but removing the oxygen would not be a sensible measure for eliminating fires. The tax policies that contributed to the financial collapse are, as a practical political matter, unalterable—part of the structure, not movable furniture within it. And imagine reducing the minimum wage in a depression, sensible as such a measure would be for stimulating production by reducing firms' labor costs, especially when, as in the current depression, unemployment has been disproportionately concentrated among the least skilled workers, those least likely to be employable at the minimum wage. As for the mercantilist policies of foreign nations, we must take the world as we find it and adapt our policies to it, including our monetary policies. The Federal Reserve never lost control over interest rates. Had interest rates risen early in the 2000s—and the Fed could have made them rise—the housing bubble would have burst while it was still small. Housing prices would not have fallen to a level that would have endangered the solvency of the banking industry because it was so heavily invested in residential mortgages.

On the basis of what we know now (our knowledge may grow with the passage of time), the financial collapse would not have occurred had the Federal Reserve followed the Taylor rule and thus kept interest rates higher in 2001–2004, or if the Fed and the other regulatory authorities, and the academic economists and political conservatives from whom they took their cue, had been more inquisitive about changes in the structure and practices of the banking industry and less complacent about the self-regulating capacity of financial markets (and hence the merits of deregulation) and the Federal Reserve's ability to "mitigate the fallout" (Greenspan's words, which I quoted in chapter 1) from a housing bubble.

8

Until the 1930s the dominant conception of how the economy as a whole operated went by the name of "Say's Law," which is commonly paraphrased as "supply creates its own demand." Workers, or the groups of workers that we call firms, produce goods in order to exchange them for goods produced by other workers. The basic concept is that of barter, and the only significance of money is that it facilitates multiparty barter by providing a standard of value. I might sell you bread but not want anything you make, so you pay me for the bread and I use the money to buy from someone else something I do want.

Say's Law was a corollary of Adam Smith's notion, encapsulated in the metaphor of the "invisible hand," of a natural harmony of economic activity. Changes in demand and supply would lead to changes in prices and wages that would restore the equality of demand and supply, and while unemployment would sometimes result because adjustments necessary to restore equilibrium were not instantaneous, it would be temporary. Workers had a reservation wage, that is, a wage below which they would either seek another job or prefer not to work at all. So some of them might stay on if their employer reduced their wage, while others would find a different job or decide not to work. The only period of real unemployment would be the time a worker spent looking for a job. Workers who abandoned the search would not be unemployed in an economically significant sense; they would simply have chosen to be self-employed, producing leisure or doing household chores in lieu of producing market income. An *aggregate* oversupply of goods (or services) or an *aggregate* deficiency in demand, and resulting persistence of unemployment—in short, a business cycle—would be unlikely, because almost everything that was produced could be sold at *some* price and everything that was produced and not consumed by the producer would be offered in exchange for other products. From the standpoint of producers, aggregate sales proceeds would always equal aggregate costs of output (wages, raw materials, cost of capital, and so forth). So even a completely unforeseen shock to the economy—say a new technology for manufacturing bread, which required much less labor than the technology it displaced —would create disequilibrium (shortage or glut) only in the very short run, as labor and other inputs got reshuffled to maintain the equality of aggregate revenues and aggregate costs.

Economists knew, of course, that there *was* a business cycle— that there were depressions (called "panics") in which problems of liquidity figured importantly (Bagehot's *Lombard Street* had been published in the nineteenth century). But there was no *theory* before Keynes that tied money, interest, and employment together in a way that explained the business cycle. Money and interest were thought of as ancillary to the "real" (that is, non-financial) economy of goods and services, rather than as factors that could bring down (or restore) that economy.

Say's Law somehow managed to survive Keynes. Its most influential current incarnation is called "Real Business Cycle Theory." The ups and downs of the economy are deemed responses to technological changes and other developments that alter relative values. The economy adjusts quickly in the efficient manner described above unless the government interferes—for example, by forbidding reductions in prices or wages. Real Business Cycle Theory cannot explain the depression that began in December

2007. The housing bubble, its bursting, and the ensuing collapse of the banking industry because of its heavy investment in housing were not caused by events such as changes in land use or population that alter relative values or by the government's messing with prices or wages. They were the result of unsound monetary policy and the risk-taking propensities of inadequately regulated banks.

Theories derived from Say's Law allow for surprise caused by unpredictable events but not for mistakes in markets undisturbed by such events. The housing and credit bubbles were the result not of shocks to the economy but of mistakes in monetary policy, and the bursting of the bubbles brought down the non-financial economy because of the inherent fragility of a largely deregulated banking system. The sequence of events was contrary not only to Real Business Cycle Theory but also to the strong form of efficient-markets theory that teaches not just that markets are hard to beat (which is true)—especially the stock market, which has been the principal focus of the theory—but that asset prices are based on sound understandings of value. The financial crisis was also inconsistent with the rational-expectations hypothesis, which teaches that businessmen and consumers have unbiased expectations concerning the behavior of the economy, and with the Barro-Ricardian equivalence theorem, which teaches that private behavior tends to cancel out the effects of fiscal and monetary policy on the nonfinancial economy.

The specific example used by Robert Barro was government borrowing. He argued that an effort by government to stimulate economic activity by borrowing would have no effect on economic activity.[1] People would realize that money borrowed by the government would eventually have to be paid back to the lenders by a hike in taxes, and so they would reduce their present consumption in order to accumulate the money they would need

1. Robert J. Barro, "On the Determination of Public Debt," 87 *Journal of Political Economy* 940 (1979).

for paying the higher taxes that they anticipated. By reducing their consumption, they would negate the intended effect of the borrowing—to increase consumption. This analysis implies not only that deficit spending is futile as a way of fighting a bust, but that low interest rates would not create a boom. People would know that interest rates would have to rise in the future in order to stop the inflation that low interest rates were bound to cause. If correct, the theory was another reason to deny the possibility of an asset-price bubble.

The broader implication was that money and interest didn't much matter; their effects on the nonfinancial economy would be undone by alert private responses. The theories had no place for such critical business-cycle behavior as hoarding cash, rather than spending it, as a hedge against uncertainty. Hoarding is a way in which the financial system can decisively affect the non-financial system by reducing aggregate demand, but hoarding is motivated by uncertainty, and uncertainty plays no role in theories derivative from Say's Law[2] except in occasional shocks to which the economy quickly and smoothly adjusts. If there is no hoarding, all financial assets are always available for investment —another reason that fiscal policy was thought incapable of affecting economic behavior other than by reducing the efficiency with which economic resources are allocated. If government borrowed to finance public works, it would be offsetting private investment dollar for dollar; there would be no effect on total investment.

This is implausible. It implies that if a billionaire decided to invest some of his money in the construction of a factory rather than keeping it all in a money-market account, there would be no increase in output. It is true that the money-market fund would have fewer assets, and suppose it had to sell Treasury securities in

2. See, for example, R. E. Lucas, "Understanding Business Cycles," in *Stabilization of the Domestic and International Economy* 15 (K. Brunner and A. H. Meltzer eds. 1977).

order to pay the check that the billionaire had drawn on his account. Then interest rates would rise slightly (for remember that an increase in the supply of bonds reduces their price and therefore increases their yield), but that would not offset the effect of the billionaire's investment on output and employment. Ridiculing the argument of the British Treasury that public spending financed by issuing government bonds was bound to diminish private spending by an equal amount, Keynes said that if this were true, it would apply to any new act of private as well as public spending, which no one believed: "In short, the fatalistic belief that there can never be more employment than there is is altogether baseless."[3]

Missing from the "classical" account criticized by Keynes—an absence that confirms that Say's Law implicitly models a barter economy—is the fact that in a money economy you don't receive a good in exchange for selling a good; you receive money. It is up to you to decide whether to use that money to buy another good or to save it, perhaps out of fear that you may need it in an emergency.

Though implausible, the modern theories derived from Say's Law were until the recent economic collapse highly influential in economic and governmental circles even though they had little empirical support, largely ignored the role of money in a modern economy, and seemed contradicted by the long history of asset bubbles, financial crises, and depressions. The theories were tenacious for reasons largely internal to the academic economics profession. As Robert Lucas, their most distinguished living advocate, admitted, they do not explain depressions.[4] Progress in economics since the days of Smith and Ricardo, Lucas argued, had been limited to increases in mathematical rigor. It was thus

3. John Maynard Keynes, "Mr. JM Keynes Examines Lloyd George's Pledge," *Evening Standard,* Mar. 29, 1929.
4. Robert E. Lucas, Jr., "My Keynesian Education," 36 *History of Political Economy* (Annual Supplement) 12, 23–24 (2003).

the profession's "internal mainstream"—its internally generated quest for ever greater rigor—that had given rise to the theories.[5] Although they rested on unrealistic assumptions about people's capacity to acquire and process information, the tendency in economics was to assume (however unrealistically) that people are "rational" in a very strong sense, and to seek to test the adequacy of economic theory by the accuracy of its predictions rather than by the realism of its assumptions.[6]

The predictions have turned out to be inaccurate—both the predictions of rational-expectations theory and those of the efficient-markets hypothesis in the strong form in which stock prices are assumed to discount future corporate profits accurately and "noise" trading, "momentum" trading, stock bubbles, and other anomalies are assumed away.[7]

The persistence of theories that did not yield good predictions was due to the absence of competing theories that could be fitted to the type of models with which modern economists were comfortable. The emphasis on mathematization drew into economics brilliant young mathematicians who might have little feel for economic phenomena.

Not that there's nothing to the rational-expectations or efficient-markets hypotheses. People don't always just blindly assume that the future will be just like the past. Naïve extrapolation ("adaptive expectations," as it is sometimes termed) is not

5. Id. at 24.

6. See Milton Friedman's paper "The Methodology of Positive Economics," in Friedman, *Essays in Positive Economics* 3 (1953).

7. See, for example, Daniel Himarios, "How Forward Looking Are Consumers? Further Evidence for the United States," 66 *Southern Economic Journal* 991 (2000); David I. Levine, "Do Corporate Executives Have Rational Expectations?" 66 *Journal of Business* 271 (1993); Michael C. Lovell, "Tests of the Rational Expectations Hypothesis," 76 *American Economic Review* 110 (1986). See also Masahiro Ashiya, "Strategic Bias and Professional Affiliations of Macroeconomic Forecasters," 28 *Journal of Forecasting* 120 (2009), finding that economic forecasters have goals other than just accuracy, such as publicity.

the only decision theory that people use. They know there's a business cycle (even if they don't know the term), which implies that the future does not just repeat the past—booms give way to busts, and vice versa, and do so irregularly (if the business cycle were perfectly regular, the future *could* be predicted from the past). Workers base expectations of unemployment on their sense of where the economy is going rather than on where it has been.[8]

The current depression, confirming earlier criticisms of macroeconomic theories derived from Say's Law,[9] has falsified those theories with a perspicuity that cannot be overlooked and so has driven many economists to reconsider the economic theory of John Maynard Keynes[10]—a theory based explicitly on the rejection of Say's Law. The analysis in this book and my prior one is based on Keynes's masterpiece, *The General Theory of Employment, Interest and Money,* published in 1936, immensely influential in its time but virtually forgotten by modern economists (including the "New Keynesians").[11] In 1992 Gregory Mankiw, a

8. Lloyd B. Taylor, "Survey Measures of Expected U.S. Inflation," *Journal of Economic Perspectives* 125 (Autumn 1999); Richard T. Curtin, "Unemployment Expectations: The Impact of Private Information on Income Uncertainty," 49 *Review of Income and Wealth* 539 (2003).

9. See, for example, Luca Pensieroso, "Real Business Cycle Models of the Great Depression: A Critical Survey," 21 *Journal of Economic Surveys* 110 (2007); Laurence S. Seidman, "The New Classical Counter-Revolution: A False Path for Macroeconomics," 31 *Eastern Economic Journal* 131 (2005), and especially Lawrence H. Summers, "Some Skeptical Observations on Real Business Cycle 'Theory,'" *Federal Reserve Bank of Minneapolis Quarterly Review,* Fall 1986, p. 23.

10. See *The Return to Keynes* (Bradley W. Bateman, Toshiaki Hirai, and Maria Cristina Marcuzo eds., Harvard University Press, forthcoming in 2010). Cf. Robert J. Gordon, "Is Modern Macro or 1978-Era Macro More Relevant to the Understanding of the Current Economic Crisis?" Sept. 12, 2009, http://faculty-web.at.northwestern.edu/economics/gordon/GRU _Combined_090909.pdf (visited Nov. 2, 2009).

11. Robert Skidelsky, the author of a superb three-volume biography of Keynes, has recently published *Keynes: The Return of the Master* (2009), in which he helpfully explains how Keynes differed from his predecessors,

prominent macroeconomist at Harvard, stated that "after fifty years of additional progress in economic science, *The General Theory* is an utdated book . . . We are in a much better position than Keynes was to figure out how the economy works."[12] Keynes's biographer goes further, stating that Keynes "was not an economist at all" (though this is intended as a compliment by the author, who is not an economist)—that he "put on the mask of an economist to gain authority, just as he put on dark suits and homburgs for life in the City"[13] (London's Wall Street). Keynes was the greatest economist of the twentieth century; to expel him from the profession is to reinforce the prejudices of present-day economists by embracing their bobtailed conception of the field.

The General Theory is a hard slog, though not for the reason that so much modern economics writing is a hard slog; for the book is not mathematical. There is some math, but it is simple and, with the exception of the formula for the "multiplier" (of which more shortly), incidental to Keynes's arguments. A

---

the "classical economists" (adherents to Say's Law), and his successors, the "new classical economists" and the "New Keynesians." He points out that the New Keynesians jettisoned the most important parts of Keynes's theory because those parts do not lend themselves to the mathematization beloved of modern economists. Paul Krugman concurs in this criticism of the New Keynesians. See his article "How Did Economists Get It So Wrong?" *New York Times Magazine,* Sept. 6, 2009, pp. 36, 42–43. Krugman's article, and the more scholarly article by Gordon, note 10 above, make sharp criticisms of the "new classical" macroeconomists (Lucas, Barro, etc.), though Krugman exaggerates. David K. Levine, "An Open Letter to Paul Krugman," Sept. 18, 2009, www.huffingtonpost.com/david-k-levine/an-open-letter-to-paul-kr_b_289768.html (visited Nov. 2, 2009). For other criticisms of the new classical macroeconomics, see Francis M. Bator, "The State of Macroeconomics," in *Employment and Growth: Issues for the 1980s* 29 (A. Steinherr and D. Weiserbs eds. 1987); Ray C. Fair, "Has Macro Progressed?" (Yale University, Cowles Foundation Discussion Paper No. 1728, Sept. 2009).

12. Gregory Mankiw, "The Reincarnation of Keynesian Economics," 36 *European Economic Review* 561 (1992).

13. Skidelsky, note 11 above, at 59.

work of elegant prose, it sparkles with aphorisms (such as "It is better that a man should tyrannise over his bank balance than over his fellow-citizens")[14] and rhetorical flights—most famously, "Madmen in authority, who hear voices in the air, are distilling their frenzy from some academic scribbler of a few years back" (p. 351). But it also bristles with unfamiliar terms, such as "labour-unit" (p. 37) (an hour's employment of ordinary labor), and references to unfamiliar economic institutions, such as "sinking fund" (a fund in which money is accumulated to pay off a debt). And it brims over with digressions, afterthoughts, and stray observations, such as "The two most delightful occupations open to those who do not have to earn their living [are] authorship and experimental farming" (p. 322). Two important chapters, dealing with the "trade cycle" (that is, the business cycle) and with mercantilism, usury, and thrift—all highly relevant to the business cycle—are deferred to the last part of the book, misleadingly entitled "Short Notes Suggested by the General Theory."

The General Theory is an especially difficult read for present-day academic economists, whose conception of economics is remote from Keynes's. That is what made the book seem "outdated" to Mankiw and led Robert Lucas, writing a few years after Mankiw, to characterize *The General Theory* as "an ideological event" rather than a contribution to economic theory.[15] The tendency of today's economists is to conceive of their field as

14. John Maynard Keynes, *The General Theory of Employment, Interest and Money* 343 (1936).

15. Robert E. Lucas, Jr., Review [of the first two volumes of Robert Skidelsky's biography of Keynes], 67 *Journal of Modern History* 914, 916 (1995). Earlier, Lucas had written that "one cannot find good, under-forty economists who identify themselves or their work as 'Keynesian'. Indeed, people even take offense if referred to as 'Keynesians'. At research seminars, people don't take Keynesian theorizing seriously anymore; the audience starts to whisper and giggle to one another." Robert E. Lucas, Jr., "The Death of Keynesian Economics," *Issues and Ideas,* Winter 1980, p. 18.

the study of rational choice.[16] The older view was that it was the study of the economy, employing whatever assumptions seemed realistic and whatever analytical methods came to hand; there is psychology as well as economics in *The Wealth of Nations*. There was a strong presumption that business firms tried to maximize profits and a weaker presumption that individuals tried to maximize utility, but how well either succeeded was left open. Keynes wanted to be realistic about decision making rather than explore how far an economist could get by assuming that people base decisions on a close approximation to cost-benefit analysis.

The General Theory is full of interesting psychological observations—the word "psychological" is ubiquitous—as when Keynes notes that "during a boom the popular estimation of [risk] is apt to become unusually and imprudently low," while during a bust the "animal spirits" of entrepreneurs droop (p. 130). He uses such insights without trying to fit them to a model of rational decision making.

Such an approach to economic behavior came naturally to Keynes because he was not an *academic* economist in the twenty-first-century understanding of the term. He had no degree in economics, wrote extensively in other fields (such as probability theory—on which he wrote a treatise that does not mention economics), combined a fellowship at Cambridge with extensive government service as an adviser and a high-level civil servant, and was an active speculator, polemicist, and journalist. He was an *eclectic* economist, a distinguished breed (think of Malthus, Mill, Schumpeter) that has since become extinct.

Keynes's theory and its application to our current economic plight are best understood if one bears in mind one historical fact and three claims made in the book. The historical fact is that

16. A notable exception is another famous English economist, Ronald Coase, of the generation following Keynes's. See my paper "Keynes and Coase," prepared for a conference on "Markets, Firms and Property Rights: A Celebration of the Research of Ronald Coase," held at the University of Chicago Law School on December 4–5, 2009.

between 1919 and 1939 England experienced persistent high unemployment—never less than 10 percent, and 15 percent in 1935, when Keynes was completing his book. Explaining the persistence of unemployment—an anomaly in theories based on Say's Law—was the major task that Keynes set himself. Though he famously declared that "in the long run, we are dead,"[17] he tried to solve a problem that, already when he wrote, had had a pretty long run.

The three claims are, first, that consumption is the "sole end and object of all economic activity,"[18] because all productive activity is designed to satisfy consumer demand either in the present or in the future. "Consumption" is not in the title of the book, however, because the only thing that interested Keynes about it was how much of their income people allocated to it—the more, the better.

The second claim is the importance (and the deleterious effect) of hoarding. People do not save just to be able to make a specific future expenditure; they may instead be hedging against uncertainty. And the third claim, related to the second, is that uncertainty—in the sense of a risk that, unlike the risk of losing at roulette, cannot be calculated—is a pervasive feature of the economic environment, particularly with respect to investment projects—projects intended to satisfy future consumption.

A nation's annual output, which is also the national income, is the market value of all the goods (and services, but to simplify the discussion I will ignore them here) produced in a year. These goods are either consumption goods, such as the food people buy, or investment goods, such as machine tools. What people do not spend on consumption they save: income minus consumption equals savings. Since income minus consumption also equals investment, savings must, Keynes insists, equal investment.

But equating savings with investment is confusing. If you stuff

17. John Maynard Keynes, *A Tract on Monetary Reform* 80 (1923).
18. Keynes, note 14 above, at 95.

money under your mattress, you are saving, but in what sense are you investing? If you buy common stock, you are investing, but the contribution of your investment to the productive capital employed in building a factory is attenuated; the money you pay for the stock goes to the person who sold it to you rather than to the factory's owner.

This confusion has to be dispelled if Keynes's theory is to be understood. The key is to distinguish between *enabling* productive investments to be made and actually *making* them; or, equivalently, between potential and actual investment. If you stuff money under your mattress, the money does not assist investment, although it may in the future, when it is removed and put into circulation (and likewise with money placed in a safe-deposit box). If you deposit money in a bank, the bank will decide whether to lend the money to a businessman to invest in his business (or to an individual to invest in buying a capital asset, such as a house)—not you.

In contrast to inert, hoarded money, money spent on consumption becomes income to the seller of the consumption good. When I buy a bottle of wine, the cost to me is income to the seller, and what he spends out of that income will be income to someone else, and so on. So the investment (again in contrast to money merely saved) that produced the income with which I bought the wine will have had a chain-reaction (what Keynes calls a "multiplier") effect. Investment leads to consumption leads to spending leads to income leads to more consumption—and to savings that may or may not be invested in the sense of being used to enable future consumption or future investment.

And here is the tricky part: the increase in income brought about by an investment is greater when the percentage of income that is spent rather than saved is higher, even if it is being saved to invest. This is counterintuitive, because one's intuition is that the more that is saved for purposes of investment, the more that national income is being increased. But this ignores the fact that spending increases the incomes of the people who are on the receiving end of the spending, and higher incomes elicit more investment because they promise more consumption, and the purpose of investment is to produce goods and services for consumption.

The multiplier effect is greater as the percentage of a person's income that he spends increases. If everyone spends 80 cents of an additional dollar that he receives, then a $1 increase in a person's income will generate $4 of consumption ($.80 + $.64 [.8 × $.80] + $.512 [.8 × $.64], etc. = $4),[19] all of which is income to the sellers of consumer goods. If only 60 cents of an additional $1 in income is spent, so that the first recipient of that expenditure spends only 36 cents (60 percent of the 60 cents that he received), the second 21.6 cents, and so on, the total increase in consumption as a result of the successive waves of spending is only $1.50, and so the investment that got the cycle going will have been much less productive. In the first example, the investment multiplier—the effect of investment on income—was 4. In the second example it is only 1.5. The difference is caused by the difference in the propensity to consume income rather than save it. But no one today thinks that investment multipliers are likely to exceed 1.5. Part of the reason is that income tax takes a big bite out of an increase in income, and only what is left over can be spent for consumption. Similarly, money spent on imported goods does not have a multiplier effect in the domestic economy, except to the extent that the price of imported goods includes domestic costs of distribution. And the net investment multiplier of a public investment project, such as a public works project in-

19. According to the formula $\Delta y = \Delta_i (MPC/1 - MPC)$, where Δ_y is the change in national income, Δ_i the initial investment, and MPC the marginal propensity to consume. This is oversimplified, ignoring as it does income tax, imports, and other effects on expenditures. Notice also that while a high multiplier makes fiscal stimulus a more effective depression fighter, it makes the economy overall less stable by amplifying the effect of a change in spending. This is another example of the topsy-turvy character of depression economics.

tended to stimulate economic growth, can easily fall below 1 if the investment crowds out private investment and thus cancels out the multiplier effect that the private investment would have had.

But the important point is not the exact size of the multiplier but that for Keynes it is consumption rather than thrift, even thrift in the form of savings that are invested, that mainly promotes economic growth. And here his second key claim kicks in—that people often save with no particular aim of future spending. Keynes mentions a host of reasons why people save that may not promote investment or consumption; he also discusses the analogous motives of businesses. Savers may want to "bequeath a fortune," "satisfy pure miserliness," "build up a reserve against unforeseen contingencies," "enjoy a sense of independence and the power to do things, though without a clear idea or definite intention of specific action" (p. 98), or, implicitly, obtain a reputation for being thrifty. (This last motive recalls the "Protestant ethic" of which Max Weber wrote.) Savings increase output, and therefore employment, only when they finance the creation of productive capital. When they are hoarded, the link between saving and promoting economic activity is broken, or at least frayed.

The third claim that I am calling foundational of Keynes's theory—that the business environment is riven by uncertainty in the sense of risk that cannot be calculated—now enters the picture. Savers do not direct how their savings will be used by entrepreneurs; entrepreneurs do, guided by the hope of making profits. But when an investment project will take years to complete before it begins to generate a profit, its prospects for success will be shadowed by unpredictable contingencies relating to costs, consumer preferences, actions by competitors, government policy, and economic conditions generally. As Keynes's biographer explains, "An unmanaged capitalist economy is inherently unstable. Neither profit expectations nor the rate of interest are solidly anchored in the underlying forces of productivity and thrift.

They are driven by uncertain and fluctuating expectations about the future."[20]

This underscores the disconnect between saving and productive investment. Thrift can reduce consumption without an off-setting expansion in investment because the investment decision is not made by the savers or influenced by the same concerns that move people to save. No matter how much or in what form income is saved, the decision to use it to enlarge future consumption rests with the entrepreneur, and only what Keynes called "animal spirits," or the "urge to action," will persuade a person to embrace the inherently uncertain prospects of investment. "If human nature felt no temptation to take a chance, no satisfaction (profit apart) in constructing a factory, a railway, a mine or a farm, there might not be much investment merely as a result of cold calculation" (p. 135).

However high-spirited a businessman may be, at times the uncertainty of the business environment will make him reluctant to invest. His reluctance will be all the greater if savers are reluctant to part with their money because of uncertainty concerning future interest rates, default risks, and possible emergency needs for cash to pay off debts or meet unexpected expenses. The greater the propensity to hoard, the higher the interest rate that a businessman will have to pay for the capital that he requires for investment. And since interest expense is greater the longer a loan is outstanding, a high interest rate will have an especially dampening effect on projects that, being intended to meet consumption needs beyond the immediate future, take a long time to complete.

Sinking funds illustrate institutional hoarding: money is accumulated to pay off a debt in the future rather than being spent, and its unavailability for investment causes interest rates to rise. Although high interest rates discourage the hoarding of cash by increasing the opportunity cost of such hoarding, they also, and

20. Skidelsky, note 11 above, at 97.

in uncertain times especially, encourage safe forms of savings, such as the purchase of government bonds, that may have only a very limited effect in encouraging investment. Institutional hoarding is illustrated in today's economy by the immense excess reserves of the banks.

Keynes's analysis is not limited to depressions but casts a particularly bright light on them. When the demand for goods and services unexpectedly falls, the economic environment becomes unsettled and even the near future becomes unpredictable. This dampens businessmen's animal spirits and causes consumers to hoard, and businessmen as well. When the urge to action deserts them, they build up their cash balances as a hedge against uncertainty. Owing to the pervasive uncertainty of the business environment, businessmen even in the best of times lack "strong roots of conviction" (p. 138) about what the future holds, and so a sudden change in economic conditions can paralyze them. When that happens, a downward spiral will develop, as falling demand and falling investment reinforce each other, causing layoffs that reduce incomes and therefore consumption and production and so induce more layoffs.[21]

But the government may be able to arrest the decline. It can push down interest rates (as by buying government bonds or other debt for cash, which increases the amount of money in bank accounts and therefore the amount of lendable money) in an effort to reduce the costs of active investment and thus encourage employment. Keynes urged this approach. But he also

---

21. The American economist Irving Fisher offered a similar analysis of the Great Depression: "These losses, bankruptcies, and unemployment, lead to (7) *Pessimism and loss of confidence,* which in turn lead to (8) *Hoarding and slowing down still more the velocity of circulation.*" Fisher, "The Debt-Deflation Theory of Great Depressions," 1 *Econometrica* 337, 342 (1933) (emphases in original). Deflation occurs when the amount of money in circulation shrinks relative to the output of goods and services. "Velocity" refers to the rate at which money circulates; the lower the rate, the less money is available for buying things. Money that is hoarded does not circulate and so is not part of the money supply that affects prices.

pointed out that it might not work well—as we have learned in the current depression. Banks might lack confidence in "those who seek to borrow from them," so that "while the weakening of credit is sufficient to bring about a collapse, its strengthening, though a necessary condition of recovery, is not a sufficient condition" (p. 142). American banks at present are hoarding most of the cash they've received from the government's bailouts.

Keynes taught that there is more that government can do to arrest a downward economic spiral than just pushing down interest rates. It can offset the decline in private consumption in a recession or a depression by increasing public investment. When we say that the government builds highways, we mean it buys highways from private contractors. And the more it buys, the more that investment—and so, because of the multiplier effect, the more that income, output, and employment—are stimulated. The $787 billion stimulus plan enacted in February 2009 is Keynes's grandchild.

And because private decisions both to invest and to consume are influenced by confidence in the future, or the lack thereof, the government must do everything it can to convince businessmen and consumers that it is resolute and competent in working for economic recovery. An ambitious public works program can be a confidence builder. It shows that government means (to help) business. "The return of confidence," Keynes explains in a key passage, "is the aspect of the slump which bankers and business men have been right in emphasising, and which the economists who have put their faith in a 'purely monetary' remedy have underestimated" (p. 288). In a possible gesture toward Roosevelt's first inaugural address ("we have nothing to fear but fear itself"), Keynes notes "the uncontrollable and disobedient psychology of the business world" (id.).

For a confidence-building public works program to be effective, the government must finance it by means that do not reduce private consumption commensurately. If it finances the program by taxation, it will be draining cash from the economy at the same time that it is injecting cash into it. But if it borrows to finance the program or finances it with new money created by the Federal Reserve, the costs of the program may be deferred until the economy has recovered to a point at which they can be repaid without undue strain. When investors passively save rather than actively invest, government can borrow their savings (as by selling them government bonds) and use the money for investment and thus economic stimulation, without crowding out private investment.

Aspects of Keynes's book disturb conventionally minded people. His emphasis on consumption as the driver of investment and hence of economic growth, and his hostility to thrift, give his theory a hedonistic flavor. Yet we have seen the damaging effects of thrift in the current downturn, in which rich people's forswearing of luxury purchases in the name of thrift has reduced employment in the retail sector, thus deepening the downturn. "Prodigality is a vice that is prejudicial to the Man, but not to trade," in the words of the seventeenth-century economist Nicholas Barbon, quoted by Keynes (p. 327). In its extreme form, this "paradox of thrift" implies that if incomes fall far enough because people are saving rather than consuming, savings, which depend on income, will actually decline.

Keynes commended Roosevelt for having destroyed agricultural stocks during the Great Depression, since sales from existing inventories do not stimulate investment but are actually a form of disinvestment. He even discussed sympathetically, though ultimately he rejected, the curious proposal of "stamped money," whereby people would be required to have their currency stamped periodically at a government office in order to remain legal tender; the bother of having to get one's money stamped would have the effect of a tax on hoarding (pp. 325–326).

All this may seem an incitement to profligacy, consistent with Keynes's rather bohemian private life as a member of the Cambridge Apostles and the Bloomsbury group. But nothing in his theory limits consumption to the purchase of frivolous private goods, or indeed to private goods of any kind. I gave the example of a public highway; other examples are the purchase of military equipment for national defense and the public subvention of education and art. And while Keynes famously (or notoriously) argued the value of unproductive projects—or so they would seem to us—such as the building of the Egyptian pyramids, on the ground that they provided employment, which increased consumption (the workers, even if they were slaves, had to be fed and clothed and housed), he preferred governments to undertake productive projects.

Correctly anticipating the rapid growth of living standards, Keynes predicted that within a century people's material wants would be satiated and so per capita consumption would stop growing. People would work less, but only because their need, and more important their desire, for income was less. And then the challenge to society would be the management of unprecedented voluntary leisure. This was a popular 1930s theme—it is central to Aldous Huxley's novel *Brave New World* (1932)—but it underestimated the ability of business to create new wants, and new goods and services to fulfill them.

That was merely a mistake; an oddity is Keynes's belief in the possibility of perpetual boom. He has wise words, which Alan Greenspan and Ben Bernanke could with profit have heeded earlier in this decade, about the need to raise interest rates to prick an asset-price bubble before it gets too large. Yet just a few pages earlier he had remarked that "the remedy for a boom is not a higher rate of interest but a lower rate of interest! For that may enable the so-called boom to last" (p. 293). (That may have been what Greenspan thought!) The statements can be reconciled by observing that as long as there is a great deal of involuntary unemployment, low interest rates, by stimulating investment and therefore production without pushing up labor costs (because workers are desperate for jobs), should not produce inflation. But we have just seen in the United States of the 2000s how even if labor costs are steady, low interest rates can produce an asset-price inflation that can precipitate an economic collapse. Keynes had earlier in his career written prophetically about the potentially disastrous effects of inflation. There is almost no mention of inflation in *The General Theory,* but he does say that when an economy no longer has any involuntary unemployment, further efforts to stimulate demand will merely cause inflation (p. 183). Volcker's breaking inflation with high interest rates in 1979–1982 was consistent with Keynes's observation.[22]

Perpetual-boom thinking illustrates the left-leaning utopian strain in *The General Theory* that has made Keynes a *bête noire* of conservatives yet charms his biographer Skidelsky, who devotes the last three chapters of his recent book to celebrating Keynes as a "green," a philosopher of limits to growth, of "the good life" lived simply, even of the end of economics. Recall Keynes's erroneous prediction that within a century people's material wants would be satiated. When that happened, the demand for capital (to finance consumption) would plummet and rentiers (people who live on income from passive investments, such as stocks or bonds, and thus are hoarders) would be wiped out—a prospect that delighted Keynes, who looked forward to "the euthanasia of the rentier" (p. 345), though of course he didn't mean this literally. He questioned free trade—that holy of holies of conventional economists—by pointing out that a nation whose people had a low propensity to consume could stimulate investment by depreciating its currency so that its exports were attractive, because that would encourage its industries to invest in producing for foreign consumption and therefore employ more workers. The nation would accumulate foreign currency that it could use to invest abroad. Keynes was foretelling the policy that China has been following lately, with good results, at

22. See Francis M. Bator, "Fine Tuning," in *The New Palgrave: A Dictionary of Economics,* vol. 2 (John Eatwell, Murray Milgate, and Peter Newman eds. 1987).

least for China. Keynes even had kind words for usury laws, arguing that they had reduced interest rates and thus made passive investment less attractive; the other side of this coin, however, is that usury laws limit the availability of credit (and by doing so make banks safer!). He favored a heavy estate tax, reasoning that it would increase consumption by reducing accumulation for bequests. The standard economic argument *against* the estate tax is identical—it encourages the substitution of consumption for saving!

Although there are other heresies in *The General Theory,* along with puzzles, opacities, loose ends, confusions, errors, hyperbole, and anachronisms galore, they do not detract from the book's relevance to our present troubles. Economists may have forgotten *The General Theory* and moved on, but they have not outgrown it or the informal mode of argument that it exemplifies, which can illuminate nooks and crannies closed to mathematics. Keynes's masterpiece is many things, but "outdated" it is not. So I will let a contrite Gregory Mankiw, writing in November 2008 in the *New York Times* amid a collapsing economy, have the last word: "If you were going to turn to only one economist to understand the problems facing the economy, there is little doubt that the economist would be John Maynard Keynes. Although Keynes died more than a half-century ago, his diagnosis of recessions and depressions remains the foundation of modern macroeconomics. His insights go a long way toward explaining the challenges we now confront . . . Keynes wrote, 'Practical men, who believe themselves to be quite exempt from any intellectual influence, are usually the slave of some defunct economist.' In 2008, no defunct economist is more prominent than Keynes himself."[23]

23. Gregory Mankiw, "What Would Keynes Have Done?" *New York Times,* Nov. 30, 2008, p. B4.

If one idea had to be picked out as central to *The General Theory*, it is the idea of uncertainty. In this chapter I elaborate on the idea and illustrate its relevance to the current crisis.

In his first inaugural address, in March 1933, Franklin Roosevelt famously said: "This great Nation will endure as it has endured, will revive and will prosper. So, first of all, let me assert my firm belief that the only thing we have to fear is fear itself—nameless, unreasoning, unjustified terror which paralyzes needed efforts to convert retreat into advance." In *The General Theory*, published three years later, Keynes wrote:

> Most, probably, of our decisions to do something positive, the full consequences of which will be drawn out over many days to come, can only be taken as a result of animal spirits—of a spontaneous urge to action rather than inaction, and not as the outcome of a weighted average of quantitative benefits multiplied by quantitative probabilities . . . Thus if the animal spirits are dimmed and the spontaneous optimism fades, enterprise will fade and die . . . It is our innate urge to activity which makes the wheels go round, our rational selves choosing between the alternatives as best we are able, calculating where we can, but often falling back for our motive on whim or sentiment or chance.[1]

1. John Maynard Keynes, *The General Theory of Employment, Interest and Money* 144 (1936).

These statements and their connection are illuminated by an economic and psychological literature on aversion to uncertainty (more commonly referred to as "ambiguity aversion").[2] The American economist Frank Knight, in 1921,[3] and Keynes in his treatise on probability,[4] published the same year, had distinguished (Knight more clearly than Keynes) between calculable risk—risk to which a numerical probability can be assigned, and of which the likelihood, direction, and magnitude by which actual outcomes may deviate from the estimated (mean) risk can also be estimated—and uncertainty, to which a numerical probability and distribution cannot be assigned with any confidence that it is correct.[5] The risk within the next five years of another

2. See, for example, Carmela di Mauro, "Uncertainty Aversion vs. Competence: An Experimental Market Study," 64 *Theory and Decision* 301 (2008); Briony D. Pulford and Andrew M. Colman, "Size Doesn't Really Matter: Ambiguity Aversion in Ellsberg Urns with Few Balls," 55 *Experimental Psychology* 31 (2008); Gideon Keren and Léonie E. M. Gerritsen, "On the Robustness and Possible Accounts of Ambiguity Aversion," 103 *Acta Psychologica* 149 (1999). On uncertainty aversion by investors, see, for example, Roman Kozhan and Mark Salmon, "Uncertainty Aversion in a Heterogeneous Agent Model of Foreign Exchange Rate Formation," 33 *Journal of Economic Dynamics & Control* 1106 (2009); Larry G. Epstein and Martin Schneider, "Ambiguity, Information Quality, and Asset Pricing," 43 *Journal of Finance* 197 (2008). For an excellent survey of the literature, although a bit dated, see Colin Camerer and Martin Weber, "Recent Developments in Modeling Preferences: Uncertainty and Ambiguity," 5 *Journal of Risk and Uncertainty* 325 (1992). Ambiguity aversion has been succinctly defined as "consumers behave as if a range of probability distributions is possible and as if they are averse toward the 'unknown.'" Irasema Alonso and Jose Mauricio Prado, "Ambiguity Aversion, Asset Prices, and the Welfare Costs of Aggregate Fluctuations" 2 (Yale Department of Economics and IMT Lucca Institute for Advanced Studies, June 26, 2008).

3. Frank H. Knight, *Risk, Uncertainty, and Profit* (1921). See especially id. at 19–20 and ch. 7.

4. John Maynard Keynes, *A Treatise on Probability,* ch. 3 (1921). Keynes, unlike Knight, does not discuss the economic implications of uncertainty.

5. See Richard A. Posner, *Catastrophe: Risk and Response* 171–175 (2004). The distinction is explicit in J. M. Keynes, "The General Theory of Employment," 51 *Quarterly Journal of Economics* 209 (1937). I should

major terrorist attack on the United States, or of abrupt global warming, cannot be assigned a quantitative probability that has any objective basis; there just isn't enough information, or a sufficiently exact theory, to enable such a calculation.

Keynes explained uncertainty in this sense more clearly in an essay published the year after *The General Theory* than he had done in that book or in his treatise on probability:

> By "uncertain" knowledge, let me explain, I do not mean merely to distinguish what is known for certain from what is only probable. The game of roulette is not subject, in this sense, to uncertainty . . . The sense in which I am using the term is that in which the prospect of a European war is uncertain, or the price of copper and the rate of interest twenty years hence, or the obsolescence of a new invention, or the position of private wealth-owners in the social system in 1970. About these matters there is no scientific basis on which to form any calculable probability whatever. We simply do not know. Nevertheless, the necessity for action and for decision compels us as practical men to do our best to overlook this awkward fact and to behave exactly as we should if we had behind us a good Benthamite calculation of a series of prospective advantages and disadvantages, each multiplied by its appropriate probability, waiting to be summed.[6]

Calculable risk and uncertainty should not be thought of as dichotomous. Often one can say that a decision is more likely, or even much more likely, to be preferable to the alternatives, without being able to quantify the probability.[7]

---

make clear that "risk" as I use the term, and as it is usually used in economics, refers simply to the probability of some event's occurring, rather than, as is common in ordinary language, the probability times the consequence (i.e., the expected cost), as when one says that mountain climbing is risky.

6. Keynes, note 5 above, at 214. On Keynesian and post-Keynesian concepts of uncertainty, see the helpful discussion in J. Barkley Rosser, Jr., "Alternative Keynesian and Post Keynesian Perspectives on Uncertainty and Expectations," 23 *Journal of Post Keynesian Economics* 545 (2001).

7. See, for example, Posner, note 5 above, at 184–186 ("tolerable windows" approach). There is also "inverse cost-benefit analysis," where a probability is inferred by dividing the expenditure on preventing some loss

Keynes argued plausibly (as had Knight) that investment decisions are often made in a setting of uncertainty, because by the time the investment can begin to yield a return the conditions determining its profitability may have changed. Some unanticipated changes can be hedged by contract, insurance, derivative securities, or other means. But rarely can all unanticipated changes be hedged, especially those that are uncertain to occur, because then it is difficult or impossible for an insurer (whether an insurance company or an informal insurer, such as the issuer of a credit-default swap) to calculate a premium. Still, businessmen do make investments in the face of uncertainty and were doing so before there were any theories of probability.[8]

Is it rational to make an investment when one's estimate of the expected net benefit is little better than a stab in the dark? The

---

(or realizing some gain) by the loss (or gain) if the outcome is not prevented. Id. at 176–184. So suppose the government spends $1 to avoid a loss of $1,000; the inference would be that the probability of the loss was at least one in a thousand. But the purpose of inverse cost-benefit analysis is not to determine probabilities but, by comparing the result of the analysis to an independent estimate of probability, to determine whether the expenditure on preventing the loss (or obtaining the gain) is cost-justified.

8. Peter L. Bernstein, "Risk as a History of Ideas," *Financial Analysts Journal* 7 (Jan.-Feb. 1995). Knight, note 3 above, at 247–251, has an excellent discussion of uncertainty in insurance. Some types of insurance involve considerable uncertainty because the degree of moral hazard is difficult to estimate, as in business-loss insurance—Herbert G. Grubel, "Risk, Uncertainty and Moral Hazard," 39 *Journal of Risk and Insurance* 99, 105–106 (1971)—or because the event insured against is unique. In the second case, a specialty of Lloyd's of London, insurance is indistinguishable from gambling. See Laure Cabantous, "Ambiguity Aversion in the Field of Insurance: Insurers' Attitude to Imprecise and Conflicting Probability Estimates," 62 *Theory and Decision* 219 (2007), and Howard Kunreuther, Robin Hogarth, and Jacqueline Meszaros, "Insurer Ambiguity and Market Failure," 7 *Journal of Risk and Uncertainty* 71 (1993), on the operation of uncertainty aversion in insurance markets. A common response to that uncertainty is bureaucratic maneuvering within an insurance company by executives who try to protect their rear ends against recriminations should disaster strike. Another response is "procyclicality"—making hay while the sun shines. Sean M. Fitzpatrick, "Fear Is the Key: A Behavioral Guide to Underwriting Cycles," 10 *Connecticut Insurance Law Journal* 255 (2004).

usual concept of rational decision making assumed in economic analysis is some form of cost-benefit analysis, which presupposes that any risk that affects expected costs or benefits is calculable within a reasonable range. But the question of rationality didn't arise for Keynes. His analysis did not depend on any very definite assumptions about human behavior. He simply had observed businessmen taking noncalculable risks. Were there no people willing to do so—people who had an "urge to action"—a capitalist economy would not function. Business is a field of activity attractive to such people—call them the bold. Timid people of equal intelligence to the bold become civil servants, middle managers, or professors instead of entrepreneurs. And indeed entrepreneurs are less averse to uncertainty than other persons,[9] and economic growth, as Keynes conjectured, is positively correlated with what would now be called low uncertainty aversion.[10]

Keynes's "urge to action" or "animal spirits" is what psychologists call extraversion and regard as a basic personality trait that includes a desire for activity and excitement.[11] At one end of the extraversion spectrum, illustrated by gambling, risk is embraced even when it has a negative expected monetary return. The opposite extreme is illustrated by the purchase of insurance without deductibles.

Extraversion and introversion are well-documented traits in a number of animal species.[12] Some guppies, for example, are ex-

9. See Luigi Guiso and Giuseppe Parigi, "Investment and Demand under Uncertainty," 114 *Quarterly Journal of Economics* 185 (1999), and references cited there.

10. Rocco R. Huang, "Tolerance for Uncertainty and the Growth of Informationally Opaque Industries," 87 *Journal of Development Economics* 333 (2008).

11. See, for example, Daniel Nettle, *Personality: What Makes You the Way You Are,* ch. 3–4 (2007); Lex Borghans et al., "The Economics and Psychology of Personality Traits," 43 *Journal of Human Resources* 972, 983 (2008) (tab. 1).

12. Daniel Nettle, "The Evolution of Personality Variation in Humans and Other Animals," 61 *American Psychologist* 625 (2006).

traverts, swim about adventurously, and as a result encounter more guppies, have more offspring, and are eaten more often by larger fish than the introverted guppies. The introverts live longer and so may produce as many offspring as the extraverts even though they will have had less frequent sexual encounters.[13]

Both Knight and Keynes emphasized the difference between a probability estimate and the confidence with which the estimate is held. The greater the confidence, the more likely it is to drive action. Confidence in one's judgment is often an expression of personality rather than a fruit of analysis. Some people are naturally confident; they consider themselves lucky. Like Christopher Columbus, as famously described by Samuel Eliot Morison, they believe in their star, their destiny, their mission.[14] They have less aversion to uncertainty in the Knight-Keynes sense than the average person. It is natural that the urge to action would be stronger the more confident one was that one's actions would be successful (perhaps successful *because* they are one's actions).

A closely related distinction is between optimists and pessimists, and a pertinent finding is that people who feel good tend unconsciously to lower their estimate of the risk of bad outcomes.[15] For my purposes an optimist is someone who tends to act in the face of uncertainty and a pessimist one who tends to pause in the face of uncertainty.

The human race would not have progressed far unless some of

13. Nettle, note 11 above, at 72–75.

14. "Their [Columbus's crew's] issue with their commander was the eternal one between imagination and doubt, between the spirit that creates and the spirit that denies. Oftentimes the doubters are right, for mankind has a hundred foolish notions for every sound one; it is at times of crisis, when unpredictable forces are dissolving society, that the do-nothings are tragically wrong." Samuel Eliot Morison, *Admiral of the Ocean: A Life of Christopher Columbus* 285 (1942). I thank Benjamin Friedman for the reference.

15. Camelia Kuhnen and Brian Knutson, "The Influence of Affect on Beliefs, Preferences and Financial Decisions" (MPRA Paper No. 10410, Munich Personal RePEc Archive, Sept. 11, 2008), http://mpra.ub.uni-muenchen.de/10410/ (visited Nov. 2, 2009). Recall Keynes's equation of "animal spirits" with "spontaneous optimism."

its members had a genetic predisposition for risk taking—were extraverts, optimists. The ancestral human environment was pervaded by uncertainty; a strong aversion by all human beings to uncertainty would have frozen activity. In a modern setting, the costs of such aversion are illustrated by the fact that the more hoarding there is, because of a weak urge to action, the less productive investment there will be (a point emphasized by Keynes, since the greater liquidity preference is, the higher interest rates must be to pry capital for investment out of people) and therefore the slower the rate at which the economy will grow. An economy in which people are afraid to take risks will sputter to a halt.

In the guppy example, personality traits enhance fitness, which is related to the economist's notion of utility. One might say that natural selection shapes utility functions to maximize fitness. Think of the quandary of Buridan's ass, a donkey who starves to death because, placed equidistant between two equally large piles of straw, he has no basis for choosing between them. Or David Hume's dictum that reason is and should be the slave of the passions, by which he meant that reason alone (as exemplified by cost-benefit analysis) cannot make decisions but can only provide information; the impetus to act on the information must come from something else. More precisely, people act on beliefs rather than on information as such, and beliefs are influenced by emotion as well as by information.[16] These philosophical insights support the evolutionary basis and rational character of the "urge to action."

This is not to say that extraversion or introversion can be deduced from the rational model of human action, as risk aversion can be by positing declining marginal utility of money income.[17]

16. See Alberto Baccini, "Edgeworth on the Fundamentals of Choice under Uncertainty," 5 *History of Economic Ideas* 27 (1997).

17. To explain: suppose one's second dollar confers less utility (happiness, satisfaction) than one's first dollar. Then if offered a choice between the certainty of having one dollar and a 50 percent chance of having two dollars,

That does not make those traits "irrational," however. Personality traits are arational; they shape a person's utility function, as in the guppy case, rather than determining whether the person maximizes it.[18] People vary greatly in how risk averse they are, and the variance cannot be ascribed to different degrees of rationality.

People deal with their uncertainty aversion in a variety of ways—trying to transform it into calculable risk when they can do so, as by improving analytical techniques or gathering additional information, and, when they can't, substituting other methods of decision making for cost-benefit analysis. The methods include extrapolating from the past, deciding according to a rule of thumb, imitating other people, flipping a coin, seeking guidance in prayer, adopting a safety-first policy, and building relations of trust (often within the family) in order to create a form of insurance that does not rely on the calculation of premiums.[19] A legal system can reduce uncertainty—for example, by requiring compensation for the taking of property by the government, since such takings are uncertain events.[20]

Uncertainty aversion, and therefore liquidity preference, are

---

one will choose the first option even though the two options are actuarially equivalent. Preferring the first option is risk aversion.

18. Compare the analysis of rational responses to fear in Gary S. Becker and Yona Rubinstein, "Fear and the Response to Terrorism: An Economic Analysis" (Economics Department, University of Chicago, Feb. 2009). Fear is treated as a given, and the issue examined—the economic issue—is how people try to minimize it.

19. See, for example, Alya Guseva and Akos Rona-Tas, "Uncertainty, Risk, and Trust: Russian and American Credit Card Markets Compared," 66 *American Sociological Review* 623 (2001); Jens Beckert, "What Is Sociological about Economic Sociology? Uncertainty and the Embeddedness of Economic Action," 25 *Theory and Society* 803 (1996); Peter Kollock, "The Emergence of Exchange Structures: An Experimental Study of Uncertainty," 100 *American Journal of Sociology* 313 (1994).

20. On the broader issue of the role of legal regulation in reducing uncertainty, see David Easley and Maureen O'Hara, "Ambiguity and Nonparticipation: The Role of Regulation," 22 *Review of Financial Studies* 1817 (2009).

thus related to option theory.[21] The greater the uncertainty, the more time it may take to learn enough about a situation to have a solid basis for investment or consumption. One pays for this valuable waiting time by accepting a zero return on a part of one's wealth.[22] But this strategy works only if the information the absence of which creates uncertainty can be acquired in a reasonable amount of time; often it cannot be.

Just as it is a mistake to dichotomize risk and uncertainty, so it is a mistake to assume that every person is either an optimist or a pessimist, the former fearless in the face of uncertainty, the latter paralyzed by it. Self-selection will alter the proportions of the different personality types in different activities. Businessmen are more likely to be optimists than librarians are; and within an investment company, traders will tend to be optimists and risk managers pessimists.

Even if we assume that optimism and pessimism are invariant to circumstances—that nothing can shake an optimist's optimism or a pessimist's pessimism—we can see that a severe economic downturn would increase pessimism. The reason is that a disproportionate fraction of optimistic businessmen will be bankrupted in the downturn; they will have tended to overcommit their resources while the pessimists were busy accumulating precautionary savings. So in the bust the relative proportions of optimists and pessimists will change in favor of the latter.

This effect is likely to be augmented, moreover, by the tendency within the same person, optimist or pessimist, of the "urge to action" to be decreasing in uncertainty. Just as people are apt to demand a higher risk premium for bearing a higher risk, they are apt to demand a higher "premium" in some form for bearing greater uncertainty. Businessmen who have an overweening con-

21. See Robert A. Jones and Joseph M. Ostroy, "Flexibility and Uncertainty," 51 *Review of Economic Studies* 13 (1984).
22. David Dequech, "Asset Choice, Liquidity Preference, and Rationality under Uncertainty," 34 *Journal of Economic Issues* 159, 166–168 (2000).

fidence in their judgment—a confidence not balanced by any fear of the unknown—are unlikely to be successful, and they will tend to be weeded out in a competitive economy. The ones who remain will have a degree of fear, and it will tend to rise as uncertainty increases because fear undermines confidence.

Uncertainty aversion explains such economic paradoxes as the fact that slack builds up in firms and other organizations during good times, providing opportunities for an acquirer or new management to cut costs, and the fact that major innovations are more likely to come from new enterprises than from existing ones.[23] These are paradoxes because in economic theory an opportunity cost—a profitable alternative forgone—is equivalent to an out-of-pocket cost. But when a firm is doing well, management is reluctant to change its business model even if it senses an opportunity to increase profitability, because predicting the consequences of a major change is fraught with uncertainty.

Uncertainty aversion is captured in such common expressions as "fear of change" and "fear of the unknown." These are evolutionarily plausible emotions, and a common (and again, an evolutionarily plausible) reaction to them is to freeze. That is a way of gaining time to analyze an uncertain situation and perhaps reduce its uncertainty; in contrast, fear of a known danger not only sharpens alertness but is likely to accelerate the response to the danger. The downward spiral that marks an economic depression increases the uncertainty of the business environment, and businessmen tend to react by freezing, that is, by hoarding instead of investing. That freezing can lead to a liquidity crisis.[24]

If liquidity preference did not increase with uncertainty, an increase in uncertainty would stimulate investment by increasing the range of possible outcomes, since limited liability—meaning

23. See, for example, Clayton Christensen, *The Innovator's Dilemma: Why New Technologies Cause Great Firms to Fail* (1997).

24. Bryan R. Routledge and Stanley E. Zin, "Model Uncertainty and Liquidity" (Carnegie Mellon University, June 2004).

that shareholders are not personally liable for corporate losses—and solvency limitations truncate the downside of a risky decision.[25] But this is not observed in a depression. Instead, liquidity preference increases, driving up the interest rates that people demand to part with cash; and higher real interest rates cause investment to decline. High interest rates also, as I noted earlier, increase the opportunity cost of holding cash. But when those rates reflect anxiety they are likely to induce conversion of cash to safe savings, such as government bonds, which do not contribute, at least directly, to increased investment.

Even in a boom one needs *some* cash, if only for transactions. But in depressions (and irrespective of expectations of deflation, though such expectations create a powerful further incentive for hoarding cash) the amount of cash that people hold increases even though the number of transactions is falling. Call this the "emergency" motive for wanting liquidity. The conventional term is "precautionary," but I wish to emphasize the particular urgency of liquidity preference during a depression, when uncertainty spikes and the demand for cash and other highly liquid assets shoots up because the likelihood of needing cash in a hurry to make up for a fall in income has increased. The need for liquidity is especially acute when, as in the current economic crisis, people are overindebted and therefore unable or unwilling to borrow, and banks, though awash with lendable money, are reluctant to lend.

Uncertainty as a motive for hoarding should be distinguished from the "unreasoning, unjustified terror" of which Roosevelt spoke in his first inaugural address. People might think that all assets were overpriced and their prices would therefore fall. This would not be an unreasoning fear during a deflationary spiral, and in fact the economy had been in such a spiral for years when Roosevelt spoke. But fear is an emotional state that can exaggerate the dangers facing a person.

25. See Guiso and Parigi, note 9 above, at 185 and n. 1.

At the opposite extreme from unreasoning fear, hoarding can be strategic, notably in a deflation, when it is really a form of investment, because in a deflation the purchasing power of cash increases just as if it were earning interest.

Optimism and pessimism can be expected to affect the behavior of consumers as well as of businessmen. Optimistic consumers will tend to have spent more and made more risky investments during the boom, and so will have fewer resources in the bust. Pessimists will have more resources, relatively, but they will have a greater liquidity preference, and so the bust will reduce personal consumption expenditures even if the average consumer's optimism quotient is unaffected. But it *will* be affected, and in the direction of greater pessimism.

The well-observed phenomenon in the current depression of wealthy people reducing their consumption of luxury goods[26] illustrates the operation of liquidity preference in a depression. Being wealthy implies that one's marginal utility of income is low (one is surfeited with goods and services), and this reduces the cost of liquidity. Even if the likelihood of ruination seems remote, a rich person knows that rich people do get wiped out occasionally, especially in a very severe economic downturn, and so it may be rational for him to reduce his consumption, just in case. "When people are uncertain, a funny thing happens: they don't look inside for answers anymore because all they see is confusion . . . They look to see what other people in this situation are doing. That's a way to reduce my uncertainty about what I should be doing."[27]

26. See, for example, "Luxury Goods to Drop as Much as 20% in First Two Quarters of 2009 according to Latest Bain & Company Luxury Forecast," *Reuters*, Apr. 29, 2009, www.reuters.com/article/pressRelease/idUS 141483+20-Apr-2009+BW20090420 (visited Nov. 2, 2009).

27. Robert Cialdini, quoted in Michael S. Rosenwald, "When You're Flush, But Acting Flat Broke: Social Cues Can Drive a Downturn," *Washington Post*, Apr. 16, 2009, www.washingtonpost.com/wp-dyn/content/article/2009/04/15/AR2009041503791.html (visited Nov. 2, 2009).

And because the rich are trendsetters, a change in their behavior will influence the less rich.[28] The persons who reduce their purchase of luxury items attribute the change in their behavior not to fear or a desire to hoard cash against possible adversity but to a recognition of the virtues of thrift and frugality. But they are not virtues, or at least social virtues, in a depression, for then their main consequence is to increase unemployment in the luxury-goods industry. There is some offset; employment increases at the lower levels of retailing as the wealthy consumers downgrade. But the increase is less, because these consumers want to reduce their overall spending.

Notice that indulging liquidity preference, in this example, presupposes discretion in consumption. People living at a subsistence level cannot shift consumption to saving. But many of the personal consumption expenditures that Americans make are discretionary, and so economic fears can spur an increase in savings. The personal savings rate has risen sharply since the crash of September 2008.

The increase in the savings rate and the correlative decline in personal consumption expenditures during a depression have been thought a challenge to the life-cycle theory of consumption and saving.[29] The theory predicts that people will use borrowing and lending to adjust their spending throughout their lifetime so that the utility of their marginal dollar will be constant. If money is worth more to them at one period than at another (maybe when they have young children to support), they will borrow in order to have additional money then, thus shifting money from the future, when its marginal utility would be less, to the present.

28. See, for example, Gary S. Becker and William M. Landes, "The Social Market for the Great Masters and Other Collectibles," in Gary S. Becker and Kevin M. Murphy, *Social Economics: Market Behavior in a Social Environment* 74 (2000).

29. See Martin Browning and Thomas F. Crossley, "The Life Cycle Model of Consumption and Saving," *Journal of Economic Perspectives* 3, 7–12 (Summer 2001).

Were it not for liquidity constraints and declines in permanent income, the life-cycle theorist would not expect consumption to be correlated with the business cycle, because the business cycle is not correlated with the life cycle. At the bottom of the business cycle a person would be looking forward to a future boom and would want to shift some of the income he expects to earn then to the present, if the present is a time when the utility of money to him is high. But if a bust renders the future uncertain and thereby increases liquidity preference, consumption even by people who are not liquidity-constrained and whose permanent income will not be reduced by the depression will fall. With this modification, the life-cycle theory predicts greater spending in a boom, at least on durables, the purchase of which would have been delayed during the bust because of the increase in liquidity preference then.

Although the aggregate loss of personal income during a bust may be recovered in the boom that follows, for many people the loss of income will be permanent. Job destruction, as I noted in chapter 6, soars during a bust—think of the automobile workers who have been laid off from their high-paying jobs with little prospect of ever being rehired. This effect will be reinforced because uncertainty increases pessimism. More people will *think* that the future is bleak and therefore that their permanent income has declined even if it has not, and so they will reduce their spending. But even people who are not pessimistic will be uncertain whether their income will recover, and this uncertainty may make them think that their permanent income is less than they thought, and so they will reduce consumption.

The effect of uncertainty aversion on investment and consumption provides a further reason why government should try to avoid (though of course with due regard to the costs of avoiding) doing things during a depression that make the economic environment more uncertain. But this is easier said than done. Harassing business by limiting bonuses or other compensation, subjecting it to new regulations, and changing the rules of the game concerning the rights of secured creditors in bankruptcy increase uncertainty. But as in the 1930s depression, measures that reduce business confidence may increase consumers' confidence if consumers blame business for their economic plight and interpret antibusiness measures as evidence that the government is combating the depression by striking at its source. This may be one reason why the government has emphasized risk taking by bankers rather than mistakes by government as a cause of the depression; another is that a confession of governmental incompetence would shake people's confidence in the government's ability to bring us out of the depression. But doubtless the main reason is politics, and the net effect of banker bashing is almost certainly to retard recovery. (Keynes had mentioned fear of a "Labour government" as a factor in the reluctance of business to invest during a depression.)[30]

Even empty threats shake the confidence of business and eventually that of the general public. An example is talk of "nationalizing" financially shaky banks rather than bailing them out. This talk comes from the sidelines rather than from the government, but at first, perhaps to put pressure on the banks, the government did not dismiss it emphatically, so that a cloud remained hovering over the banks while offering no balm to an anxious public.

Government should seek to allay the fears, unreasoning and otherwise, of consumers and businessmen, but not by lying about the economic situation—rather by projecting, as Roosevelt did so successfully (though in fact neither he nor his advisers knew how to arrest the depression), an aura of confidence, command, and determination. A wrinkle here, however, is that uncertainty aversion appears to decrease with increases in the ominousness of an uncertain event.[31] If you were told that you probably are dying, you would prefer the prognosis to contain

---

30. Keynes, *The General Theory* 162–163, note 1 above.
31. W. Kip Viscusi and Harrell Chesson, "Hopes and Fears: The Conflicting Effects of Risk Ambiguity," 47 *Theory and Decision* 153 (1999).

a large error term.[32] This suggests a downside to efforts by government to encourage spending by understating the gravity of the economic situation. Businessmen who believe that their businesses probably are doomed will have an incentive (given limited liability and limited solvency) to make risky investments in the belief that only by "throwing long" is there any chance of survival. And inducing investment is the central goal of efforts to speed recovery from a depression.

Government should not try to do too much—it should not try to superimpose reform on recovery, for by doing so it will increase the uncertainty of the business environment. As Keynes explained in an open letter to Roosevelt,

> Recovery and Reform—recovery from the slump and the passage of those business and social reforms which are long overdue. For the first, speed and quick results are essential. The second may be urgent too; but haste will be injurious, and wisdom of long-range purpose is more necessary than immediate achievement. It will be through raising high the prestige of your administration by success in short-range Recovery, that you will have the driving force to accomplish long-range Reform. On the other hand, even wise and necessary Reform may, in some respects, impede and complicate Recovery. For it will upset the confidence of the business world and weaken their existing motives to action, before you have had time to put other motives in their place. It may over-task your bureaucratic machine, which the traditional individualism of the United States and the old "spoils system" have left none too strong. And it will confuse the thought and aim of yourself and your administration by giving you too much to think about all at once.[33]

The Obama Administration has not taken this advice to heart; nor did Roosevelt.

32. Id. at 155.
33. "An Open Letter to President Roosevelt," *New York Times,* Dec. 31, 1933, http://select.nytimes.com/gst/abstract.html?res=F70A11FB3C55137 38DDDA80B94DA415B838FF1D3&scp=1&sq=keynes%20open%20let ter%201933&st=cse (visited Nov. 2, 2009).

Another implication of my analysis is that generous unemployment benefits may, by reducing individuals' economic uncertainty, contribute to recovery from a depression. True, they will also lengthen the period of job search. But if there is little hiring, the principal effect may be that more newcomers to the workforce, who are not eligible for unemployment benefits, will be employed, rather than that unemployment will rise.

More important, a stimulus program that reduces unemployment, even if only slightly, may increase economic activity by reducing the fear of the still employed of losing their jobs and by convincing people that the government is indeed determined to speed recovery from the depression.[34] But unless carefully designed and limited in size, such a program, by increasing the national debt and therefore inducing expectations of higher taxes, inflation, devaluation, or other adverse future economic developments, may cause people to reduce their estimate of their permanent income and thereby curtail their spending.

34. The role of stimulus programs as confidence-builders is overlooked in the otherwise excellent argument for the need for such a program in our current economic troubles in Martin Feldstein, "Rethinking the Role of Fiscal Policy," 99 *American Economic Review Papers and Proceedings* 556 (May 2009).

THE CRISIS OF MACROECONOMICS

10

One thing we've learned from the economic events of the past two years is that macroeconomics, or at least the part of macroeconomics that studies the business cycle, is a weak field. With only a few exceptions, macroeconomists, including the most illustrious, did not anticipate the current depression.[1] And the profession cannot agree what to do about it, or, more precisely, what to do next—continue fighting it or move to head off the possible aftershock of inflation and related deficit-engendered woes. "When asked the question: 'Can you explain what has happened?' Robert Solow, a winner of the Nobel Prize in Economics, simply shakes his head and says: 'No, I don't think that normal economic thinking can help explain this crisis.'"[2] A remark made many years ago by another Nobel Prize–winning macroeconomist, Robert Lucas, has been confirmed: "As an advice-giving profession we are in way over our heads."[3] In part this may be because macroeconomists' advice tends to a suspi-

1. See Richard A. Posner, *A Failure of Capitalism: The Crisis of '08 and the Descent into Depression*, chs. 4, 8 (2009).
2. "Is 2009 the New 1929? Current Crisis Shows Uncanny Parallels to Great Depression," pt. 5, "Underestimating the Crash," *Der Spiegel*, Apr. 29, 2009, www.spiegel.de/international/world/0,1518,621979-5,00.html (visited Dec. 12, 2009).
3. Robert E. Lucas, Jr., *Studies in Business-Cycle Theory* 259 (1981).

cious degree to be correlated with their politics. "Because non-economists often favor one policy or another based on their own interests, or prefer economic advice that pretends to certainty, there is an incentive for economists to become contending advocates of theories, rather than cool assessors of the state of knowledge."[4] Usually if you know whether an economist is liberal or conservative, you know whether he favors or opposes the $787 billion stimulus plan and whether he worries more about unemployment than about inflation. This is not the sign of a mature science. Furthermore, the neglect of the informal economic approach taken by Keynes in favor of mathematical models of the business cycle has been a mistake, but so too, as we shall see in this chapter, is the attempt to marry Keynes to the new field of "behavioral economics."

I have been moved to criticize a number of economists in this book because there has been so little self-criticism by economists—a bad sign. Instead we have defensiveness, as in a May 2009 article by Gregory Mankiw that offers the following defense of his profession's disappointing performance:

> It is fair to say that this crisis caught most economists flat-footed. In the eyes of some people, this forecasting failure is an indictment of the profession. But that is the wrong interpretation. In one way, the current downturn is typical: Most economic slumps take us by surprise. Fluctuations in economic activity are largely unpredictable. Yet this is no reason for embarrassment. Medical experts cannot forecast the emergence of diseases like swine flu and they can't even be certain what paths the diseases will then take. Some things are just hard to predict.[5]

There *is* reason for embarrassment—"caught flat-footed" may be an unconscious acknowledgment of that. Mankiw's de-

4. Christopher A. Sims, "Macroeconomics and Methodology," *Journal of Economic Perspectives* 105, 107 (Winter 1996).

5. Gregory Mankiw, "That Freshman Course Won't Be Quite the Same," *New York Times*, May 24, 2009, p. B5.

fense of his profession misses the point, which is not forecasting error but obliviousness to danger. The medical profession knows that it can't predict the emergence of a new pandemic and, knowing this, takes precautions, such as the creation of a global early-warning network, the adoption of protocols for minimizing the spread of a new contagious disease, and the development of new vaccines and treatments. And when a new disease appears, the profession swings into action.

The Federal Reserve is not the equal of the Centers for Disease Control, or macroeconomics comparable as a scientific discipline to public health, medicine, or biology. An economic disease that was not new—namely, the metastasis of housing prices—appeared in the early 2000s and was largely ignored by the economics profession. The bubble burst in 2007 and a recession ensued, the dangerousness of which the profession missed. The near-collapse of the banking industry in September 2008 came as a shock to economists both inside and outside the government, as did the failure of the economy to respond to the orthodox treatment—reducing the federal funds rate.

We have discovered that despite the centrality of banking to the economy of a modern commercial society, macroeconomists know little about modern banking and that an understanding of the business cycle continues to elude them as well. If I may again quote Mankiw, writing in February 2009, "I don't pretend to be enough of an expert, or to be close enough to the facts, or to have a large enough staff, to know what should be done with the banking system, which is at the center of our current economic turmoil. But I am confident that fixing it should be the main focus of policy efforts."[6]

The economics of the business cycle is a weak area of economics because of the difficulty of conducting cogent empirical stud-

6. "Greg Mankiw's Blog," Feb. 16, 2009, http://gregmankiw.blogspot.com/2009/02/nationalization-or-pre-privatization.html (visited Dec. 8, 2009).

ies, because of stubborn theoretical disagreements (a problem related to the empirical difficulties—the rival theories can't readily be confirmed or falsified empirically), because of the complexity of the economy, and because of the high ideological stakes and resulting tendency to the politicization of academic controversy. These are inherent difficulties of business-cycle economics, for which economists should not be blamed. But they can be blamed for underestimating the difficulties and overestimating their understanding. In 2002, referring to Milton Friedman's theory that mistakes by the Federal Reserve had turned a recession triggered by the stock market crash of October 1929 into the Great Depression, Ben Bernanke, addressing Friedman and his collaborator Anna Schwartz, said: "Regarding the Great Depression. You're right, we [the Federal Reserve] did it. We're very sorry. But thanks to you, we won't do it again."[7] They've done it again. In his presidential address to the American Economic Association the following year, Robert Lucas announced that the problem of depressions had been solved and macroeconomists should move on to other subjects.[8]

Speaking of Milton Friedman, I am put in mind of a remark in his monetary history with Anna Schwartz about the Great Depression:

> The literature, and particularly the academic literature, on the banking and liquidity crisis is almost as depressing as that on the contraction in general. Most surprisingly, those whose work had done most to lay the groundwork for the Federal Reserve Act or who had been most intimately associated with its formulation . . . were least perceptive, perhaps because they had so strong an intellectual commitment to the view that the Federal Reserve System had once and for all

7. "Remarks by Governor Ben S. Bernanke at the Conference to Honor Milton Friedman," University of Chicago, Nov. 8, 2002, www.federalreserve.gov/BOARDDOCS/SPEECHES/2002/20021108/default.htm (visited Dec. 8, 2009).

8. Robert E. Lucas, Jr., "Macroeconomic Priorities," 93 *American Economic Review* 1 (2003).

solved problems of liquidity. One can read through the annual Proceedings of the American Economic Association or of the Academy of Political Sciences and find only an occasional sign that the academic world even knew about the unprecedented banking collapse in process, let alone that it understood the cause and the remedy.[9]

Plus ça change, plus c'est la même chose.

In November 2008, shortly after the banking crash, Queen Elizabeth II visited the London School of Economics and asked the faculty why "nobody [had] noticed [before September 2008] that the credit crunch was on its way." Responding in the unhurried English fashion, on June 27, 2009, seven months after the Queen's visit, the British academy convened a forum to answer her question. The answer was delivered in a July 22 letter to the Queen written by two professors at LSE, Tim Besley and Peter Hennessy.[10] The letter is complacent. Responsibility for the oversight is attributed to "a failure of the collective imagination of many bright people, both in this country and internationally, to understand the risks to the system as a whole." In other words, everyone was to blame, which means no one was to blame. "Everyone seemed to be doing their [*sic*] own job properly on its own merit," but no one realized that the individual activities of the "many bright people" had endangered the solvency of the entire global financial system. On the contrary, people were lulled into believing that "financial wizards" had purged risk from the system.

The letter does not mention the economics profession, although one of the authors is an economics professor (Besley; Hennessy is a political historian). The only economic models referred to appear to be "value at risk" models for calculating the risk of loss in an individual transaction.

---

9. Milton Friedman and Anna Jacobson Schwartz, *A Monetary History of the United States, 1867–1960* 410–411 (1971).

10.   http://media.ft.com/cms/3e3b6ca8-7a08-11de-b86f-00144feabdc0 .pdf (visited Dec. 6, 2009).

On August 10 another letter was written to the Queen responding to her question, this one signed by ten English and Australian economists.[11] This letter criticizes Besley and Hennessy's letter. It charges that "their overall analysis is inadequate because it fails to acknowledge any deficiency in the training or culture of economists themselves." It continues that "in recent years economics has turned virtually into a branch of applied mathematics, and has . . . become detached from real-world institutions and events." Education in economics has become too narrow, "to the detriment of any synthetic vision," and Besley and Hennessy say nothing about "the typical omission of psychology, philosophy or economic history from the current education of economists" and mention neither "the highly questionable belief in universal 'rationality' nor the 'efficient markets hypothesis.'"

A more focused criticism would have been more effective. The Queen was asking about the failure to foresee the financial collapse of the previous September rather than about the health of modern economics in the large. That failure was due in significant part to a concept of rationality that exaggerates the amount of information that people—even experts—have about the future and to a disregard of economic factors that don't lend themselves to expression in mathematical models. The efficient-markets theory, when understood not merely as teaching that markets are hard to beat even for experts and therefore passive management of a diversified portfolio of assets will almost certainly beat stock picking, but as demonstrating that asset prices are a dependable gauge of value and therefore that there are no asset "bubbles," blinded most economists to the housing bubble of the early 2000s and the stock market bubble that expanded with it.

And in modeling the business cycle economists ignored not

11. www.feed-charity.org/user/image/queen2009b.pdf (visited Dec. 8, 2009).

only vital institutional details (such as the rise of the shadow banking industry), because such details are difficult to accommodate in mathematical models, but often money itself, on the ground, derived from Say's Law, that it doesn't really affect the "real" (that is, the nonfinancial) economy. They ignored key concepts in Keynes's analysis of the business cycle, such as hoarding, uncertainty, business confidence ("animal spirits"), and workers' resistance to nominal (as distinct from real) wage reductions in depressions. Lessons of economic history were ignored too, reinforcing the belief that there would never be another depression. Even when the banking industry imploded, many macroeconomists denied that the implosion would lead to anything worse than a mild recession. The measures that the government has taken to recover from what has turned into a depression owe little to post-Keynesian economic thinking, and economists cannot agree on what more, if anything, should be done and which of the government's recovery measures has worked or will work.

Granted, the study of business cycles is only a part of modern economics. Other parts, such as labor economics, bear significantly on the study of business cycles without being implicated in the failures of response to the current crisis. But the management of the business cycle had until the present crisis been regarded as a triumph of modern economics and a justification for regarding economics as the queen of the social sciences.

In May 2009 *Knowledge@Wharton,* the online journal of the University of Pennsylvania's Wharton business school, published an article entitled "Why Economists Failed to Predict the Financial Crisis."[12] Like the second letter to Queen Elizabeth, the article criticizes economists for having committed themselves to a model of human behavior that exaggerates rationality. This is a surprising criticism coming from a business school, since so

12. http://knowledge.wharton.upenn.edu/article.cfm?articleid=2234 (visited Dec. 8, 2009).

many business school professors advocate efficient-markets theory in a very strong form. I agree with the criticism but would prefer to avoid fussing over the meaning of "rationality" and its cognates. It is an extremely vague word. A serviceable definition is responding logically and consistently to whatever relevant information can be obtained at a cost less than the expected value of the information. Emphasis needs to be placed on the limited availability (high cost) of information bearing on many economic decisions, whether by businessmen or consumers, and as a result the frequent presence of uncertainty in the sense of risks that cannot be calculated. Uncertainty can lead to "herding" behavior—following in another's tracks in the hope that the other knows more than one does—or, what amounts to the same thing, "momentum" trading of common stock and other assets. This kind of behavior is sometimes irrational but often is a rational second-best response to inability to obtain good information to guide a decision.

The Wharton article cites a report by eight European economists (known as the "Dahlem Report") on the failure of the economics profession to foresee the financial crisis.[13] The report states that "the economics profession appears to have been unaware of the long build-up to the current worldwide financial crisis and to have significantly underestimated its dimensions once it started to unfold. In our view, this lack of understanding is due to a misallocation of research efforts in economics. We trace the deeper roots of this failure to the profession's insistence on constructing models that, by design, disregard the key elements driving outcomes in real-world markets."[14] The report notes that "as the crisis has unfolded, economists have had no choice but to abandon their standard models and to produce hand-waving

13. David Colander et al., "The Financial Crisis and the Systemic Failure of Academic Economics" (Kiel Institute for the World Economy Working Paper No. 1489, Feb. 2009).
14. Id. at 1.

common-sense remedies."[15] There is indeed a striking contrast between the formalism of modern economic models of the economy and the advice that economists have been giving since the crisis erupted. Essentially they have advised the use of remedies that have been known and applied since the nineteenth century— or disparaged those remedies.

Three articles in the July 16, 2009, issue of the *Economist* magazine criticize the economics profession for its failure to anticipate the financial crisis and for its inability to agree on what should be done to speed recovery.[16] Like mine, this is criticism from outside the profession. The articles are worth reading, but they rely too heavily on criticisms from within economics itself, notably from Joseph Stiglitz and Paul Krugman, whose positions are extreme. Unlike conservative economists who oppose any stimulus package, left-leaning economists such as Stiglitz and Krugman argue that the stimulus is too small. They began agitating in June 2009 for a *second* stimulus of perhaps $1 trillion.[17] Without analysis and explanation that they did not offer their readers, the proposal was irresponsible. With the national debt soaring, the question whether the nation could afford another $1 trillion debt was acute. And what would the money be used for? When would it come on line? How would the program be deformed as it wended its way through Congress? The states are facing an aggregate budget shortfall of at least $100 billion, and there is an argument for a federal loan to tide them over. But the

15. Id. at 2. For amplification of the analysis in the Dahlem Report, see David Colander et al., "The Financial Crisis and the Systemic Failure of Academic Economics," 21 *Critical Review* 249 (2009).

16. "What Went Wrong with Economics," *Economist*, Jul. 18, 2009, p. 11; "The State of Macroeconomics," *Economist*, Jul. 18, 2009, p. 65; "Efficiency and Beyond," *Economist*, Jul. 18, 2009, p. 68.

17. See, for example, Paul Krugman, "The Stimulus Trap," *New York Times*, July 9, 2009, p. A25; Joseph Stiglitz, "Stimulus or Bust." *Guardian*, Aug. 10, 2009, www.guardian.co.uk/commentisfree/cifamerica/2009/aug/10/economy-stimulus-bailout (visited Dec. 8, 2009). See also Paul Krugman, "Mission Not Accomplished," *New York Times*, Oct. 2, 2009, p. A31.

other $900 billion? Could it be spent in the near term, or not until 2011 and 2012, when it might have a strong inflationary effect?

Supporters of fiscal stimulus claim that to the extent it increases output and therefore tax revenues, the contribution that its cost makes to the deficit is exaggerated. But this is imprecise. The deficit is increased by the full cost of the stimulus, though it may make future deficits smaller than they otherwise would be, which is just to say that deficit projections should take account of the effect of stimulus on government revenue. But the stimulus will not reduce the annual structural deficit—$500 billion and growing—or the deficits likely to be created by the Administration's health-care and climate-change initiatives, or by other ambitious social-engineering programs still to be announced.

Neglect of essential details also shadows the left-leaning economists' proposal to nationalize (that is, confiscate), rather than bail out, the banks whose risky lending and resulting near-collapse precipitated the depression. Government ownership of the immensely complex big banks, even if intended to be temporary, could well be a disaster. Certainly it would have a baleful effect on business morale, and this should worry followers of Keynes, as the leftist economists purport to be. The day the government took control of the board, management would be wondering, What happens to us? And who will the government appoint to the board? And what will the board do—whom will it appoint to run the company? Who are the smart bankers? And how long will it take the new management to get up to speed? And will the board be profit-maximizing, or will it pursue political objectives, as in other nationalized industries? Will it want profits sacrificed to mortgage relief, for example?

Krugman's uncritical enthusiasm for universal health insurance reflects an internal struggle between his economics and his politics, in which the latter usually prevails. He is not a health economist and has offered no analysis of the likely costs of the changes that he favors, which would go much further than the

Administration's current thinking. On the basis of current long-term interest rates on bonds, he insists that the threat of inflation is negligible in the foreseeable future and infers from this that the nation can well afford even bigger deficits than it is running. His analysis is cursory.

Robert Lucas, from the other end of the political spectrum, responded to the *Economist*'s criticisms of the profession.[18] But his response is technical. He argues that economists will never develop models that can forecast "sudden falls in the value of financial assets, like the declines that followed the failure of Lehman Brothers in September [2008]." The reason is efficient-markets theory, which teaches that the prices of financial assets impound the best information about their value. But Lucas's detour into efficient-markets theory is wide of the mark. The criticism of macroeconomists and financial economists is not that they failed to predict that the collapse of Lehman Brothers would lead to a fall in stock prices (they were already falling). It is that they disbelieved in asset bubbles and so were oblivious to signs that the rise in housing prices in the early 2000s was a bubble phenomenon—oblivious even though there were plenty of warnings by reputable people[19] and a history stretching back to the Great Depression of bank failures, precipitated by risky lending, that had destabilized or threatened to destabilize the economy of the United States and other countries.[20]

Lacking interest in institutional detail (a lack related to the in-

18. Robert E. Lucas, "In Defense of the Dismal Science," *Economist*, Aug. 6, 2009, p. 67.

19. See, for example, Dirk J. Bezemer, "'No One Saw This Coming': Understanding Financial Crisis through Accounting Models" (MPRA Paper No. 15892, Munic Personal RePEc Archive, June 16, 2009), http://ideas.repec.org/p/pra/mprapa/15767.html (visited Dec. 12, 2009).

20. Nicole Gelinas, *After the Fall: Saving Capitalism from Wall Street—and Washington* (2009), is a lucid account of the long string of precedents for the financial collapse of September 2008. A more comprehensive account is Carmen M. Reinhart and Kenneth S. Rogoff, *This Time Is Different: Eight Centuries of Financial Folly* (2009).

creasing mathematization of economics and to the type of person attracted to the field by that mathematization), the economics profession did not understand how deeply the banking industry was invested in housing and that it might collapse along with housing prices when the bubble burst. The profession mistakenly believed, moreover, that at the first sign of trouble the Federal Reserve could avert a serious recession by reducing the federal funds rate.

Lucas's version of efficient-markets theory shares with his own distinctive contribution to macroeconomics—the rational-expectations hypothesis—an exaggerated belief in the knowledge and foresight of investors and other economic actors. (And here his conservatism shows; conservatives believe that markets are robust and government intervention in them rarely justified.) Not that any economist believes that markets are omniscient. The steep rise in oil prices in the wake of the 1973 war of Egypt and Syria against Israel had macroeconomic consequences yet could not have been foreseen. But that is an example of an external shock. No external shock caused the fall in housing and stock prices and the collapse of the banking industry in 2008. The housing bubble, the risky capital structures of the banks, lax regulation, and the low personal savings rate were internal U.S. economic phenomena that had been building for many years. Neither the markets nor the economists foresaw the consequences.

Lucas argues that until the collapse of Lehman Brothers, the risk of a financial crisis was so small that to have recommended "pre-emptive monetary policies on the scale of the policies that were applied later on would have been like turning abruptly off the road because of the potential for someone suddenly to swerve head-on into your lane."[21] The probability of such a sudden swerve is indeed too slight to justify the costly preventive measure of not driving at all. But the financial crisis had been building since mid-2007 and had turned acute in March 2008

21. Lucas, "In Defense of the Dismal Science," note 18 above.

with the collapse of Bear Stearns, yet the Federal Reserve and most economists, including Lucas, did not notice the crisis that was swerving head-on into their lane. Just a few days *after* Lehman collapsed, Lucas expressed skepticism that the economy would slip into a recession[22] (where it had already been for ten months), and a few days *before* the collapse he had expressed skepticism that the subprime mortgage crisis would contaminate the mortgage market.[23] Even though he disbelieves in forecasts, he was making forecasts, and they were erroneous.

Lucas says in his *Economist* piece that the Federal Reserve saved the day by pumping cash into the banking system and persuading the Treasury Department to do likewise. He does not mention the other measures taken by the government. He praises Bernanke for having "formulated contingency plans ready for use when unforeseeable shocks occurred." In fact the Fed made no contingency plans to deal with possible housing and stock market collapses that might shake the economy to its foundations. Its response when the shocks hit with full force in September 2008 was prompt but also improvised and spasmodic, and included the calamitous failure to bail out Lehman Brothers.

That was one blunder Bernanke made, and there are others, none of which Lucas—who is unstinting in his praise of Bernanke—mentions. Nouriel Roubini, while urging Bernanke's reappointment as Fed chairman, had pointed out that Bernanke "supported flawed policies when Alan Greenspan pushed the federal funds rate . . . too low for too long and failed to monitor mortgage lending properly, thus creating the housing and credit and mortgage bubbles"; "kept arguing that the housing recession would bottom out soon"; "argued that the subprime problem was a contained problem when in fact it was a symptom of

22. Matthew Benjamin, "Hundreds of Economists Urge Congress Not to Rush on Rescue Plan," *Bloomberg,* Sept. 25, 2009, www.bloomberg.com/apps/news?pid=20601087&sid=aNKGD.bJwmRA (visited Dec. 8, 2009).

23. Robert E. Lucas, Jr., "Mortgages and Monetary Policy," *Wall Street Journal,* Sept. 19, 2007, p. A20.

the biggest leverage and credit bubble in American history"; "argued that the collapse in the housing market would not lead to a recession"; "argued that monetary policy should not be used to control asset bubbles," and "attributed the large United States current account deficits to a savings glut in China and emerging markets, understating the role that excessive fiscal deficits and debt accumulation by American households and the financial systems played."[24] This long string of mistakes, surprising in the economics profession's foremost student of the Great Depression, highlight the weakness of business-cycle economics.

Lucas has responded to my criticism of his article in the *Economist* in an e-mail that he has authorized me to quote. He says:

> I think you are making a big mistake in dismissing the efficient market hypothesis. [Eugene] Fama is not just a theorist: He is a meticulous statistician and data guy. The CRSP [Center for Research in Security Prices] data set on stock prices that he put together years ago was a great achievement by itself. He and his students and hundreds of others have tested the implications of the EMH [efficient-markets hypothesis] on these and other data. I think you owe it to yourself to look at some of this evidence before you write it off . . .
>
> The logic is very commonsensical too. If I have information that an asset I hold will decline in price between today and tomorrow, I am going to sell today. If lots of others have the same information I do, they will sell too. But then the entire price decline will occur today. (This does not rule out the possibility of a Warren Buffett, who processes way more and better information than others do.)
>
> Don't be put off by the term "efficient" in the EMH. The EMH is completely value-free, like the gas laws.
>
> I think if you try to write down exactly what your imaginary bubble-popper will do when he goes to the office every day—maybe provide a little institutional detail—you will see that he is just a fantasy.

24. Nouriel Roubini, "The Great Preventer," *New York Times Week in Review,* July 25, 2009, p. 12.

I have been defending the efficient-markets theory for more than thirty years, since I first argued that trustees should be permitted to adopt a buy-and-hold strategy for their trust portfolios and to rely on diversification to minimize risk, rather than trying to evaluate the prospects of each individual stock in the portfolio or to time market turns.[25] (That is now the accepted understanding of the law's "prudent man" rule of trust investment.) But my understanding of the theory is not that the stock market consistently discounts corporate earnings accurately. Just the fact that stock prices gyrate much more than the value of the companies whose stock is traded refutes the notion that the stock market is "efficient" in a strong sense.[26] As a matter of theory, moreover, as Grossman and Stiglitz explained long ago, "because information is costly, prices cannot perfectly reflect the information which is available, since if it did, those who spent resources to obtain it would receive no compensation."[27]

The weaker notion of efficient markets—that the market is hard to beat—is consistent with the existence of bubbles and of the "momentum" trading that underlies them ("the trend is my friend").[28] One of Keynes's insights was that many people trade

25. See, for example, John H. Langbein and Richard A. Posner, "Market Funds and Trust-Investment Law," 1976 *American Bar Foundation Research Journal* 1; "The Revolution in Trust Investment Law," 62 *American Bar Association Journal* 887 (1976); Posner, "The Prudent Investor's Powers and Obligations in an Age of Market (Index) Funds," in *Evolving Concepts of Prudence* 19 (Financial Analysts Research Foundation 1976); also in 5 *Journal of Contemporary Business* 85 (Summer 1976).

26. Lawrence H. Summers, "Commentary on 'Policies to Curb Stock Market Volatility,'" paper delivered at Symposium on Financial Market Volatility, Federal Reserve Bank of Kansas City, Aug. 17–19, 1988, www.kc.frb.org/publicat/Sympos/1988/S88SUMME.PDF (visited Dec. 8, 2009).

27. Sanford J. Grossman and Joseph E. Stiglitz, "On the Impossibility of Informationally Efficient Markets," 70 *American Economic Review* 393, 405 (1980). Fama has conceded the point. See Eugene F. Fama, "Efficient Capital Markets: II," 46 *Journal of Finance* 1575 (1991).

28. When the Dow Jones Industrial Average appeared to be approaching

on the basis of what they think other people are trading on. You see prices rising and think the people paying the higher prices may know something about values that you don't know. You may even be rather confident that rising housing or stock prices are a bubble phenomenon, but if you think that other traders will keep pushing them up, you may rationally decide to buy as well, since if you bail out before the bubble bursts you may be leaving a lot of money on the table.

Eugene Fama has criticized me in correspondence for arguing that the rise in housing prices in the early 2000s was a bubble. He points out that real estate prices rose in many other countries as well, including countries in which subprime mortgages are not offered, and that the prices of other assets, including publicly traded stocks and commercial real estate, also rose. Since bubbles have to be financed with savings, he is skeptical that the market value of *all* assets could have been pushed up just by low interest rates that drained savings into asset purchases. He argues that the so-called bubble in U.S. housing prices was based on expectations of higher future values and that the fall in prices discounted future losses that were expected to result from a recession caused by "real" (that is, nonfinancial) events. He acknowledges, however, that macroeconomics has never been good at explaining why the shocks that lead to economic downturns occur; he gives as examples efforts to explain the Great Depression and the current downturn.

Fama is correct that the bubble was worldwide. Low interest rates were a global phenomenon, and low interest rates caused the bubble. Subprime mortgages contributed to it by increasing

---

the magic number 10,000, an equity strategist was quoted as saying: "Will 10,000 make a difference to some people? . . . It's psychological, but if enough people act on it, it's meaningful. The higher the market goes, the more that those on the sideline sit there and are concerned they're missing something. It takes a while for their fear to wear off." *New York Times,* Sept. 29, 2009, p. B1.

the demand for housing. But they were not essential; low interest rates alone increase the demand for housing because houses are bought mainly with debt. And it is not true that an increase in the market value of some class of assets can't exceed the total savings available for buying the assets. If the price of a house rises, the market value of the other houses in the neighborhood may well rise too even though there aren't buyers for all those houses.

The current downturn does not appear to be the result of some event in the "real" economy, like the oil-price hikes of the 1970s. It is the product of a sharp fall in housing and stock prices that reduced people's wealth dramatically so that they started spending less, which caused a recession, which became catastrophic when the banking industry collapsed in September 2008.

Defending the Fed's inaction in the face of asset-price inflation, Fama expresses skepticism that the federal funds rate influences anything other than the inflation component of interest rates. I disagree (see chapter 1), but even if he is right, that more limited influence is critical, because changes in the federal funds rate signal the Fed's inflation expectations and likely response and so influence long-run interest rates. When the Fed raised the federal funds rate to 20 percent in 1981, market interest rates quickly followed; the prime rate rose to 21.5 percent that year and the thirty-year mortgage rate to 16.63 percent.

The Fed's failure to dig the economy out of the hole into which it fell in September 2008 by expanding the money supply to reduce interest rates persuaded much of the economics profession to support fiscal stimulus—the Keynesian prescription for speeding recovery from a depression. In a recent book two distinguished liberal economists, George Akerlof and Robert Shiller, reflecting on the current depression, marry Keynes to "behavioral economics" (which we encountered in chapter 5 in discussing the proposed Consumer Financial Protection Agency) and offer the resulting union as a replacement for the conventional failed monetarist economics.[29]

The title of the book reflects the authors' belief that by "animal spirits" Keynes meant "noneconomic motives and irrational behaviors" and that he wanted government to "countervail the excesses that occur because of our animal spirits."[30] That is a misreading. The passage in which Keynes mentions animal spirits, as we know from chapter 8, is not about excesses and does not argue that "animal spirits" should be damped down. It is about the danger of paralysis in the face of uncertainty ("If the animal spirits are dimmed and the spontaneous optimism fades, enterprise will fade and die"). Because businessmen, especially when investing in projects that will not yield an immediate return, are operating in an uncertain environment, they need a spurt of confidence—a willingness to take a plunge into a body of cold economic water—in order to steel themselves to invest. Their confidence and hence willingness to invest, and the confidence of workers and hence their willingness to spend on consumption, are diminished when unemployment is high. So, Keynes argued, government should step in and replace lost private demand for goods and services with increased public demand. That would make businessmen more willing to hire and invest and by thus reducing unemployment would increase the willingness and ability of consumers to spend.

Keynes did worry about stock market speculation, because he thought that speculators based their decisions on guesses about the psychology of other investors rather than on which companies had the best prospects and therefore should attract new investment. But he did not relate speculation to an excess of animal spirits.

29. George A. Akerlof and Robert J. Shiller, *Animal Spirits: How Human Psychology Drives the Economy, and Why It Matters for Global Capitalism* (2009).

30. Id. at x.

Since the publication of their book, Akerlof and Schiller have acknowledged that they "cannot say definitely to what degree Keynes would have been sympathetic to our view. *Nor does it really matter what he would have thought.* We are presenting a new theory of macroeconomics which we think is in the spirit of Keynes, but it is a new theory."[31] Yet in their book they had ascribed to him the claim central to their own analysis that "these *animal spirits* are the main cause for why the economy fluctuates as it does. They are also the main cause of involuntary employment . . . Keynes's animal spirits are the keynote to a different view of the economy—a view that explains the underlying instabilities of capitalism."[32]

The irony is that the authors rightly criticize mainstream economists for having so far forgotten Keynes that present-day "Keynesian economics" (usually called the "New Keynesian Economics") bears little relation to Keynes's actual views. It seems that Akerlof and Shiller are among the forgetful ones. This is surprising, because Keynes is a powerful antidote to the kind of overformalized mainstream macroeconomics that the authors decry.

They list "confidence," "fairness," "money illusion," the temptation to "corruption," and susceptibility to "stories" as manifestations of "animal spirits" that create bubbles that lead eventually to recession or depression. Only "confidence" comes within shouting distance of the meaning Keynes assigned to "animal spirits." People buy common stock when stock prices are rising, and they (notoriously) bought houses during the early 2000s, when house prices were rising. Since no one (with the rarest of exceptions) can predict the ups and downs of the stock market or the housing market, these purchases must have been

31. George A. Akerlof and Robert J. Shiller, Letter to the *New Republic,* May 8, 2009, www.tnr.com/article/books-and-arts/disputations-our-new-theory-macroeconomics (visited Dec. 8, 2009) (emphasis added).

32. Akerlof and Shiller, note 29 above, at ix (footnote omitted; emphasis added).

motivated, the authors argue, by something other than rational utility maximization. But that is not obvious, or implied by Keynes's usage. Common stocks have generally been a good investment. And since no one is able to time market turns, no one knows when the market is overpriced and therefore when one should sell rather than buy. Indeed, the idea of selling at the "top" of the market is incoherent, because if it were known that stock prices had peaked, no one would buy.

There are plenty of dummies who play the stock market; there is momentum trading by people fearful of missing out on a bonanza; the overwhelming evidence that index funds outperform managed mutual funds has not weaned most investors from the managed funds; newspapers still print, presumably because there is a readership for, stock forecasts by analysts and money managers who have no record of being able to outperform the market; and there is Keynes's point that smart speculators may trade not on the economic prospects of companies but on their sense of how other traders will behave. But few sophisticated investors thought that the stock market was overpriced when it peaked in 2007; had they thought that, they would have reduced the amount of stock in their investment portfolios. The problem was not irrationality; the problem was rational ignorance, including ignorance of the Federal Reserve's limitations as a systemic regulator.

Akerlof and Shiller rightly associate booms with "new era" thinking[33] but wrongly deem such thinking irrational. Stocks soared in the late 1920s because it was a period of rapid economic growth based on new products such as the mass-produced automobile, new methods of retailing such as the chain store, and new methods of finance such as installment buying and the purchase of common stock on margin. There was no compelling

---

33. A point that Irving Fisher had made about the boom that preceded the stock market crash of 1929. See Fisher, "The Debt-Deflation Theory of Great Depressions," 1 *Econometrica* 337, 349 (1933).

reason to think that existing stock prices reflected an exaggerated expectation of increased wealth in the new era. The late 1990s were likewise heralded as a new era, this time on the basis of expectations that dot-com marketing would transform the economy. In both cases the expectations were premature rather than erroneous, exaggerated (ex post) but not unreasonable when formed.

The early 2000s seemed to most observers still another new era, this one based on the seemingly magical conjunction of low interest rates with low inflation, rising asset values, and new financial instruments believed to reduce risk and thus enable greater lending and borrowing. In all three cases the new eras turned out, at least in the short run, to be false dawns, and an asset-price crash ensued. Given the uncertainty of the economic environment, stressed by Keynes, such mistakes are not evidence that investors are irrational.

Nor are booms the result, as Akerlof and Shiller curiously argue, of "corruption scandals." A crash exposes frauds; rarely is it caused by them. Cheap credit and, as a consequence, soaring house values were the immediate causes of the housing bubble and all that followed when it burst. The underlying causes were the deregulation of financial services, lax enforcement of the remaining regulations, unsound decisions on interest rates by the Federal Reserve, huge budget deficits, the globalization of the finance industry, the financial rewards of risky lending—and competitive pressures to engage in it—in the absence of effective regulation, the overconfidence of economists inside and outside government, and the government's erratic, confidence-destroying, off-the-cuff responses to the banking collapse. These mistakes of commission and omission had emotional components. The overconfidence of economists might even be thought a manifestation of animal spirits. But the career and reward structures and ideological preconceptions of macroeconomists are likelier explanations than emotion for the economics profession's failure to foresee or respond effectively to the crisis.

Like Akerlof and Shiller, I believe in bubbles, but I hesitate to seek an explanation for them in such ill-defined and miscellaneous concepts as "variations in the level of trust," "storytelling and human interest," "perceptions of corruption or unfairness," "anger and optimism," and "social epidemics causing changes in gut instincts and feelings."[34] What happened to Occam's razor? Do we really need such an assortment of "inconstancies of human thinking"[35] to understand how an investment bubble forms? Isn't it enough to note that risk and return are positively correlated, that there are different levels of aversion to risk, including negative aversion (risk preference), and that averters tend to be pessimists, risk preferrers optimists?. Some optimists are born gamblers, believers in their lucky star drawn to finance because of the positive correlation of risk and return. Some born gamblers are home buyers rather than financiers and decide to buy a house in circumstances in which if prices fall or even just stop rising their investment will be wiped out. Nothing is gained by calling such businessmen or such consumers irrational; they simply attach different values to the prospect of gain relative to the prospect of loss. Fraud, conflicts of interest, misunderstanding of complex transactions, dumb mistakes, and other human failings were certainly features of the housing and credit bubbles, but these are constants in human behavior.

While for Keynes "confidence" ("animal spirits") was the key to getting out of a depression, for Akerlof and Shiller it is something to be chilled down in order to prevent booms that might turn into busts. This turning of Keynes upside down may explain the most surprising statement in the book: that "both presidents are heroes of ours"[36]—for the two presidents are Herbert Hoover and Franklin Roosevelt. Both are heroes to Akerlof and Shiller because they ran budget deficits and created new agencies

34. Akerlof and Shiller, note 31 above.
35. Id.
36. Akerlof and Shiller, note 29 above, at 95.

to regulate the economy. But in the three and a half years of depression during which Hoover was president, confidence drained out of the economy. The depression touched bottom at the end of his term and turned around within weeks of Roosevelt's inauguration. Hoover's adherence to the gold standard, and his determination to keep government small (so no Keynesian stimulus) and raise taxes to try to balance the budget, created a rational expectation of continued economic contraction, dampening the economy's animal spirits. Roosevelt's decision, made promptly upon his taking office, to go off the gold standard, push up prices (in order to end deflation), and engage in massive (for the time) deficit spending created an expectation of economic recovery. This expectation had positive effects on the economy even before the new policies could take effect.[37] Roosevelt restored confidence, which Hoover had killed, and renewed confidence restarted the economic engine.

It is curious that critics of rational-choice economics should fail to register the *emotional* difference between Hoover's and Roosevelt's responses to the depression. Yet it would be a mistake to equate rationality with absence of emotion. The word "emotional" has overtones of irrationality, but emotion itself is at once a form of telescoped thinking (it is not irrational to step around an open manhole "instinctively" without first analyzing the costs and benefits of falling into it) and a prompt to action[38] that often, as in the case of investment under uncertainty, cannot be based on complete information and is therefore unavoidably a shot in the dark. We could not survive if were afraid to act in the face of uncertainty.

Irrationality is not the courage to act. Irrationality is to be found in behavior impelled by the cognitive quirks that we owe to the human brain's having evolved in a very different environ-

---

37. Gauti Eggertsson, "Great Expectations and the End of the Depression," 98 *American Economic Review* 1476 (2008).

38. On both points, see my book *Frontiers of Legal Theory,* ch. 7 (2001).

ment from our present one. Why else are we frightened by scary movies even though we know there is no rational basis for fear? There were no movies in the ancestral human environment. We are poor at evaluating low-probability events because there was little in that environment that could be done about such events. The irrational sense, which merchants exploit, that a price of $5.99 is significantly less than $6.00 illustrates the limited value in that environment of ability to evaluate fine differences. Identifying these quirks is a significant contribution of cognitive psychology and behavioral economics to the understanding of human behavior. But they do not explain depressions as well as rational-choice economics does, provided that people are not assumed to be hyperrational.

And provided that we do not give up too soon in searching out the self-interested motives of human behavior. Apparent irrationalities can often be seen as rational once one looks inside the "black box" of an institutional setup and sees the play of self-interest bringing about results that, while individually rational, disserve institutional goals. While it *seems* irrational for an investment company to sell underperforming stocks in its portfolio disproportionately at the end of years and quarters (a common practice), we saw in chapter 1 that it may be entirely rational from the standpoint of the portfolio manager.

The complexity of a modern economy has defeated efforts to create mathematical models that would enable depressions to be predicted and would provide guidance on how to prevent or, failing that, recover from them. But the insights of behavioral economics have not done the trick either. Shiller is greatly to be commended for having spotted both the dot-com bubble of the late 1990s and the housing bubble of the 2000s, and for his penetrating criticisms of extreme versions of the efficient-markets hypothesis.[39] But few if any other behavioral economists noticed

---

39. See, for example, Robert J. Shiller, *Irrational Exuberance* (2nd ed. 2005).

the bubbles, and he and Akerlof offer no concrete proposals for how we might recover from the current depression and prevent a future one. They want credit loosened, but so does everyone else—so did Keynes, who criticized our government for tightening credit in the early stages of the Great Depression.

Akerlof and Shiller invoke "fairness" and "money illusion" in an attempt to explain the behavior of employment and wages in a depression, such as workers' resistance to wage cuts even when deflation is causing real wages to rise. The authors ascribe such resistance, which in the depression of the 1930s produced a sharp rise in real incomes for many workers while others were on breadlines, to workers' sense of "fairness" and to "money illusion." By "fairness" the authors mean the workers' sense of entitlement to their existing wage, and by "money illusion" they mean the workers' failure to distinguish between the amount of money received as a wage (the nominal wage) and the purchasing power of the money (the real wage). They also argue that employers deliberately "overpay" their workers in order to boost morale and loyalty. But this does not explain why nominal wages are not cut during a depression in order to maintain (not cut) real wages.

As we saw in chapter 3, there is no need to invoke the hopelessly vague word "fairness" in order to explain these phenomena. A worker who rather than being paid a flat wage is paid a percentage of his firm's income would be unlikely to complain when his wage dropped in a depression; he would know that his wage was variable and he would plan his life accordingly. But if paid a fixed wage, he is likely to count on it as a steady source of income. Since depressions are rare and have unpredictable consequences, he won't have been able to protect himself in advance from the consequence of a depression-induced cut in his wage. He is going to be upset to find that he's working just as hard or harder but being paid less, and he won't be reassured by being given a lecture on deflation and purchasing power, because he will not understand or believe it. He will be less upset if, while his nominal wage remains unchanged, rising prices reduce his real wage. Prices may not be rising in a depression; and reductions in nominal wage are especially resisted because of suspicions of favoritism or discrimination or simply failure to appreciate the quality and importance ot the worker's work—the last being a particularly serious problem when workers work in teams, which makes it difficult to determine the contribution of each worker to the employer's profits. And whereas wage cuts make the entire workforce unhappy, layoffs make just the laid-off workers unhappy, and since they are no longer on the premises, they do not demoralize the remaining workforce by their unhappy presence. This explanation for the high rate of unemployment in a depression gives weight to cognitive and emotional factors (workers do not understand deflation, they may be unduly suspicious of the motives for cuts in nominal wages, and unhappy workers can demoralize the workplace) but does not assume irrational behavior.

Airplane manufacturers conduct stress tests on a new airplane's wings to determine their resilience in the worst turbulence that the plane might encounter, and the Federal Reserve in the spring of 2009 conducted stress tests on major banks to determine whether they could survive a further large decline in the economy. A depression is a stressor. It exposes weaknesses. It exposed the Madoff fraud and it exposed the weaknesses in economics that I have been discussing in this chapter and previous chapters. "The disintegration of financial globalization has produced an intellectual crisis for economists who had been gripped by the idea of market perfectibility and rational foresight."[40] The economists assured government officials, businessmen, and the general public that everything was fine—they knew how to prevent

40. Harold James, *The Creation and Destruction of Value: The Globalization Cycle* 144 (2009).

depressions; there would never be another one. But when the depression hit, they said that by the way they hadn't actually known how to prevent a depression or dig us out of one; they had only pretended to have understood depressions—depressions are too complicated for economists to model.

We may need the concept of an "economics cycle." The Great Depression discredited the macroeconomic theories built on Say's Law, and laissez-faire more generally. Economists became keen to identify macroeconomic and microeconomic market failures. Fiscal policy and monetary policy were assigned the job of eliminating involuntary employment, and regulation was imposed to assure efficient and equitable economic performance in markets that fell far short of the stringent conditions of perfect competition and were in many cases suspected of monopolistic tendencies. Government thus was given ambitious economic tasks but was assumed capable of performing them at tolerable (in some versions at negligible) cost to society.

Then came the "stagflation" of the 1970s, when monetary and fiscal policy signally failed to achieve full employment with or without inflation. Instead it was an era of lackluster economic growth and sharply higher inflation. Skeptics argued persuasively that regulatory and antitrust policies were having the opposite of the intended effect: they were impeding competition, and without achieving offsetting benefits. The pendulum swung the other way, in favor of deregulation, privatization, antitrust retrenchment, and macroeconomic policies that stressed price stability.

Conservative critics of the interventionist era touched off by the Great Depression and the New Deal had complained that the interventionists had succumbed to the "Nirvana fallacy": that instead of comparing imperfect markets with imperfect regulation, they had assumed that government could correct market imperfections infallibly. The critics were right, but succumbed to their own Nirvana fallacy by persuading themselves that markets were perfect, which is to say self-regulating, and that government intervention in them almost always made things worse.[41] The cycle seems about to take another turn, in favor of regulation, but it may be arrested by the conspicuous failures of government revealed by the current depression and the efforts to fight it. Of course, government was also thought to have failed in the run-up to the Great Depression and the initial (pre-Roosevelt) efforts to mitigate it. But the government that failed conspicuously, the government of Herbert Hoover and the Republican Party, was thought, a little unfairly, the government of no government. The many mistakes made by Roosevelt and the Democrats in fighting the depression were obscured by general satisfaction with the New Deal.

Economists need to curb their ideological preconceptions, but that is not enough. They will not have a good grasp of business-cycle economics until economics is fused with psychology (so Akerlof and Shiller are on the right track, though they are well short of their destination) and political science. The psychology of boom and bust and the political consequences of booms and (especially) busts are fundamental to understanding the business cycle, and to moderating it.

41. I have succumbed to this second Nirvana fallacy myself in some of my work in economic analysis of law.

THE WAY FORWARD

III

11

The pressure on government to "do something" to prevent a repetition of the financial collapse is irresistible, even if the "something" is closing the barn door after the horses have escaped—closing it so violently that the barn collapses. The pressure has already produced questionable statutory changes, such as the new credit card law, plus a raft of ambitious proposals by the Administration that are under consideration by Congress at this writing. The pressure has produced an informal tightening of banking regulation at the very time when it should be loosened to encourage lending. Tight regulation is what we want for booms, loose for busts, consistent with the proposition that depression economics is normal economics turned upside down. But private incentives (including the incentive of regulators eager to show that they've learned their lesson—and their even greater incentive to prevent at whatever cost an *exact* repetition of the last crisis, for which no excuses would be accepted) move in the opposite direction from public need in a depression. Just as people hoard when we want them to spend, regulators get stricter when we want them to loosen up.

Ambitious reforms are premature, as I argued in chapter 5, pending a rigorous inquiry into the causes of the depression, pending recovery from it and with that recovery the restoration of a modicum of certainty to the business environment—and pending the return of regulatory complacency, for until then the regulators will be hyperalert for signs of another financial crisis. A major cause of the financial collapse of September 2008 was that the regulators were asleep at the switch. They are now insomniac.

Before ambitious plans are hatched, with the inevitable delays and confusion and unintended consequences, there is first the need to assure that the regulators are employing their existing powers to the full. The Securities and Exchange Commission had all the statutory authority it needed to prevent the broker-dealers from taking on more risk than was safe for the economy.[1] Already the commission, under a new chairman appointed by President Obama, has announced that it will impose on money-market funds reserve and capital requirements that would have limited the systemic consequences of Lehman Brothers' collapse had they been in force in September 2008; for we recall that it was Lehman's role as an intermediary between the money-market funds and issuers of commercial paper that made its collapse disrupt both the money-market and commercial paper markets. The proponents of radical reform should hold their fire until we see what more the fresh crew of regulators installed by the new Administration can do.

Another preliminary need is for a study in depth of the causes of the financial crisis. The study commissioned by Congress (see chapter 5) is not that study. It is proceeding at a leisurely pace with meager staff and a membership that is bipartisan rather than nonpartisan and has limited expertise. Unfortunately, it's hard to find people who understand the issues presented by the economic crisis yet are not compromised by having committed themselves to one diagnosis or another or been complicit in the failures suspected of having caused the crisis—like some of the

---

1. Michael J. Halloran, "Systemic Risks and the Bear Stearns Crisis," in *The Road Ahead for the Fed* 151 (John D. Ciorciari and John B. Taylor eds. 2009).

authors of the Administration's proposals. I have my own views of the causes of the financial crisis, obviously, but they are not definitive. Until a properly staffed study of the causes of the crisis is conducted, proposals for reform—all of which are designed to prevent the next crisis by eliminating the practices that caused this one—should be tabled.

But that is the counsel of perfection. The pressure for near-term reform is too great to be resisted entirely. I shall therefore discuss possibilities for reform that, unlike those I have criticized, seem to me to deserve serious consideration, whether or not their merits are sufficient to warrant actually adopting them; for no government reforms are easy to accomplish. I array these possibilities in reverse order of complexity and cost, so simplest first. Think of the array as a ladder with rungs; the reader can stop climbing when he or she feels that the crossover point has been reached between the benefits of reform and the costs. Thus I begin with suggestions that would be easy to implement because they would not require altering the regulatory structure, and I then turn to more problematic possibilities, of which the most promising is the separation of commercial banking from proprietary trading and other high-risk financial activities.

1. *Establish an* executive *commission to study the causes of the crisis and suggest reforms.* The 9/11 Commission, although it did a better job than the Financial Crisis Inquiry Commission is likely to do, was far from an unalloyed success.[2] Like the FCIC, it had been created by Congress. When the next intelligence failure occurred—the mistaken belief that Iraq had weapons of mass destruction—the President created and staffed a commission to investigate the failure and make recommendations. The members and staff of the commission were more expert than their counterparts on the 9/11 Commission had been, and the commission received (naturally) better cooperation from the executive branch

2. See Richard A. Posner, *Preventing Surprise Attacks: Intelligence Reform in the Wake of 9/11,* ch. 1 (2005).

and completed its work faster.[3] President Obama should create a nonpartisan expert commission to study the causes of the current depression and to suggest reforms. It is not too late to do so.

2. *Consider limited legal reforms.* We recall from chapter 2 that the Federal Reserve Act authorizes the Fed to lend money to a nonbank only if the loan is "secured to the satisfaction" of the Fed. Lehman Brothers lacked good security for the loan it needed, but I argued that in the emergency circumstances created by a collapsing global financial system the Fed could have declared itself "satisfied" with whatever security Lehman could have offered, since the statutory term "secured to the satisfaction" is not defined either in the statute or in regulations issued by the Fed. To clarify the Fed's authority and deprive a future Fed chairman of an excuse, Congress could amend the Federal Reserve Act to add "in the circumstances," or "in the sole discretion of the Federal Reserve," after "satisfaction," or it could delete the reference to security altogether.

While Congress is at it, it might take a look at section 363 of the Bankruptcy Code—the provision for the sale of assets of a bankrupt firm—which was the vehicle for the de facto reorganization of General Motors and Chrysler. Those reorganizations, as we saw in chapter 4, violated the spirit of the absolute-priority rule, which puts secured (and other senior) creditors ahead of the other creditors of a bankrupt firm. Not that the rule should be considered sacrosanct; and violation of it probably was justified by the economic crisis, which was still extremely grave when the bankruptcies took place (it is still grave). But fixed-income (bond) investors fear that the use made of section 363 in the auto bankruptcies may operate as a precedent for bankruptcies in nor-

---

3. See *Report of the Commission on the Intelligence Capabilities of the United States Regarding Weapons of Mass Destruction* (Mar. 31, 2005). I disagreed with much of the report but acknowledged its analytic superiority to the 9/11 Commission's report. See my book *Uncertain Shield: The U.S. Intelligence System in the Throes of Reform,* ch. 2 (2006).

mal economic conditions, and their fear could result in higher interest rates for no good reason. Their anxieties could be allayed
by an amendment to the Bankruptcy Code that protected secured creditors in a section 363 sale unless the sale were pursuant
to a government bailout of the bankrupt company. Then secured
creditors would demand higher interest only in lending to companies that might be candidates for a bailout—and those are the
companies that *should* pay higher interest rates, in order to curb
their appetite for taking risks that endanger the economy and
counting on being bailed out should the risks topple them.

Among other legal issues that might benefit from a legislative
resolution are whether a bankruptcy court should be permitted
to cram down the mortgage on a primary residence (that is, reduce the mortgage to the current market value of the mortgaged
property); whether in a bankruptcy that may have macroeconomic consequences government bailout loans should be given
priority over claims of secured creditors; whether there is any
constitutional limitation on the federal government's abroga-
tion of a private contract—for example, a contractual obligation to pay bonuses to employees of American Insurance Group;
whether in cases in which a depression prevents a firm from honoring a contract the firm can ever appeal to such doctrines of
contract law as impossibility and frustration, or to such common
contractual provisions as *force majeure* clauses and "material
adverse conditions" clauses, to be excused from performance
without incurring legal liability; whether bankruptcy law should
be amended with respect to nonbank banks to bring it closer to
the "resolution" procedure by which the Federal Deposit Insurance Corporation winds up the affairs of commercial banks that
fail; and what the priorities of creditors should be in a rehypothe-
cation (see chapter 2).

3. *Rotate staff of financial regulatory agencies.* A program of
rotating financial regulatory staff among the different financial
regulatory agencies might help to broaden the perspectives of

regulators, reduce the "stovepiping" of information that may relate to a wide range of companies and financial markets, expose regulators to new ideas, reduce turf warfare based on misunderstandings, and make a career in financial regulation more interesting and challenging and thus attract a better quality of financial civil servant. The model would be the military reforms instituted by the Goldwater-Nichols Act of 1986, which made service in joint commands a prerequisite to promotion to a senior level. Some nations have merged the historically separate branches of their military (in our military these are the army, the navy, the air force, and the marine corps, though confusingly the marine corps is also a part of the navy), and some proponents of financial regulatory reform would like to eliminate the separate federal financial regulatory agencies. But the success of the Goldwater-Nichols Act suggests that improved coordination of separate agencies can achieve adequate performance while avoiding the delay and disruption and infighting and turf warfare and general confusion that would be sure to attend a merger of major agencies.

4. *Consider changing the financing of financial regulatory agencies.* Consideration should be given to financing the banking agencies out of congressional appropriations rather than, as at present, out of fees paid by the regulated firms. The fee system puts the agency and the regulated firms in the approximate relation of seller to customers. Let's not forget the slogan that the customer always knows best: there is always a danger that regulated firms will exert undue influence over their regulators, and the danger may be enhanced if the regulators are financed by those firms. A particular danger is that by configuring its structure in a particular way, a regulated firm will bring itself under the jurisdiction of an agency that wants to increase its fee income and so will offer (implicitly, of course) a softer regulatory touch. This unedifying practice is called "regulatory arbitrage" and is illustrated by the maneuver in 2006 by which Countrywide Finan-

cial Corporation, at the time the nation's largest mortgage bank, was able to substitute the notably lax Office of Thrift Supervision for the Federal Reserve as its regulator (also lax, as we know, but less so). So it's not a good argument for the fee system that it fosters competition among regulators. They vie to be chosen by a firm to be its regulator by the need to obtain fees. But the only way they can attract a firm is by lightening regulation—hence regulatory arbitrage.

There is the further danger, when an agency is supported out of fee income, of a mismatch between the penalty function of fees and the revenue function. Fees set at the right level to deter risky practices may generate too little or too much income to finance the agency at its optimal size.

Against abolishing the fee system it can be urged that the system gives the agencies a degree of autonomy from Congress and so can actually liberate them from undue influence by the regulated firms, which form interest groups that pressure Congress for lighter regulation (though sometimes for heavier regulation, aimed at preventing competition). Fee-financed agencies don't have to go hat in hand to Congress every year asking for an appropriation. This consideration is particularly important in the case of the Federal Reserve, which needs some insulation from congressional (and also presidential) control in order to be able to perform its essential function of maintaining economic stability. But the Fed's financial independence stems not from the fees that it charges the banks it regulates but from its ability to create money.

Furthermore, if an agency's budget is determined by Congress, budgetary considerations may cause Congress to reduce the appropriation for a regulatory agency's staff and by doing so impair the agency's ability to carry out its regulatory duties effectively. I am left uncertain whether abandoning the fee system would be a good idea.

5. *Establish a financial intelligence agency.* In recent years I

have written about the reform of national security intelligence and responses to catastrophic risks generally,[4] and this writing has influenced my views about the reform of financial regulation—the financial crash of September 2008 was sudden, catastrophic, unanticipated. Reflection on intelligence and crisis management leads me to suggest the creation within the Federal Reserve, the National Economic Council, or the President's Council of Economic Advisers of an office that would conduct financial intelligence. It would emphasize warning signals, such as surges in housing prices—a frequent precursor of a banking crisis[5]—and emergency financial planning.[6] State banking and insurance regulators, who are well placed to be early detectors of impending financial crises, would be knitted into a nationwide system of financial intelligence coordinated by the new federal office.

The regulatory failures that underlie the current depression were not due to a lack of legal authority, as the regulators have argued in attempting to excuse their failure, or from the structure—overelaborate though it is—of regulation of the financial industry. They were due to lack of foresight and knowledge, and they can be rectified, at least to some degree, by a sharper focus on information collection and analysis and on contingency planning.

These are separate tasks. The first is the pure intelligence task. The Treasury Department already has an intelligence office, the duties of which include detection of financial transactions for the

4. See, for example, my books *Catastrophe: Risk and Response* (2004); *Preventing Surprise Attacks,* note 2 above; *Uncertain Shield,* note 3 above; *Countering Terrorism: Blurred Focus, Halting Steps* (2007).

5. Carmen M. Reinhart and Kenneth S. Rogoff, *This Time Is Different: Eight Centuries of Financial Folly* 270–281 (2009).

6. Paul Volcker has proposed the creation of the position of Vice Chairman of the Federal Reserve for Regulation and Supervision. Statement by Paul A. Volcker before the Committee on Banking and Financial Services of the House of Representatives, Sept. 24, 2009, www.house.gov/apps/list/hearing/financialsvcs_dem/volcker.pdf (visited Dec. 8, 2009).

support of terrorists. Keeping track of lawful but possibly risky transactions, collating financial data from varied sources, including financial journalists and independent analysts, and scrutinizing balance sheets carefully should be easier than dismantling terrorist funding networks. Nor is the pooling of information concerning risks to the overall financial system a task that can be left to the private sector. Considerations of trade secrecy and concerns that exchanging information with a competitor might get a firm accused of trying to collude in violation of antitrust law limit the amount of information that firms are willing to share either with each other or with credit-rating agencies, academics, and forecasters. The government can require that sensitive information be divulged to it under promise of secrecy, and after scrubbing it of details can share it with the financial industry in order to make the industry aware of industry-wide risks that no individual firm would have enough information to be able to discover.

Contingency planning is not wholly alien to financial regulation—think of the stress tests conducted on major banks in the spring of 2009. Stress tests are designed to identify financial weaknesses before they cause actual bank failures; the object, as the name implies, is to determine whether a bank can survive if it is stressed by adverse economic developments. If it flunks the test, there is time to take precautionary measures to avert failure should the stressful conditions materialize.

A grim but instructive parallel to my proposal is the COG (continuity of government) plan. That is the plan for ensuring the survival of the U.S. government in the event of a nuclear attack, or comparable catastrophe, that destroys Washington, D.C. First formulated early in the Cold War, it has been updated periodically since. As far as I know, no counterpart plan has ever been devised to deal with the possibility of a catastrophic failure of our financial system. (One is put in mind of the fact that at the time of the Pearl Harbor attack, the United States had no foreign intelligence service.) It is not as if such a failure were unprecedented; it happened in the United States and other countries during the Great Depression, and in Japan as recently as the 1990s. Warnings by journalists and economists of a housing bubble and a possible ensuing banking collapse were issued as early as 2002 and gained in frequency and urgency as the bubble expanded and burst. By 2007 a deterioration of the financial system was evident to many observers. The Federal Reserve expressed concern and took some limited precautionary measures, yet when disaster struck in September 2008 the government was taken unawares and had no remedial plan. The Federal Reserve and the Treasury Department reacted vigorously, but in a haphazard fashion that undermined the confidence of businesses and consumers.

It is essential that the Financial Intelligence Agency be separate from all regulatory authorities. The combination of financial intelligence with regulation would undermine performance of the intelligence function. Regulatory objectives shaped by presidential and congressional politics, pressures from the regulated firms, and the regulators' own sense of their mission would deform intelligence collection and analysis. Regulators wearing their intelligence hat would look for and find just the information that would conform to their regulatory plans. The belief that Iraq had weapons of mass destruction was supported by intelligence collected in support of the preconceptions of the intelligence agencies' political masters. We should not let that happen with respect to financial intelligence.

Not that the regulatory agencies should eschew analysis. In particular, the Federal Reserve needs better macroeconomic models for understanding the interactions that can bring down the financial system. The need is not for ever more refined mathematical models of the economy, however; it is for "agent-based models." These are not mathematical models. They are computer simulations of how persons (or organizations) can be expected to react to each other's moves, and so are appropriate for modeling "runs."[7] They enable the effects of uncertainty, different attitudes toward risk, differences in leverage, and different patterns of interdependence among firms to be studied in ways that elude conventional mathematical models.

6. *Regulate off-balance-sheet contingent liabilities.* The weakness of the banks in the years and months leading up to the collapse in September of 2008 was obscured by the extent to which they had undisclosed contingent liabilities—for example, contingent liabilities resulting from the issuance of credit-default swaps. Congress seems on the verge of requiring that standard credit-default swaps be traded through clearinghouses; many are, but at present there is no requirement that they be because they are an unregulated part of the securities market. Credit-default swaps are, as we know, both a form of credit insurance and a vehicle for speculation, corresponding respectively to forward contracts and future contracts. There is nothing wrong either with insuring debt or with speculating on the risk of default. The problem is a law (the Commodity Futures Modernization Act of 2000) passed toward the end of the Clinton Administration that forbade the Commodity Futures Trading Commission to regulate credit-default swaps and other novel derivative securities. The law was motivated by a concern that U.S. financial firms would lose business to foreign firms, particularly English firms, which would continue to offer unregulated swaps. But the opacity of the unregulated market in swaps made it difficult to assess the creditworthiness of the issuers, and this was a factor in the credit freeze that followed the collapse of Lehman Brothers. Lenders who had bought swaps to insure against defaults by their borrowers became uncertain whether the issuers of the swaps would be able to

7. See Mark Buchanan, "Meltdown Modeling: Could Agent-Based Computer Models Prevent Another Financial Crisis?" 460 *Nature* 680 (2009); J. Doyne Farmer and Duncan Foley, "The Economy Needs Agent-Based Modelling," 460 id. 685.

cover the default, and so became insecure about their own solvency. An unrelated problem was that credit-default swaps could be and were securitized and yet the securities were extremely difficult to value, adding to uncertainty about the solvency of the financial institutions that had invested in them.

The clearinghouse solution is incomplete, because even a fully regulated insurance market can collapse. Insurance is effective against independent risks but not against correlated ones. A further shortcoming of the clearinghouse solution is that it presupposes uniform swap contracts, which can be traded without the traders' having to master the details of complex contracts. Many credit-default swaps are custom-designed to fit particular circumstances. The more of these there are (weighted by value), the less the clearinghouse approach will succeed in making the commitments embodied in swaps perceptible to the markets and the regulators.

There is suspicion that a major reason for the custom-designed swaps, and indeed for opposing regulation of swap derivatives generally, is that off-exchange trading offers more profit opportunities than trading on exchanges, which facilitates price comparison. But there are advantages to custom-designing a swap; I do not know whether they outweigh the costs from reduced competition.

The issue of design reflects the fact that even when they are used to provide insurance, credit-default swaps are not insurance policies issued by insurance companies. (It was happenstance that American Insurance Group, which ran aground on the sale of credit-default swaps that it had sold without having adequate reserves or posting collateral, was an insurance company rather than a bank or a hedge fund.) They can be as idiosyncratic as the terms in a contract for the sale of goods that determine how the risk of fire or delay or a product defect is to be allocated between the parties. The methods of regulating standardized futures contracts or insurance policies don't make a smooth fit with credit-default swaps, which is one reason why they were removed from the Commodity Futures Trading Commission's authority.

Even at the most acute phase of the banking crisis, not only were many credit-default swaps being traded through clearing-houses, but most swap obligations were honored—though in the case of AIG, by the government after it took over the company. But because the credit-default swap market was unregulated, its financial solidity in a period of crisis could not be gauged, and this uncertainty had its usual effect in chilling financial activity.

Yet even AIG, it has been argued, could have honored its swap obligations had it not invested very heavily in mortgage-backed securities, with the result that its capital was severely impaired.[8] It had done that, the argument continues, because the risk of bankruptcy created by selling swaps to the purchasers of mortgage-backed securities was correlated with the risk of bankruptcy created by the fact that AIG owned such securities. If they did not tank, the sale of the swaps would be profitable. If they did tank, AIG might go broke by reason of its ownership of mortgage-backed securities, but if so the shareholders would incur no *additional* loss from the company's defaulting on its credit-default swaps. The sale of the swaps would have no downside.

This (to digress for a moment) is an example of how limited liability (shareholders' insulation from personal liability for the debts of their corporation) can induce risky corporate behavior. There was a time when if a bank went bankrupt its shareholders could be assessed a sum of money, equal to the purchase price of their shares, to meet the claims of the bank's creditors, so that the cost of the bankruptcy to the shareholder would exceed the loss of the prebankruptcy value of his shares. And investment banks used to be organized as partnerships, and partners, unlike

8. Richard Squire, "Shareholder Opportunism in a World of Risky Debt" 24–31 (forthcoming in *Harvard Law Review*).

shareholders in a corporation, do not have limited liability; as a result, financial partnerships are managed more conservatively than financial corporations.

But it is unrealistic to suppose that banks of the scale of the major modern banks could attract sufficient equity capital as partnerships—precisely because of the greater financial risk borne by a partner than by a shareholder. A prominent example of a financial company organized as a partnership—Brown Brothers Harriman—has partnership capital of only about $500 million. Goldman Sachs's market capitalization of almost $100 billion is two hundred times greater. There are proposals to shrink big banks, but not to the size of a Brown Brothers Harriman.

But I have wandered from the main point, which is the desirability of fuller disclosure of contingent liabilities. For credit-default swaps and other derivatives that are traded either on exchanges or through clearinghouses, the information is public and the only needs are for aggregation and for disclosure in intelligible form. For customized swaps, the problem of disclosure is difficult to solve because the issuer's potential liability may hinge on details buried in a lengthy contract. In the case of the SIVs (structured investment vehicles; see chapter 2), simply requiring the creator of a SIV to consolidate the SIV's balance sheet with its own balance sheet should do the trick.

There is a danger in focusing obsessively on credit-default swaps as a source of contingent liabilities, and not only because SIVs are also an important source. Apart from their insurance function, credit-default swaps are instruments for speculation, and they have close substitutes that can create equivalent risk. Purchasing a swap, which pays off if the debt the swap protects against falls in value by the amount specified in the swap, is equivalent to selling the debt short. Selling short is both a way of speculating and a way of hedging; taking a long position (the value of the swap) is equivocal in the same way. Tightening up on credit-default swaps could deflect speculation into forms as difficult for regulators, or markets, to keep track of.

7. *Reform credit rating.* Credit-rating agencies have taken a public relations beating in the wake of the financial crisis because of the conflict of interest inherent in the agencies' being paid by the issuer of the securities that they rate and for the other reasons discussed in chapter 5, but above all just because the tranches of debt securities rated triple-A bombed. There is thus a wisdom-of-hindsight flavor to the criticisms, and it remains an abiding puzzle that *sophisticated* investors, who after all were the purchasers of tranches of securitized debt, would rely on credit ratings, knowing as they must have the limitations on the agencies' objectivity. Still, plausible explanations have been offered. One is that many institutional investors, such as pension funds, are forbidden to buy debt that does not receive at least an "investment grade" rating, so that if the credit-rating agencies were too chary about awarding such ratings there would be a shortage of debt for such investors to invest in. In addition, some institutional investors are not *very* sophisticated; this is especially true of the pension funds of the smaller states and cities.

And then there is the quasi-official status of what are called the "Nationally Recognized Statistical Rating Organizations." Ten credit-rating agencies have been given this designation by the SEC, including the leaders—Moody's, Standard and Poor, and Fitch. The SEC allows issuers of debt rated by an NRSRO to provide prospective investors with a less elaborate offering document. That led some swap customers of American Insurance Group to allow AIG to substitute its triple-A rating for collateral to back the credit-default swaps that it had sold. In addition, insurance companies, pension funds, and other investment entities that are permitted to invest only in investment-grade securities cannot be sued for investing in securities rated triple-A by an NRSRO. This puts the NRSROs under pressure to give the sellers of securities a high rating and thus weakens market discipline. It also, and more ominously, reduces the incentive to the investor to use care in making investment decisions rather than relying blindly on an NRSRO's credit rating.

There is no reason for giving a federal stamp of approval to *any* credit-rating agencies or for granting them any other privileges denied competitors, just as there is no reason to have the government sponsor mortgage companies (Fannie Mae and Freddie Mac). Elimination of NRSRO certification would be a worthwhile reform.

The Administration has advanced other proposals regarding the credit-rating agencies, such as forbidding them to provide consulting services to any company they rate, requiring them to disclose the fees they receive for a rating, and forbidding "ratings shopping," the practice by which a company solicits "preliminary ratings" from multiple agencies but only pays for, and only discloses, the highest rating that it receives. Other proposals, however, are downright silly, such as requiring the agencies to use different symbols for securitized debt than for corporate bonds, on the ground that the former is riskier than the latter, which of course is not always true. The SEC has already promulgated rules forbidding executives of credit-rating agencies to provide both ratings and advice on how to structure securitized debt, forbidding the executives who actually rate an issuer's debt to discuss the fee for the rating, and limiting gifts from the issuers to employees of the rating agency.

These rules and proposals probably are unnecessary. Once burned, twice shy: investors will be more cautious about relying on ratings, and the agencies will be more careful, especially if they are stripped of their legal privileges; that is the only reform of credit rating that is worth fighting hard for.

8. *Tie capital requirements to the business cycle.* Another reform that deserves (and is receiving a great deal of) consideration is gearing banks' capital requirements to the different phases of the business cycle. There are many high-risk industries, ranging from airlines to restaurants, but only one—banking—poses systemic (economy-wide) risk. One way to limit risk is to place a ceiling on leverage—the ratio of borrowed capital (debt) to owned capital (equity), the latter acting as a cushion against the

bank's defaulting in the event of losses. Another way is to increase the bank's required reserves.

The ratio of debt to equity in a bank's balance sheet tends to rise in boom periods because values are rising then (house values, for example), and this reduces defaults, increases the value of the collateral for loans, and for both reasons makes the bank's loan portfolio seem less risky, and this encourages the bank, feeling safer, to borrow more so that it can make more loans, thus increasing its leverage. At the same time loan quality is actually declining because in a boom borrowers and lenders alike believe that rising values will prevent default even if the borrower is not creditworthy in the usual sense.

The factors that drive up the market value of bank assets and reduce loan quality during a boom set the stage for catastrophe during a bust. A fall in the value of houses or other collateral precipitates defaults, aggravated by declining loan quality (more defaults). And with the market value of the banks' assets falling, their debt-to-equity ratio, already high, rises dangerously. If a bank has $100 in assets, $90 in debt, and therefore $10 in equity, and the value of its assets falls to $95 with its liabilities unchanged, its equity will be worth only $5 and so its debt-equity ratio will have risen from 9 ($90 ÷ $10) to 18 ($90 ÷ $5).

There are various methods of dealing with the problem of risk in banks' capital structures,[9] some of which I discussed in chapter 5. These methods are well within the authority of the federal agencies that regulate commercial banks, and though imperfect, as we saw, would have some value in supplementing a program of required disclosure of off-balance-sheet contingent liabilities. We must bear in mind, however, that there is no free lunch in a program of reducing systemic risk by restricting risk taking by bankers. If banks are required to issue bonds convertible to common stock should the bank's solvency be threatened, the bond-

9. For good discussions, see the articles by Andrew Crockett, Richard J. Jerring, and Myron S. Scholes in *The Road Ahead for the Fed*, note 1 above.

holders will lose the protection of bankruptcy (for they will be converted from creditors to owners) and this prospect will increase the bank's cost of borrowing. Anything that reduces leverage will reduce profitability, and anything that reduces profitability will hurt competition for staff even if the government imposes no limitations on bankers' compensation.

And what about nonbanks, such as the big broker-dealers that were at the heart of the banking collapse? They are regulated as we know by the Securities and Exchange Commission, and in the case of insurance companies by state insurance commissioners. Both the SEC and the state commissioners lack expertise in matters of systemic risk; hence the argument for empowering the Federal Reserve not only to identify financial institutions that create the kind of risk illustrated by Long-Term Capital Management's debacle[10] but also to minimize that risk by limiting their leverage or imposing other restrictions. The problem is that besides the broker-dealers, the largest of which are now parts of bank holding companies and therefore regulated by the Federal Reserve rather than by the SEC, there are some 10,000 hedge funds (though most are foreign or small or both), not to mention countless other financial institutions that can create systemic risk; American Insurance Group is the poster child for such firms.

Since nonbank financial intermediaries are so much like

---

10. The collapse of Long-Term Capital Management, a large though not immense hedge fund, almost caused a global financial collapse. The hedge fund was bailed out by a consortium of Wall Street firms organized by the Federal Reserve. It was highly leveraged by hedge fund standards; its debt-equity ratio was 25 to 1. When the value of the securities in which its capital was invested suddenly plummeted, it had to start selling them to meet margin calls, and by dumping a large number of these securities in a short time it created a serious imbalance between supply and demand. That imbalance forced down the value of the securities, which compelled other owners of the securities to sell to meet their margin calls, causing the value of financial assets to spiral downward and by doing so to jeopardize the solvency of a large number of financial institutions.

banks, it is temping to put the Federal Reserve in charge of *all* financial intermediation; but the objections that I discussed in chapter 5 seem to me compelling. An alternative would be to beef up the SEC's solvency-regulating staff and create a federal insurance regulatory agency—perhaps inside the SEC.

But a better solution, to which I now turn, might be to separate commercial banking from the shadow banking system.

9. *Return to the Glass-Steagall Act.* In the spirit of the Public Utilities Holding Company Act and the Glass-Steagall Act, both passed in the 1930s and since repealed, commercial banking (and closely related activities such as lending by thrifts and by money-market mutual funds) could be separated from proprietary trading and other high-risk financial activities.[11] The reasons are several. One is the contagion of the kind that brought down Lehman Brothers. Unless the risky and safe banking activities are conducted in strictly separate subsidiaries—which is difficult to do without sacrificing whatever benefits flow from having both types of activity in the same enterprise—the assets involved in the safe activities will be available to the creditors of the risky ones. And remember how the banks felt obligated by considerations of customer relations to honor the debts of the SIVs they had created, though they probably had no legal obligation to do so unless they had guaranteed those debts.

Another reason for separating out commercial banking is the awkwardness of trying to merge disparate business cultures in a single firm. The combination is likely to be unstable if the different cultures have different risk profiles. A safe, conservative banking operation attracts a different kind of executive from a speculative trading operation. The banker will be more cautious and, because risk and return are positively correlated, will be less munificently rewarded (the less risk, the lower the return). The greater profitability and more generous remuneration of the traders will nudge the bankers (or induce top management to

11. As suggested by Volcker. See note 6 above.

pressure them) to increase the profitability of their own operations, which will require their taking greater risks. So separation would automatically solve the problem for which limiting the amount or the structure of compensation of financial executives is proposed as the solution.

This is just the beginning of the benefits of forcing banks to divest their risky, nontraditional banking activities, thus building a dike against inundation of commercial banking by a collapse of other parts of the financial system. Although nowadays commercial banks supply less than a quarter of the total amount of credit in the United States, they play a unique role. They provide essential financing for small and medium-sized businesses (what is called "external finance")—businesses too small to meet their own financing needs out of retained earnings or by issuing bonds or commercial paper, or to be attractive to a lender that lacks an established relationship with the borrower, which would enable the lender to assess the borrower's creditworthiness. If a bank fails, though other lenders remain, borrowers from the bank may be unable to establish the kind of personal relationship with a new lender that would reassure the lender that the borrower is creditworthy.

Relationship lending has declined during the current depression not only because of fear of default and a falloff in demand for loans but also because the relationships that sustain relationship banking had withered in banks that had embraced the new model of originating and purchasing securitized debt. Creating securitized debt for a fee, or buying securitized debt, involves no relationship with the debtor. This is an argument for restricting securitization by commercial banks. And it underscores the point that the required separation is not between divisions of a conglomerate financial intermediary but between activities: traditional banking and risky modern banking.

Banks also provide standby lines of credit that provide emergency funding when other sources of credit fail, as happened when the commercial-paper market froze in the wake of the collapse of Lehman Brothers and the near-insolvency of other broker-dealers that had been intermediaries in that market. Issuers of commercial paper arrange for standby lines of credit from commercial banks in case the usual purchasers of their paper, and thus lenders to the issuers, stop buying it, as Lehman did. Banks back up riskier lenders. (Standby lines of credit are, by the way, another example of banks' off-balance-sheet contingent liabilities, which can constrain their lending—which did constrain it at the outset of the banking crisis, when the commercial-credit market froze.)

A further point is that commercial banks are the normal conduit by which the Federal Reserve pumps cash into the financial system in order to increase the amount of lending, whether by lending money to banks directly or, more commonly, by buying short-term Treasury securities (or lending money to the banks, taking the securities as collateral by means of repossession agreements), thus increasing their lendable cash. More broadly, commercial banks are the instruments by which the Fed controls the money supply and hence interest rates. When they endanger their solvency because they stray beyond their traditional banking activities, they cease to be dependable instruments for the implementation of monetary policy. That point was illustrated by the ineffectuality of the Fed's normal open market operations in the financial crisis of 2008 and the Fed's need to resort to "credit easing," whereby in effect the Fed *became* a commercial bank yet was unable to replace the commercial banks as a source of credit for small businesses and consumers; the Fed is in no position to engage in relationship banking. Weakened by their unsafe lending practices, the banks are hoarding the cash with which the Fed flooded them rather than lending it.

Even when a nationwide housing bubble bursts and mortgages are a significant component of the asset portfolios of most banks, with the result that the capital of most commercial banks is impaired, the Fed can prevent the collapse of those banks by pumping cash into them. It thus is not a surprise that the primary victims of the banking collapse of September 2008 were not commercial banks but other financial intermediaries. Part of the reason is federal deposit insurance, which protected most commercial banks[12] from the runs that brought down Bear Stearns and Lehman Brothers and might well have brought down Merrill Lynch, Morgan Stanley, and Goldman Sachs within days of Lehman's collapse had the government not intervened by arranging the sale of Merrill to the Bank of America and the conversion of the other two firms to bank holding companies. The conversion placed them under the Federal Reserve's regulatory authority and thus gave them access to the "discount window"— in other words, made it easy for them to borrow money from the Fed—and also enabled them to shore up their capital with federally insured deposits. The conversion reassured investors and stopped the run that was threatening to deprive the firms of the short-term capital they needed in order to continue in business.

It is also much easier for the Fed to recapitalize a bank than to recapitalize other types of financial institution, for the Fed's lending money to commercial banks is less controversial than its lending to nonbanks. And the Federal Deposit Insurance Corporation has authority and expertise that enables it to close a failing bank and transfer its assets to another bank with minimal disruption to depositors and other creditors of the failing bank. The streamlined resolution authority that the FDIC uses in lieu of bankruptcy to minimize the disruption of credit markets caused by a bank failure does not work well if a bank trades and invests all over the world and as a result has assets subject to a multitude of separate bankruptcy or resolution authorities.

With the commercial bank industry sealed off from other financial intermediation, the Federal Reserve's independence would be protected. It would be operating, as it did until the financial crisis of 2008, solely within the orbit of commercial

12. Not all, because some commercial banks had borrowed heavily from short-term lenders other than demand depositors.

banking—quietly regulating commercial banks and moving interest rates up and down by esoteric means (how many people know what "open market operations" are?). The Fed would not be making life-and-death decisions regarding huge Wall Street firms, as when it refused to administer financial CPR to Lehman Brothers—firms that, whether called banks or bank holding companies or something else, are engaged primarily in speculation rather than in banking in the sense described above. There is nothing evil about speculation, but it can create macroeconomic risk, and that is a reason for separating it from commercial banking.

Money-market funds, like thrifts (mortgage banks), are so similar to commercial banks that all three types of financial institution probably should be regulated on the same principles, emphasizing safety. This would require shifting regulatory authority over the money-market funds from the SEC, and over the thrifts from the Office of Thrift Supervision, to the Federal Reserve. These would be incremental organizational changes that should not overburden the Fed. On the contrary, these changes, along with the separation of commercial banking from high-risk financial activities, would diminish the need for a "systemic risk regulator," a dubious position that the Administration wants the Fed to fill.

But making commercial banks, thrifts, and money-market funds safe would leave much of the banking industry—which is to say financial intermediation in whatever form—unsafe. This is a problem of functional versus institutional regulation. Our system of financial regulation is primarily one of institutional regulation. It thus places broker-dealers under the SEC's regulatory authority even though they are functionally banks, while the "real" banks are regulated by banking agencies. The problem has been solved for the moment by the conversion of some of the major broker-dealers to bank holding companies and by the acquisition of the others by commercial banks. But that is at best a temporary solution, and maybe no solution at all, because the

Federal Reserve doesn't know much about broker-dealers, even if they are parts of banks or bank holding companies. And a great many financial firms, such as hedge funds, remain under the SEC's aegis, and there will be more as new firms arise and existing firms alter, merge, and diversify. Broker-dealers comparable in size and interconnectedness to those that cratered in September 2008 may emerge. There are also big industrial loan companies, such as GE Capital, a part of a nonfinancial company, General Electric. There are the money-market funds. There are insurance companies, like American Insurance Group. There doubtless are forms of financial institution not yet invented. And we know from the experience of Long-Term Capital Management that a hedge fund can create systemic risk; recall too that the London office of AIG, which was responsible for AIG's collapse, was functionally a hedge fund.

We are now to imagine the big shadow banks separated once again from commercial banks and bank holding companies and so restored to the SEC's regulatory jurisdiction. If the commission, as suggested earlier, is made responsible for protecting the solvency of other shadow banks, it would make perfectly good sense to return the big shadow banks to its regulatory control rather than having the Fed and the SEC divide regulation of broker-dealers between them.

Although the separation of commercial banking from other financial intermediation merits very serious consideration, it is not something that should be ordered forthwith. It would be a formidable undertaking, entailing as it would the breakup of such giants as Citigroup and Bank of America. It would be fiercely opposed. The argument that separation would sacrifice significant economies of scale and scope, while unsubstantiated and rather implausible (the travails of Citigroup and Bank of America seem to have been amplified rather than diminished by the scope of their activities), would have to be carefully appraised.

Moreover, merely reenacting the Glass-Steagall Act (and repealing the statute that repealed it)—the New Deal statute that separated commercial from investment banking—would not avoid the complexities involved in the divestiture of banks' nonbank divisions and affiliates. As explained by Robert Pozen, "Even under Glass-Steagall commercial banks could invest in bonds, manage mutual funds, execute securities trades on the order of their customers and underwrite government-related securities. The main thing they couldn't do was underwrite corporate stocks and bonds. Even that prohibition was loosened, as regulators permitted bank holding companies to set up special subsidiaries devoted in part to underwriting corporate stocks and bonds. In other words, the main impact of repealing Glass-Steagall was to allow banking organizations to become more active in underwriting."[13]

So a greater rollback of financial deregulation than merely reenacting the Glass-Steagall Act would be necessary for a clean separation of commercial banking from other financial intermediation. (Greater, but in one respect lesser, as there is no good reason to forbid commercial banks to underwrite new issues of securities, a central prohibition of Glass-Steagall.) Such a rollback is conceivable, if barely, but there is a further hitch, as Pozen goes on to explain:

> The repeal of Glass-Steagall facilitated the rescue of four large investment banks and thereby helped reduce the severity of the financial crisis. When Bear Stearns and Merrill Lynch got into serious trouble, they were promptly acquired with federal assistance by JPMorgan Chase and Bank of America, respectively. These rescues happened only because banks could own full-service broker-dealers. When Goldman Sachs and Morgan Stanley were challenged to find adequate short-term funding, they were allowed to quickly convert from

13. Robert Pozen, "Stop Pining for Glass-Steagall," *Forbes*, Oct. 5, 2009, p. 24.

broker-dealers into bank holding companies. Banks have a significant advantage over broker-dealers in obtaining short-term financing in illiquid markets. A bank can rely on insured deposits and Fed loans as well as short-term financing in the form of commercial paper. Commercial paper buyers are a fickle bunch. Bank depositors are more stable retail customers.[14]

All true; but we know from chapter 2 that the Federal Reserve can lend to a firm that is not a commercial bank, even if the borrower has lousy collateral; it can also guarantee the borrower's debts. It is not obvious that these are inferior solutions in an economic emergency to forcing a merger with a bank.

The biggest objections to separating commercial banking from shadow banking come from having to decide what is and what is not commercial banking and, what is really the same problem, from the difficulty of preventing the commercial banking sector from shrinking to dangerously small size under competitive pressure from more loosely regulated shadow banks. The less flexibility commercial banks have with regard to lending practices, the more business they will lose to the shadow banks unless the latter are strictly regulated by the SEC, which remains an unlikely prospect in light of the SEC's history and culture, and would be undesirable because a modern economy depends on risky as well as safe lending.

Remember that commercial banking until the 1980s was safe but that the rise of shadow banking led to relaxed regulation of commercial banks to enable them to compete with the shadow banks. If commercial banks are again made safe—if we push the clock back to 1980—we may find that we have restarted the deregulatory cycle.

10. *Reorganize the regulatory structure.* Any thoroughgoing consideration of financial regulatory reform should address regulatory structure. Regulation of financial intermediation is di-

14. Id.

vided among more than a hundred federal and state agencies, and some consolidation of these would eliminate duplication and stovepiping—agencies hate to share information, because in bureaucracy information is power—and therefore reduce cost, which might enable agencies to pay higher salaries to regulators, to get a better quality of regulator. For example, the creation of a Consumer Financial Protection Agency is a bad idea for the reasons I gave in chapter 5, but given the similarity of the consumer financial products offered by different financial institutions, there is a case for entrusting one agency with responsibility for consumer financial protection rather than dividing that responsibility among a number of separate agencies. The consumer protection divisions of the Federal Reserve and the other banking agencies could thus be reassigned to the Federal Trade Commission and consolidated in a new Financial Regulation Division of the commission. Another useful reform related to protection of consumers of financial products would be to make the SEC the protector of all such consumers and the Commodity Futures Trading Commission the regulator of all exchanges.[15]

Notice how these reforms would shift financial regulation from an institutional toward a functional orientation. This would reduce duplication and hence regulatory arbitrage, but at the cost of possibly enlarging a regulatory agency's responsibilities beyond its capacity. That is the objection to designating a single agency as the systemic risk regulator of the entire financial sector.

Some thought should be given to reorganizing the Federal Reserve itself. Why are there regional banks—why is there not a single central bank in Washington? And why should the regional banks, whose presidents participate in the establishment of the nation's monetary policies, be quasi-private institutions? Is the

15. John C. Coffee, Jr., and Hillary A. Sale, "Redesigning the SEC: Does the Treasury Have a Better Idea?" 95 *Virginia Law Review* 707, 839 (2009).

structure of our central banking system (which as far as I know has no foreign counterparts) rational, or is it just a fossil remnant of Andrew Jackson's suspicion of a national bank?

I am not entirely happy with the suggestions that I have made in this chapter. The only ambitious proposal that I have discussed sympathetically—the separation of commercial banking from other forms of financial intermediation—is fraught with problems. The more numerous unambitious proposals that I have advanced may hold, singly or even in the aggregate, only modest potential for reducing the risk of another financial collapse. These doubts underscore the need for a serious, neutral, patient, well-funded inquiry into the causes of the crisis and the optimal directions for reform, conducted by an elite presidential commission.

12

Arguably, the true legacy of banking crises is greater public indebtedness.[1]

Richard Cheney is reported to have said, when he was Vice President, that "deficits don't matter."[2] Certainly the Bush Administration ran big ones, as a result of which the public debt (the national debt less federal liabilities to Americans created by Social Security and other entitlement programs) doubled. It has continued mounting as the deficit continues growing. It has now reached $7.5 trillion, an amount equal to more than half the (annual) gross domestic product.

It will continue to grow rapidly, because of the fall in federal tax revenues as a result of the economic downturn; because of the aging of the population, which, along with the continued acquisition of advanced medical technology, is causing a continuing rapid increase in Medicare costs; because of the reluctance of Congress to raise taxes or cut spending programs, and because of the cost of the ambitious new programs of the Obama Administration, though how much money will actually be spent on those programs, such as health-care reform and climate control, and when, is at this writing unclear.

1. Carmen M. Reinhart and Kenneth S. Rogoff, *This Time Is Different: Eight Centuries of Financial Folly* 170 (2009).
2. Jonathan Waisman, "Reagan Policies Gave Green Light to Red Ink," *Washington Post,* June 9, 2004, p. A11.

If the United States were an autarchy—if it had no trade, or any other commercial relations, with any other country—the recovery from a depression would be readily manageable. Even a sharp aftershock would do no more than delay the eventual recovery. Restrictions on risky lending by banks would not divert banking business to foreign banks, because foreign banks would not compete in the United States. They might recruit talented bankers from the United States, but nothing those bankers did in their new foreign jobs could hurt American banking, because it would have no foreign competition. The collapse of foreign economies would have no effect on our economy, because the United States would neither export nor import, neither borrow abroad nor lend abroad. So no stimulus money would be "wasted" on imports—that is, would go to stimulate production and therefore employment in foreign countries.

All debt would be owned by Americans. If the government decided that in order to jump-start the economy it would eliminate overindebtedness by inflating the currency, there would be no impact on dollar holdings by other countries, or on the dollar as the principal international reserve currency, because dollars would have no value outside the United States. No matter how high the rate of inflation, there could be no devaluation of the dollar, because there would be no trade between the dollar and other currencies.

But that is not the world we live in, and because it is not, we cannot be confident that after any aftershock that may protract or disrupt our recovery from the current depression the economy will regain its past luster. Our public debt is funded by Treasury borrowing, and 45 percent of the borrowed money is lent by foreign governments and other foreign entities. (At present our borrowing is less tilted toward foreign lenders. Because of the increase in the personal savings rate of Americans coupled with the decline of private investment, more of Americans' savings are loaned to the government.) The U.S. economy is deeply entangled with foreign economies in other ways as well, and those economies are deeply entangled with each other.

These entanglements limit the ability of the United States either to prevent or to mitigate economic crises. An illustration to which I've already alluded is that international trade complicates stimulus efforts by causing what is called "leaky Keynesianism": to whatever extent a stimulus program funds projects that require imports, it stimulates foreign economies rather than the domestic economy. Concern with such leakage reinforces what is anyway a tendency in a depression, which is for nations to erect trade barriers in order to limit imports so as to encourage domestic production (to replace imports) and therefore employment. The goal is unlikely to be attained. A country imposing such restrictions *hopes* other countries won't retaliate, because it wants its exports to grow as well as imports to shrink, since exports enlarge domestic production. But probably the countries harmed by the restrictions *will* retaliate—especially in a depression, when the pressure to increase production and therefore employment is acute—so that in the end the main effect of trade barriers will be to reduce economic efficiency everywhere. For countries like the United States that export much less than they import, however, import substitution by domestic producers may more than offset the loss of foreign markets for domestically produced goods.

The prospect of retaliation does not prevent the erection of trade barriers, as history shows. Fear of retaliation is overcome by the political influence, amplified in a depression, of domestic producers hurt by imports and unable to take the long view.

And protectionism sometimes works. A good example is China's policy of maintaining a rate of exchange between Chinese currency and the American dollar that by overvaluing the dollar makes Chinese goods cheap in the United States and American goods dear in China.[3] This protectionist policy has

3. Suppose the purchasing power of one American dollar is equal to that

persisted because few American producers are interested in producing the products that China exports or that Chinese consumers are interested in buying, while American consumers are happy to be able to buy Chinese products on the cheap and our government is happy to be able to finance much of the public debt of the United States by borrowing from China and other countries that run trade surpluses. But consistent with the point that economic downturns stimulate protectionist policy, in September 2009 the United States in response to union demands placed heavy duties on Chinese imports of tires and China promptly retaliated by imposing duties on some U.S. exports to China.

International trade is nothing new, obviously; but what is relatively new, and until the current depression was growing, is the globalization of financial services—their merger into a single world market, and inherently a volatile one because of the rapidity with which money can be shunted from one country to another. It is an accident that our banks were pushed to the brink of insolvency (and some over it) by loans made in the United States; had they been heavily invested in a bubble in another country, their balance sheet might have taken the same hit, though the harm to the U.S. economy would have been less—for that harm was due in part to the fact that the bursting of the bubble reduced the market value of Americans' savings.

It is natural to think that enlarging the scope of a market reduces risk—that if the entire world is a market, economic adversity in one part of the world will be set off by prosperity in another. But diversification increases risk at the same time that it spreads it. An insurance pool, for example, reduces risk to the insured by spreading his risk among the members of the pool; but

---

of 10 Chinese yuan, but because China fixes the exchange rate at 20 yuan to the dollar, a Chinese producer sells in the United States for a dollar a product that the producer spent 20 yuan to produce. That is the equivalent of an export subsidy combined with a tariff on imports.

that means that each of the other members now bears a piece of his risk. The risk of a default in Bangladesh can thus become a risk to the American economy if the default was on a loan by an American bank.

There is, in short, a house-of-cards quality to the global integrated economy of trade and finance. Suppose a developing country that is a heavy borrower of foreign capital gets into economic trouble and decides to jack up interest rates in order to reduce the flight of capital, but many foreign lenders pull out their money anyway, much as in the case of a bank run, forcing interest rates still higher and bankrupting local businesses in droves. Then demand for imports will fall and so exporting nations will be hurt. That will trim their demand for imports and thus reduce the exports of other nations. Meanwhile lenders will have taken a hit from having made risky loans that have gone sour, and the hit will reduce their capital and thus inhibit their lending, reducing the amount of credit in the world economy.

We can keep our banks from making risky foreign loans that can trigger the kind economic downturn that I have just sketched, even if the banks make them through foreign subsidiaries. And we can prevent foreign banks from making risky loans in the United States. What we cannot prevent is foreign banks from making risky loans outside the United States, so if we prevent our banks from doing so by piling on restrictions designed to prevent a recurrence of the financial crisis they will lose business to those banks. To protect American banks from being outcompeted by foreign banks subject to fewer restrictions would require an international convention on standards of bank lending. We thought we had one, in the Basel II Accords,[4] which set standards designed to prevent excessively risky lending. Basel II failed. It decreed that in determining whether a bank had sufficient capital its assets should be weighted by their riskiness. Because the triple-A tranches of mortgage-backed securities were

4. www.bis.org/publ/bcbs107.htm (visited Oct. 22, 2009).

thought safer than ordinary loans, the Basel II Accords encouraged banks to invest in those securities.

The deeper problems with Basel-type accords are that an international accord is likely to adopt a lowest-common-denominator approach to assuring the safety of banks and that assuring compliance with financial standards would require an inspections regime that governments are unlikely to permit. A further problem is that it is not enough to get the major nations to agree to tighten lending; because of the mobility both of money and of financial talent, even a very small country can aspire to become a major banking center.

Realistically, then, the choice for the United States is between permitting its banks to meet the competition of foreign lenders that take the kind of risks that precipitated the present economic crisis and losing some of our financial business to foreign banks. Such a loss (and one would like to see an estimate of how big it is likely to be) would not be a trivial long-term consequence of the present crisis, for even after the crash, financial services contribute a great deal to U.S. national income (5.8 percent in the second quarter of 2009).

A further entanglement of the United States with foreign nations arises from the fact that foreign contracts are often denominated in dollars rather than in the local currency. If an oil producer in a Middle Eastern country sells oil to a refinery in a South American country, neither party may be happy to have payment made in the currency of the other party's country, because by the time payment is due the value of the currency may have changed to the advantage of that other party. By providing that payment will be made in U.S. dollars, the parties can hedge against changes in the value of the local currencies. For such hedging to be effective, however, the value of the dollar has to be stable. At the height of the financial crisis the dollar's value rose because of fear that other countries would devalue their currencies or even default on their debts. The rise created potential hardship for parties on the buying side of contracts—they needed more of their local currency to buy the dollars that the contract obligated them to pay to the other party. As the economic outlook has brightened, the value of the dollar relative to other currencies, particular the euro, has fallen sharply, harming the selling side of international contracts.

The dollar's instability could imperil its status as the principal international reserve currency, accounting at present for almost two-thirds of total international currency reserves. The temptation to reduce the national debt by inflating (inflation being the debtor's friend) will rise as the national debt rises, and we may yield to the temptation, as we have done in the past. U.S. inflation in the 1970s, though substantial, did not affect the dollar's standing as the leading international reserve currency. But that was because there was no alternative, in part because the inflation was worldwide. Today there are alternatives: the euro, the Japanese yen, and in time the renminbi—for China is on course to become the world's leading economic power, though it may falter, as did Japan, an earlier contender for that distinction.

The loss of the dollar's status as the leading international reserve currency would be a blow to the United States, because that status allows the United States to run a trade deficit (up to a point) costlessly. Foreign countries need to hold U.S. dollar reserves in order to supply dollars in exchange for local currencies to businesses that have dollar-denominated contracts. If we had a trade surplus, we would be importing dollars rather than exporting them and as a result the rest of the world wouldn't have enough dollars for their transactions. Dollars not only are a U.S. export item but cost nothing to produce, and this increases the benefit to the United States of supplying the leading international reserve currency.

The dollar won't lose that status in the near term, because foreign countries hold so many dollars, which would plunge in value if demand for dollars fell; because other currencies, including the euro, the yen, and the renminbi, are distrusted; and because investors have lately been buying dollars in great quantity to conduct the "carry trade," discussed below. But if we continue our heavy borrowing abroad to finance our growing public debt, the interest rate that our government pays holders of that debt will rise, compounding the effect of greater borrowing on the government's interest expense; and interest paid to foreign as distinct from domestic borrowers reduces American wealth. And because public and private debt are substitutes, higher interest rates will slow economic activity; productive investment will be competing with lending to the government to pay its mounting debts.[5]

As a growing balance-of-payments deficit reduces the value of the dollar relative to other currencies while making imports more expensive, American exports should grow, implying a shift of workers and capital from services to manufacturing. But the shift, reversing a long-term decline in manufacturing relative to services, may be a painful and protracted one, just as China's transition from an export-led manufacturing economy to a domestic consumer economy is likely to be painful and protracted, as I noted in chapter 1. Any major restructuring of a nation's economy will produce heavy unemployment as a by-product until the restructuring is complete. We have grown accustomed to financing our consumption by borrowing heavily abroad to pay both for manufactured imports and for our elaborate systems for distributing goods and providing other services (warehouses, malls, etc.). Our economic productivity has become heavily dependent on the immigration of high-IQ professionals, but one casualty of the depression has been the imposition of restrictions on that immigration designed to protect jobs.[6]

5. On these dangers to the U.S. economy, see, for example, Augustin Landier, David Sraer, and David Thesmar, "Financial Risk Management: When Does Independence Fail?" 99 *American Economic Review Papers and Proceedings* 454 (May 2009); Martin Feldstein, "Rethinking the Role of Fiscal Policy," 99 id. 556.

6. See Harold James, *The Creation and Destruction of Value: The Globalization Cycle* 198, 211 (2009).

As our dollar falls in value, imported goods such as oil, the price of which moves inversely to the value of the dollar because oil is priced in dollars (an example of the use of the dollar as an international reserve currency), will become more expensive. The added cost may exceed any greater dollar earnings from increased exports.

All this will be of little consequence if the U.S. economy grows as fast as federal expenditures. But that is unlikely to happen soon enough (if at all) to prevent our public debt from growing out of hand as a result of the growth of the annual deficit caused by reduced tax revenues and continued stimulus and post-stimulus recovery spending, spending on new programs, and the inexorable growth of entitlement spending. The economy is expected to grow by only about 3 percent in 2010, which would leave GDP more than 6 percent below its trend line (see chapter 6).

The adjustments that will be needed, if the economy does not outgrow an increasing burden of debt, to maintain our economic position in the world may be especially painful and difficult because of features of the American political scene that suggest that the country may be becoming in important respects ungovernable. The perfection of interest-group politics seems to have brought about a situation in which, to exaggerate just a bit, taxes can't be increased, spending programs can't be cut, and new spending is irresistible. If one may judge by the Bush Administration's profligacy and the impact of that profligacy on the public debt, these tendencies are bipartisan. This leaves borrowing and inflation as the only ways of defraying the growing costs of American government.

As Auerbach and Gale explain, "Under current estimates, the long-term fiscal gap is about 9% of gross domestic product . . . The fiscal gap measures the size of the immediate and permanent tax increases or spending cuts that would keep the federal government in balance over the long term. *The current gap represents about as much revenue as the income tax generates in a good year, so we would need to double our income tax collec-*

tions to solve our fiscal problems using the income tax alone."[7]
We are not going to double our income tax collections in the
short term; in the long term, they may double as a function of
economic growth, but government spending probably will more
than double.

Radical measures that would reduce spending and raise government revenues, such as means testing for Medicare and Social
Security benefits, on the spending side, and a federal VAT (value-
added tax), a financial transactions tax, a carbon emissions tax,
an online sales tax, or a combination of these taxes, on the revenue side, would close the fiscal gap. So would the repeal of popular but distortionary tax deductions such as the income-tax deduction for interest on mortgages. But all these measures would
encounter—some have encountered already—ferocious political
opposition. And the VAT—simple in execution, vast in revenue-
generating potential, attractive from an antidepression standpoint because it would reduce consumption and thus encourage thrift in boom times (it could be reduced in a bust, when we
don't want thrift), and free from the disincentive effects that raising marginal income tax rates would have—is objectionable on
Keynesian grounds because reducing consumption reduces the
return to investment and so retards economic growth.

At this writing, Congress seems about to enact an ambitious
program of health-care reform, dramatically expanding health
insurance coverage, which will cost the federal government $100
billion a year. This is supposed to be paid for in full by cost savings and by higher taxes on rich people; that is unlikely, but suppose it happens. Those offsets, having gone to reduce the cost
of expanding health insurance coverage, will not be available to
reduce the federal deficit. The government appears to have no

7. Alan J. Auerbach and William G. Gale, "Fix Health Care. But Fix the
Deficits, Too," www.taxpolicycenter.org/publications/url.cfm?ID=1001313
(visited Oct. 22, 2009) (emphasis added). See also Daniel Shaviro, "The
Long-Term U.S. Fiscal Gap: Is the Main Problem Generational Inequity?"
77 *George Washington Law Review* 1298, 1301–1315 (2009).

plans for reducing the deficit, as distinct from its not-very-credible plans to prevent health-care reform from increasing it.

What is saving us for the time being is the large current-account surpluses of China and other export-emphasizing countries—surpluses that are largely in dollars, not only because the dollar is the principal international reserve currency but also because the United States is such a huge borrower of dollars. There are plenty of foreign dollars available for the purchase of U.S. government securities, and this makes it easy for the United States to borrow at reasonable interest rates to fund its public debt even though Americans are not big savers. Actually they're saving more nowadays (4.7 percent of their disposable income at last report, though this is less than half what the personal savings rate was as recently as the 1980s), with the result that in fiscal 2009 a higher percentage of lending that financed the public debt came from Americans than in previous years—62 percent rather than 55 percent. But this may change as the economy recovers.

For now we can continue to fund our public debt at reasonable interest rates. But for how long? The public debt is growing very fast. As the economy recovers, federal tax revenues will rise, but federal expenditures will be rising too, if only because of the growth of Medicare and other entitlement programs, and they will rise all the faster if a significant part of the Administration's ambitious program is authorized by Congress.

At some point the wheels may start coming off the chassis. Assume that the public debt continues to grow more rapidly than the economy. The Treasury will have to borrow more and more, yet at a time when recovering economies need investment capital, creating competition for the world's limited capital and therefore forcing interest rates up and hence deepening our deficits and slowing our economic growth. We already pay more than $400 billion a year in interest on the public debt, and that amount will grow rapidly as both the size of the public debt and interest rates rise. According to the Congressional Budget Office, if the Bush tax reductions are not permitted to expire and the alternative minimum tax is indexed for inflation, growing deficits, combined with rising interest rates on borrowing to fund the deficits, will push the public debt to 200 percent of GDP in 2038.[8] At that point an interest expense of 5 percent would mean that we were paying $1.2 trillion a year to service the debt. Little weight should be placed on remote economic forecasts, but they do indicate the potential threat to American prosperity and power.

Suppose that before interest rates begin to climb as the economy recovers, political pressures prevent the Federal Reserve from raising those rates in order to head off inflation caused by the banks' finally deciding to lend the huge excess reserves that they have accumulated as a result of the Fed's monetary response to the current economic crisis. Fear of inflation will push up long-term interest rates, including rates paid by the Treasury to fund the growing public debt. Fear of inflation will also make foreign countries worry about the value of their dollar reserves and wonder whether the dollar should continue to be the dominant international reserve currency.

A partial solution to the threat that inflation poses to the dollar's standing in the world economy is the TIPS program (Treasury Inflation-Protected Securities). TIPS are Treasury bonds that are tied to the consumer price index. If all Treasury securities were TIPS, inflation would not be an effective method of liquidating the nation's public debt, because the amount owed the owners of the debt would rise in proportion to the increase in inflation. But it is unlikely that TIPS (at present a small fraction of all Treasury debt) will displace federal debt that is not indexed to inflation, and of course the Treasury could stop issuing TIPS. Moreover, TIPS would not protect the dollar as a reserve currency, because they would not prevent inflation; they would just

8. Testimony of CBO Director Douglas W. Elmendorf, July 16, 2009, www.cbo.gov/ftpdocs/104xx/doc10455/07-16-Long-TermOutlook_Testimony .pdf (visited Oct. 22, 2009).

protect bondholders against inflation. (Unsurprisingly, therefore, the Chinese, who hold $800 billion in Treasury bonds, are enthusiastic about TIPS.) But the program would put pressure on the government to finance the debt by taxation or spending cuts rather than by inflation.

As the dollar falls in value, the public debt will become cheaper to repay, the demand for U.S. exports will grow, and our demand for imports will fall. The increase in the ratio of exports to imports will reduce the current-account deficit and thus the rate of increase of the public debt. But increasing exports relative to imports, by tending to reverse the long-term decline in U.S. manufacturing relative to services, may, as I suggested earlier, be a painful and protracted process. And even with a reduced current-account deficit, U.S. public debt will continue rising because of increasing unfunded expenditures on social programs—and for all one knows on military activity as well, because the United States remains the world's policeman. Lenders will charge higher interest rates to continue to fund our public debt if they think the dollar is losing value. If inflation persists, the dollar will decline as an international reserve currency, and with the demand for dollars thus reduced, its value will fall further.

As real interest rates rise as a consequence of a growing public debt and declining demand for the U.S. dollar as an international reserve currency, U.S. savings rates will rise and, by reducing consumption expenditures, slow economic activity. Economic growth may also fall as more and more resources are poured into keeping alive elderly people, most of whom are not highly productive members of society from an economic standpoint. The United States may find itself in the same kind of downward economic spiral that developing countries often find themselves in. As an economic power, we may go the way of the British Empire, which occupied approximately the same position in the world economy in the nineteenth century as the United States does today.

Further grounds for concern are found in a recent study by a pair of financial analysts at Morgan Stanley.[9] Noting the surprising fact that personal consumption expenditures by Americans are not declining despite the significant decline in labor incomes in this depression and the significant increase in the personal savings rate, the analysts point out that transfer payments by the government to individuals and families (Social Security, unemployment benefits, tax credits, etc.) now exceed the taxes being collected from the household sector. At the same time, private investment net of depreciation is negative. This means that private savings are being borrowed by the government, combined with the government's foreign borrowing, and transferred to households to enable them to maintain their accustomed level of consumption. People are saving more, but government borrowing overwhelms their saving, with the result that aggregate saving—public plus private—is negative.

Negative savings, negative private investment, an incredible ratio of household debt to disposable income (1.25 to 1, though down from 1.39 to 1 in 2007), massive government borrowing to finance private consumption—these are not the signs of a healthy economy. Of course, we're in a depression, but our public finances are in such disarray that one cannot contemplate the future without foreboding. "The US economy, and the world economy, cannot recover sustainably by propping up consumers for yet another binge."[10] But that is what we are doing.

I have emphasized problems with our political culture, but the broader social culture may also prove an impediment to renewed economic progress. America's growth has been promoted by the "can do" attitude of its people, their rejection of fatalism, their individualism—qualities conducive to innovation, ambition, and

9. Gerard Minack and Jason Todd, "The New Imbalances," *Downunder Daily*, Dec. 7, 2009.

10. Jeffrey D. Sachs, "Rethinking Macroeconomics," 4, 3 *Capitalism and Society* 3 (2009), www.bepress/com/cas/vol4/iss3/art3 (visited Dec. 17, 2009).

hard work. But the rejection of fatalism is also a major factor in our soaring medical costs, as our old people (and often their children) insist that every effort be made, at taxpayer expense, to extend their lives. As a result, 25 percent of Medicare costs are incurred in treating elderly people in the last few months of life. American individualism is a barrier to fiscal belt-tightening through tax hikes or spending cuts. A "can do" attitude can and often does express itself in a refusal to worry about looming crises. Americans can overcome any challenge. So not to worry!

No country is fated to rule the roost forever. Qualities that promote a country's fortunes in one era may undermine them in another. Consider Japan, which in the 1980s was believed to be well on the way to overtaking the United States economically. Japan spent the 1990s unsuccessfully trying to recover from a collapse of its banking industry caused by the bursting of a housing bubble.[11] It adopted aggressive monetary and fiscal policies to spur recovery. The policies did not work well[12] and caused the public debt to soar. But the debt was financed mainly internally, because of the high Japanese personal savings rate. And with its large surplus of exports over inputs Japan accumulated dollars (and other currencies), which also reduced the debt burden. Interest rates remained very low, in part because of chronic deflation. The low interest rates stimulated the "carry trade": investors would exchange Japanese yen for local currencies in countries in which interest rates were high. That is a form of arbitrage, but because of government interventions in the currency

11. The story of Japan's long struggle to recover from its precursor to our September 2008 financial collapse is told succinctly and well in Matthew Bishop and Michael Green, *The Road from Ruin: Reviving Capitalism for Renewed Prosperity* 136–144 (2010).

12. "In Japan, open market operations for a time did little but add to banks' excess reserves." Stephen H. Axilrod, *Inside the Fed: Monetary Policy and Its Management, Martin through Greenspan to Bernanke* 127 (2009). Sounds familiar! More on the parallels between the Japanese economic crisis of the 1990s and our current crisis below.

markets it tends not to erase international interest-rate differences, as one might expect arbitrage to do.

Japan's economic growth slowed dramatically. But the consequences for the economic situation of the average Japanese were cushioned by an increase in productivity, which kept Japanese incomes up[13]—and by doing so dampened political pressure for economic reform.

Japan has been hard hit by the current economic crisis, in part because of its dependence on exports. Once again it has responded with aggressive monetary and fiscal measures—this time with potentially disastrous long-term effects on its debt.[14] The International Monetary Fund predicts that the ratio of Japan's national debt to its GDP will reach an astronomical 2.27 to 1 in 2010. (The U.S. ratio is .94 to 1.) Though interest rates and hence the cost of serving Japan's debt remain low because Japan is again experiencing deflation, credit-rating agencies have reduced Japan's bond rating to AA−.

Yet the government evinces no sense of urgency about the country's mounting debt burden, a burden aggravated by the rapid aging of Japan's population. International financial markets agree with the rating agencies that there is a nontrivial probability that Japan will default on its public debt, for the "CDS spread" (the percentage of a debt that a creditor desiring insurance against default must pay for the insurance) on Japanese public debt is almost 1 percent (.75 percent).

The United States differs in many respects from Japan but is looking more and more like it. We too experienced a banking collapse in the wake of the bursting of a housing bubble. Our monetary and fiscal responses too, though aggressive, may not have been highly effective. Our fiscal stimulus started late and is

13. "Japan's Troubles and Some Lessons for the U.S.," *Bank Credit Analyst* (BCA Research Article, Nov. 2009).
14. See Richard Barley, "Japan: The Land of the Rising CDS," *Wall Street Journal,* Nov. 11, 2009, p. C20.

poorly designed, and some think too small. And there is concern that, like Japan, we are babying our weak banks by allowing them to overvalue their assets and underestimate their liabilities. Banks will not do much lending as long as they are undercapitalized, and they will remain undercapitalized as long as their balance sheets are heavy with overvalued assets. That was a major factor in the sluggishness of Japan's recovery in the 1990s from its housing bubble, which had pulled down the banks when it burst, just as the bursting of our housing bubble did.[15] The stress tests that the Federal Reserve conducted in the spring of 2009 underestimated the stress that the banks were experiencing (by assuming an unemployment rate—unemployment being highly correlated with bank-loan defaults—substantially lower than it became within a couple of months after the tests). The tests also disregarded likely defaults of bank loans that will mature after 2010. Banks have been increasing their loss reserves in anticipation of further defaults, and this has further weakened their balance sheets. And because one way in which they rebuilt their balance sheets in the wake of the financial collapse was to take out an unusual number of short-term loans, they are facing uncertainty with regard to their ability to roll over those loans at reasonable rates of interest as the loans come due in two or three years. Yet they are being pressed by the government to make loans, which in a depressed economy would weaken them further. And the government's efforts to prop up housing prices may just be postponing the day of reckoning when the housing surplus precipitates a new round of price declines that wipe out home buyers lured by tax credits and other emergency measures.

Our government, like Japan's, is lulled by the prevailing low interest rates into believing that it can continue to run huge deficits without raising taxes or cutting spending but simply by borrowing. We are maintaining our high level of consumption by

15. See, for example, Richard Katz, *Japanese Phoenix: The Long Road to Economic Revival,* ch. 5 (2003).

borrowing rather than by working and investing. Like Japan, we have an aging population, which is pushing up entitlement costs. Our government seems not to have any economically realistic or politically feasible plans either to raise substantial revenue or to cut spending substantially. Instead it plans ambitious unfunded spending programs. There is an air of complacency about deficit spending and public debt—again like Japan.

China's economic policy plays a role here. For reasons explained in chapter 1, China is likely to recede from its mercantilist policies only very gradually. For the foreseeable future, its currency will remain undervalued relative to the dollar, and so China will be continuing to finance U.S. consumption. Our ability to borrow seemingly unlimited amounts of money from the Chinese relaxes the pressure on our government to pay down our immense and growing public debt either by raising taxes or by cutting spending. American politicians, their policy horizons foreshortened by their limited terms of office, refuse to trade present pain for future gain. They prefer to kick the can down the road, as if their motto were "sufficient unto the day is the evil thereof."[16] That's why we're in danger of imitating Japan's lost decade. We would rather limp from year to year with the aid of Chinese money than place our fiscal house in order.

Because of our low inflation rate and the Federal Reserve's easy-money policy, which has kept interest rates very low, the dollar has become a favorite currency for the carry trade: U.S. dollars borrowed cheaply and exchanged for foreign currencies generate a spread more or less effortlessly from the interest on investments made in those currencies, though not without risk. The carry trade may be a factor in recent rises in commodity prices; indeed there is fear of new bubbles as a result of all the dollars sloshing around in the world economy. This poses dangers for the global economy, because the carry trade is susceptible to runs. If a speculator borrows dollars short-term to mini-

16. Matthew 6:34.

mize interest expense and uses them to buy rupees, say, and the dollar surges in value relative to the rupee, the speculator may have to sell his rupees in a hurry to repay his lenders. If so, the value of the rupee will fall farther relative to the dollar, which may precipitate a run on rupees as the speculators unload them. Because of the integration of the world's financial systems, a run on a foreign currency can harm the economies of other countries.

Remember Greenspan's promise, when in 2004 the Fed began raising interest rates, that the increase would be gradual, and how such a promise would tend to keep housing prices rising (see chapter 1)? History may be repeating itself. Bernanke has made clear that the Fed will keep short-term interest rates low for some time. The Greenspan put of the early 2000s has become the Bernanke put of 2009, reassuring the carry traders that the Fed is not going to pull the rug out from under them by open market operations designed to reduce U.S. bank balances, a policy that would increase the value of the dollar in relation to other currencies by reducing the amount of money in circulation (the U.S. money supply is essentially the sum of all U.S. bank balances), and by doing so would increase interest rates on dollar loans. Our government is doing nothing, moreover, to prevent the dollar from falling in value relative to other currencies—the government *wants* it to fall in order to spur exports, import substitution, and a mild inflation—and a falling dollar makes the carry trade more profitable. The carry trader borrows dollars with which to buy currencies that can be invested at higher interest rates than the cost of borrowing the dollars—and then, after cashing out the investment, he returns to the lenders dollars worth less than when he borrowed them.[17]

Only if the U.S. economy grows more rapidly than the public debt will we be okay. That's a big if, because the Administration's

17. See Steven Pearlstein, "The Fed's Airheaded Bubble Orthodoxy," *Washington Post,* Nov. 13, 2009, www.washingtonpost.com/wp-dyn/content/article/2009/11/12/AR2009111210788.html (visited Nov. 25, 2009).

focus is not on economic growth but on redistribution (the major goal of health-insurance reform) and on creating at least an aura of prosperity, at whatever cost in deficit spending and future inflation, ahead of the November 2010 congressional elections. The major exception is the Administration's emphasis on educational reform: education is key to economic growth. But redistributive policies, whether they take the form of encouraging unionization, discouraging free trade, raising marginal income-tax rates, increasing subsidies for health care, or retarding immigration—especially but not only immigration by highly educated persons—will make it more difficult for the United States to escape Japan's fate.

The speed-up of the electoral cycle is an aggravating factor. By the second year of a U.S. President's first term the attention of his political advisers becomes fixated on the forthcoming midterm elections, viewed as a referendum on the first half of his presidency. True, the President's party can do badly in the elections yet the President be reelected two years later; Reagan and Clinton are examples. Clinton actually benefited from the fact that the Republicans wrested control of Congress from the Democrats in the first midterm elections of his Presidency, because it enabled him to govern thereafter from the political center, where he was more comfortable and enjoyed broader public and political support. But a President with a legislative agenda as ambitious as Obama's doesn't want to lose control of Congress. A President's temptation to inflate the currency on the eve of an election in order to create the appearance of prosperity, however fleeting, is one of the strongest arguments for an independent central bank. The recent growth in the Fed's unpopularity may make it quail from exhibiting independence in the run-up to the November 2010 elections.

Two relatively minor incidents in the fall of 2009 illustrate what might be called the political-economy obstacles to a clean recovery from the current depression—a recovery that will spare the nation unmanageable debt.

The surprise tariff on imports of Chinese tires that I mentioned was imposed under a heretofore unused law that authorizes the President to impose a tariff without a finding that the imports were a form of "dumping" or were otherwise "unfairly" competitive. The tire tariff was pure protectionism, transparently a payback to the unions for their strong support of Obama in the 2008 election. Protectionism is a special temptation in a depression because money spent on imports stimulates foreign economies rather than the U.S. economy and higher prices of imports create opportunities for domestic producers. Hence the "Buy America" provisions in the fiscal stimulus law.

But the broader significance of the tire tariff is what it reveals about the outsized influence on American economic policy of industrial unions that control only a small fraction of the American workforce, and in turn about the quirks of our political system. All but two states award all their electoral votes to the candidate who obtains a plurality of the popular vote in the state. This makes winning that vote, however narrowly, in states rich in electoral votes disproportionately important to a successful strategy for a presidential candidate, and in turn amplifies the power of interest groups in those states. States in which unions, despite their modest fraction of the labor force overall, are electorally powerful include major swing states, such as Ohio. Since unions lean to the Democrat Party, courting unions is a sensible political strategy for a Democratic President even when it means offending, and inviting retaliation by, a nation—China—that owns a large fraction of our public debt.

A feature of our eighteenth-century Constitution that has survived into the twenty-first century is the extraordinary decentralization of American government. Power is divided among the states, between the states and the federal government, and within the federal government among the President, the Congress, and the federal judiciary. Congress itself is effectively tricameral because of the President's veto, and the Senate requires a supermajority vote to pass any legislation that steps on big political

toes and is governed much of the time by a de facto rule of una-
nimity. A huge federal bureaucracy limits political initiatives.
Campaign contributions—insulated in the name of the Constitution by a conservative Supreme Court from effective limitation—
make the legislative system one of quasi-bribery. Modern com-
munications technology and marketing techniques, along with
the expense of modern elections, amplify the influence of interest
groups, especially their influence in blocking change. The short
electoral cycle (major federal elections every two years) truncates
the government's policy horizon.

So we have a structural political problem. There is also a
problem with our political culture. It used to be that we had a
liberal and a conservative party, though both were loose coali-
tions lacking European-style rigid ideological uniformity. The
Democrats, the liberal party, favored big government and therefore big government spending—and therefore high taxes to pay
for the big spending. The conservative party, the Republicans,
opposed big government and big government spending and
therefore favored low taxes. These were coherent positions. For
Democrats, however, favoring heavy taxes was an albatross,
while for Republicans the albatross was opposing big government spending. Beginning with Reagan, and continuing with the
second Bush, Republicans squared the circle by abandoning their
opposition to big spending while redoubling their commitment
to low taxes. Belatedly, the current Democratic Administration
has decided that while still favoring big government spending
(indeed more than recent Democratic Administrations have favored it) it too wants to keep taxes low—not so low as the Republicans want, but low enough that deficits that swamp those of
the Reagan and Bush years are looming. From the standpoint of
economic policy we have only one party, and it is the party of
profligacy.

Another political evolution should be noted. Beginning in the
1970s, the traditional opposition of the parties with regard to

economic regulation waned. Democrats lost their zeal for common carrier, public utility, and antitrust regulation—in short, for regulation based on the premise that unregulated markets were prone to monopoly or other failures of competition. At the same time, Republicans bowed to political pressures for regulation aimed at promoting the new, as it were "post-economic," liberal causes of the environment, safety, and protection of workers against discrimination on invidious grounds. The gradual convergence of the parties on regulatory issues set the stage for the financial collapse and ensuing depression, while their convergence on taxes (hostility) and spending (welcoming) has undermined the prospects for the economy after recovery from the depression.

The structural problems of our government are less serious than the problems of political culture that I have just discussed, in the following depressing sense: solving the structural problems might not improve the government's performance. Parliamentary governments, such as that of the United Kingdom, are more centralized than ours and have longer electoral cycles, yet do not seem to manage the economy any better than our government does. What could solve our problems of political culture, I have no idea.

Second example: In October 2009 the President announced that $13 billion of the $787 billion stimulus plan that had been enacted in February would be used to pay every Social Security annuitant $250 in 2010, to compensate for the fact that there would be no cost-of-living (inflation) increase in Social Security benefits that year. There would be no cost-of-living increase for the excellent reason that the consumer price index did not increase in the year ending September 30, 2009, and the Social Security law makes that the relevant index and relevant period for determining the entitlement of Social Security recipients to an increase in benefits in 2010 and, if so, of what size. In fact the CPI decreased slightly over the relevant period and so Social Security benefits should fall, not rise. But they cannot fall, because the So-cial Security law has a ratchet: benefits increase when the cost of living increases but do not decrease when the cost of living de-creases. Remember too that transfer payments are an inefficient form of fiscal stimulus, because they are at two removes from production and hence from stimulating employment (see chapter 4); and so the $250 windfall cannot easily be justified on macro-economic grounds.

The measure is further evidence of fiscal imprudence. But not just the Administration's fiscal imprudence. The political parties play leapfrog when it comes to spending. The Republicans shed crocodile tears for recipients of Social Security and Medicare. Each party tries to outdo the other in generosity to any powerful voting group in states that are politically competitive. The most powerful such group is the elderly; they are numerous, they have a high propensity to vote, and they have a keen sense of their stake in specific government policies. The costs of both Social Security and Medicare are increasing rapidly as the population ages, and as the population ages the voting power of the elderly can only increase, placing additional pressure on a budget al-ready disproportionately devoted to supporting society's least economically productive members (on average—an important qualification).

In the foreword to the German edition of *The General Theory,* published during the Nazi era, Keynes wrote that "the theory of aggregated production, which is the point of the General The-ory, . . . can be much easier adapted to the conditions of a totali-tarian state [*eines totalen Staates*] than the theory of production and distribution of a given production put forth under condi-tions of free competition and a large degree of laissez-faire." By "aggregated production," Keynes seems to have meant private plus government production, the latter being particularly impor-tant in a depression to take up the slack created by the drop in private demand for goods and services.

Keynes was a liberal democrat, not a fascist, though labeling him a fascist is a staple of right-wing extremism.[18] He was correctly implying that a totalitarian state can control the business cycle more effectively than a democratic one. This is not only because a totalitarian state can implement measures to prevent a depression more rapidly and decisively than a democratic state can, but also because it is likely to adopt autarchic policies in order to minimize its citizens' contact with, and its own dependence on, an outside world deemed a threat whether as a potential enemy or as a tempting example. These points do not make totalitarianism superior to democracy or suggest that it is more efficient; judging by the communist experience, it is much less efficient, and all in all an odious flop. But democracy does make it difficult, as we are seeing, to control the business cycle without doing long-term economic damage.

The question I want to leave the reader with is whether the United States has an institutional structure and a political culture equal to the economic challenges facing it. Cumbersome, clotted, competence-challenged, even rather shady as our overall governmental system is, it can react promptly and effectively to a genuine emergency. We saw it doing that in response to the financial collapse of September 2008; the tendency in a crisis is for all branches of government to defer to the President. But when there are huge challenges but no emergency, our political system tends to be ineffectual. Limited terms in office (with or without term limits) truncate politicians' horizons; and interest-group politics, operating with vast sums of money on a complex decentralized system of government strongly biased to the status quo, has little trouble pushing needed reforms off beyond those horizons. The financial collapse and the ensuing depression (as I insist we must call it) have both underscored and amplified grave problems of American public finance that will not yield to the populist solutions that command political and public support. The problems include the enormous public debt created by the decline of tax

18. See Google entries under "was Keynes a fascist?"

revenues in the depression, the enormous expenses incurred by government in fighting the depression, and the boost the depression has given to expanding the government's role in the economy. These developments, interacting with a seeming inability of government to cut existing spending programs (however foolish), to insist that costly new programs be funded, to limit the growth of entitlement programs, or to raise taxes, constitute the crisis of American-style capitalist democracy.

INDEX